Masters of the Universe

Masters of the Universe

WINNING STRATEGIES OF AMERICA'S GREATEST DEAL MAKERS

✳

DANIEL J. KADLEC

HarperBusiness
A Division of HarperCollinsPublishers

HarperCollins books may be purchased for educational, business, or sales promotional use. For information please write: Special Markets Department, HarperCollins Publishers, Inc., 10 East 53rd Street, New York, NY 10022.

FIRST EDITION

Designed by Interrobang Design Studio

Library of Congress Cataloging-in-Publication Data

Kadlec, Daniel J.
   Masters of the universe : winning strategies of America's greatest deal makers / Daniel J. Kadlec. — 1st ed.
    p. cm.
  Includes index.
  ISBN 0-88730-933-X
   1. Businessmen—United States—Biography.   I. Title.
HC102.5.A2K34 1999   98–53438
650'.092'273—dc21

99 00 01 02 03 ❖/HC 10 9 8 7 6 5 4 3 2 1

For Kim, the only editor I could love; Lexie and Kyle, for understanding the demands of this project; Danielle, who was diligent in keeping her button-framed portrait propped squarely alongside my computer screen; and Toots, who kept my feet warm.

Contents

Introduction

THE GROUP OF DEAL MAKERS FEATURED in this book represent some of the very best in the world today. Creativity, endurance, and a willingness to stick to one's convictions, even in the face of conventional wisdom, have marked the careers of these bold and successful men. Writing the introduction about these nine business leaders has been a humbling endeavor. These men are legendary in the world of deal making, and their knowledge and experience are certainly top-rate. Their stories are fascinating portions of business history from which a great deal can be learned.

Our business team has been fortunate to be involved in more than one thousand deals, both buying and selling companies over the last forty years. During one nine-month period while we were building Waste Management, we bought one hundred companies. This sometimes required breakfast, lunch, and dinner meetings in three different cities on the same day, an experience that made us believers in private transportation. The lessons from this book would have been a great tool in the early days of making deals. The school of hard knocks is definitely overrated.

In all my years of doing deals a few rules and lessons have emerged. Most important, always try to put yourself in the other person's shoes. It's vital to try to understand in depth what the other side really wants out of the deal. You have to treat the other person fairly and honestly, just as you would want to be treated. It has to be a win-win situation for both sides. The other players in the deal can't feel they've lost. This is especially critical if the two parties are going to continue to work together. In today's world of mega-deals you never know when you will find yourself sitting across the negotiating table from that person again.

Deal making is negotiating, as Viacom's Sumner Redstone says. My experience has suggested that virtually every phase of life is filled with the process of negotiating. People negotiate throughout their lives: marriage, buying a car, finding a bargain at a garage sale, agreeing on what movie to rent for the evening, finding the right company to round out a corporate vision.

While we were building Blockbuster Entertainment we were acquiring companies rapidly and growing internally. For six years we opened a new Blockbuster store every seventeen hours. And today at AutoNation USA, we are focused on selling and leasing new and used cars. Thus far we have purchased more than four hundred new car dealerships, acquired National and Alamo car rental companies, and opened forty AutoNation USA superstores.

One area of negotiations that many people have participated in to one degree or another is buying an automobile. Historically, this has been an uncomfortable process for most people. It is not what you would call a fair negotiation because the salesperson has the numbers and the customer is at a decided disadvantage.

This process of negotiation for buying a car is one that we believe one day will be drastically different. Already at our AutoNation USA superstores vehicles are sold under a one-price, no haggling method. The price on the car is fixed and there is no negotiation. And the age-old method of involving a trade-in doesn't have to be part of the process. We believe that eventually this will be the system throughout the automobile business. You should feel comfortable sending your children to buy a new or used automobile. After all, automobile manufacturers have increased the quality of their product for more than fifty years; however, the sales method has remained quite antiquated.

How do you spot a great deal? What do most deals have in common? And do great deals have losers? These are questions that frequently arise during discussions of being an entrepreneur and a deal-maker.

Many times when we are attempting to acquire a company we are also looking for a new partner. We want people to join our team, not just sell us a company. Typically, we are trying to convince a seller to buy into our vision of the big picture. We look at an industry and try to see where that industry could be in three, five, and ten years down the road. We want sellers to share that vision and help us reach the future by offering their unique experience. It is here that a win-win situation is absolutely critical, because in the process of buying a new company were also inheriting a new partner.

Sometimes you can't see a deal, but others help you see it before it becomes obvious to you. That was the case with Blockbuster, when at the time we took control of the company, my wife, Marti, and I didn't even own a VCR. A close friend, John Melk, was an investor in a Blockbuster store in Chicago, and he had to literally plead with me to come take a look at this video store. And ultimately Blockbuster went on to become known as one of the great American business stories. We were in the right place at the right time but had to be persuaded to take a closer look.

As you will glean from the business accounts in this book, there is a certain time in every deal where you have to trust your gut instincts. You have to do what you think is the right thing because when you're making a deal you have to live with the consequences and the many lives that are going to be affected. There definitely is a greater good than simply the profit to be earned from the transaction.

Enjoy this wonderful book about some of the great business deals of all time. The stories and experiences compiled in the chapters ahead are insightful and fascinating and offer a unique glimpse into the men who have negotiated some of the most interesting deals of our day.

H. Wayne Huizenga
Chairman, Republic Industries

Masters of the Universe

chapter one

Deal Makers

IT'S NO STRANGE THING THAT GREAT DEAL makers trip over one another at every turn. When Kohlberg Kravis Roberts bought the battery maker Duracell for $1.8 billion in 1988, Ted Forstmann and Joe Rice were standing in line just a few million dollars shy. When Sumner Redstone bought the cable company Viacom, the yet undistinguished owner of MTV and Nickelodeon, his 1987 deal incidentally minted $110 million for Carl Icahn, who had looked over the company a year before and held stock warrants that were given to him as part of a package to make him disappear. Sandy Weill took a run at BankAmerica before Hugh McColl finally got it. Gary Wilson and Stephen Bollenbach both did stints as top financial executives at Marriott and Disney. Henry Silverman and H. Wayne Huizenga competed for the same car rental companies in the 1990s. And on and on.

For all the millions to be made buying and selling corporate assets, the "deal" community just isn't that big. When you whittle down the club to those who really excel at it—and have for years—the number shrinks to maybe a few dozen. That's why the same names pop up continually in any discussion of the money men behind the bustling practice known on Wall Street as M&A (mergers and acquisitions). It's unlikely that any major U.S. bank that was sold in recent years wasn't looked at by Hugh McColl. The same thing goes for any major diversified financial services firm and Sandy Weill. You think any large company looking to unload an underperforming division doesn't immediately think of Ted Forstmann and Joe Rice? Think again.

These are the great deal makers of our day. There are, of course, others. Henry Kravis, Leon Black, Sam Zell, and Ronald O. Perelman. A book like this one cannot begin to profile them all. But those I have selected, who talked to me about their peculiar line of work, represent the gamut of deal-making styles. Each is a veteran of three distinct decades of merger mania: the 1970s, which provided the origins of bank and brokerage consolidations and leveraged buyouts; the 1980s, which gave us heated bidding wars and corporate raiders; and the 1990s, when a roaring bull market made high-priced stock swaps the strategy of choice.

As a new decade dawns, it's not yet clear what distinction it will claim. There are modest hints that the mega-merger—a deal worth $20 billion or greater, so common in the latter half of 1990s—will fade from sight for a while as it did after the $29 billion blockbuster for RJR Nabisco in 1989. Of the nine deal makers profiled here, four—Gary Wilson, Hugh McColl, Sumner Redstone, and Sandy Weill—say they've probably done their last really big one. Weill (Citigroup), Redstone (Viacom), and McColl (Bank of America), especially, have built their companies through acquisitions, each of them more than once doubling the size of his company with a single transaction. Now, their companies are finally so large that there just isn't much left for them to buy that would have that kind of impact. So the mega-merger business could be in for a slowdown as these titans of takeover digest the prizes they've captured in a hectic period that produced a mind-boggling $2.4 trillion in takeovers around the world in 1998. No other year came close.

The biggest year of the renowned 1980s merger decade was 1989, which produced only $568 billion in deals. The biggest year for deals before 1998 was the previous year, with about two-thirds the volume.

Besides, as 1998 closed, the stock market had hit a rough patch. Numerous large deals, such as the one between chemicals giants American Home Products and Monsanto, had fallen apart. In some cases, the values were no longer there as one stock declined more than

LARGEST DEALS EVER (WORLDWIDE) BY DOLLAR VALUE AT ANNOUNCEMENT

Buyer	Seller	Value	Year
Exxon	Mobil	$86.4 billion	1998
Travelers	Citicorp	$72.6 billion	1998
SBC Communications	Ameritech	$72.4 billion	1998
Bell Atlantic	GTE Corporation	$71.3 billion	1998
AT&T	Tele-Communications	$69.9 billion	1998
NationsBank	BankAmerica	$61.6 billion	1998
British Petroleum	Amoco	$55.0 billion	1998
WorldCom	MCI Communications	$43.4 billion	1997
Daimler-Benz	Chrysler	$40.5 billion	1998
Norwest Corp.	Wells Fargo	$34.4 billion	1998

TOTAL VALUE OF MERGERS AND ACQUISTIONS WORLDWIDE, BY YEAR

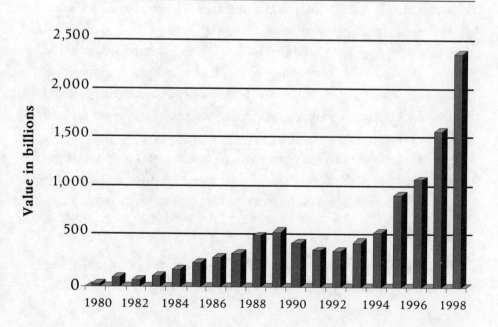

another. Weill's blockbuster deal to merge Citicorp with his Travelers Group was completed anyway. But that deal still serves as an example of how steeply prices had fallen. When the deal was announced in the spring of 1998, the market was just peaking and the merger was valued at $72 billion. By the time the deal was completed in the fall, both companies' stocks had plunged, and it turned out to be "just" a $39 billion deal. As stocks slump, companies look more skeptically at the partners they are marrying. The deals typically get fewer and smaller.

Counteracting that force, though, is the group known as financial buyers, investors who scan the market for undervalued assets and pay in cash—borrowed, to be sure, but cash nonetheless. Financial buyers with some $80 billion in unleveraged, untapped war chests were licking their chops as they surveyed the wreckage of the 1998 stock market pullback. Some were clearly thinking that the turn of the century might belong to them. If so, the volume of deals probably won't fall off much and could even pick up around the world. It would be just another turn in the ever-changing business of shuffling companies and their various parts.

And I wouldn't look for the likes of Redstone, Weill, and McColl to sit completely still. Once a deal maker, always a deal maker. I asked Weill point-blank if he had done his last deal. His return was a simple telltale grin. McColl is no different. Just months after our interview, in which he told me that his final mission was to integrate NationsBank and BankAmerica and then retire, he had already switched gears and persuaded the board to extend his tenure two years beyond his planned retirement date. Redstone may not be done either. He believes the entertainment industry has consolidated about as far as possible for now, but he's quick to note that if some unforeseen force changes the nature of his business, he'll be quick to jump back into the fray.

HOW TO MAKE MONEY: CHANGE THE RULES

Whatever the new millennium brings, you can be sure of one thing: The deal community will adapt. Great deal makers do so constantly.

Carl Icahn was a "value" investor in the 1970s and a leveraged raider and vocal advocate for boardroom change in the 1980s. In the early 1990s he dallied in corporate bonds and made a living as a vulture investor, fighting for the assets of distressed companies that were going through bankruptcy proceedings. Forstmann and Rice have undergone several transformations as well, in their early days relying on double-digit inflation to help them secure big profits and later focusing on revenue growth in the low-inflation 1990s. Henry Silverman paid cash for most of his early acquisitions, but when his company's stock took off, he quickly realized that paying at least partly in stock was the smart play. Later, when he ran into trouble, he stopped paying in stock and called off deals. As bank consolidations intensified, McColl was the most willing to throw out the old rules of valuation and pay big premiums to get the marquee banks he coveted. Bollenbach and Wilson changed all the basics of running the books of a big corporation, exploiting financial restructurings to their fullest to help shareholders realize greater value.

The ability to adapt is just one asset of successful deal makers. These deal makers have many and, I believe, their strengths can be acquired and used by ordinary investors and everyday businesspeople. Among their common characteristics is clearly the deep-seated desire to be fabulously rich. There's no denying it, money motivates. But far more important to their success is a collective level of brazenness that would bust the brazometer. I call them brazen, not merely confident, because, to my great surprise, I found in my interviews that doubts occasionally plague this group of achievers and they lean on one another. Stephen Bollenbach called Henry Kravis for advice when he got caught in a showdown with institutional bondholders over his breakup of Marriott Corp. Sumner Redstone sought the advice of savvy deal maker Laurence Tisch in structuring his bid for Viacom.

But despite their doubts, which tend to be fleeting, they find a way to push on—almost always over objections by the ubiquitous army of naysayers who are present at all deals of size and vision. And that's why

I say they are brazen, even cocky. This quality is rooted in confidence, but it reaches a higher level. Confidence is knowing that a deal is right; brass is having doubts but doing it anyway, knowing that you're smarter than the next guy and will somehow find a way to win. Pushing forward in the face of uncertainty and criticism is a common trait among great deal makers and, I'd venture, successful entrepreneurs at any level.

Of course, cutting great deals takes much more than merely the chutzpah to believe in yourself against long odds. Those odds exist for a reason, and brass alone is the road to ruin. Great deal makers back their supreme confidence with a tireless passion to maneuver around obstacles. That passion, in fact, is what gives them the fortitude to move forward against the advice of friends and colleagues. They know that with hard work, they will prevail. Ted Forstmann's decision to run corporate jet maker Gulfstream is a perfect example. Forstmann had never run an operating company in his life. He was an investor who left management to others. But when his deal for Gulfstream went so sour that it threatened to obliterate his reputation and the health of his firm, he assumed command, worked long hours, and eventually nursed the company back to health. Icahn's persistent "shuttle diplomacy" was a key factor in getting Texaco and Pennzoil to reach a historic court settlement that unlocked the value of Texaco's beaten-down shares. Bollenbach's split of Marriott unleashed a torrent of fury in the bond market, but there was no turning back for him. McColl looked at BankAmerica three times over a period of years before the timing was right. Sometimes patience is the hardest work of all.

Another great asset of great deal makers is their vision for what a company can be—not what it is today—and a keen eye for how change can create value. Sumner Redstone looked ten years into the future to muster the will to pay a huge premium for Viacom. Not only did he like the underrecognized MTV and Nickelodeon networks, he correctly saw that content would become more important than hardware as media, computer, telephone, and entertainment companies collided in the 1990s to take advantage of new technologies that would wire the home as if it were Air Force One. Henry Silverman had the foresight to see that fundamentals in the car-rental industry were turning. He bought Avis and led the recovery. Gary Wilson bought Northwest and changed the business model of the airline industry, shrinking to profitable routes and partnering with other airlines to fill in missing pieces. Forstmann also changed the basic business plan of an industry. On his watch, Gulfstream began making an active market in used jets, initiated a time-share program, dramatically lowered production time, and redirected the company's sales efforts and advertising. Much of what he did has been copied by competitors. Rice made a similar difference at the printer company Lexmark, where strategic and management support, as well as new investment, were required to transform the company into a powerhouse. Henry Silverman put it poignantly in our conversation: "You make money by changing the rules and being there first."

PARANOIA PLUS

Casual observers of Wall Street and business in general may assume that it's a clubby atmosphere in which wealth begets wealth and anyone worth millions must somehow have had it handed to him or her. That's certainly true in some cases. Family businesses are still handed down. But deal makers are, by their nature, street fighters without a lot of friends or, at least, with a fair number of enemies. Many of them have clawed their way from humble roots and serve as an inspiration to all those who started life with little more than their own great expectations. The nine ultrasuccessful deal makers who are profiled in this book come from various backgrounds. Henry Silverman, Hugh McColl, and Ted Forstmann were born well-off, but Carl Icahn, Sandy Weill, Gary Wilson, and Sumner Redstone hail from modest beginnings.

Likewise, some (Redstone and Icahn) were outstanding students. But others like the surfer dude from California, Stephen Bollenbach, and the proud ex-Marine McColl were unspectacular academically. That, too, is an inspiration of sorts. You don't have to be book-smart to be successful.

Among the more curious traits of this group is a general loathing of the Wall Street banker community, the legion of highly paid advisers who are quick to put other peoples' money on the line but are interested mostly in what they'll get out of the deal for themselves. Redstone says he learned early on not to trust his advisers. Icahn would rather act on gut instinct than anything he heard from an investment banker. For a dozen years McColl refused to throw any business to venerable Goldman Sachs because he thinks the firm put its interests ahead of his—the client's—in a deal years ago. Another common trait is the group's love of competitive sports. Rice, Forstmann, Weill, and Wilson all attained notable athletic success early in life. On competition of another sort, Icahn and McColl both earned seed money playing high-stakes poker. Bollenbach and Forstmann were gambling bridge players.

There's also a collective paranoia, the feeling that if a new deal failed, it would spell the end of their days as deal makers. They may feel this way because most deals tend to be bigger than the last one and there's so much more on the line each time. Or maybe it's that Wall Street is a friendless place, where the only thing that counts is your most recent results. Blow a deal, and you lose your investors. Reputation is everything—reputation for success, that is. In perhaps the clearest example of the downside to this blood sport, Henry Silverman saw his company's stock fall from $41 to $7 in 1998 because a deal went sour. It is this well-grounded paranoia that keeps great deal makers working so hard even though they are immensely and irreversibly wealthy. The collective net worth of the deal makers in this book is more than $12 billion.

HIGHS AND LOWS

Before I move on to the deal makers and their stories, I'd like to offer one disclaimer. The purpose of this book is to explore deal-making techniques and the qualities of successful deal makers. My method was to focus on the greatest deals by great deal makers. I asked each subject to identify what he considers his most outstanding transaction. We then talked about how it came to be and the decisions he made along the way. These are largely one-sided stories that the deal makers told me in one-on-one interviews. I have interjected context and some commentary. I have also held their versions up to the scrutiny of press accounts and other factual reports of each deal at the time it was done. In some cases, but not all, I have contacted other people named in the book for their versions of events. But mainly the conversations and the accounts are presented as the key subject of each chapter remembered them.

This book, by its nature, tends to point up the positive aspects of deal making and deal makers. Clearly, the subjects are human beings with faults. They have made mistakes. And though they all are undeniably successful, many have critics who will take issue with the positive light I shine on them. For balance, I have included some discussion of failures and missteps. But because the book is about great deals and what to learn from them, it is mainly a study of success and thus inherently complimentary.

There were several low points in this project. The lowest was when I flew to Charlotte to interview Hugh McColl, who had flown to New York to announce his takeover of BankAmerica. Within a week, an interview with Sumner Redstone was also canceled. But both men wound up spending generous amounts of time with me and provided immense insights into their line of work. It was no fun watching Henry Silverman's stock dive in the summer of 1998—after I had interviewed him about the Avis takeover. Silverman's problems were no reflection on Avis, which stands today as one of the great deals in history. But his failed deal for the marketing firm CUC put a damper on his previously unspotted reputation, and it changed his style and strategy dramatically as he looked forward to selling more businesses than he bought.

In a similar vein, the implosion at small appliance-maker Sunbeam Corp. rocked my plans. Al Dunlap, the Sunbeam CEO and veteran of many deals, was going to be the focus of one chapter—with Sunbeam as the deal of choice. That plan had to be scrapped when accounting questions surfaced and Sunbeam's stock sank from $51 to under $10, and Dunlap was sent packing.

The high points are too numerous to mention. I'm extremely proud of having an insider's view of two of the biggest deals in history: Weill's merger creating Citigroup and McColl's takeover of BankAmerica, both of which occurred in 1998. But each chapter, I think, offers special insights and practical advice. I encourage the reader not to skip over the brief question-and-answer sections that follow each chapter. They contain some of the most entertaining stories and keenest insights straight from the mouths of these masters of the universe.

chapter two

Carl Icahn

Raider with a Pulse

HE'S BEEN CALLED MANY THINGS IN HIS LIFE: trader, investor, raider, tough-as-nails negotiator, good-for-nothing agitator, emotionless profiteer, greenmailing son of a bitch—things better, things worse. Just name it. But what Carl Icahn is, above all else, is a master deal maker. That is to say, he's all the above and perfectly unapologetic about any of it. He's a pure capitalist. The end always justifies the means. Winning is everything, and in Icahn's endless world of deals, winning means only one thing: Who got the money?

So it's no surprise that the middle-class kid from Queens, a medical school dropout, regards his late 1980s skirmish with mighty Texaco as the greatest of his many big deals, which probably number a couple of dozen over three decades. It's the one that made him the most money the fastest, an astounding $500 million for eighteen months' work—a raider's reward for having the foresight to see Texaco as a grossly undervalued stock following the October 1987 stock market crash, and both the genius and the guts to inject himself into one of the most costly and contentious lawsuits in history. That suit was the landmark case brought by Pennzoil in 1984, alleging that Texaco had illegally interfered in Pennzoil's planned merger with Getty Oil. After three years, a Texas jury finally sided with Houston-based Pennzoil and slapped White Plains, New York–based Texaco with a stunning $11.2 billion judgment including interest. Texaco, the proud oil giant, filed for Chapter 11 bankruptcy protection in 1987 to buy time while preparing an appeal.

And that's when Icahn made his move. Never one for exhaustive due diligence, Icahn knew instinctively that the judgment would be negotiated sharply lower during the appeal process. He wasn't alone. The blockbuster judgment was widely viewed as an abomination or, at least, an aberration that would never stand. But what was the real number? $3 billion? $8 billion? Nobody knew. The confusion left Wall Street paralyzed, glued to its collective seat with inertia. But not Icahn. In a palpable show of certainty, he bought 30 million shares of Texaco's slumping stock. Icahn's trader's instinct is one of his chief assets and as much as anything what sets him apart from others in the big leagues of investing and cutting deals. Icahn would later sell those shares and more, bought in the low $30s, for $49 each—but not until after he had brokered a historic court settlement, taken a full-fledged run at Texaco, intimidated Pennzoil by buying some of its "cheap" shares as well, and generally raised the ire of anyone and everyone connected to the oil patch.

"I'VE BEEN BUYING YOUR BONDS"

The first time I met Icahn was during those Texaco days. It was a brief encounter. He had just emerged from a closed-door pitch to the influential shareholder group, the Council of Institutional Investors. He was seeking the group's support in his bid to buy Texaco for $60 a share, or $12.4 billion. At the time, Icahn's bid was a long shot, and it was far from clear where the council stood. But Icahn was at his brash best as he confidently led a famously small entourage down the hall of a Washington, D.C., hotel jammed tight with representatives of the media. Other than his right-hand man for many years, Al Kingsley, Icahn kept few confidants. His disdain for investment bankers, brokers, analysts, and other advice givers is legendary. He prefers people of action.

"Carl," I called out as he approached my stakeout point. "How'd it go in there?" For some reason, reporters (I was covering Wall Street for *USA Today*) always felt comfortable with Icahn. Calling him "Carl," even on a first encounter, didn't seem at all odd. Icahn's approachability is another of his unusual assets. Icahn has used the press as his personal public relations machine for years, if not floating pure rumor, at least seeing to it that arguments favorable to his causes were well aired in the *Wall Street Journal*, the *New York Times, Businessweek, USA Today*, and other influential newspapers and periodicals. On that day, as Icahn walked a hall intermittently illuminated with camera flashes and searing TV lights, he had little to say. "OK. OK. I made my point," was his answer to a reporter he'd never met. Then he glided down the corridor, tossing out one-line morsels in a lightning-filled forest of ravenous news-hounds.

Since that unspectacular introduction, Icahn and I have met a half dozen or more times. We speak by phone irregularly. I never get tired of his stories, his posturing, his style. In 1989, when I was the business editor of the *St. Louis Sun*, Icahn was the controlling shareholder of TWA, the troubled airline he bought in 1985. One day I visited him at his headquarters, then in Mt. Kisco, New York. I was accompanied by my editor-in-chief, Ralph Ingersoll, who happened to own the *Sun* and had a small newspaper empire with properties in the Midwest and East—all of it financed with high-yield, high-risk corporate "junk" bonds. Those were the speculative securities of the day, providing easy money to borrowers who had the confidence to invest that money knowing they'd have to earn back enough to pay annual interest expenses of 13 percent to 16 percent and hoping they would have enough left over to make it all worthwhile. Finding lenders was no problem. This was the heyday of Michael Milken and junk-bond pow-erhouse Drexel Burnham Lambert, an outfit (later discredited and driven out of business) that could find the capital to finance a jet with one wing.

St. Louis is TWA's fortress-hub. The airline controls some 75 percent of the gates at Lambert International Airport. So it was a good story for our paper when the unions and Icahn fought bitterly over Icahn's insis-tence that the unions relax some of their onerous work rules if they expected him to reinvest TWA's cash flow in new aircraft. We flew to Mt. Kisco for an interview. The way Icahn quickly set the tone for the meeting was masterful.

That year had been a tough one for any enterprise financed with junk bonds. In the fall, a proposed union buyout of United Airlines' parent UAL, to be paid for partly with money raised through the sale of junk bonds, fell apart, and the whole market for such debt collapsed. It saddled certain junk-bond issuers, those like Ingersoll with "reset" bonds that roll over at prevailing rates, with increasingly higher interest payments. As the credit risk grew, big bond investors sold their positions and drove the prices of many of these publicly traded bonds to 40 cents on the dollar or less. I didn't know then how much trouble my employer was in. (Ingersoll's bonds were getting cheap, like many others, and the *Sun* ultimately folded less than a year later.) But Icahn did. When he stepped into the spacious leather-and-mahogany boardroom, where Ingersoll and I had been waiting, Icahn hit my boss with a monstrous zinger. "Ralph," Icahn began. "What kind of story are we planning here? Because, you know, I've been buying your bonds."

It was a joke, or so we all assumed. We chuckled. But Ingersoll's chuckle was a little less heartfelt than that of others in the room. Whether Icahn was really buying Ingersoll's bonds, and thus giving himself leverage to take over the budding media concern if Ingersoll missed an interest payment, was not important—at least not to me. We did the story the way we set out to do it. But it was vintage Icahn. Grab the upper hand as quickly as possible, even in a simple interview.

Years later, while at *USA Today*, I met Icahn for lunch at one of his favorite New York restaurants, Il Tinello, an Italian haunt on Fifty-sixth Street, half a block from Fifth Avenue. The place was busy, and Icahn had arrived ahead of me. He was waiting at a round table tucked neatly into a corner. The table was big enough to seat eight but was set for only two, and it had the attention of everyone in a white jacket. Clearly, it was *his* table. After lunch Icahn rose and began to leave. I asked him about the check. He shot me a quizzical glance and said he'd take care of it. "No, Carl," I said. "Let me buy." My offer had nothing to do with generosity or even journalistic integrity. I wanted my boss, who kept a close watch on my expense account, to see that I had taken Icahn to lunch. But it struck Icahn's funny bone, and given that he's worth about $2.8 billion, I guess I can see why. Icahn wouldn't let it go. He stood up in the middle of the restaurant and, speaking for all to hear, bellowed to the maître d': "Look at this, Mario, he wants to buy *my* lunch. When is the last time somebody bought my lunch in here?" Funny thing, though. He didn't argue. If there's a dollar to be made— or saved—Icahn will take it. I bought the meal.

A final personal anecdote about Icahn was our chance meeting one evening in New York's swank 21 Club. I spotted him at the bar and, sensing an opportunity to get some insight, maybe even a quote for a story I was working on, approached him. The story was fairly mundane, having to do with whether the stock market was overvalued. Icahn, who has believed that to be the case since about 1993, gave me his thoughts. When I asked him about a comment for the record, he mulled it over a good twenty minutes before he finally gave me something I could print. "What's in it for me?" he kept asking. "Why should I be in this story?" The quote was a simple one-liner, having to do with the pack mentality of individual investors and his unshakable belief that the mutual-fund-buying hordes would one day get slaughtered in the market. But he had to negotiate each word of the quote. No deal— indeed, no detail down to a quote in the newspaper—is too small to negotiate.

When I met with Icahn for this book, it was the spring of 1998, and he hadn't pulled off any front-page coups in about a decade. But that doesn't mean that he hadn't been busy or that he lost his touch. In an epic confrontation with another great deal maker, Ronald O. Perelman, Icahn had just gotten the upper hand in a bankruptcy-court battle for control of the comic book company Marvel Entertainment, home to Spiderman and the Incredible Hulk. A couple of years earlier, he had backed Bennett LeBow in a failed attempt to take over RJR Nabisco, the picked-over tobacco giant that was such a disastrous investment for Henry Kravis in 1989. Icahn made $100 million trading RJR shares even though the LeBow takeover never happened. Earlier in the 1990s, Icahn made money trading in distressed junk bonds; during this time he frequently butted heads with ex-Drexel banker and sometimes poker chum Leon Black, now doing deals for himself under the name Apollo Management.

The truth, though, is that Icahn hasn't been nearly as active or as visible as he was in the wild days of 1980s merger mania. Here's a guy who struck fear into corporate America for a decade, taking runs at Tappan, Simplicity Pattern, Owens Illinois, Marshall Field, Chesebrough Pond's, ACF Industries, American Can, Dan River, Phillips Petroleum, TWA, and USX. In the 1990s, Icahn—always a value player—has preferred to build a cash hoard of more than $1 billion, waiting, waiting, waiting for a relentless bull market to come crashing down, at which time he would deploy those resources to build large stakes in the scads of companies that would surely become artificially undervalued in a careening market. At the time of this writing, the fall of 1998, the Dow was showing signs of weakness and possibly entering a bear market after an amazing run to 9300 since the 1990–91 recession had pushed it as low as 2365. The run, which at one point lasted six years without so much as a 10 percent pullback, left Icahn and other value players baffled. Icahn was dabbling with some oil stocks, which as a group had been underperforming the market, and giving the tobacco stocks another look (RJR had fallen back to the levels he first invested at on his way to making the $100 million). "I look for that kind of stuff because I don't buy the market," Icahn said. "The market is just ridiculously high for somebody like myself. I think it's way too high. These multiples [of earnings, book value, and dividends] are crazy, and sooner or later all these people flowing money into mutual funds—something's going to go wrong." So for the most part, Icahn was holding fast to his cash, confident as ever that his time would come again.

FROM POKER TO BROKER

Such patience is a virtue that this sixty-three-year-old raider didn't always have. In his younger days, words like *aggressive, eager,* and even *pushy* better described Icahn. And while it's never easy to tell what shapes the values of a man like Carl Celian Icahn, it is clear that he needed an assertive side if he was ever to break out of the humdrum life to which he was born on February 16, 1936, in Brooklyn, New York. His parents, Michael and Bella Icahn, moved a year later to the neat, middle-class section of Bayswater in Queens. Michael had a law degree from Fordham University but never practiced law, preferring to chase in vain after his lifetime dream of singing on the stage. Bella was a school-teacher. Carl was their only child, and both parents were extreme liberals who viewed excessive wealth as a social disease. But Bella had a younger brother who married money and moved to Scarsdale, an exclusive northern suburb where the families have house help and the children drive shiny new BMWs to high school. Visiting Bella's brother, Uncle Elliot Schnall, provided young Icahn with his first glimpse of real money, and Icahn, the irascible A-student who graduated second in his class at Far Rockaway High School (a public school) and stunned everyone by gaining a scholarship to haughty Princeton University, never let that vision get too far out of sight.

At Princeton, Icahn was a premed student mainly to keep peace with his mother. He never stopped thinking of Uncle Elliot's wealth and how he might attain such status himself—without taking a lifetime to do it. In many ways, Icahn, the working-class Jew from New York, was out of his element at Princeton. But his intelligence rarely was in question. He excelled at philosophy and became one of the best chess players on campus, and his senior thesis was judged the best in his class. After Princeton, Icahn enrolled in New York University Medical School but soon realized that he was sickened by the sight of blood and quickly, to the great disappointment of his mother, left the school never to return.

He became an army reservist. It was during basic training that he developed a love for poker, and although real blood made him nauseated, the make-believe red stuff that spills when you slay someone across the poker table invigorated Icahn. With his gift for bluffing and calculating odds, Icahn managed to build a chest of poker winnings worth about $4,000 over just a few months of active duty at Fort Sam Houston in San Antonio, Texas. Then he decided to take the money and put it and his considerable skills to work in the stock market.

It was Uncle Elliot who found him his first job, in 1961, as a broker trainee at Dreyfus, where Icahn displayed an uncanny knack for picking winning stocks. But when the market tanked in 1962, Icahn lost everything he had managed to make in the previous two years. To pay the rent, he occasionally "leased" his apartment in New York to an acquaintance who used it for romantic interludes. But Icahn quickly recovered, landing a job at Gruntal, where he built a hugely profitable options business. In 1968, Uncle Elliot loaned Icahn $400,000 to buy a seat on the New York Stock Exchange, and thus was founded Icahn & Co., which continued to exploit gaps in the underdeveloped options market and later struck riches buying and selling similar securities in different markets at wide price differences, a practice known as arbitrage. By the mid-1970s, Icahn had progressed to full-fledged raider, hooking up with Kingsley to look for "undervalued" companies, or those selling in the stock market for less than the value of their assets.

To talk about Texaco, Icahn and I met in his dark-paneled boardroom on the forty-seventh floor of the General Motors Building in New York, at Fifth Avenue and Fifty-ninth Street. The office looks out over New York's Central Park, which was turning a pale spring green. From the boardroom, you get a fantastic view, looking north over the park all the way to Harlem. Inside, Icahn's office has a blue carpet, dark wood, and loads of macho art—statues of horses and lions and paintings of more horses and lots of historic battle scenes. He also decorates with deal memorabilia. In his lobby is the framed letter from Pennzoil chief J. Hugh Liedtke, dated December 24, 1987, congratulating him on getting Texaco to settle the landmark case.

As is typical of Icahn, our conversation started slowly, with the usual quizzing. What is the book about? Would he have any control over the final version? (Answer: very limited.) And could he stop the tape recorder? (He did so just once.) Icahn talks much as he conducts his business, often resorting to sweeping generalizations and leaving the details to underlings. Fortunately, there is an extensive public record on his battle with Texaco, so it was no problem filling in the gaps. I should note that an unauthorized biography, *King Icahn,* by Mark Stevens was an immense help.

OPPORTUNITY CALLS

The Texaco deal began inauspiciously enough. Its roots date to the mid-1980s, when Icahn one day fielded an unexpected call from the wealthy Australian investor, Robert Holmes á Court. Holmes á Court was seeking an audience with Icahn, who promptly obliged. "He came in and he was very soft-spoken, very reticent, hardly even talked," Icahn recalled. "And he just came up and he goes, 'You know, Carl, you should look at a company called Texaco. It's very undervalued." Icahn knew Holmes á Court by reputation. His trader's instinct told him that if Holmes á Court was pushing Texaco, there had to be a reason, and he, Icahn, would absolutely take a look. He suspected that the Australian wanted him to buy a stake and start rattling cages in an effort to get a special dividend or some other "shareholder enhancement." That's OK. Icahn doesn't mind being used, not if there is a chance that he can turn the tables and use the user. So he resolved to look at the company the next day, and that's about all that was said about Texaco. The two passed some minutes talking generally about deals and investing, when it dawned on Icahn that Holmes á Court seemed to be bragging a lot. It deepened his suspicions about the Australian and ticked him off to boot.

"He tells me that he flies around in a 727 like some kind of satellite," Icahn recalled. "He stops in so many different cities he hardly knows what cities he's in—to look at his many investments. And then he goes back to Melbourne or Sidney and then comes around again. And then he said to me that he had about $12 billion he was looking to invest, and he was real proud of that number. But I asked him if it was his or if it was lines of credit, and he says to me, 'No, no, it's lines of credit with banks. But they're all my friends, and whenever I have to call on it for any type of deal, they'll give it to me.'" Icahn respected Holmes á Court but could barely contain his amusement. Here was one of the world's best-known deal makers trying to tell him that a line of credit was as good as money in the bank. "You know, Sir Robert," Icahn said in a deflating tone. "When you need the money, they won't give it to you. The banks won't give it to you." The two laughed lightly and then parted company.

Icahn woke the next morning and scanned the numbers on Texaco. Sure enough, the company seemed underpriced, considering its vast oil reserves and stellar brand name. Still, in the $40s, it was no raging buy. Icahn bought a few hundred thousand shares, enough to keep him watching. And he did nothing for more than a year. Then opportunity beckoned. First came the Pennzoil judgment and then the April 12, 1987, bankruptcy filing by Texaco. With that considerable cloud hanging over the oil company, its stock was hard hit in the October 1987 stock market crash, slumping to $28 from the low $40s. Icahn started buying again, this time with a vengeance. He amassed some 6 million shares by mid-November 1987. He still didn't have a plan. He simply viewed the stock as cheap relative to Texaco's assets, and he was dead sure that the staggering court judgment would be reduced. His goal at that point was to make a little noise only if necessary, but basically to wait for the stock to rise and then cut and run.

But then fate played a role. In mid-November, Icahn boarded a small plane for Martha's Vineyard, where he planned to shop for a house for the summer. On the seat was a New York city tabloid, which carried a headline to the effect that the Australian billionaire Robert Holmes á Court was having financial problems and would probably have to sell assets, including his 24 million shares of Texaco. That stake was equal to 10 percent of the oil giant's outstanding shares. Icahn wasted no time. When the plane landed, he called Holmes á Court in Australia. The two failed to hook up, so Icahn went house hunting and returned to his home in Bedford, New York, that night. When he got home, the Australian returned his phone call. "Sir Robert," Icahn began, "it's none of my business, I realize, but it says here in the papers that you're having trouble."

Holmes á Court sheepishly returned, "You were right, Carl. The banks won't give me the money, and I need it." Icahn leaped at the opportunity. Others, including the raider Sir Jimmy Goldsmith, had been sniffing around Texaco. If Icahn was going to make a big play, this was his chance, so he floated an offer. "Look, Sir Robert, I'm not going to try to take advantage of you," Icahn began, as he tried to take advantage of the Australian. "The stock is $29, and if you want to sell it to me at that price, I'll buy it, all of it or part of it. I'm not trying to get it for $26 or $27. On the other hand, I don't want to pay you $29 and an eighth. Further, I'm giving you permission to go out and tell everybody that Icahn will give you $29. If it helps you get more, hey, you owe me dinner. But I need an answer in forty-eight hours." It was a perfect preemptive strike. Holmes á Court called back in twenty-four hours and agreed to sell Icahn 12 million shares at $29. That was in November. By January, Icahn had bought the other 12 million shares for $37 and had thus donned full battle gear.

DRINKS IN THE MORNING

Now, for the first time, Icahn had big money on the line in Texaco, and he was determined to play a role in settling the litigation and boosting shareholder value. It wouldn't be easy. Texaco and its tough new CEO James W. Kinnear, a lifetime Texaco man, rightly thought that they had gotten a raw deal in the Texas courts. They let everyone know that they felt certain that a higher court would vacate the judgment entirely and that they were prepared to go to the Supreme Court if they had to. Pennzoil CEO Hugh Liedtke, for his part, insisted that he would settle for nothing less than full payment.

It was, of course, a pair of poker bluffs of the highest order. Liedtke knew full well the judgment would be reduced on appeal, and Kinnear wasn't about to bet the ranch, all of Texaco, on a reduced judgment— no matter how likely that outcome seemed. But the two showed no signs of giving an inch, so Icahn became determined to play the mediator, forcing both sides to reach a deal before they all grew old. Icahn quickly began meeting and phoning all the key people in the case, the equity committee, the creditor's committee, the bankruptcy attorneys, and Pennzoil's character of a lawyer, the King of Torts, Joe Jamail, a close friend of Liedtke who had represented Pennzoil in the suit against Texaco. That suit arose from an internal dispute at Getty Oil Co., which essentially was put in play—considered ripe for takeover—when Gordon Getty (the firm's largest stockholder) began to push for change. Liedtke allied himself with Gordon Getty and made a push for control. After a twenty-five-hour board meeting, Liedtke was sure he had a deal for Getty Oil, but a few days later Texaco stepped in and bought the whole company. Liedtke was bitter and dejected. Since his early days as George Bush's partner in the oil patch, he had wanted to build a big oil company. Getty Oil would have let him realize that dream. He felt he had been cheated, and he convinced the King of Torts to take the case, alleging that Texaco had conducted "tortious interference with a contract." For his efforts in the case, Jamail ultimately collected $500 million. So Jamail, a gun for hire, was feeling pretty good the morning he and Liedtke went to New York to visit with Texaco's new largest shareholder, Icahn, to try to put a deal together.

"OK, Carl, you're the guy who can settle this," Jamail began.

"Yeah, yeah," Icahn shot back. "But there's no way you are going to get $4 billion or $5 billion."

That quickly, Liedtke snapped. He had been insisting on the full $11.2 billion, and here Icahn was opening the talks by refusing even half of that amount, which hadn't even been offered. "C'mon, Joe, let's get out of here. I told you this guy Icahn can't help us." Jamail, still wearing the Stetson hat he had arrived in, was in sync with his friend.

He was upset, though not so much at Icahn's opening salvo as with the air of finality in which it was presented. "This is bullshit, Hugh," he said to his friend. "We're leaving." He then told Icahn to "get fucked" and began to leave.

Deep down, Jamail knew that Liedtke really wanted to settle and that $4 billion or so was in the ballpark. So he was relieved when Icahn quickly asked them not to charge off before they could talk some more. Liedtke was having none of it. He left. But employing his deepest Texas drawl, Jamail turned to Icahn and said, "You know, heyall, I think you can help me, boy. You can help me. Let's us go have a drank."

Incredulous, Icahn noted that it was 10 A.M., and he didn't know where they could find the martini that Jamail was looking for at that hour. "But I used to go to the Parker Meridien on Fifty-sixth Street a fair amount, so they knew me," Icahn recalled. "So we go there and it's like a Bogart movie. The chairs are up on the tables, and people are cleaning up. We convince them to set a table, and they start bringing over martinis for Jamail." Icahn was drinking Bloody Marys. Over a couple of rounds, the two exchanged small talk, Icahn explaining why he likes tennis, that he disappointed his mother by dropping out of med school, and that when he travels he often flies coach. The last item practically made Jamail spit out his martini. "You are one cheap son of a bitch, Icahn," said the King of Torts. The two laughed and became friendly. Icahn would later ask Jamail to represent him in unrelated matters. Finally, Jamail got down to business.

"You heard the fat man in thar," he said, referring to the portly Liedtke. "He ain't gonna take less than four and a half or five billion. C'mon. That Kinnear is so dumb, you want to spit when you see him. You're going to have to talk to him and help us out here. You got a big position."

"Kinnear will never pay $4 billion or $5 billion," Icahn repeated. "I have talked to him." Then, to Icahn's surprise, Jamail opened the door for a much lower number. "How much do you think he *will* pay?" the Texas lawyer asked.

"$3 billion," Icahn said, not missing a beat.

Happy to hear a number, Jamail told Icahn he had a deal.

Of course, there was no deal until Icahn could sell it to Kinnear and Jamail could sell it to Liedtke. But at least here was a hard number to work around, with sponsorship on both sides. Jamail, tasting his own $500 million windfall, was by now feeling so good that he started telling Icahn about another case he was working on. He was representing the driver of a pickup truck who had run into a ditch forty miles east of Houston and caused extensive property damage. "I think my guy was a little drunk," Jamail confided. "The suit was for $11 million, but we settled for $7 million."

"Well, that's great," Icahn said. "You got them to take only $7 million."

"Oh no," Jamail said, busting with a grin the size of Texas. "They paid *us* $7 million."

The King of Torts was, indeed, a man of persuasive powers. He convinced the jury that another truck, one owned by a nearby commercial firm, had crossed the yellow line and forced his drunk client off the highway. The commercial firm had to pay. But no less persuasive was Icahn, who, shortly after the meeting, bought 2 percent of Pennzoil's stock, just for good measure, in a not-so-subtle message that illustrated to Liedtke how easily trouble can come knocking.

Icahn and Jamail parted company that day as the lunch crowd started arriving. They were feeling good about their chances, determined to broker this settlement at $3 billion. About the same time, other interested parties—including the influential equity committee, which represented the interests of all shareholders in bankruptcy proceedings—were fast concluding that something around $3 billion just might be the right number, too. Still, Icahn was having trouble talking Kinnear into taking the deal. Kinnear, though heartened by how low the figure was, wasn't absolutely convinced that he shouldn't take his shot in court with the appeal, and that drove Icahn crazy. He tried to land a spot on the equity committee, to push the settlement. But he was turned down.

It didn't matter, though. The equity committee also had its eye on $3 billion, and when Judge Howard Schwartzberg, overseeing the bankruptcy case in the Southern District of New York, ruled that to move the process along, the equity committee would be invited to propose a reorganization plan for the court to consider, Kinnear finally had to think seriously about taking the deal. In the end, it was the equity committee and Liedtke who came to terms for $3.4 billion. And they might have ended up at that figure all on their own anyway. But Icahn's persistent "shuttle diplomacy" and Jamail's early behind-the-scenes insistence that $3 billion—the figure he and Icahn agreed to over martinis and Bloody Marys at 10 A.M.—was a good number certainly didn't hinder the process. And they probably moved it along far faster than would otherwise have been the case.

THE BATTLE IN TULSA

The settlement was only the beginning of Icahn's oil strike. It got the stock moving again into the high $30s. But Icahn had just whetted his appetite, and he was far from content with his quick winnings. Texaco was perhaps the most mismanaged of the big oil companies, and when Icahn bought the second half of the Holmes á Court block of shares in January 1988, he was determined to force wholesale change at the company and get the stock even higher—to $50 or even $60.

It was about that time, and with that goal firmly planted in his mind, that Icahn took another unexpected call, this one from his buddy Leon Black. At the time, Black was an investment banker for Drexel, which had helped Icahn raise the money to buy TWA two years earlier. He was in town with a client, the elderly Armand Hammer, chairman of Occidental Petroleum, and his heir apparent to run the company, Ray Irani. Would it be OK for the three to visit Icahn at his Bedford home to talk about Texaco? Black inquired. Icahn, always one to listen to a deal, welcomed the meeting, and the four sat around his fireplace one wintry evening discussing the value of Texaco.

After Black made the introduction, Irani did most of the speaking for his side. They wanted Icahn's stock and were willing to pay $45 a share. Icahn, thinking he could get the stock to $60 with a little effort, wasn't interested. So, with Hammer nodding off in front of the fire, Irani went a little higher. "$50," he said. Then Hammer woke up and began to berate Icahn. "$50 is a great offer," he said. "You're a stupid young man not to take this offer. If you say yes, we'll go talk to Texaco, and we'll do it right away. It is ridiculous for you not to take it."

Then Hammer nodded off again, and Icahn, who had doubts about how serious the offer was anyway, told Irani no deal. With that, Irani began to protest: "Carl, we've done all the numbers, and I'm telling you, I'm telling you as sure as I'm living, I swear to you we can't do a penny more than $50." Icahn turned him down again, and with that, Hammer emerged from dreamland once more, looked at Icahn, and—undermining all of Irani's efforts—asked: "So, did you take the $55?"

But even the price of $55 would not have compelled Icahn to sell. He wasn't sure what Black was doing there with the inattentive Hammer, but he had become convinced that there was no deal to be done. He agreed to the meeting because, well, you never know. It doesn't hurt to hear somebody out, especially if he is accompanied by a known player like Leon Black. It's one of Icahn's traits: Hear them out because everything is for sale; every deal can be done at the right price. This meeting ended with nothing more to show for it than a hearty chuckle at Hammer's expense. Even if the offer had been a firm one, Icahn at that time was convinced that he could unlock even greater values by playing the agitator, a role he had by then perfected, and probably would have turned it down.

After the Hammer meeting, Icahn went on the attack. In the newspapers, he criticized Kinnear as slow to respond and inept at running a large company. In court, he opposed the equity committee's plan to reorganize and submitted his own plan, which would strip away Texaco's takeover defenses and make the company vulnerable to an outside buyer. Icahn thought that maybe he would be such a buyer, or at least pretend to be such a buyer, though he told no one of that plan right away. Ultimately, Icahn's reorganization plan was shot down by the equity committee but not before the committee, which harbored no love for Icahn, had been persuaded that some of Icahn's proposals made sense. The committee's plan included provisions to remove the takeover defenses, though in Icahn's view it did not go far enough.

Still, the door was now ajar, and Icahn was ready to pry it wide open. When Texaco's management dragged its feet on the sweeping change that he wanted, Icahn, who had been lobbying for quick asset sales and a onetime special dividend to shareholders, announced that he would launch a proxy fight to place his own candidates on the board of directors. Still, Texaco refused to placate Icahn, and in May 1988 Icahn floated a $60-a-share bid for all of Texaco. "I never thought I could win it," Icahn now concedes. "At least I didn't think I'd have much of a chance. But I figured the worst is that the company would have to do some things to get the stock price up in order to get the votes to beat my slate of directors. I just wanted to see the stock go higher."

Nevertheless, Icahn played his hand to the hilt. Texaco's management may have had its doubts about Icahn, suspecting all along what the raider today freely admits. But Kinnear and company still had to respond to Icahn's challenge. It became a sordid affair, both sides hiring private investigators to try to dig up dirt, and both sides swapping insults in full-page ads that ran in the *New York Times* and other newspapers.

Amid all the nastiness, Icahn was briefly engaged on another front. The unions at TWA, a company Icahn controlled, had learned that Icahn was funding his Texaco foray partly with TWA's cash, and they were livid. TWA's cash, they argued, was not for speculative investment. It was for investment in new jets and the airline business, they insisted. "I bought maybe 10 million shares, at $36 or $37, with TWA money," Icahn said. "What's the difference? I own TWA. But I'm hearing all this crap from the unions, and I tell them, OK, I'll buy the stock from you. I had the money, and by now the stock was at $45, so that's the price I paid." The airline booked an $80-million investment gain, and the issue disappeared—for a time. But, Icahn said, when he ultimately sold out at $49, "the unions were upset, saying that they should get the top price for those shares, that I had taken money from them. They're raising hell to this day even though I took all the risk."

Back on the Texaco front, Icahn was busily putting together a strategy. Texaco's main argument against him was that he could not raise the money needed to finance such a large buyout. So Icahn began searching for partners, from fellow raider T. Boone Pickens to the international conglomerate Hanson PLC of Britain. Ultimately, though, no partners would be found. In some cases, Icahn feared he'd have to give up too much control, and in others, the chemistry just didn't seem right. Without a partner, the influential pension-fund managers, who collectively owned most of Texaco's stock and would thus decide whether Icahn's slate of directors would win, weren't likely to support Icahn. But it wasn't necessarily a lost cause. A few big shareholders were eager to tweak Texaco's management, which hadn't delivered solid financial performance for years. Others thought that Icahn was right—that entrenched managers had no stake in the company other than their jobs. They wanted Icahn's bid put to a vote.

Still, Icahn knew he was coming up short on votes. Then, a miracle, or at least a possible miracle, occurred. In the weeks just before Texaco's June 17, 1988, annual meeting in Tulsa, Oklahoma, the epicenter of oil country, a block of stock equal to 4.9 percent of Texaco was put on the market. Whoever controlled that block just might be the key to helping Icahn over the top, or so he thought. But Icahn had a problem. He already owned 14.9 percent of Texaco at that point, and under the law in Delaware, the state where Texaco and hundreds of other large companies are incorporated, he couldn't go past 15 percent without triggering onerous filing requirements and limiting his flexibility to buy and sell more shares. In the end, Icahn identified the owner as none other than Kohlberg Kravis Roberts, which found a way to the middle of so many 1980s deals. Icahn pleaded with Henry Kravis to deal him the voting rights over the block. But no deal was forthcoming.

To this day, Icahn remains furious about the way Kravis treated him. Sometime before the June 17 proxy vote, Kravis managed to sell his 4.9 percent block, but it wasn't until after the date of record for voting on Icahn's director's slate had passed. What that meant was that Kravis, who had no economic interest in Texaco, still had 4.9 percent of the vote. King Henry, as he was known, waited until the last minute and then submitted his ballot. The final tally revealed that Kravis had supported Texaco's slate.

That all but ended the skirmish. The final tally was 58.6 percent for Texaco's slate of directors and 41.4 percent for Icahn's. To casual observers, Icahn came nowhere near winning. But his efforts weren't in vain. Texaco focused on the votes it had failed to get and realized that the outcome was much too close for comfort. It could not risk another battle and so quickly decided to deal with Icahn before he came back at them—not just with a proxy contest for control of the board but with an outright hostile bid for the entire company.

After months of quiet negotiation, in January 1989, Texaco announced special dividends totaling $8 a share to be funded by the sale of some $7 billion in assets. In return, Icahn agreed not to buy any more Texaco stock and, in effect, not to vote his block as long as he owned it. Both sides dropped all litigation. On June 1, 1989, Icahn sold his entire stake, which had reached 42.3 million shares, for $49 each, or $2.1 billion. It was and still is the second largest single trade in the history of the New York Stock Exchange, behind a 48.8-million-share block of Navistar traded on April 10, 1986. Three prominent brokerages—Goldman Sachs, Shearson Lehman Hutton, and Salomon Brothers—bought the Texaco block, which they divided and resold to clients.

THE ONE THAT GOT AWAY

If Icahn was the big winner in Texaco, so, too, were its millions of shareholders, who not only saw their stock rise 30 percent in less than two years but shared in the special dividend as well. In the end, even Icahn's bitter enemies in the Texaco struggle came to appreciate what the raider had accomplished. And even Kinnear acknowledged Icahn's helpful role in forcing Texaco to get back on track. Speaking at the Waldorf Astoria in New York in March 1989—soon after the final settlement with Icahn—Kinnear was asked point-blank if Icahn had made a contribution to the renewed health of Texaco. "You'd like to say no," he told a reporter from the *New York Post*. "Can you say that it galvanized and got the attention of the rest of the organization? I'd have to say that's possible."

Who were the losers? Certainly not Texaco, which was revitalized. Neither were Liedtke and Pennzoil victims. They might have gotten a better settlement if not for Icahn, but it would have taken longer. You could argue that the investors who failed to reach a deal to partner with Icahn missed out. But then they didn't have anything on the line and might have done just as well wherever they turned to invest after they failed to reach terms with Icahn. Was Kinnear a loser? Maybe. He had to acknowledge how poorly the company had been run. But the main losers, and this is true in all deals that work, were the people who sold their stock too soon. That means the finger points squarely at Holmes á Court, who let go of his 24 million shares at an average price of about $33. In so doing, he missed out on an eighteen-month profit of $384 million. It was essentially a transfer of wealth to Icahn, and it came about largely because the Australian had become overextended in other investments and couldn't get the banks to stake him any longer.

For his part, Icahn remains philosophical about the success. Some of it was luck, he knows. Like picking up that newspaper on the commuter plane to Martha's Vineyard. "I've always said that luck comes and goes, luck comes to everybody," Icahn said. "But it's the guy who's worked hard who is able to take advantage of the lucky break who gets ahead. So the hardest worker is suddenly the one who is always getting lucky. So, you see, the harder you work, the luckier you get. Is that really luck? I don't know, but that's the way it works."

Icahn hasn't always been lucky. I asked him to name some of the deals that went sour on him. He squinted and came up blank. He lost on a few stock trades, but said that's not really losing because in trading it's how you do overall that matters. A baseball player who hits .300 doesn't think of himself as a loser because he misses on seven of ten chances. If there's an opportunity that got away, it was in the early 1970s when he pioneered the discount brokerage business along with Charles Schwab. "I had this great idea," Icahn said. "Why the hell not keep the commissions down and do the trades cheaper? Why should these goddamn analysts matter? There's no great value there. Why not knock them out and charge less? So I did a little of it, but basically I was so busy investing that I never got the right guys to run it."

Ultimately, he gave up on the retail brokerage business after he lost a personally wrenching $500,000 lawsuit. A client had bought a lot of stock on margin—that is, with borrowed money. When the market suddenly plunged, Icahn's brokers tried to reach the client to tell him he needed to put up more money or his stock would be sold to pay off the margin debt. They never reached the client, and sold all his stock. "We tried to reach him ten times," Icahn said. "But the guy was an alcoholic, and he was in an institution drying out. Get this. The judge wouldn't let us tell that to the jury. He said it was prejudicial. So I lost the case. I couldn't believe it. I said what the hell do I need this for? And I sold. That was really stupid. I should have stuck with it. Shit, it probably would be worth $2 billion today."

Icahn the trader, the philosopher, the storyteller, has an engaging manner on many subjects. I'll close this chapter on King Carl with a series of questions and answers that, since you've read this far, I figure you'll enjoy.

Question: *Carl, how do you know when a deal is right?*

Answer: Every once in a while in business, and this is what you have to wait for, if you're the guys with the most money or the knack or understanding, you get a no-brainer. It hits you over the head. It's so good that you act immediately. I don't know if it's instinct or experience. It's both. You see that something is just being given away for one reason or another, and the smart guy knows how to take advantage of that. Something inside just goes click, and you know it. Remember that movie *The Hustler,* with Jackie Gleason as Minnesota Fats and Paul Newman as Fast Eddie Felson? Newman was talking about why he loves pool. He hits some crazy shot and it goes in, and he says to some girl, "It's a great feeling when you're right and you know you're right. Like all of the sudden I've got oil in my arm. Pool cue's part of me. You know, it's a pool cue. It's a piece of wood but it's got nerves in it. You can feel the roll of those balls. You don't have to look. You just know. You make shots that nobody's made before. And you play the game the way nobody's ever played it before." That's the way it is with great deals, something goes click. I mean you're not always going to be right. Luckily, I've been right most of the time.

Question: *Was there ever a point in the Texaco deal when you thought you might lose money?*

Answer: Never. This one was never going to be a loser. It was one that just hit you over the head. I mean, really, this was just a question of how much I was going to make. I'm telling you, I couldn't lose in this one. Still, when I bought the stock, a lot of people were saying I was stupid. Friends of mine would say, "How can you buy this thing? It's going to blow up." "C'mon," I'd say. "That's absurd. It's too valuable. It's just too good." And you know, that's always the case when you do these deals. There's always somebody saying you can't do it. It's wrong. It's going to blow up. It's terrible.

Question: *How would you describe your style? You talk about instinct and opportunity without doing the due diligence . . .*

Answer: No, no, no! I never said I don't do due diligence. We had done a lot of work on Texaco before the opportunity ever came. So we knew something about it already. What I'm trying to tell you is that in these deals where you make these big investments, you have to have the instinct to say I'm going. You can't just sit there. When you buy into these things, there's a lot of calamity going on. So if you wait for all the numbers, you never do it. You just have to know that the basic value is there. I didn't have to do a lot of due diligence to know that Texaco was worth more than $29 a share.

Question: *How has that instinct served you in the 1990s?*

Answer: In the 1990s I bought all these junk bonds, and it was kind of the same. Everybody was telling me, "Oh, they're terrible." They're this and they're that. They're going to blow up. But you don't have to be a genius to analyze these things. I mean, look at [Donald Trump's] Taj Mahal [casino in Atlantic City]. When the bonds were 25 cents on the dollar, everybody was saying, "Oh God, no, the Indians are coming. The Indians are coming. It's no good." [Taj bonds became depressed when the casino filed for Chapter 11 bankruptcy protection and legalized gambling on Indian reservations in Connecticut was taking hold and about to start cutting into the Taj's revenues.]

  Well, I'm looking at these bonds and saying, you know Trump just built this thing for $1.1 billion. The value is there. So I start buying the bonds, and there are days when

I'm the only buyer. And my friends keep yelling at me about the Indians. "The fucking Indians are coming. There's going to be gambling built up all over, and you're going to have nothing. You're crazy, Carl." And I said, "C'mon, bullshit." So I bought every bond I could get. They kept telling me about the fucking Indians.

You know, I made a deal with Trump, and to this day Trump will tell you that I saved his ass, and in a way I did because I supported him [in bankruptcy proceedings]. He got to keep the Taj even though the equity committee wanted revenge. Yeah. The equity committee wanted revenge. Wilbur Ross [who represented the equity committee] told me that. I said, "What? They want revenge? What is that all about? This is business."

So I got them on the phone and said, "Look, you know I'm a tough guy, and I'm taking this deal [the reorganization plan]. How can you not take it? It's a great deal. You're getting everything without having to go through the war." So, anyway, we ended up getting the deal done, and a few years later the bonds are back up to 96 cents on the dollar. Everything is going great at the Taj, and I sell my bonds, after they went from 25 to 96, and one of those guys who was calling me a few years earlier saying what an idiot I was calls me again and says, "Carl, I just bought some of those bonds you're selling at 96. Those are great bonds. They're going to 100. Why are you selling?" And I said, "You know, can I ask you just one question? What ever happened to the fucking Indians?"

Question: You've spent a fair amount of time battling over assets in bankruptcy court in the 1990s. Did the Texaco experience open your eyes to some of these bankruptcy deals?

Answer: Yeah. I've learned a lot, and we've done a lot there. But, God, they were giving those bonds away in the early 1990s. Those deals were so good they hit you over the head, and yet there's always a problem. There's always a reason not to do it. You just have to get past that.

Question: *To this day, there is some question as to how big a role you actually played in getting Texaco to settle with Pennzoil. The people on the Texaco equity committee believe they had much more to do with it.*

Answer: You know, that doesn't really matter to me. I didn't care. I just wanted to see a deal done. I didn't care who got the credit. The deal, I believe, was going to be done no matter what. I always believed that. It was just a matter of what price. I figured $3 billion was about where Liedtke would come in, and it was. You're never sure about these things. But I don't care who gets the credit. My philosophy in these great deals is that you get involved and then you strategize, find ways to make it happen quicker. You make sure that the greatness comes out. You've got to be able to ride with it for a while, take some bad breaks, and not let your emotions get involved. You can't let emotions get into it if you're a professional at this stuff. People are going to do stupid things. You can get mad for a few minutes, but then you have to let it go. The idea is to buy things cheap. But you have to see why it is cheap. Generally, I find there are emotions involved when something is being given away cheap. And that's when it all goes click. Then, you have to make sure the value comes out one way or another.

Question: *When did you start to realize that you were a pretty shrewd deal maker?*

Answer: It's funny. I was always good at certain kinds of logical thinking. Like the philosophy course in school. I won awards for that. I always wanted to go on with philosophy. I was going to go to medical school. I was always a very good student. In certain areas, I was really quite good. I mean, without having to do much work I was always able to think logically, you know, and that kind of thing fits on Wall Street. But it's funny that I learned the hard way. I made a lot of money, and then the market crashed in 1962, and that's when I realized that you have to work, really work. You can't just play the market. So I guess that was the time it hit me, if there was a time. Now I'm always at work. I'm a workaholic. To this day I don't play the market. I mean, I play a little, obviously, with all the money I have. But I always like to look at asset plays, stuff that makes sense no matter which way the market goes.

Question: *You talk about luck that you make. What about genuine luck? Ever get any of that?*

Answer: I'll give you a quick story, one that will make you laugh. It's always better to be lucky than smart, right? Leon Black and I were fighting it out over E-II, the company that has Samsonite and Culligan. I won't bore you with the details, but I end up owning like 3 million shares, and Leon is running the company. He says to me, "Why don't you come on the board?" He's got these bright guys on the board, you know, Harvard MBAs, but he says, "Why don't you sit on the board?" So I decide OK. I'll sit watch on the board. One day, one of these Harvard MBAs says, "Hey, we ought to open up some plants in India, sell water, you know, through Culligan." I said, "India? What the hell do we know about India?" I looked at Leon, and I said, "C'mon, Leon. Buy me out. The stock is at $22. You can have my 3 million shares at $20." But these geniuses look at Leon, too, and say, "No way. Forget it, Icahn, you're a minority investor. You sit on the board. You suffer with it. Screw you. We're not buying you out." You know what I ended up getting for that stock about a year and half later? $80. All those Harvard geniuses, right? They should have taken the deal. I was lucky.

chapter three

Hugh McColl

Southern Dynamite

WHEN YOU DO DEALS FOR A LIVING AND
you're good at it and the object is to build a business—not simply to
take out a profit, as is the case with raiders like Carl Icahn and "financial engineers" like Ted Forstmann and Joe Rice, whom you'll meet in
later chapters—the nature of deal making is that each transaction gets
successively larger, and the most recent one generally is the most
impressive. Ask any great deal maker who has built an empire what his
best deal was, and often he will shoot back either that it hasn't been
done yet or that it's the one he is working on now—the one that will
take his empire to the next level and provide more scale to crush the
competition.

This, by the way, takes nothing away from the singularly profit-
minded. Raiders like Saul Steinberg, T. Boone Pickens, Irwin Jacobs,
Ronald Perelman—all familiar 1980s names—perform a vital economic function, forcing managements to keep improving the value of
their companies or risk the meddling of unwanted agitators. The presence of a raider generally benefits all shareholders by keeping stock
prices on the rise. Raiders, except for the best, have slipped below the
radar in recent years, largely because an unprecedented bull market
through the 1990s has kept the stocks of even inept managers' companies surging forward. Raiders are most active, and their economic benefits most visible, when prices are down, not up. Late in a strong bull
market, there just isn't a lot of management prodding to be done.

Financial engineers, on the other hand, tend to find deals in any market environment and serve the equally critical function of policing corporate assets—in effect, making sure that the assets that come under their wing reach full flower. How do they do it? Through leveraged buyouts, or LBOs, specialists like Rice and Forstmann (as well as Henry Kravis, Tom Lee, and others who are not in this book), stand ready to take control of misfit and underperforming divisions commonly found in many large companies. They are a kind of lonely hearts club for unwanted properties, borrowing heavily against the properties they buy and then working feverishly to mold them into profitable stand-alone entities. They trim fat and purge operating problems, always with an eye toward finding a buyer at a much higher price three to seven years down the road. In later chapters, you'll see how Rice did that with IBM's cast-off typewriter division, now the bustling electronic printer company Lexmark, and how Forstmann did it with the ailing jet builder Gulfstream.

Raiders and LBO artists are opportunists in ways that empire builders can never be. Their deals don't necessarily get bigger because ultimately the only thing they are out to build is a personal track record of making money, which they do by picking off wounded game of all sizes and varieties—one at a time. For LBO guys, the goal is not to layer synergy on top of synergy but, rather, to fix what's there and sell it. Raiders try to persuade boards of directors to enhance shareholder value through asset sales and special dividends; then they sell their stock and move to the next gimpy duck.

Those are, to say the least, vastly different endeavors from the one that Hugh McColl embarked on four decades ago, when he entered the banking business determined to gobble up, assimilate, and continue to operate every available chartered bank between North Carolina and California. McColl's hell-bent acquisition spree started in 1983, the year he became CEO of regional banking power NCNB (later renamed NationsBank), and now includes the purchase of more than fifty banks, each generally larger than the last and culminating in the $48 billion blockbuster deal for BankAmerica in the spring of 1998. (McColl's bank is now called Bank of America.) It was the largest bank deal ever. No surprise: McColl, whose net worth is about $55 million, tabs the BankAmerica deal as his best in a long and unparalleled career. For an empire builder like McColl, each deal must land him pieces to fill out part of a puzzle, and because size itself is a goal, each deal tends to leverage off the last and adds progressively more heft to his asset base and market value. Big. Bigger. One day, the biggest. It's a simplistic strategy that has been tried in many different industries, but few have mastered it. Count as one H. Wayne Huizenga, who built trash company Waste Management and video king Blockbuster Entertainment that way. But it's a short list after that, and none has done better at this high-stakes game of addition than the ex-marine from Charlotte, North Carolina, arguably the greatest bank deal maker in the greatest era of bank mergers in history.

Between 1988 and 1998, the number of banks in the United States dropped by a third from 15,000 to under 10,000 in a consolidation wave fueled by years of reckless lending that ended in a full-scale banking crisis in 1990. In the four years ending in 1991, more than 750 banks failed, including a record 206 in 1988 alone. But bank-merger fever wasn't just about insolvent banks running to the arms of healthy banks. There was a growing view among visionaries in the banking industry, and eventually in Washington, that U.S. banks would have to bulk up—and that meant link up—if they ever hoped to gain the size needed to compete in the global economy with international behemoths like Japan's Dai-Ichi Kangyo and Germany's Deutsche Bank. The U.S. economy may be the largest in the world, but by most measures none of its banks ranked in the global top 10. Indeed, in the late 1980s, of the 50 largest banks in the world, only three—Citicorp, Chase Manhattan, and BankAmerica—were from the United States.

Other factors spurred bank consolidation, too. Not least were the crumbling fire walls that had kept brokerage firms out of the business of commercial banking since the 1930s. Those barriers don't exist throughout much of the world, and, again, U.S. banks would need a level playing field to compete in the world economy. A new age was fast approaching in which size would be the key to survival. McColl knew it early on, but he was hardly alone. For years he's been challenged in the bank-takeover game by the likes of John McCoy, who runs the super regional powerhouse Banc One in Columbus, Ohio. Another takeover rival is Ed Crutchfield, who runs the superregional First Union just down the road from McColl in Charlotte. Virtually every bank of any size in the United States was put together with mergers in the 1980s and 1990s. The largest U.S. bank prior to 1988, Chase Manhattan, is largely the product of a merger in 1996 with Chemical Banking, a deal that was brought about by another great deal maker—though not a banker—Michael Price, the activist money manager at the Mutual Series of mutual funds. If there's an exception in the banking world, it would be Citicorp. It generally has grown without a steady diet of big acquisitions. At least, that is, until 1998, when Chairman John S. Reed hooked up with another star deal guy named Sanford I. Weill at the insurance and brokerage powerhouse Travelers. The two agreed to one of the largest mergers ever: $39 billion worth of international banking, insurance, underwriting, trading, brokerage, and credit-card clout. That deal and Weill are the focus of the next chapter.

NO PRISONERS

Even before he became CEO of NCNB, McColl had made a name for himself as one of that bank's aggressive senior executives. McColl was so comfortable gobbling up banks that he once entered into a merger pact without his boss's approval. He had to call it off. But it was through many other acquisitions in which McColl had a hand that his bank quickly became the biggest in North Carolina, surpassing its much-loathed rival Wachovia Bank. After McColl finally landed the CEO title in 1983, this proud southerner staged a kind of Sherman's march straight through the belly of America—buying banks in fifteen states, including Florida in 1982, Texas in 1988, Georgia in 1989, and Maryland in 1992, and the $9.6 billion acquisition of Boatmens in 1997, adding nine Midwest states, including Missouri, Kansas, Oklahoma, Arkansas, Iowa, and Illinois. BankAmerica in 1998 was the capstone to his amazing career: the deal that gave him the distinction of having a bank with branches in contiguous states that stretch from his beloved Carolinas to the Pacific Ocean. No other bank can make a coast-to-coast claim, and though McColl says that he's done buying— that it will take until 2001 to assimilate BankAmerica fully—I'm not so sure. His creation still could use a New York bank, but McColl has always insisted that the Northeast is not a growth market and that he prefers to stay south of the Mason-Dixon line. He could also use an international bank, something that might not have seemed important just a few years ago. But with the globalization of the economy and the current wave of mega-mergers in banking, the concept of hooking up with a big international partner has currency.

When I interviewed McColl for this book, one of my main concerns was that by the time it was published, McColl would already have inked another, even bigger, deal that would change his company in bigger ways than the BankAmerica deal. "I don't think that can happen, nor do I want it to happen," McColl assured me in the summer of 1998. "And we're really committed to not having it happen." But once a deal guy, always a deal guy. In our conversation, McColl made it clear that he precludes nothing. "Having said that," he deadpanned, "I must acknowledge that the last four deals I did came when I wasn't ready."

Before I started working on this book, I had never met McColl, who speaks with a deep southern accent—one that he is known to exaggerate in the company of New Yorkers as a kind of signal that the world is changing and the damn Yankees have nothing on those good old boys from down South. So deep is his accent, even when he's not exaggerating, that he openly wondered if my New York–based transcriber would record our conversation accurately. He joked that I should send my three hours of tapes to North Carolina for transcription. I should note here, by way of disclosure, that I've had a special interest in McColl's career since late 1996, when he announced plans to buy Boatmens Bancshares. I was a shareholder of that Midwest bank and have held on to my stock through each reincarnation—first Nationsbank and then Bank of America.

My one-on-one relationship with McColl got off to a rocky start, though. Months in advance, he had agreed to meet me in his office in Charlotte on Monday, April 13, 1998, to discuss his favorite deal of all time, that being (at the time) the 1988 takeover of venerable First RepublicBank in Dallas. It was a landmark deal. First Republic had assets of $32.5 billion while McColl's NCNB had assets of only $29 billion. First Republic was in dire need of a partner, having slipped into insolvency during the Texas real estate collapse. But tiny NCNB was competing against the biggest banks in New York and California. That McColl was even willing to bid is testament to his ego. In the end, though, ego won. McColl's team from North Carolina discovered a tax loophole missed by everyone else and walked away with the biggest prize in Texas. That one deal doubled McColl's asset base, and did so on terms so generous that virtually no one in the industry argues that it wasn't one the savviest bank deals ever. McColl managed to heave over $1 billion of the acquisition costs on to taxpayers, and in so doing managed to spend beyond normal capacity and thus enter the expansive Texas market. For the first time, he and his team were seen as players who were not to be taken lightly by even the biggest banks in New York.

I was eager and had prepared extensively for the interview. My plane tickets were ordered far in advance, and I was set to leave the airport at Newark, New Jersey, at about 6 A.M. on April 13—the Monday following Easter Sunday. When I arrived at the airport, though, I got my first glimpse of that day's *Wall Street Journal,* and there on the front page was the startling headline: "NationsBank to Merge with BankAmerica." I realized that this proposed merger might mean that my interview with McColl was off, so I checked my office. No word. I checked at home.

No word. I wasn't quite sure what to do, but I certainly didn't want to be responsible for blowing the interview, so I got on the plane and flew to Charlotte.

Somewhat predictably, in retrospect, I was greeted by a public relations type who told me that McColl was unavailable, that he was in, of all places, New York, to meet with analysts and the press—the very city I had just left. McColl, or at least his press people, didn't want to cancel my interview even though McColl would be out of town. Why? He thought it would tip his hand—signal that something big was in the works. I am, after all, a journalist. He didn't want to risk any leaks. Still, I was upset. There are many ways to call off an interview without tipping your hand. Journalists get put off all the time, and we don't automatically run to the phones to check out the excuse. After venting my frustration and making a few phone calls, I went back to the airport and flew home. Upon reflection, and after spending subsequent time with McColl, I have come to understand the treatment. A man like McColl takes no prisoners when closing a deal. If a few people are inconvenienced, so be it. He'd take that treatment just as readily as he metes it out. He plays by his rules and takes no unnecessary chances. Once the deal is closed, he goes back to smooth out any bumps. The first order of business, though, is always to get the deal done. Weekends, holidays, missed commitments. No matter. When there's a deal in the air, all else is expendable.

Some weeks later, possibly the most powerful banker in the nation more than made up for what I had considered unnecessarily cavalier treatment. On a trip to New York, he set aside ample time and came to my office to make good on his commitment to sit for an interview. There was no mention of the earlier blown meeting, and the interview went well. McColl arrived at the Time/Life building on Fiftieth Street at the Avenue of the Americas with only one aide, his top PR person Lynn Drury, whose southern accent may be even deeper than McColl's. McColl was wearing a blue suit, white shirt, and a colorful tie dotted with elephants. (He likes ties with elephants and often buys one or more while traveling with a merger in the making.) McColl has intense powers of concentration, near total recall, and a writer's eye for detail. After I asked him to relate the story of the BankAmerica deal, I had only to listen. Often he would seem to go off on a tangent only to wend his way back to the point five or even ten minutes later, stitching together every lose end as tight as the skin on a baseball.

BANKER'S BLOOD

Hugh Leon McColl Jr. was born on June 18, 1935. He came by his competitiveness naturally and early, and it has stayed with him. He was born and raised in Bennettsville, South Carolina, a quiet town of about ten thousand in Marlboro County, two hours southeast of Charlotte. In this sleepy southern setting, his favorite childhood book was *The Little Engine That Could*. Today, on a pillow in his office is stitched: "The trouble with being a good sport is you have to lose to prove it." The McColls were a prominent family in those parts and even have a town named after them north of Bennettsville near the state line. McColl's father, Hugh Sr., or "Big Hugh," was a banker. So was his grandfather. So was his great-grandfather, Duncan Donald McColl, a Civil War veteran who founded the Bank of Marlboro and brought the first railroad and textile mill to this town of farmers. Duncan McColl guided his bank through the Great Depression and then sold it to become a cotton broker. McColl's father and grandfather eventually invested in another bank, Marlboro Trust Co., which is where young Hugh worked as a teenager.

Hugh was the oldest of four—three of them boys. His mother, Frances Carroll McColl, instilled the same competitive spirit and sense of community in all three. She was an artist who studied in New York and then returned to Bennettsville, where she set up a studio behind the McColl home near the center of town. She was also a musician and something of a daredevil, who once dove off a trestle bridge into a river just for fun. Hugh, who climbed Mount Kilimanjaro at age sixty, must have inherited some of that spunk. The McColl boys grew up battling one another in backyard football and pickup basketball. They didn't watch a lot of TV. Their mother wouldn't have it. Instead, she encouraged them to read and made *Beau Geste,* a romantic novel about brotherly love, a rite of passage for all three. True to their heritage, they all became bankers. The youngest ended up at C&S/Sovran in Atlanta and stayed on after big brother Hugh took the bank over in 1991, the deal that morphed NCNB into NationsBank.

Throughout his academic life, McColl was a so-so student. But he was immensely popular and was elected president of this high school student council and later voted Best All-Round Boy in his senior class. He lettered in four sports. His yearbook quote reads: "He who is talented in leadership holds the world's dream in his grasp." McColl left Bennettsville to attend the University of North Carolina at Charlotte, where he majored in business administration. Upon graduating in 1957, he entered military service (two years as a marine), where, like Carl Icahn, he took a fancy to no-limit poker. Tales abound. One night, having lost everything he had brought to the game, he ran upstairs to borrow $10 from a friend and came back to win $3,000. McColl's years as a marine were uneventful, though he served briefly in war-torn Lebanon. He returned home after his stint in the U.S. Marines, which he calls his school of management, planning to take up the family calling—banking. Big Hugh had big plans for Hugh Jr.; he sent him to the big city of Charlotte to start his banking career.

McColl's first full-time bank job was in 1959 as a trainee at American Commercial, a small bank that within a year would become known as North Carolina National Bank, later to become NCNB. Always ambitious, he made steady progress up the ladder, becoming senior vice president in 1968. In 1974, at age thirty-eight, McColl was named president of NCNB and was then a clear candidate to succeed his mentor, Tom Storrs, as CEO. The recession of 1974–75 stalled his career, as it did for nearly everyone at the bank. NCNB, which had a reputation for risk taking and this time had made a big, bad bet on the direction of interest rates, nearly fell into insolvency. But the bank survived; a few years later, Storrs retired and McColl was crowned CEO. McColl was in the right place at the right time. Interstate banking laws were beginning to crumble, and the greatest bank merger era on record was about to occur. McColl, the acquisition-minded banker; the mountain climbing ex-marine; the five-foot, seven-inch man with the ten-foot ego, would be there to lead the charge.

CALIFORNIA DREAMING

Hugh McColl knew for most of his professional life that he would one day end up owning a California bank. He didn't know when. But much of what he built in the 1980s was geared toward amassing the bulk that he would need to get a California bank and whatever else he needed to fill in the pieces in between. "We always perceived that this sunbelt strategy we were following had to include California," McColl said. "One of eight Americans lives there. The GDP, if it was its own country, would be in the top ten in the world. The numbers are phenomenal. It's so persuasive that it's not worth talking about anything else." Like many banks in the early 1990s, BankAmerica ran into trouble with bad real estate loans in a slumping economy. McColl's earliest recollection of fancying a deal with BankAmerica was in that period— in 1991. It was, at the time, a pipe dream, one that included visions of buying Wells Fargo or First Interstate instead. Never a small thinker, McColl, in the depths of the worst banking crisis since the Great Depression, had his eye on California's largest banks.

But he was years from bagging such a quarry. At home in Charlotte, the newly named NationsBank was having problems of its own. It had just acquired C&S/Sovran, and the stock was deeply depressed as Wall Street adopted a wait-and-see attitude toward the aggressive McColl in this era of bad real estate loans and mounting uncertainty over the economy. The depressed stock deprived McColl of the currency he needed to make any further deals of any kind, much less to move on a California trophy. But, as early as 1991, McColl had thought about buying BankAmerica.

Slowly, the recession of 1990–91 lifted. The banking crisis eased a few years later, buoyed greatly by a generous Federal Reserve policy that held short-term interest rates abnormally low—under 3 percent— while long-term rates drifted higher. The net effect was that at a time when there was virtually no demand for loans, banks paid little for deposits and then invested the proceeds in ultrasafe treasury securities at far higher yields, locking in an easy profit. It was, as I wrote in a column back then, an unofficial bank bailout. Depositors were screwed. The economy was on track, and they should have gotten better returns on their deposits. But the Fed chose to delay raising short-term rates to let banks fatten up after some scary lean years.

Early in 1995, the economy was solidly on track, and the banks were healthy again. And the California fire was burning hot in McColl's soul. By then, bank consolidations had gained momentum and the deals were getting bigger than ever. In February, McColl took an unsolicited call from an investment banker at Merrill Lynch. Would McColl and NationsBank be interested in sitting down with BankAmerica and its CEO Richard M. Rosenberg? The call came to NationsBank's chief financial officer (CFO), Jim Hance, who took it directly to McColl. "Yes," was McColl's quick, one-word response. And with little more than an expression of interest delivered through a third party, he boarded a jet for San Francisco to meet with Rosenberg at BankAmerica's headquarters. That McColl would jet to the West Coast on a thin promise is a measure of the man. "Part of my own style and confidence level is that I'll go anywhere at any time to talk to some-body about anything," McColl said. "I've learned not to consider it a concession to go. If a deal is going to work, it'll work anywhere. So I didn't mind flying out there." On this point, McColl clearly was not blowing smoke. The very fact that I was interviewing him in my office was testament to his go-anywhere philosophy. It was also testament to his cocksure ego. A lot of executives feel they are giving up something psychologically if they go to the other guy. McColl's point is that it doesn't matter. If you know what you're doing and have confidence in your strategy, meet the guy in his backyard. Why not? You don't lose a chess game on the first move. If he wants it, give it to him.

So McColl met with Rosenberg for about three hours in Rosenberg's office, and then the two went to dinner. They met again in March and a third time in April, this time in Pensacola, Florida. Both men could sense what McColl calls "the wonder of it all," his phrase for a perfect bank fit. NationsBank hadn't yet bought Barnett Banks (January 1998) to become dominant in Florida. Nor had it yet bought Boatmens (January 1997) to become a big player in Missouri and surrounding states. But it was already in Texas and nearly every state from there back to North Carolina. Merging with BankAmerica then would pretty well have given McColl the coast-to-coast franchise he so wanted. But there were obstacles, and both men sensed that the deal wasn't likely. Still, they kept talking. It's another McColl tactic. Keep the lines open. Stand firm on the things you must have but don't say no to anything unless pushed. There's nothing to gain in shutting off the talks before all the issues are on the table, and knowing all the issues, as you'll see in this case, can help a great deal later on.

Both men were hesitant before the Pensacola talks. Things weren't progressing, and since Pensacola is a fairly small town, they worried that two hotshot bankers would be noticeable there together and that it might send the stock market the wrong message. They agreed to keep a low profile.

"So the two of us jet in on private airplanes, get picked up by stretch limo, and go downtown to the best hotel in town," McColl recalled with a disbelieving laugh. "It was a very poor low profile, I'll be the first to say. It turns out nobody in Pensacola knew who we were, but they must have known we were some big dogs. I'll never forget it." Word of the meeting never leaked, and it's a good thing because that meeting is where McColl's second hankering for BankAmerica ended in disappointment. "All I had to do was reach out my hand," McColl later wrote in a note to himself, "and I would be the most powerful banker in the world." But he just couldn't do it.

At the time, BankAmerica was the bigger of the two, with assets of $215 billion. NationsBank's assets totaled $170 billion. That gave Rosenberg the presumed negotiating leverage that comes with size. In the course of the talks, McColl had learned just how Rosenberg planned to use his edge. Essentially, McColl was being offered the job of CEO, but only for the next three years, at which time a BankAmerica executive would succeed him. The successor that Rosenberg had in mind was his ambitious senior executive at the time, David Coulter, who would later take the reins from Rosenberg at BankAmerica and finally, in the spring of 1998, cut the deal that joined the two banks and completed McColl's march from the East to the West Coast. The succession issue didn't sit well with McColl, a fiercely loyal man who didn't want to sell out his management team, none of whom would ever get a chance to be CEO. Beyond that, Rosenberg wanted to move the headquarters to Chicago and keep the BankAmerica name.

It wasn't a bad deal for McColl. But aside from the issue of selling out his management team, he felt he would be selling out the city of Charlotte—indeed, the entire South. McColl never said no to the deal. He simply did not say yes, and the wonder of it all, for a while longer, remained a slippery slope that McColl could not ascend. He was as determined as ever to get to the top, but only on his terms. McColl was showing tremendous patience.

To understand why McColl turned down the BankAmerica deal in 1995, you have to understand his love of the South. Ultimately, when he finally cut a deal with BankAmerica, he agreed to a name change—something he and his predecessors had done several times before. So that was not the real deal breaker. And in any true merger, a CEO's favorite managers face longer odds of being the eventual successor to the corner office because there are that many more high-quality executives in the fold. These matters weighed on McColl in 1995. But what really zapped the deal was the proposed move to Chicago. Rosenberg wasn't asking a lot. After all, he was proposing to meet McColl halfway—not in San Francisco, not in Charlotte. Chicago, Rosenberg must have assumed, was the perfect place for a national bank—smack dab in the heart of the nation. But that is the point, McColl now says, "that we cratered on."

Why? McColl freely admits that he carries the flag for the South. Not in the sense of any confederate ideals, but in the sense that he's a southerner with tremendous southern pride and believes he owes it to it his part of the country to stay there and let the economic benefits and prestige of running one of the world's largest banks accrue to his native region. "We are entrepreneurs who built this bank," McColl said. "We built it in the South. I was not willing to move the headquarters of this company out of the South then, now, or tomorrow—never. Why should I? Is there someplace in the world better than where I am? Show me somebody that's been more successful than me while I've been operating out of Charlotte, North Carolina. You don't have to be in Chicago or New York to have all the brains in the world."

McColl often turns reflective when asked about his loyalty to the South. He's clearly studied southern history, noting in some detail how the North inflicted crushing economic sanctions on the South after winning the Civil War. The North, for decades, managed to usurp through discriminatory rail taxes most of the South's natural resources, using them to industrialize and modernize while the South stagnated. "My part of the world was economically disadvantaged," McColl says. "And it exacerbated its problems with segregation, trying to maintain two separate school systems." In the 1960s, when the South threw off the shackles of segregation, McColl said, was "when the economy really exploded against the rest of the nation, and it's been a growth machine ever since. And we've done well by staying in the South all these years."

The BankAmerica deal died in Pensacola in spring 1995, mainly over the issue of where the new company would be located. But McColl wasn't giving up. On a European trip with some of his top managers later that year, McColl's thoughts began to drift, obvious for all to see. Knowing his boss well, CFO Hance turned to him at one point and said: "Don't worry about it, Hugh. One day we'll buy BankAmerica."

Indeed, that day was approaching. First, though, came the $9.6 billion deal for Boatmens, then the $15 billion deal for Barnett. McColl still had his eye on California, but he wasn't about to remain idle, waiting for a deal to come to him. Buying Boatmens gave him a huge Midwest presence and, more important, blocked his acquisitive competitors from landing this enviable franchise with business in nine states in America's heartland. Banc One, for example, could have used Boatmens to connect its Ohio base with its Texas operations, giving it a smooth geographic presence from the Midwest to the South. The Barnett deal solidified NationsBank's preeminent position in the South and finally made McColl number one in the critical state of Florida. Best of all, though, is that the two deals bulked up NationsBank, adding $25 billion of market value to the bank and, not lost on McColl, making it a bigger bank than BankAmerica. Thus the next time McColl sat down with an executive from the California giant, he would have the leverage in determining such deal-breaking issues as succession and whose headquarters to keep.

AN INSULT AND A NEAR DEAL BREAKER

In November 1997 McColl and his NationsBank brain trust had their plates full. The Boatmens acquisition wasn't yet a year old, and the Barnett deal had just been announced. There was much work still to be done to combine the banks' computers and other systems. McColl hadn't lost sight of his California dream, but he was plainly so busy that it was, temporarily anyway, out of his mind. Then out of nowhere his top strategic planner, Greg Curl, who came to him from Boatmens, approached him one day and said, "Hugh, you know I've looked at the numbers. Here's what Wells Fargo looks like. Here's what BankAmerica looks like, what First Chicago looks like, and what Fleet National looks like. There is no combination that gets us close to what BankAmerica can do for us. This is it. This is your answer. This is California."

From that day on, McColl thought about little else. Not that the information from his top planner was any surprise. After all, McColl had been flirting with BankAmerica for six years. But now he had size, reputation, and market clout—much more than just the ego and unbridled confidence that had been his calling card in 1991. Finally, McColl thought, it was time really to pursue this goal. So while the operations people at NationsBank had barely started integrating Barnett and NationsBank, McColl and his top dogs turned their focus to BankAmerica.

Maybe the word leaked. Or maybe the brass at BankAmerica, which for six years had been doing a mating dance of its own, simply refocused on NationsBank at the same time. It's not clear. But what is clear is that McColl didn't have to wait long for things to happen. On February 26, 1998, the well-known Wall Street lawyer Ed Herlihy, from the venerable law firm Wachtell, Lipton, Rosen & Katz, called McColl's trusted CFO, Jim Hance. "Would you be interested in talking to BankAmerica?" It was déjà vu, for sure. But this time, McColl told himself, the prey would not escape. McColl knew well that BankAmerica, though it had a strong franchise west of the Rocky Mountains, had become locked into a regional bank role. Its Texas franchise was slipping, and that was supposed to be its key for future growth. Meanwhile, it faced huge technology costs getting its branches up to speed and preparing for the year 2000 issue. That issue was a serious one for the banking industry, which could ill afford to risk massive computer failures and information gridlock when the calendar flipped over to 2000.

Indeed, BankAmerica and its new CEO David Coulter had looked at a number of potential partners: American Express, Citicorp, Chase Manhattan, First Union, and NationsBank. Only NationsBank gave the bank the fit it needed, both geographically and in terms of superior technology. So there it was again, and seen from the other side: the wonder of it all.

McColl gave Hance the go-ahead to start talking with BankAmerica, whose CFO, Michael O'Neill, was a friend of Hance's. Over the phone, the two hashed out all the old issues related to name, location, succession. McColl gave Hance explicit instructions not to cave on any of those issues. He and Hance also worked out the details of how such a transaction would be financed: a stock swap. For a deal this size, a stock swap seemed obvious. But would the deal have a clear buyer, someone who would pay a premium over the other bank's market value? Or would it be a merger of equals? These questions were all dealt with by Hance and O'Neill over the phone, a nifty strategy on both McColl's and Coulter's parts because it saved the decision makers from having to confront the issues head-on, a situation in which egos might get in the way.

After a series of lengthy phone conversations over the course of a month, Hance and O'Neill finally had their first face-to-face negotiation on March 27, 1998. At that meeting, which lasted nearly four hours, the two came to terms on a financial structure. By then, BankAmerica's Coulter, a twenty-two-year veteran of the bank, had more or less caved on the issues of succession and location, though those points would have to be formally addressed later. It was clear that his primary goal was to create value for his shareholders, which he had been doing via asset sales and the dispatching of underperforming business lines since he was named CEO. No way did Coulter want to pay a premium for NationsBank, which might have dropped his stock lower. McColl, too, was reluctant to pay a premium. So both CFOs agreed: It would have to be a merger of equals. Neither side would tolerate the payment of a premium price that, although it would enrich one side's shareholders, would leave the ongoing bank—one in which both banks' shareholders would have a stake—in a weakened state.

The two CFOs studied both banks' stock prices during the previous thirty days and found a constant relationship: If the two banks were one, on the basis of market capitalization, NationsBank would be 54 percent of the company, and BankAmerica would be 46 percent. They agreed that each set of shareholders would have that level of ownership after a deal was done. To accomplish that, the NationsBank board authorized McColl to seek a deal in which NationsBank's shareholders would continue to own one share of the new company for every share they owned of NationsBank while BankAmerica's shareholders would get 1.1316 shares for every 1 share that they held in BankAmerica. Finally, it was time for McColl and Coulter to meet.

At this point, the basis for a deal was well known, and conceptually both sides had signed off. The wonder of it all was right there, and both sides were eager to lock it in. But the deal itself was a long way from complete. Many is the deal that gets squashed at the last minute by a clash of egos at the top. In 1997, computer-company acquirer Eckhard Pfeiffer at Compaq had all but inked a deal to buy Gateway 2000, when Gateway's idealistic founder and CEO, Ted Waitt, got bad vibes about how his loyal employees would be treated and nixed it all minutes before he was to sign the papers. Everything now hinged on how McColl and Coulter would get along. And on March 28, only a day after the two negotiators had so masterfully put together a frame-work, the whole thing threatened to blow up. Hance met with McColl at McColl's house to brief him on the discussions that had taken place and to prepare him for his first encounter with Coulter. At the end of that briefing, Hance told his boss that there might be one little prob-lem. BankAmerica's brass, it seemed, didn't want its company to be known as a "southern bank." No one had said it directly. But it was strongly implied.

McColl, a second-to-none banker, hard-charging deal maker, and firmly rooted southerner, boiled over inside. "At that point I really had concluded, 'Screw them. I don't need this. I won't take that insult.'" It was Saturday. McColl didn't sleep a wink and was up early on Sunday to take his venom out on the weeds in his garden. After he jogged seven miles, he and his wife went to the 8 A.M. service at Covenant Presbyterian Church in Charlotte, where he had been spending part of his Sundays for thirty-eight years. As he was flipping through the Bible during the service, he came upon a passage (Matthew, xxvi, 52): "All they that take the sword shall perish with the sword." Long before, McColl had taken to looking for signs to push him onward in tough deals. While working on the First RepublicBank deal and struggling through one of the low points, he stumbled upon a $10 bill on the sidewalk. There was a bookstore nearby. He went in and bought a prominently displayed book entitled *Texas*. That was his sign to press on and get the Texas bank.

On this Sunday, McColl took the Bible's words as another sign. He decided he would not take up the sword; he would let the "southern bank" insult pass and move ahead. After church, he went to an old friend, Joe Martin, who lived across town. Martin had been with McColl in the early days at NCNB and was a trusted adviser. He encouraged McColl to press forward. Hance, meanwhile, had been urging McColl to move in the same direction. So on Monday morning, March 30, McColl called the highest-level meeting at NationsBank. He met with his three top executives: William F. Vadber, the head of risk management; Kenneth D. Lewis, president of NationsBank; and James H. Hance, vice chairman and CFO. One of them was destined to succeed McColl if no big changes occurred. Each knew that a merger with BankAmerica would greatly expand the pool of eligible successors and lessen his own chance of running the bank. But they all encouraged McColl to go make the deal with Coulter.

MEETING OF THE MINDS

From his vantage as reigning king of bank deals, McColl knew well what was at stake in the meetings to come. He studied his eventual partner—but for now adversary—in detail, right down to knowing that Coulter's favorite drink was a Tanqueray martini. McColl's research told him that Coulter was a thinker, that he liked to proceed slowly and consider everything carefully. This would not be an easy negotiation for McColl, the fiery ex-marine whose deal-making style, in his words, "is to stay in one room until we have a deal. Lock all the doors, don't eat, don't drink, don't go to the bathroom until you've got a deal."

The two men had agreed to meet in Phoenix at the annual Bankers Roundtable on April 2–5. But with the blessing of every key person in his organization, McColl, who had long been scheduled to give a speech at the University of Kansas on March 31, accelerated the meeting to April 1, the following day. Hell, he figured, he was halfway across the country already. Why not go the extra two thousand miles and get things rolling? It was McColl's willingness to meet on the other guy's turf and his penchant for action at work again. After his March 31 speech, McColl answered questions for about thirty minutes. It was an astute gathering of business students, professors, and the press. But they totally missed it when McColl answered one question from the floor. "Mr. McColl," the questioner began, "you have always spoken of your yen to buy a bank in California. What can you tell us about those plans today?"

"Nothing," he responded coolly.

Practically every time that question had come up publicly or privately for the previous seven or eight years, McColl would unleash a torrent of reasons why California made sense and why he had to get a bank there. But not this time. When the question was asked this time, McColl was neck-deep in negotiations for the biggest bank merger ever. His answer was as truthful as it could be. He could say absolutely nothing.

Had another banker been present, he or she might well have understood that McColl was on the verge of something big. Had an astute money manager or savvy investor been present, he or she might have run out and bought shares of every California bank with publicly traded stock. But the moment passed without further comment. That night, McColl boarded a jet for San Francisco, checked into the Mandarin Oriental Hotel, and endured his fourth consecutive night of little or no sleep. He was to meet Coulter at 9 A.M. the next morning, April 1.

McColl arose early that day. He sent out for his customary breakfast of two four-minute eggs, bacon, and toasted rye bread. A diabetic, he took only a swallow of orange juice and some coffee. He paced. He wrote himself notes about what to say and what not to say. At two minutes to nine, he finished dressing and strangled his tie into a knot. At 9 A.M.: no Coulter. At 9:05: still no Coulter. McColl, already on edge from the lack of sleep, felt several cups of coffee working over his stomach and a slow anger started to build. At 9:07: no Coulter. McColl was three minutes from checking out in a boil. At 9:08, the bell finally rang. McColl opened the door. Coulter apologized for being late. McColl, his near tantrum already receding—though not yet dissipated—shot back: "Well, I thought maybe it was an April Fool's joke and you weren't coming."

"It was the hardest thing I've ever had to do to punch that elevator button," Coulter said in complete seriousness. With that, McColl softened and replied: "Well, I've been nervous myself." He confided that he hadn't slept well for nearly a week. The two sat down at a small breakfast table and shared stories about their careers and personal lives. McColl spoke of his younger days growing up in North Carolina, then some about his tour with the Marines. Coulter spoke of growing up in rural Pennsylvania, where his father was a long-haul truck driver without the means to put him through college. If he hadn't been able to obtain a full scholarship, he might never have gone to college, Coulter said. He ended up as a researcher for the Federal Reserve. That last point caught McColl's attention. His former boss and mentor, Tom Storrs, had the same job early in his career. Was this one of those signals? McColl was becoming convinced that this deal would happen, possibly sooner than anyone could have thought.

McColl, perhaps betraying his eagerness, then fine-tuned the conversation. "So, David, why would you do this deal? I'm happy to be here talking. But why do this?" Coulter then went through the logic. McColl was relieved that what he heard jibed perfectly with his own thoughts. That is, there was "the wonder of it all," and Coulter was on board. Geographically, competitively, and culturally, the deal just made perfect sense. But Coulter went beyond these issues, to an area that

McColl found surprising. And it revealed Coulter as a man who had given a great amount of thought to his company's future. In his two years as CEO, Coulter had personally made the rounds to meet the top two hundred people in his organization. "He had concluded that about a third of his team were A players, about a third were C players, and about a third were sub-C players," McColl recalled. "He didn't have the management to take him where he needed to go. And he had picked us as best of class. We had the management and the aptitude to take the expanded company forward."

The meeting ended about noon. The two hadn't made any specific strides, but they had made the intellectual and emotional contact that it takes to get a deal done. Coulter also had mentioned that he and his wife would be willing to move to Charlotte, something McColl hadn't asked for but that he considered a big step toward reaching a meeting of the minds. Before running off to another commitment, Coulter asked McColl to come to dinner at his home that night. McColl agreed. He then went off to lunch with Hance and Herlihy. Things were moving along pretty well. So the three started talking about a management team. After three hours, McColl dressed casually for a walk about town. He picked up a couple of elephant ties, one of his strange rituals during negotiations for deals, and then went back to the hotel for a shower. Coulter's car picked McColl up in front of the Mandarin and whisked him to his ninth-floor apartment in Pacific Heights at 7 P.M. sharp.

Coulter, his wife, and McColl engaged in light conversation before they sat down to a light, catered meal. Then, Coulter and McColl got down to business. What would the management team look like? The two weren't sure if it should be six or eight, and then Coulter, the math whiz and deep thinker, shocked McColl. "I intuitively think it should be six," he said. McColl, on red alert, took note. He had studied Coulter, and the man rarely did anything "intuitive." McColl, on the other hand, was as intuitive as they get. Was Coulter playing to him? What would he want in return?

Ultimately, what Coulter really wanted was to get the deal done. He and McColl parted company that night without having even discussed their own roles or who would be on the management committee. But in meetings between the CFOs and lawyers the next morning, it became clear that Coulter wanted to move fast. The BankAmerica side was talking about time lines leading to the completion of the deal. McColl still wanted to firm up the basics, like who would be the CEO, even though that was pretty much a given. The two agreed to meet again on Thursday, April 2, at the Bankers Roundtable, a high-profile conference in Phoenix, the night they had originally intended to meet for the first time. Only now things were moving so fast that both men didn't want to spend any time at the conference; they wanted to get on with the deal.

McColl and Coulter decided they should skip cocktails and dinner on the opening night and meet in Coulter's room at the Ritz Carlton. As McColl was ducking out, wearing traveling attire and carrying a briefcase chock-full of merger notes, he ran into Ed Crutchfield, who was just arriving for the conference. Crutchfield heads the nation's sixth-largest bank, First Union, which just happens to be McColl's cross-town rival in Charlotte. McColl noted that the banker "would have just thrown up if he had known what I was doing."

McColl carefully steered his way around Crutchfield, lying about how he had just arrived, too, and saying that there was nothing big going on. Then he bolted for his car and made straight for the Ritz, where he was about to put the last touches on the biggest bank deal in history. At the Ritz, McColl had taken two rooms. He was late. When he arrived at room 835, the room number he had given Coulter, he found that his personal secretary, Pat Hinson—a woman who had been at the bank longer than McColl, some forty-four years—had put a note on McColl's door, directing him to the second room, 940, where Coulter was waiting. Over hamburgers and several drafts of McColl's favorite drink, Lagavullin straight up, the two finally got around to hashing out the real issues. There were five of them, and sometime between 7:30 P.M. and when the meeting broke at around 11 P.M., these issues were resolved; they constituted the official memorandum of understanding that would frame the merger. The exact words of the memorandum follow.

Point one: "It is the desire of the boards of directors that Mr. McColl be elected chairman and chief executive officer and that Mr. Coulter be elected president of the corporation and a member of the board of directors. It is the present intention of the boards of directors for Mr. Coulter to succeed Mr. McColl."

Point two: "The new company will be managed by a team of six executives: Hugh L. McColl Jr., David A. Coulter, James H. Hance Jr., Kenneth D. Lewis, Michael J. Murray, Michael E. O'Neill."

Point three: "The executive headquarters will be in Charlotte, North Carolina, which will be the principal office of the chief executive officer. The headquarters of the Global Bank will be in San Francisco, which will be the principal office of the president. It is our intention that the senior management team will be located in the principal cities within the franchise."

Point four: "Both banks have good patriotic names which will be retained in one form or another. The name of the holding company shall be BankAmerica Corp. It is anticipated that the company will operate with both brands for a period and ultimately will converge the brands after careful study. In any case, our colors will be red, white, and blue and will take advantage of the greatest franchise in American banking."

Point five: "The board of directors will number twenty, with eleven from NationsBank, inclusive of Mr. McColl, and nine from BankAmerica Corp., inclusive of Mr. Coulter, reflecting the respective ownership percentages in the new company."

This last point was a major coup for McColl. Up to that meeting, it had always been envisioned as 10–10 split. But as the two men began naming names during that meeting, they struggled to fill out the BankAmerica side. McColl convinced Coulter that they could go outside the bank to fill those slots. Coulter worried about how that would look. Then McColl spoke up. "Here's how we'll sell it," he began. "Our shareholders will own 54 percent of the company, and yours will own 46 percent after the merger. Why not an 11–9 split? It's the logical thing to do." Coulter went for it. McColl then sent for his secretary, and in both men's presence the dutiful Pat Hinson typed up the memorandum, which both men read and signed. The deal was all but done that evening of April 2, 1998.

BOARDROOM BRAWL

The next day, Saturday, April 3, McColl left the conference early for Charlotte. A small group of confidants, including mentor Joe Martin, met McColl and the NationsBank team at the airport with bagpipes and champagne for McColl's first real celebration of the event. But early the next week, for one excruciating day, all the meetings and plans and agreements of the previous week seemed as if they would go for naught. Both the BankAmerica and the NationsBank executive committees instantly approved the merger, but it still had to pass muster with the boards of directors. No problem at NationsBank. But the BankAmerica board was hung up on the 11–9 director split. On Wednesday, April 7, McColl boarded a jet for San Francisco, thinking that the BankAmerica board was ready to rubber-stamp the deal the next day. He was all set for a ceremonial board meeting and a round of cordial congratulations. When he arrived at the Mandarin hotel, it was 11 P.M. He called BankAmerica's lawyer Ed Herlihy to let him know he had arrived, and Herlihy, still half asleep, dropped a bombshell on McColl. "We've got a problem," the lawyer said. "The board is trying to renegotiate the whole deal."

It was an overstatement. But besides not liking the 11–9 split, the board was uncomfortable with the succession issue. The members wanted more assurance that Coulter would be the next CEO—after McColl. So on Thursday morning at 9 A.M., McColl went to face the board. He had no intention of letting the deal collapse, but he wasn't going to give an inch either. A deal is a deal, and that morning Coulter was assuring him that he would deliver the deal as they had agreed in Phoenix. McColl counts his encounter with the BankAmerica board among his most inspiring performances. Not that he was acting. There was an element of bluff to what he told the board, but this proud southerner might well have walked if the board attempted to take back anything he and Coulter had agreed on. McColl summoned his resolve and marched into the boardroom. He spelled out the logic of an 11–9 split the way he had spelled it out to Coulter. Then he confronted the succession issue and told the board that he personally did not have and did not want an employment contract. "My job is good for the day," he told them. "I'll be here as long as you and the new board want me, and when you don't, I'll be gone."

McColl sensed positive body language from several of the directors. He was winning, so he continued. "To be very candid," he said, "this is a huge undertaking, this company that Dave and I are creating. And it has the backing of both managements. But if we don't have the backing of the board, it isn't going to work. If you all aren't behind me 100 percent, we won't do the deal. I'll just get on a plane and fly back to Charlotte." It was what the BankAmerica board wanted to hear from the next CEO of one of America's largest bank companies: charisma, fortitude, ability, leadership, salesmanship, mental toughness. After an hour without McColl and Coulter present, the board called the men in for formal handshakes. There was no applause, as there had been at the NationsBank board meeting earlier. This was, after all, a company being acquired. But at long last the deal was done. McColl didn't linger. He boarded the next flight to Charlotte. "When you've made the sale, it's time to go," he says.

The deal was formally announced on Monday, April 13. On September 24, 1998, shareholders from both companies formally approved the merger, and the new BankAmerica was born. After seven years, McColl finally had his California franchise. It was the second biggest bank holding company in the country, with $580 billion in assets, behind the newly merged Citicorp/Travelers, now called Citigroup, which had $751 billion in assets. BankAmerica had 8.1 percent of all U.S. bank deposits—more than any other bank. It had 4,800 branches and 14,700 automatic teller machines in twenty-two states, including Alaska. Even though McColl had agreed as part of the merger agreement that he would retain the BankAmerica name, he had left open the possibility of keeping that name for the bank holding company only and putting a variation of that name on his many branches— something like NationsBank of America. The NationsBank name was, indeed, dear to him. But not letting his pride get in the way, McColl asked for extensive market research and found, somewhat to his surprise, that BankAmerica had unequaled name recognition for a bank. That equity is part of what McColl had bought, and he wasn't about to fritter it away. He had changed names before, and he would do it again. On October 1, the new bank's board met and formally agreed that the holding company and all its branches would be called Bank of America, harking back to the early days when legendary founder A. P. Giannini started the company by making small loans to working-class immigrants at a makeshift desk on the loading docks of San Francisco.

To get the deal done McColl and Coulter came together like countrymen at war. But it seems clear that no real friendship ever developed. Indeed, less than a month after the shareholders formally blessed the NationsBank-BankAmerica union, Coulter, the erstwhile heir apparent to run this coast-to-coast banking giant, resigned. Chalk it up to turbulent world markets in the summer and fall of 1998, if you like. Before the merger, Coulter's bank had entered into a controversial investment relationship with the New York firm D. E. Shaw, which made a number of bad bets and ultimately resulted in BankAmerica's posting $1.4 billion in writedowns and losses in the third quarter—the first reporting period for the newly merged entity. The hit sent the bank's quarterly earnings tumbling 78 percent, and its stock followed with a quick 11 percent drop. Surprised and incensed, McColl asked for Coulter's resignation with lightning speed.

Astute McColl watchers figure that Coulter's number was up long before the earnings problems surfaced, though. McColl has long eschewed mergers of equals in big part for one simple reason: he's fiercely loyal to his own team and does not believe that any group anywhere can run a bank better. Recall that the succession issue was a critical sticking point in McColl's earlier mating dance with then-CEO of BankAmerica, Richard Rosenberg. Shortly after Coulter stepped down in October 1998, McColl got the board to grant him a two-year extension that will keep him in power until 2003. The swift ouster of Coulter, and McColl's extended term as CEO, may be the clearest examples of why, when dealing with a deal maker, there really is no such thing as a merger of equals, and the smart money is always on the deal maker to emerge on top.

Here are some outtakes from my conversation with McColl, the fiery ex-marine and arguably the greatest bank deal maker ever:

Question: *Hugh, when would say that you first realized you were very good at buying banks?*

Answer: Well, I think that without question I went through a period from 1982 to 1985 when I was a new CEO, when I was not successful in merging banks. We got into Florida through a loophole, and we acquired some things. But they were very small and, you know, in a way we failed, which we never like to say, but we failed in those years to bring down a big one, which we really wanted to do. And so I think that the point I first realized it was when I did a landmark deal. When we did Texas in 1988. [McColl routinely refers to First RepublicBank as "Texas." It was the deal that got him into that state.]

Question: *You've bought a lot of banks in your day. Have you ever considered being bought?*

Answer: No. Never have and never would.

Question: *Do you share your feelings about the South and your unwillingness to leave it, even for a prize the size of BankAmerica, with others in your organization?*

Answer: Absolutely. I hide nothing. No secrets from my teammates. We are as tight as can be, and there are no secrets. My board and my executive committee know how I feel. I didn't try to make that decision by myself. I put all the issues on the table with my executive committee, and there is nobody on the board who would vote to leave the South. It could not be done. There is no CEO who could deliver this company outside the South. The board would never let it happen, so it ain't ever going to happen. It's like saying you're going to move the University of Texas out of Austin or Yale out of wherever it is.

Question: *You have a tremendous energy level. Is that the key to your success?*

Answer: We have very high handicaps at this company. The reason is that we don't play much golf. And, in fact, the last thing anybody would say to me is that he's got a low handicap. I mean they wouldn't want me to know. When I was much younger, I actually got rid of people who smoked pipes on the grounds. I figured anybody who had enough time to mess with pipes had too slow a metabolism for me. The BankAmerica deal closed on Easter weekend. They wanted to keep it for another week because of everything happening over Easter. I said, "Easter weekend? What does that mean? We do all our deals on holidays." You know, that's my attitude. It never occurred to me that a holiday might get in the way of a deal. We've never been on holiday. We

don't know what those are. So it never occurred to us that
Easter might be a problem.

Question: *Doesn't that pose a problem, culturally, when you acquire other
companies?*
Answer: No, because people whose metabolism won't keep up won't
be there. It will be an issue for people who are used to
delaying decisions. They will find that they are swept aside.
We are people who believe in going into our war room and
saying anything you want to say about something, disagree-
ing sharply with each other. But when we leave the room
after the decision had been made, we are in lockstep, and no
one is allowed to deviate from that course after that. In
other words, you get your day in court to make your point.
If your point carries, fine. If it doesn't, then either you support the team or you're out. There's no deviation from that.
Some companies don't do that; some companies have club-
house lawyers who then fight a decision either passively or
otherwise. But you can't do that in our company. It doesn't
work. We don't allow it. All our energy has always been
externally focused, that is, competitive energies rather than
competing with each other internally.

Question: *Explain "the wonder of it all," a term you use in describing the benefits of merging with BankAmerica?*
Answer: This is a tremendous fit. It's dynamite. There is essentially
no overlap, and it's a mammoth business when you put them
together. We became the largest banking service company in
the country. Number one small lender. Number one middle-
market lender. Number one in terms of corporate accounts.
In other words, I told my people, "The only number you got
to remember is one."

Question: *It's been said that you can really rip into your executives.*

Answer: I know myself very well. I have what I call escalating anger. It's sort of circular and it's random and extremely violent, verbally anyway.

Question: *What have you learned about deal making? What are the little things that make it work?*

Answer: Well, it was not an accident that I had my secretary at the meeting with Dave Coulter the night we agreed to the merger. I learned from both my prior CEOs that if you've got something important, write it down so there's no mis-understanding. And I knew she was highly dependable and accurate. So I had her there. Most people would not have had her there. They'd have had lawyers there to handle it. But I wrote it all down myself, and then gave it to Mrs. Hinson. If we'd had two sets of lawyers there, we'd still be negotiating. I've learned that I used to feel important saying no to things. But I don't feel that way anymore. It's just that I don't say yes, which is a different thing. You know, you can say, "Oh, that's interesting, but here would be one of the difficulties" without saying, "I won't do it."

chapter four

Sandy Weill

Another Year, Another Office

WHILE HUGH MCCOLL WAS SWALLOWING banks with the gusto of a vampire at the blood bank, Sanford I. Weill—"Sandy" to most of the world—was pursuing a similar business plan on Wall Street. For Weill, the geographic challenges were less daunting. Wall Street in the strict sense is a fairly confined area of Lower Manhattan. So he didn't have to travel far to stage his assault on the brokerage industry. And the pickings were relatively easy. This was in the 1970s, and times were tough for anyone trying to make a buck in the market. Oil prices were soaring. The inflation rate was in double digits. Corporate profits were lackluster. A president was forced from office in midterm. The Cold War raged. The stock market, numb from perpetual bad news, limped through its worst decade since the Great Depression. By the grace of dividends, stock investors managed to eke out a gain. But it wasn't much. The Standard & Poor's 500, with dividends reinvested, returned a piddling 5.9 percent a year for the decade. Few were interested, and the brokerage business, in a word, sucked. But Sandy Weill was smitten.

A consummate bottom feeder, Weill, the Brooklyn-born son of immigrants from Poland—whose first job on Wall Street was as a lowly messenger—built his empire by buying out-of-favor businesses on the cheap and then slashing costs. He's actually had two careers on what associates and friends joke is "Weill Street." In the first, he was a consolidator of the shaken, disorganized, and highly fragmented brokerage industry during the oil-shock seventies. He presciently bought more than a dozen firms just ahead of a soaring bull market that would revitalize the brokerage business. His second career started after he sold his carefully cobbled brokerage firm, Shearson Loeb Rhoades, to American Express in 1981. As one of American Express's largest shareholders following that deal, Weill quickly moved up from the brokerage subsidiary and became president of American Express. But he lost a 1985 power struggle to James D. Robinson III, and although Weill left with a fistful of dollars, he no longer had a company to call his own. He had to start building from scratch.

The setback was a rare one for Weill, and since then he's more than made up for it. He eventually bought Shearson back from American Express as part of a spree that included the purchase of Primerica with its mass-market-oriented brokerage firm Smith Barney, and later bond trading powerhouse Salomon Bros. En route to building a giant insurance and brokerage company at Travelers Group, Weill grabbed other financial services companies as well. By 1998 Travelers had joined American Express as one of the prestigious thirty stocks making up the Dow Jones Industrial Average and had overwhelmed it financially with assets of $387 billion, versus American Express's assets of just $120 billion. It's a comparison that still makes Weill smile.

Weill's second tour of success cemented his reputation as one of Wall Street's savviest deal makers. Many in his place would have called it a career after leaving American Express. But Weill rarely idles for long. Just ask his secretary, who because of her boss's penchant for buying bigger and better brands—and adopting their names and office space as his own—has had five offices in three buildings in the nineties alone. At a charitable event in New York City late in 1997, Weill met up with Citicorp CEO John S. Reed, and the two had a fateful conversation. It would lead to the greatest deal in Sandy Weill's life, the merger of Travelers Group with Citicorp to form the insurance, brokerage, money management, credit card, and global commercial banking colossus now known as Citigroup. The deal was so compelling that Weill made the unusual concession of agreeing to a merger of equals, rather than his being the acquirer. That concession meant that Weill, for the first time in a decade, would no longer be supreme ruler of his kingdom. He would share the title of co-CEO with Reed. But it was worth it. Citigroup became a banking company of unchallenged size in the United States, with assets of $751 billion. "Pure magic," Weill says of the combination.

When the stock-swap deal was announced in April 1998, it had a market value of $72 billion and was the largest merger ever announced. Some of the magic that Weill saw faded into grim reality in ensuing months. Shares of both Travelers and Citicorp took a pounding as the stock market suffered its worst spill in seven years. Global financial services stocks, roiled by credit problems in Asia and Russia, were hit hard across the board before the deal could close. Travelers was riding a down wave brought on in part by its new partner's vast exposure to foreign markets. It led to a chorus of second-guessing within Travelers. But Weill, though concerned, never wavered. That foreign exposure, after all, was one of the things he coveted. This just happened to be a rough patch, and he'd have to get through it. By the time the deal was completed in the fall, the stocks had fallen so far that the value of the stock swap was "only" $39 billion—not even as big as the NationsBank-BankAmerica marriage at about the same time.

But the magic that Weill first noted was about more than mere size in the stock market. Citigroup today has 100 million customers in one hundred countries—unparalleled global reach. Hugh McColl's deal may have bulked up his bank and spread it from coast to coast, which was his life's ambition. But Weill's deal challenged the status quo in a far more urgent manner. So breathtaking was this deal that he would personally confer with the popular and powerful Federal Reserve chairman, Alan Greenspan, before going forward. The president of the United States would have to be notified. This was not merely two banks hooking up to dominate a bigger territory. Been there, done that. This was a very large bank being joined at the hip with a very large brokerage and insurance business. They were in different lines of work.

No overlap. The deal's success would rely more on "cross selling" of products and building revenues than the more common merger synergies of achieving big cost savings by getting rid of duplicate staff and functions.

Moreover, under the laws at the time it wasn't even a legal combination. Insurance and commercial banking under one roof is a federal no-no, as decreed in the Bank Holding Company Act of 1956. Weill was given two years (the Fed has authority to extend the period to five years) to divest the insurance businesses, and the clock began ticking when the deal was completed. But it was Weill's fervent hope that the divestiture would never occur. His not-so-modest plan from the start was to change federal law; to mold it around his unique creation. Talk about brass. Weill inked history's largest deal knowing that it was an illegal combination of businesses but figuring that he could persuade lawmakers to change the rules of the game before his grace period expired.

How's it going? At the end of 1998, no imminent changes were in store. At least one House bill to Weill's liking had been in circulation but with little momentum, and Weill lost a powerful ally when Senate Banking Committee Chairman Alfonse M. D'Amato, the Republican from New York, lost his bid for reelection in November. D'Amato's place on the committee, and with it jurisdiction over banking laws in the United States, fell into the less friendly hands of Sen. Phil Gramm, the Republican from Texas. Weill wasn't panicking, though. He still had plenty of time. He also had a fallback plan. Divesting the insurance businesses was only one possible solution. Weill had hatched another plan as well—to "de-bank" his giant bank. It would mean transferring a lot of banking activities to nonbank entities and losing his U.S. bank charter. It would be a massive undertaking. But clearly it could be done, and Weill planned to use that possibility as part of his argument for why legislators should change the archaic restrictions in the 1956 Bank Act.

It's impossible to assess the long-term financial impact of the deal on investors at this early date. Clearly, in the short run, the deal—when coupled with the market's overall problems and investors' perception in the fall of 1998 that banks were especially vulnerable—had led to lower values. Weill, a passionate believer in being an owner as well as a manager, was hurt more than most. His personal net worth is a function of where his company's stock trades on any given day. Before the April merger agreement, Travelers traded at around $62 and Weill's 16 million shares were worth $990 million. After the announcement his stock rose to $73, giving him a net worth near $1.2 billion. Weill continues to own 16 million shares, now of Citigroup. Near the end of 1998, the stock had fallen to the low $50s, lowering his personal net worth to $830 million. He remained optimistic that the bank's fortunes would change for the better, that the combined heft of Travelers with Citicorp would in the long run create value that neither company could create on its own. He's been right with such judgments so often in the past that it seems pointless to take issue. We'll just have to see.

As this book went to press there were many unanswered questions about Weill's deal for Citicorp. The insurance issue was only one. It wasn't clear who was actually running Citigroup. Was it Weill or Reed? In our conversations, Weill steadfastly insisted that the co-CEO arrangement was working beautifully, that he and Reed were seeing eye to eye on most issues. Weill's executives seemed to have the upper hand early in the integration process, but Weill later had been forced to let go of his protégé and longtime number two, Jamie Dimon. It was a sign that Reed, a respected banker and a man of great intelligence, was making his presence felt. So some rifts were developing.

The big risk from Weill's perspective was that he might lose the corporate infighting. It happened to him thirteen years earlier at American Express. But most of Wall Street was still handicapping the horse race in Weill's favor. He's a veteran and survivor of some twenty-plus deals in his long career, and it seemed a long shot that Reed, a neophyte at the takeover game, would force him out. Who knows? Maybe the co-CEO arrangement would actually work. But even if it didn't and even if Weill ended up taking a back seat to Reed, Citigroup was unmistakably Weill's idea. It was grand. It was visionary. It challenged convention. It was a signature deal for a Wall Street legend.

MANAGEMENT HE *REALLY* LIKES

I've known Sandy Weill, professionally, since the middle 1980s; and while it's said that he is ruthless and abrasive in running his business, he is, on the basis of my experience, always generous and cordial. One of my early encounters with Weill came while I was at the *St. Louis Sun* in 1990. Weill had only recently bought Primerica Corp., the financial services firm that owned the brokerage Smith Barney. That deal put him into the brokerage business, which he dearly loves, for the first time in more than three years. Weill was touring his newly acquired branch offices and agreed to see me on his way through town. I was eager to get reacquainted. It was clear by then that Weill was in the early phases of building a second empire, and I was eager to get his view from Wall Street and nurture our relationship.

I'll never forget that interview. Even in those dark days for junk bonds and the economy, Weill was an optimist. Businesses were failing all over. St. Louis, home to assembly plants for each of the Big Three auto makers, was especially hard hit by a slump in car sales. But Weill spoke of the collapse of communism and other global forces that he believed would lead the world economy out of peril. Optimism is one of his enduring traits, and it wasn't until years later that I recognized how valuable that positive attitude was to him. Think about it. Weill is a bargain hunter. He buys businesses on their deathbed, so out of favor that they are practically being given away. He's got to be an optimist. The nature of his bet is that the assets he has bought will recover and gain value.

Another striking thing about Weill is his discomfort during interviews. Weill insists on having one or more aides present no matter how well he may know the reporter. He's deeply concerned about making the right impression, to the point where he'll sometimes ask a reporter after an interview if his answers were useful. It's a genuine gesture by an improbably humble man. Certainly Weill has a big ego. You don't get where he is without one. But despite his success and his wealth and his power, he's not terribly comfortable talking about himself. After our last interview for this book, I couldn't help asking him if he ever thought about what he had achieved and pinched himself to make sure he's awake. "Every day," he told me. "I'd hate to have to do this all over because I'd never be able to do it this well again."

Weill hates confrontation. It's one of the things that set him apart from many of the deal makers in this book. He'd rather move an under-performing executive over than out. If that seems to run counter to the shareholders' best interests, you'd never know it by the way his stock has risen. Beginning with Weill's reincarnation in 1986, the stocks of his companies have increased tenfold, outrunning by a factor of three the strongest bull market in a generation. Consider also that a human touch at the top may not be such a bad thing. Weill, as I've noted, is no stranger to head-lopping after an acquisition. But that's part of the cure for any troubled company, which early in his career was the only kind he'd buy. Weill is active in children's charities. He has a recital hall named after him at Carnegie Hall. He also is a role model and benefactor for students at New York City's High School for Economics and Finance, an outgrowth of the Academy of Finance curriculum that Weill has sponsored since 1982—and that is now being used in 136 high schools across the country.

A few years ago, for one of my columns in *USA Today*, I talked Weill into accepting a challenge from the high school kids: they would pick a stock portfolio to go up against his in a one-year contest. Weill was a good sport. There was nothing in it for him, except possible embarrassment if the kids beat him. But he felt that participating would draw attention to the school, which he had established to emphasize the importance of financial literacy. In vintage Weill form, he tried to change the rules of the contest. He wanted his entire portfolio to be in one stock: Travelers. I wouldn't let him. He had to pick five and so did the kids. So he ticked off the best five managers he could think of, and their stocks constituted his portfolio. Yes, Travelers was in the portfolio. He *really* likes management there. To make it interesting, Weill offered to take the kids to one of his favorite restaurants if he lost: Stick to Your Ribs in Long Island City, Queens, where the Texas-style barbecue is smoky, spicy, and hearty. But he never had to make good on the bet. His "management" portfolio won the day.

For this book, I met Weill twice—once in his rambling office at Travelers headquarters at 388 Greenwich Street in lower Manhattan. It was a beautiful room with expensive furniture and a striking view of the Empire State Building and most of midtown. That interview came just two days after his blockbuster Citigroup deal was announced. Weill was beaming. There's little pleasure for a deal maker greater than engineering the biggest deal in history. My second meeting with Weill came in late October—in his new offices at the Citicorp Center on Fifty-third Street and Lexington Avenue. The new digs were less grand, on the fourth floor with a terrace and a so-so view looking south down Lexington. Weill hadn't yet moved all his furnishings. But a large framed photo of the modest Brooklyn house he grew up in was there—hanging over his couch as a constant reminder of his roots. The merger was completed by then. The stock market had beaten down his shares. He was elbow-deep in the tough part—making the two companies one. With everything that was going on—my meeting with him was just days before he announced the departure of protégé Dimon—it must have been difficult for him to answer my questions. But he did, making good on a promise made months earlier. Weill wore a blue-striped shirt with a solid white collar and a blue suit. His red tie was populated with a legion of multicolored Travelers umbrellas. With his world swirling, and just days into his new, still-barren office, Weill sat on the big leather couch beneath his childhood home and recounted the highlights of his most amazing deal.

GOOD MANAGER, NEEDS WORK

Sanford I. Weill was born on March 16, 1933, in Brooklyn. (Like Harry S. Truman—who for many years insisted that his middle initial not be punctuated because it didn't stand for an abbreviated name— Weill has a middle initial that stands for nothing. His mother had wanted to name him after her father, Isaac, but didn't care for the name. So she gave him the *I* and decided to let him take a name beginning with the letter *I* later in life. (Weill never finished the job.) He and his sister, Helen, grew up in the Bensonhurst section of that New York City borough, in a yellow stucco house on Bay 26th Street near Gravesend Bay. It was in those days a pleasant middle-class neighborhood. His father, Max (sometimes called Mac), was a dressmaker who emigrated as an infant to the States from a town in Poland near Warsaw. His mother, Etta, was a homemaker who had immigrated from Poland about the same time. Max was a modestly successful businessman, who at one point owned a steel importing company. But his was an up-and-down career that took the family to Miami Beach for three years. When Max and his family returned to Brooklyn, they moved in with relatives. Max vented his frustrations on young Weill, nagging him about his mediocre grades. Sandy spent many days playing stickball in the streets and delivering newspapers for pocket money. In a neighborhood filled with rabid Dodgers fans, Weill called himself a Yankee fan. No street tough, he has in fact referred to himself as something of a "sissy" in his youth—someone whose mother occasionally had to rescue him when an argument with the neighborhood kids threatened to turn into a street brawl.

Weill attended public schools until high school, when his parents shipped him off to Peekskill Military Academy in rural New York, about three hours north of the city. Being on his own in that environment, he toughened fast and learned how to take as well as mete out punishment. He took up tennis, became the team captain, and was good enough to compete in the Junior Davis Cup. He graduated in 1951, when he enrolled at Cornell University. There he briefly considered becoming an engineer but found the curriculum too difficult. He majored in liberal arts, and for family reasons—not scholastic ones—he very nearly failed to graduate. His father had run into trouble and closed the steel business. When Weill was a senior, his father left his mother for a younger woman. Weill tried to get his parents to patch things up; in the process he missed a crucial exam and was later informed that he did not have enough credits to graduate that spring.

At the same time, Weill was preparing to marry Joan Mosher, a Brooklyn College student whom he met on an April Fool's Day blind date that had been set up by her father and his aunt. Her family became upset with the troubles at the Weill household—not the least being Sandy's scholastic setback—and tried to call off the wedding. But Joan Mosher stood up to her family and the two were married in June. Max Weill was so caught up in his new life that he missed the wedding and then married his mistress the next day. (He would eventually remarry a second time.) Ultimately Weill got the credits he needed and graduated in September 1955, becoming the first in his family with a college degree. His marriage to Joan remains strong in its fifth decade. She is a perfect partner for Sandy. He takes care of business; she takes care of important relationships. He relies on her opinions on a wide range of business matters, not least on executives that he is considering hiring. He is fond of making cliché comments on the husband-wife relationship. In my first interview with Weill, I asked him how it would feel to be co-CEO with John Reed, pointing out that it had been years since he'd had a boss. "I wouldn't say that," he said to me, smiling. "I've been married forty-three years." Months later, in my follow-up interview, I had repeated a question to Weill for the third or fourth time, and prefaced it with a comment to the effect that I was sorry to keep pushing him on the same point. He smiled again and said, "You know, I do have a wife."

Weill left Cornell with a commission as a second lieutenant in the Air Force and expected to be trained as a pilot. But he reconsidered and began looking for work on Wall Street, where he was promptly turned down for training programs at Merrill Lynch, Bache, and Harris Upham. (The latter was bought by Smith Barney, which was bought by Primerica, which was bought by—you guessed it—Sandy Weill.) He eventually was hired at Bear Stearns as a messenger making $150 a month. By studying for his broker's license on the side, he turned that humble start into the beginnings of a storied career. He soon moved to a better-paying job at Burnham & Co., where I. W. "Tubby" Burnham took him under his wing. Weill might have made partner and gone on to run that firm in time. But in 1960, at twenty-seven and living in a rented apartment with two young children at home, he and Joan agreed to pool their down-payment money with $30,000 from Sandy's mother and other funds from friends and partners totaling $200,000, and opened the doors of Carter, Berlind, Potoma & Weill. It was quickly renamed Cogan, Berlind, Weill & Levitt, and it became a stiff proving ground. Marshall S. Cogan is a famed deal maker in his own right. He's an art collector who once owned the 21 Club restaurant in New York and more recently has been trying to build an auto dealership empire. Roger Berlind is one of the most successful producers on Broadway. Arthur Levitt Jr. became chairman of the Securities and Exchange Commission. Another early partner, Arthur L. Carter, is a big-time publisher who owns the *New York Observer*.

In 1960 Weill's start-up firm, with the initials CBWL, had just one office in midtown Manhattan and was known on Wall Street somewhat derisively as Corned Beef with Lettuce. The firm did deals on behalf of clients. It was Sandy Weill's little firm that helped Saul Steinberg buy Reliance Insurance in the late sixties, creating a platform for that investor/raider to make millions in the go-go eighties. Weill recalls cashing Steinberg's $750,000 check for advisory services rendered and thinking then that it was a nice check but that Steinberg had something better: a bigger company as a base to do bigger things. Weill had to go out and find another client and start all over again. "That's when I said to myself, I think I'd rather be a deal person for our own company and help grow it rather than just be a deal guy on the outside,"

Weill recalls. Not long after that he began doing deals for himself. In 1970, Weill's group bought the brokerage Hayden Stone, seizing on that firm's troubles stemming from a bear market in 1969. Hayden Stone was thirty times bigger than Weill's fledgling outfit. So he adopted its name. In the next ten years, which included the worst bear market since the thirties ('73–'74), Weill would gobble up other troubled brokerages, including Shearson Hammill in 1974 and Loeb Rhoades Hornblower in 1979. His modus operandi was to buy not only bigger firms with more customers but firms with better brand names and adopt those names as his own. It's a successful practice that continues to this day, and explains why he willingly accepted the "Citi" name when he and Reed agreed to their 1998 blockbuster. By the end of the '70s, Weill, who emerged as the leader of his partnership in 1973, commanded one of Wall Street's largest retail brokerages, called Shearson Loeb Rhoades, with 280 offices worldwide.

In those tough days, Weill was merciless and cheap. He quickly eliminated hundreds of jobs after each acquisition and thought nothing of checking into $50 items on an expense report. Survival was the name of the game, and he was not only surving but growing by capitalizing on other firms' inability to cut their own overhead. To some he went too far. Arthur Carter's newspaper once called Weill "a disgrace to the business community." But from the ashes of the brutal seventies no one emerged as a bigger success on Wall Street. The stock of Weill's firm rose almost a hundredfold. Weill was the reason. He was a hands-on manager who paid attention to details. After one acquisition he showed up in the back office late one night in his pajama top just to make sure that the transfer of customer accounts was accomplished without hitches. Long before Weill sized up Citicorp for a merger partner he had come to believe that size mattered. He worried that his firm would be left for dead unless it found deep pockets to align with. So in 1981 he sold his firm to American Express for $930 million. He stuffed $30 million into his own pockets as a result of stock that he owned and was truly rich for the time in his life.

Weill quickly grew to love the perks of a big-company executive: chauffeurs, limos, private jets. But he was no good at being number two—"deputy dog," he says of his American Express days—and in the clubby atmosphere at American Express he couldn't muster the support he needed to land the top job against the more refined and politically adept James Robinson. Weill, along with the sage from Omaha, Warren Buffett, tried to buy 60 percent of the Fireman's Fund insurance business from American Express. Dispatched there by Robinson, Weill had turned that business around by installing new performance measures and making management more accountable. In what's known as the "December debacle," he let go 10 percent of the staff. But his deal for Fireman's fell through, and Weill, having made his play, felt he had to leave. He set up an office with his young assistant, Jamie Dimon, and started looking for companies to buy. At first the two were thinking big. A real estate bust in California had taken a toll on the venerable Bank of America. Its stock was trading at about $8. Weill sent the board a letter saying he'd like to buy a chunk of stock, put together a $1 billion equity infusion to clean up its balance sheet, and take over as CEO. But the board told him to shove it and Weill, interested only in a friendly deal, went away quietly. Just a few years later, Hugh McColl would take a fancy to the California bank, and he would not go away.

Weill, out of work for more than a year, caught a break in May 1986. *Fortune* magazine ran a glowing story under the headline "Sanford Weill, 53, Exp'd Mgr, Gd Refs." Management at a little-known and troubled Baltimore lending company, Commercial Credit, owned by Minneapolis-based Control Data, read the article and asked Weill if he'd consider buying the business. Control Data had already made it clear that it wanted to unload the division. Weill by then was thinking slightly less grandly and agreed to invest $7 million of his own money and become CEO after Control Data sold 82 percent of the company to the public in an IPO. It wasn't much. But Weill was back in business, and he multiplied Commercial Credit's net income eight times in six years—from $25 million to $193 million. He also very quickly began hunting for larger game. In 1988 he bought for $1.5 billion the financial services company Primerica, which owned Smith Barney. In 1992, he bought 27 percent of Travelers. In 1993, he paid $1.2 billion to American Express and regained ownership of the brokerage firm that he helped build, Shearson Lehman Brothers. He also bought the rest of Travelers for $4 billion. In 1996, he bought control of Aetna's property and casualty insurance business for $4 billion. In 1997, he bought Salomon Bros. for $9 billion. Then, in 1998, came the $39 billion monster for Citicorp.

For a deal of such size and extreme complexity, the Travelers-Citicorp merger fell together in the planning stage quickly. A mere five weeks after Weill first approached Reed with the idea, both boards had signed off on it and a merger pact had been inked. No bidding wars. No threats. No dawdling. No real controversy. No muss, no fuss. It was a deal the way Weill liked deals. Both sides saw the benefits and both sides felt they were winners. But as with many deals, the walkup would prove to be much easier than the act of making the deal work after the companies combined.

"REMEMBER OUR CONVERSATIONS LAST SUMMER?"

It was in the spring of 1997, six months before Weill bought Salomon Bros., that the idea of buying a big international bank first surfaced inside Travelers. Weill doesn't recall exactly how it surfaced. But by then Travelers had fully integrated its most recent acquisition—the property and casualty insurance operations of Aetna—and it was time for another. Weill and his top planners knew that if Travelers was going to keep growing it would very soon have to vault into foreign markets. At this point, with annual revenue of $37 billion and a market value twice that size, it was still essentially a domestic company in an economy that had been going global for years. The priority was the brokerage operations as capital markets developed in Russia, China, India, Thailand, Indonesia, Brazil, Argentina and scores of other "emerging markets." U.S. investors wanted access to those markets and those markets had an emerging middle class that would want to invest at home and in the United States. Merrill Lynch, Morgan Stanley, Goldman Sachs, and other brokerages had already bought foreign firms, formed overseas alliances, or expanded well beyond the United States on their own. If Weill's pride, Smith Barney, was going to compete, it would need greater reach.

How to accomplish that? The obvious solution was to buy another brokerage with a foreign presence and merge it with the Smith Barney subsidiary. But doing the obvious isn't a Weill trait. He and his top planners, including Jamie Dimon, began to discuss the possibility of buying an international bank that would not only give Travelers an overseas presence but catapult it into a bunch of new businesses as well. There was no discussion of exactly what banks might be candidates; it was more conceptual at that stage and set the Travelers brass to thinking about how it might work and what businesses they most wanted to be in. By the summer of 1997, though, Weill's group was considering names and was deadly serious. Things progressed far enough with one bank that Weill alerted Alan Greenspan, who as chairman of the Federal Reserve is the top regulator of banks doing business in the United States. "The thing never got beyond first base," Weill says. "So I never disclosed the name." His discussions with Greenspan were hypothetical. But Greenspan paid attention. He knew that today's hypothesis could quickly become tomorrow's reality, especially where Sandy Weill was concerned. A year later, Weill still won't talk about which bank he had looked at. But *Fortune* magazine in May 1998 identified the near partner as J.P. Morgan—big, but no Citi.

So in the summer of 1997 Weill had been trolling for a large commercial bank and came up empty. But just a few months later—in September—he partly sated his appetite by buying Salomon Bros., a global bond sales and trading firm that got Travelers to really start thinking international. No sooner had Weill announced the $9 billion deal for Salomon, however, than he had potential cause to regret it.

Global stock, bond, and currency markets fell into a swoon. A currency crisis had begun in Thailand over the summer, when that nation's spiraling trade deficit and mushrooming debt sent its currency, the *baht*, into free fall. Its stock market followed, and a recession soon set in. Most thought the damage would be contained. But it wasn't. The contagion spread to a wider circle of emerging Asian markets including India, Indonesia, Korea, and Malaysia. As those markets toppled in the fall of 1997, a genuine panic began to build around the globe, and it took a toll on the profits of any firm associated with foreign markets. Salomon was one of those. Meanwhile, U.S. markets buckled but quickly rebounded, reinforcing a fast-growing theory among many U.S. investors in the '90s: There's no need to send your money abroad when the markets at home are so much more stable and profitable. Weill, having just agreed to buy Salomon and now getting a firsthand look at the inherent risks of being a global player, knew that he would have some explaining to do. Shareholders might well ask: Who needs global markets? You were doing just fine without them.

But Weill was unfazed. Nearly forty years on Wall Street had taught him that from panic comes opportunity. His only question: How big would Travelers have to be to play in global markets and not only not worry about getting wiped out by severe difficulties in any one region, but be able to exploit calamity by sucking up weaker competitors in order to grow? A fair question, and one without a precise answer. It's what was on Weill's mind the evening of November 18, 1997, when he hosted the annual dinner for the Jewish Theological Seminary in New York City, a dinner at which John Reed of Citicorp would be a special guest of honor.

Weill and Reed had known each other for more than twenty years. They met in the middle seventies, when both served as outside directors of a company called Arlen Realty, which fell on hard times and demanded a fair amount of interaction from its directors. Both Weill and Reed were living in tony Greenwich, Connecticut, and they ended up spending a string of Saturdays together dealing with Arlen's problems.

Since those days the two had seen each other only sporadically—
maybe three times a year. Weill had been a guest at Reed-sponsored
functions a few times. He was also a valued Citibank customer. But the
two were nowhere near being buddies. They were acquaintances with
common business interests. "But if he called me or I called him the call
would be answered," Weill says, perhaps underestimating his own
clout. It's a short list of folks, indeed, who wouldn't take a call from
Sandy Weill—or John Reed, for that matter.

The two, accompanied by their wives, engaged in light conversation
most of the evening. Weill, with the Salomon purchase still fresh, mentioned in passing his emerging fascination with global markets and the
apparent opportunities developing in Asia. But mostly the banter was
casual. Weill specifically recalls complimenting Reed on the job he had
done taking Citicorp from the brink of a government bailout in the '90
banking crisis to being one of the largest banks in the world. "I think
the surprise was the chemistry between us," Weill says. "We really
hadn't spent a lot of time together. But this night there was an especially good feeling" (even the wives got along). That chemistry played a
huge role in the eventual merger. Weill has long had a penchant for
mixing business with pleasure; he likes working with people he knows.
This, Weill thought, was a man he could do business with.

Two and a half months later, in January 1998, Travelers' highest-
ranking managers, a group of eighteen, were holed up at the company's
spacious planning center in Armonk, New York, for an annual three-
day New Year's strategy session, and the idea of buying an international bank came up again. The group, obviously conscious of their
acquisition of Salomon Bros. just months earlier and the still-unsettled
nature of foreign markets, nonetheless believed that this might be the
year that they would land the big one. Weill & Co. pondered the
prospect. That's what this annual big-think-a-thon was all about. All
ideas are welcome, and this one was more welcome than most. The
group began creating a list of potential targets, including the twelve to
fifteen biggest financial institutions in the world; names like J.P. Morgan,

Goldman Sachs, ING Barings—and added somewhat late, Citicorp. "When Citicorp was finally mentioned I remembered back to how I felt with John at the Seminary dinner," Weill recalls. "I said that I would call him. Everybody thought it was a wheel-spin, so nobody really bothered me about it. They thought it could never happen. I like a challenge, so I called John the next day."

Reed picked up the phone. It was a quick conversation. Weill was planning to attend the prestigious Business Council meeting in Washington, D.C., in late February. He figured Reed would be there too and asked the Citicorp boss if he'd set aside some time and meet with him. Reed said sure. He assumed the Travelers chief was going to hit him up for a table at some charity, and was prepared to go as high as $50,000. "I've yet to collect on that one, and probably never will," Weill now jokes. The idea of a merger never crossed Reed's mind. It rarely left Weill's. But there wasn't much point obsessing over it before talking to Reed. Citicorp was too big to try to buy on a hostile basis, and that's not Weill's style anyway. He had walked away from Bank of America—an ailing institution at the time—when its board gave him a cold shoulder. Citicorp, a thriving bank with an enviable international brand, wasn't worth another thought without some expression of interest from Reed.

At the conference, Weill called Reed in his hotel room and made a date for Wednesday evening, February 25. Reed would meet Weill at his suite in the Park Hyatt after dinner, about 9:30 P.M. As he knocked on Weill's door that night he had no clue of what he was about to hear. Weill greeted him and Reed started with a light opener. "I feel a little strange coming into a gentleman's bedroom late at night," he quipped. Weill chuckled and offered the Citicorp boss a glass of wine. "No, thank you," Reed responded. Then Weill got straight to the point.

"John, I have been thinking about this for a long time. I'm not sure how to say it so how about I just start at the end?"

"Fine," Reed answered, by now suspecting this would be no ordinary charity that Weill was putting the arm on him for.

"I think it is a great idea for our companies to merge," said Wall

Street's deal king, who then watched as a shock wave washed over Reed's face. It lasted just an instant.

"I never thought of that," the Citi boss returned, unruffled. "It could be a good idea."

With the nature of the meeting in the open, Reed and Weill moved further inside the room and began to relax. Weill was on. He had to lay out the reasoning for such a blockbuster deal, the same thinking that he and his board had thoroughly aired at their planning meeting in Armonk a few weeks earlier. Weill was heartened that Reed seemed eager to hear him out. Weill's case centered on the ongoing global market turmoil and how it might create opportunities in the near future. The turmoil was certain to spell disaster for some firms. A global powerhouse the size of a merged Citicorp and Travelers would be strong enough to survive and scoop up business at the expense of smaller and weaker foes. Beyond that, Weill explained, this would be a merger of true equals. The two men would serve as co-CEOs and co-chairmen, and they each would have the same number of board seats.

That setup would work because the merger did not create a lot of opportunity to build profits through cost cuts. There would be little overlap in their businesses. What there would be, though, was an unprecedented array of financial products for sale under one name. The cross-selling opportunities were virtually limitless and both men's expertise would be needed. Suddenly, Citibank's vast customer base would become prime targets for mutual funds and insurance sold by Travelers, whose customers might be peddled stocks and bonds from anywhere in the world—wherever Citibank was doing business. The combination also would give them a leg up in the race to win foreign corporate clients setting up extensive private pension systems, an outgrowth of the global shift away from communism and state-run retirement systems toward market-based economies and private money management.

Cross-selling financial products has met with considerable resistance in the past. Sears found it difficult to sell mutual funds after it bought

Dean Witter years ago, and Weill himself had trouble mixing credit cards with retail brokerage in his stint at American Express. But that doesn't mean it can't work. In his own empire Weill has generated billions through cross-selling. For example, Travelers manufactures annuities and Salomon Smith Barney sells them. "All of a sudden, from nowhere, Travelers annuities sales are up 40 percent, overnight," Weill says. "That's $1 billion of new annuity sales because we have Salomon Smith Barney."

As Weill spoke that night, Reed listened carefully. He was buying it. Yet he knew very little about Travelers' diverse financial businesses, and he wouldn't be able to give Weill's idea serious consideration without a close look at the company that Sandy Weill had put together. Getting such a look would be impossible anytime soon. He was set to leave on a three-week trip around the world the next day. "Let's sleep on it," Reed finally told Weill. "We can talk more in the morning." Reed then stunned Weill with his parting comment. "Should I be thinking about canceling the trip?" he asked. Weill was blown away by that level of interest after a twenty-five-minute conversation. He told the Citicorp chief not to cancel anything. The process had just begun, he said, and it couldn't possibly proceed so fast that immediate plans were in jeopardy. It was apparent right then, though, that Reed had one foot on board. "I really thought, from that moment, that this deal would work," Weill recalls. "And as I look back, there was never a time since the conversations began that John and I went off on diverse tracks."

Before Reed and Weill met the next morning, Reed had confided in his wife about the conversation. She thought it was worth pursuing. He also had called his chief confidant, Citi Vice Chairman Paul Collins, who was in Dallas attending a board meeting as an outside director for Kimberly-Clark. Reed and Weill agreed that Collins would become the point man for discussions while Reed was traveling during the next few weeks. That was fine with Weill, who knew Collins and in fact some years earlier had gotten him to join the board at Carnegie Hall. So for the next ten days, Collins worked with a small contingent from

Travelers: Weill, Jamie Dimon, and the former Kidder Peabody CEO who would later become co-head of Citigroup's investment banking operations, Michael A. Carpenter. They swapped financial information and began to discuss personnel. "We were trying to get a sense of how things might fit," Weill says. "How would the people come together?"

On his trip Reed was giving the matter plenty of thought. From Singapore, he faxed Weill a five-page stream-of-consciousness letter describing his thoughts on the world, the future of banking, and how Citicorp and Travelers might work together. Weill found those thoughts to be pretty well aligned with his own. The planning sessions then widened to include more senior executives and lawyers. Between March 5 and March 23 this group met several times. Toward the end, Reed had returned from his trip and gotten involved too. In fact, on Thursday, March 19, Reed and Weill met for dinner at Travelers planning center in Armonk. It was just the two of them. They were at this point discussing in some detail who the top managers would be and really getting a sense of the combined company. "I expected us to talk late and stay over until Friday, when our associates would join us," Weill says. "But after dinner John got up and said he was going home, that he really loves spending the evenings with his wife but would be back the next morning at 7 A.M. So my roommate turned out to be just me."

Joined by senior executives the next day—Dimon and Carpenter on Weill's team; Collins and Vice Chairman and Corporate Secretary Charles E. Long on Reed's team—they talked until 6 P.M. They had agreed on a structure. Other than both sides having the same number of board seats and Reed and Weill sharing the top job, Citi and Travelers shareholders would each own 50 percent of the new company, which would be called Citigroup. Things were moving extremely fast, too fast even for Weill. At the end of the day, Reed put his arm around Weill and said, "I look forward to working with you, partner." But Weill, out of character, returned, "How about we sleep on it and see if we feel the same way tomorrow?" This was his deal. He wanted it badly. But even a deal king needs time to think. Not all that much time, it turned out. The next morning felt a lot like the past evening, so Weill and Reed forged ahead. It was time to alert the regulators and fully brief directors at both companies.

"That was really the meeting where the deal was done," Weill recalls. "All the terms, why we should do it, who does what to whom, the positioning of key people. The only questions we had were what kind of reaction we'd get from the Fed, because if it was not encouraging we might not have gone on, and from our boards, because this was really a very big deal for both of us."

Reed had already prepped some members of his board informally. By Monday, March 24, he had officially prepped them all, and they had given him the go-ahead. On that day, Weill placed a call to his longtime acquaintance, Alan Greenspan, at his office at the Federal Reserve in Washington, D.C. He had no trouble getting through. After some pleasantries the conversation was brief and crisp.

"Alan, you remember our conversations last summer?" Weill began, focusing Greenspan on that hypothetical merger with a global commercial bank.

"Yes."

"I'd like to have a meeting with you to talk about the specifics of doing something like that."

"Okay," Greenspan said.

"It's important that we have the meeting this week on Wednesday or Thursday because this thing is really moving fast," Weill said, and then taunted the demure Fed chief. "Would you like to know who I'd like to come see you with?"

"I'm not sure," Greenspan quipped.

"Well, you're going to see him so I might as well tell you. I'd like to come see you with John Reed."

"Let me get back to you," Greenspan said.

An hour later, after having consulted with the Fed's lawyer, the very businesslike Greenspan called back and told Weill he'd like to see him sooner rather than later. A meeting was set for Wednesday, March 26. Weill also called Treasury Secretary Robert Rubin and told him he had a deal to tell him about. Rubin joked: "You're buying the government?" On Tuesday, March 25, Weill presented the merger to his board, which authorized him to move forward. The next day he and Reed and their top executives and lawyers met with Greenspan and others on the Fed's board of governors to discuss regulatory issues. Weill remembers walking away pleased. "You never know what a regulator is going to end up doing," he says. "He wasn't blessing it right away. But he was not negative. From our conversations it seemed worthwhile going ahead."

"WHY THE HECK WOULD I BE HERE WITH YOU?"

So Weill and Reed swung into full motion. The two sides fully exchanged legal, tax, accounting, financial, and other information. They met several times to go over the material and called in outside legal and accounting consultants to analyze it all. From March 27 through April 3 they went over the details of the merger agreement. On April 2 the Travelers board gave the deal its preliminary blessing. On April 3 the Citi board did the same—after a seven-and-a-half-hour marathon meeting in which Citi's directors heatedly debated the co-CEO arrangement. "There were a ton of questions from both the boards about our being co-CEOs," Weill says. "Obviously we were able to convince our respective boards that we think we're up to it, and that if they think we're not behaving they should throw us out."

On April 3–4, the exchange ratio was negotiated directly by top executives at both companies. Technically, Travelers would buy Citicorp, issuing 2.5 new common shares for every Citi common share. Existing law made that the obvious way to get the deal done. Banks are not allowed to engage in most forms of insurance underwriting. But under the Bank Holding Act, an insurance company can buy a bank and apply to become a bank holding company by agreeing to get into compliance with the law within a specified period—in this case a minimum of two years and a maximum of five years. Weill, as I've noted, believes that banking laws will be dramatically different in five years, providing banks in the United States with the ability to engage in much wider arenas of finance. If he turns out to be correct on that score it will be at least partly because his deal forced lawmakers to look around the world and see that banks elsewhere have such freedoms already. Congress doesn't want to appear out of touch with the changing nature of high finance.

Still, there was no guarantee that anything would change. The Dutch financial services conglomerate ING, with offices in the United States and around the world, had felt, nearly a decade earlier, that U.S. laws in this area were about to bite the dust. So it went ahead and bought the Dutch insurance company Nationale Nederland in 1990. After a two-year grace period and then three separate one-year extensions, little had changed. Insurance and commercial banking remained an unlawful mix. So in 1994, the company gave up its U.S. bank charter—and with it access to cheap money from the Federal Reserve and the right to accept consumer deposits. That same fate may well await Weill, and he knew it on the evening of April 4, when both company's boards formally approved the merger. The deal was signed on April 5, when Weill and Reed placed a joint phone call to President Clinton. The next morning, April 6, they let the world in on their secret.

And it had been a secret. "There was not a single leak, which was wonderful," Weill says. "That meant to me that the people involved must have liked the deal; otherwise, it would have been in their interest to leak the thing. That's what happens. You know what they say: Loose lips sink ships. So we took that as a real positive sign. And after we announced the deal on a Monday morning the stocks went up 20 percent, which was incredible. It created $30 billion of market cap in one day."

It was an enthusiastic response without staying power, however. Travelers stock, after shooting to $73 from the low $60s, would begin to fall back within days, and over the summer it sank as low $28.50. The decline was partly a result of a slumping stock market overall, and partly the result of weak economies in Asia that threatened to drag the U.S. economy down as well. But there were nagging questions about the Citi-Travelers merger. How would these two behemoths really fit together? Who would run the company? And with few cost-cutting opportunities, could the promised cross-selling generate additional revenue quickly enough and significant enough to add incremental earnings? Given the checkered past of cross-selling efforts, many wondered if it would really work.

For five months Fed staff and officials put questions to Weill's group almost daily. They were pushing for detailed information on how Travelers works, what kinds of risks it takes in underwriting and in its cash management practices. "We showed them whatever they wanted," Weill says. "The more they know the better they can regulate. This went on for a long time." Meanwhile, both Citi's and Travelers' exposure to Asia was beginning to hurt. All hell broke loose in the third quarter, when Russia defaulted on billions of debt. Stock and bond markets around the world plunged in August. Again, the U.S. markets didn't get hit as hard. The Dow Jones industrial average fell nearly 20 percent—its biggest slide in eight years. But emerging markets were hit far harder, and Weill spent some tough weeks worrying about his deal. "Shareholder groups, arbitrageurs, speculators, who the heck knows who else," Weill says. "They were all starting to ask why we were taking on all this emerging markets risk with Citibank. We already had considerable exposure through Salomon. In fact, we reported a loss for the quarter because of Salomon. People were asking why we didn't walk away from the Citibank deal, or at least try to renegotiate it."

For the third quarter, losses at Travelers' Salomon Smith Barney unit and at Citicorp's global relationship bank totaled $500 million, helping sink Citigroup's net income for the quarter by 53 percent—to $729 million from what would have been $1.5 billion had the two companies been together a year earlier. But Weill wasn't any more interested in turning back than he had been a year earlier when overseas shock waves has tossed his Salomon purchase into question. "My only comment, and I'm glad it got picked up on the wires," he says, "was that the only thing you have in this world is your word. My word is my bond. We are going to complete this thing." Reed felt the same way. The two CEOs pushed forward knowing, as Weill says, "that on the other side of this problem is a really great opportunity." Weill recalls being in Hong Kong meeting with a group from both Citicorp and Salomon. "It was about midnight, and it was just when things in the markets were their wildest," he says. "I remember looking at this group and saying to them, 'Jeez, what are all these questions? If I wasn't going to do this deal why the heck would be I here with you at twelve o'clock at night?' "

A month later, on September 23, 1998, with scores of needed approvals already in hand from various insurance and other regulators, the Federal Reserve and the Justice Department finally weighed in with their nods. The merger was official, and on October 8, 1998, the two stocks began trading as one.

Here's a brief Q&A with Sandy Weill, the deal king whose word is his bond:

Question: *Everyone knows about your disappointment at American Express, getting pushed out after you had built one of the largest brokerages in the country and sold it to them. Was that the deal you shouldn't have done?*

Answer: I think from all deals you get certain things. From the point of view of a lot of my associates, it's the deal I shouldn't have done because the latter part of the '80s were pretty painful for them, having stayed at American Express. From my point of view, I had been the chairman of this company from 1965. I had been the CEO since 1973. I was doing the same things over and over again. The world was going to change. I could see that. Securities companies, I thought, had to get more permanent capital and so were going to become parts of other businesses. And that has, in fact, happened. I thought American Express looked like the most interesting partner that one could have in financial services. I thought they had a lot less bureaucracy. So some of the things that I thought were wrong. But I wanted to broaden my own thought process and grow. That didn't work out for me right then.

Question: *What would be the deal that you didn't do? The one that got away?*

Answer: That would be Bank of America. But my wife is very happy that one got away because she was not thrilled about moving to San Francisco.

Question: *Just think: If you had bought Bank of America you'd be working for Hugh McColl right now.*

Answer: Oh, well, I don't think so.

Question: *How do you spot a good deal?*

Answer: That comes from decades of reading and operating and having knowledge of the industry. Then, when something happens it may look like a disaster to someone else but it looks like an opportunity to you. All the deals we do, they don't all turn out to be easy. One of the toughest for us was buying Primerica, where they had management problems at some of the insurance companies. We ended up focusing those companies, though, and took some write-offs, and ended up with some very great businesses.

Question: *What's the hardest part of getting a deal done?*

Answer: It's the people.

Question: *What do you mean?*

Answer: Trying to satisfy all the needs and feelings, providing they are appropriate, of all the people that you are doing business with. Now, up until Citicorp most of the companies that we bought were underperforming. Commercial Credit was an underperforming part of Control Data. Primerica was underperforming a lot. Travelers had lost money in real estate and gotten hit with Hurricane Andrew. Aetna's property and casualty business was not performing that well. You have to recognize that companies' problems aren't necessarily caused by all of the people who work there, but by just a few of the people who work there. So you have to treat the people with respect, and they have to know that you are going to make your decisions based on who in your judgment is the better person to have the job and that not all of your people are going to be winners and all of their people losers.

Question: *Is it possible, Sandy, for a deal maker to stop doing deals?*

Answer: Sure.

Question: *Is this your last deal?*

Answer: Is this your last story?

Question: *Really.*

Answer: Well, we have a lot to do to get this thing to come together. That's our focus. But we will always be looking for things to do when the opportunity is right to increase our market penetration.

Question: *But in terms of building the company, which you've done numerous times by acquisitions that doubled your size or more—that surely must be over.*

Answer: I can't imagine another deal that would double our size. But listen, you've got to see what happens. You wake up in the morning, you see what's going on in the world, and you have to be willing to change your thoughts.

Question: *It's hard to believe that planning the Citi deal went as smoothly as you say. It's such a huge deal. Wasn't anybody telling you it was a bad idea or that it couldn't be done?*

Answer: It went very smoothly. It was unbelievable. Really. You know, it's the biggest deal I've ever done and it was just unbelievable from day one.

Question: *What did you see that made it such a slam dunk?*

Answer: I think that John saw an entrepreneurial firm with great execution capability and a great track record. And what we saw was, gosh, it would take many lifetimes to accomplish what he's been able to build in terms of a consumer franchise all around the world. And so many pieces just fit. And there was nothing to fight about because we both had about the same amount of common equity, and earnings were pretty close and so were our market caps. There were no fights. No arguments. Nothing.

Question: *How unusual is it for you to suggest a merger at one of your yearly planning meetings?*

Answer: We have spoken with our people on our planning committee of all the things that we are planning to do before we do them, and there never has been a leak, which I think is very good. We are all shareholders of the company. All of us have an agreement with each other that as long as we are part of the planning group we will never sell our stock. So I think it's only fair that we have an open discussion. People get a chance to express their opinion. If anyone's against it there is a lot of jousting. But we try to get to where it's a complete buy-in before we go ahead and do it. That's called team-work.

Question: *That's also been called the "blood oath," I believe?*

Answer: That's an agreement—it's not written and there is nothing signed, but it's described in our proxy—where we on the planning committee and our board of directors agree not to sell any stock.

Question: *Any parting words for would-be deal makers?*

Answer: I have a habit of most mornings getting up positive. I think that's good. And we are having this interview in the morn-ing. So I am positive. But I think you should never get too cocky. When you get cocky, you get shot down.

chapter five

Stephen Bollenbach

Treasurer for Hire

HUGH MCCOLL, THE CONSOLIDATOR AND pure stock-swap artist whom you met in Chapter 3, represents the newest breed of deal maker in America. Not that there is anything novel about issuing shares of your own company and trading them for the shares of a target company, making the two into one. Whenever possible, acquirers have done things that way for decades. But in the 1990s, a roaring bull market made it possible pretty much all the time—at least for any CEO with a fast-rising stock and a keen eye for prey that made sense. Folks like McColl; H. Wayne Huizenga (building his third empire, this one car dealerships); Barry Sternlicht (hotels); and, to a certain extent, Henry Silverman, the up-and-down franchise king whom you'll meet in Chapter 9, have been among the sharpest and boldest at that game. Take McColl. In his remarkable string of bank acquisitions since 1983 virtually all the big ones had a stock-swap element. As long as Wall Street kept pushing his stock higher, he had the inflated currency needed to buy bigger and bigger banks whose earnings and stock weren't growing quite so fast. All other things being equal, if McColl's stock rose 25 percent in a year while a target company's stock rose only 10 percent, McColl was able to buy the target by issuing 12 percent fewer shares than would have been required a year earlier. The deal actually got cheaper.

That kind of math, coupled with the push for size to win clout in the global economy, has propelled merger activities to unprecedented levels. In 1998, deals totaling $1.6 trillion were announced in the United

States alone, overwhelming the previous record of $907 billion the year before. But even with Wall Street and corporate America gaga over stock swaps, there will always be room for creativity, and perhaps the most ingenious deal maker of his day is the treasurer for hire, Stephen Bollenbach.

To call him a treasurer is, of course, a huge understatement. Bollenbach is now the CEO of Hilton Hotels, where in the middle to late 1990s he put together a string of impressive deals, including the $3 billion acquisition of Bally's just six months after he took the top job in February 1996. He was Disney's chief financial officer in 1995 and engineered the $19 billion takeover of Cap Cities/ABC. He's also spent time as Donald Trump's top financial mind, helping that notorious deal maker regain his footing after some missteps in the 1990 recession, and as the CFO of Holiday Corp., parent of Holiday Inn, where in the 1980s he fought off a hostile takeover attempt by none other than Donald Trump. Treasurer. Yeah, right. And Hugh McColl is just a loan officer.

But the fact is that Bollenbach's brilliance springs from his loosely defined treasurer's role. He's attained higher titles. But his knack for creating shareholder value through financial maneuverings is what makes him special. Bollenbach has split companies, sold assets, taken on large amounts of debt, swapped debt for equity, paid special dividends, and restructured loans—all in the name of shareholder value. And a pretty fair job he's done. A *Fortune* magazine article in March 1997 noted that if you had invested $1 in Bollenbach's employers beginning in 1982 and moved your money each time he switched jobs, you would have $38.76—an annual growth rate of nearly 28 percent. More than most keepers of the legerdemain, Bollenbach has been responsible for elevating the treasurer–chief financial officer (CFO) role from mere steward of the vaults to strategic thinker and value-added decision maker. It's no small thanks to Bollenbach that CFOs are now routinely considered suitable successors to the CEO's job. His mentor, Gary Wilson, who hired him at Marriott Corp. in 1982, is another who has achieved great things as a financial strategist and is the subject of the next chapter.

In his career, Bollenbach has landed only a handful of really big deals like the Cap Cities deal for Michael Eisner and Disney and the Bally's acquisition at Hilton. But for pure volume, he's in a league with the best. Bollenbach has bought and sold literally hundreds of hotels, including trophy properties like the two-thousand-room Marriott Marquis in New York's Times Square. What does he consider his greatest deal ever? Oddly, it wasn't a takeover or hotel deal at all, and it was a transaction that fostered more ill will on Wall Street than did Babe Ruth's historic trade to the Yankees on the streets of Boston. In 1993, Bollenbach, the CFO, persuaded legendary hotel magnate J. W. "Bill" Marriott to split the then-struggling hotel and food services company Marriott Corp. into two companies—one with the company's most desirable assets (management contracts on hundreds of prime hotels) and one with the least desirable assets (scores of unsalable properties burdened by billions of dollars in debt). The two pieces would become known as the Good Marriott and the Bad Marriott.

The split raised hackles among Marriott's bondholders because it placed the company's best assets out of reach should the company ever default on its bond obligations. But it was a pure joy for the stockholders, who finally were liberated from troubled assets that had been overshadowing all other developments at the company for years. A corporate bond basically is an IOU. Companies take money from bond investors and agree to pay them interest for a set amount of time, at the end of which they return all the money they had borrowed. Bond investors are a risk-averse lot. Before agreeing to lend the money they demand collateral, just in case the company runs into hard times and cannot make the interest payments. That collateral is the tangible assets of the company itself—planes, equipment, real estate, and so on. In creating two companies out of one, and lumping most of the debt with the least valuable assets, Bollenbach significantly raised the risk of Marriott's bonds. The bondholders had less collateral. That additional risk drove down the value of the bonds. Coincidentally, Marriott's stock took flight. A stockholder's main concern is future corporate profits. With the debt and poor-quality assets stripped away, management was free to focus on the things that were working well and the stock market was more willing to give them a higher value. There was name-calling; second-guessing; back-stabbing; lying; and, ultimately, about a dozen lawsuits. But in the end, the bondholders never missed a payment, and the lawsuits were settled for peanuts. The stockholders, of course, rode a magnificent and enriching turnaround that signaled Bollenbach's arrival as a financial mind with few peers. One share of Marriott in the winter of 1992, when Bollenbach came aboard for his second stint there, traded for about $15. If you held it and all the subsequent shares of companies spun off through spring 1998, you would have had stock worth about $120—an eightfold increase that blows away most stocks during an incredible bull market.

The deal personally enriched Bollenbach by several million dollars because of the stock and stock options he held. His employer, the Marriott family, did even better. It made some $90 million in less than a year as the stock surged higher in 1992 and 1993. But more important than the money, for Bollenbach anyway, was that this deal landed him his first job as CEO of a large corporation—at Bad Marriott, called Host Marriott—and opened the door for all other CFOs who aspired to running a company.

"LIKE ASKING TO BUY HIS CHILDREN"

In a 1996 interview with *Financial Executive* magazine, Bollenbach reflected on the importance of his ascent to the corner office and the forces that made it happen: "When I was very young, a bank paid 5 percent interest on savings accounts, and every other bank in the country also paid 5 percent interest. The rules were absolutely fixed. The markets were tightly regulated, both domestically and abroad. You couldn't transfer currencies to other countries. If you borrowed in other countries, there were special taxes on the money. Because of the regulations, there was no real opportunity for financial people to create value for shareholders in the same way that other departments, such as marketing, engineering, or manufacturing, could. All that changed in the 1960s and into the 1970s. Today we have unregulated financial markets virtually around the world. That gives financial people an opportunity to develop their skills, learn how the markets work, and deal with them. Just as the marketing people can outmarket their competitors or the manufacturing people can produce the same high-quality product less expensively than another company, the financial people can create value for the shareholders. That's what has changed. From a financial person's perspective, the opportunity to be a major contributor at a company, in terms of creating value for shareholders, is unlimited."

And Bollenbach is living proof.

I met with the ex-surfer and California native in New York while he was in town for a board meeting at Time Warner, where he is a director. He invited me to his suite in the ultimate trophy hotel, the elegant Waldorf Astoria on Park Avenue at Forty-eighth Street. The Waldorf is owned by Hilton, where Bollenbach has been CEO since 1995. Our meeting was in late March 1998. The ever-on-the-hunt Bollenbach was deep in negotiations to buy parts of the casino company Circus Circus. These negotiations would later come to naught. Seated on a leather couch in the spacious second-floor executive's suite, Bollenbach patiently took me through the events of six years earlier. He was gracious and outgoing. He wore a white shirt and striped tie and had a cast on his right hand, the result of corrective surgery for tendon damage.

On the pudgy side and with a full head of silvery white hair, Bollenbach looks, at a glance, a bit like a young Boris Yeltsin. It's an amusing comparison because no one ever had to convince Bollenbach of the virtues of capitalism, as at some point doubtless was the case with the Soviet leader. And while Bollenbach may not be a reformer of worldly and historic significance, his innovations in finance will leave a lasting mark on Wall Street.

Stephen Frasier Bollenbach was born on July 14, 1942, in Los Angeles. His father, Walter, was a milkman, and his mother, Betty, worked in a factory. His was a decidedly working-class upbringing, but the Bollenbachs wanted for nothing during young Stephen's teenage years in the 1950s, a prosperous time in the United States, particularly in California. Bollenbach once described his childhood as the West Coast equivalent of *Happy Days*. Bollenbach was anything but inspired as a student. He spent most of his days playing sports and surfing, figuring he would follow in his father's footsteps and become a milkman. From a kid's point of view, he said, what could be better? You're done working at 2 P.M. and can spend the rest of the day at the beach.

After Bollenbach graduated from Lakewood High School in 1960, his father got him a job scooping ice cream at Disneyland, where he stayed just long enough to earn money for a new surfboard. He still figured he would end up at the Carnation Milk Co. but elected to give college a go and so drifted to Long Beach City College, which wasn't much tougher than high school and where beer-bash parties were a core part of the curriculum. At Long Beach, though, a keen-eyed professor saw Bollenbach as a kid with promise but no direction and took him under his wing. The professor with vision saw to it that Bollenbach enrolled in UCLA, where Bollenbach earned a B.S. in finance in 1965 before working days and earning his MBA from California State University at Northridge in 1968.

Fresh from graduate school, the ex-surfer dude went to work for publicity-shy mogul and investor Daniel K. Ludwig, one of the richest people in the world, with interests in shipping (he pioneered the development of the supertanker) and savings and loan associations, to help run his S&Ls in the western states and other properties in Australia. While working for Ludwig, Bollenbach met and married Barbara Christeson, with whom he would later have two sons who would grow up to be investment bankers. Barbara was an avid tennis player, which impressed the sports-minded Bollenbach. But he would later give up tennis to focus his recreational time on golf, fishing, and skiing.

Bollenbach also enjoys fast cars and historical novels, especially about the Civil War. He once bought a $113,000 Ferrari on an impulse.

Bollenbach became CEO of Ludwig's Phoenix S&L in 1980. He left the mogul in 1982, hired away by Gary Wilson, the creative CFO at Marriott Corp., who was looking for a treasurer. The early 1980s were heady days for Marriott Corp. The real estate market was booming, and, partly at Bollenbach's behest, the company was building ten thousand hotel rooms and spending about $1 billion a year. But Marriott had no interest in actually owning the real estate, a capital-intensive business. So it sold hotels to investment partnerships, insurance companies, and other institutions as fast as it could build them and then took the capital and went on to build the next hotel. The key to the company's success in those years was that it would retain the management contract at each hotel. Those contracts paid Marriott 3 percent of the revenues and a cut of the hotels' profits. They were Marriott's core business—not building but running the hotels.

The strategy worked marvelously until 1986, when sweeping tax reform put the crunch on what had already become an overbuilt hotel industry. Illustrating the value of good timing, Bollenbach had left Ludwig's Phoenix thrift—his first CEO post—not long before it failed and was seized by the government in the S&L disasters of the late 1980s. His timing was even better at Marriott. He left the firm in 1986 before tax reform was implemented. He had no way of knowing that the tax changes would devastate the development business, and he had only an inkling that too many hotels were being built. He switched jobs simply because he was offered a better position at Holiday Corp., owner of Holiday Inn hotels. Bollenbach became the CFO, whereas he had been only the treasurer at Marriott.

Clearly, though, there were no hard feelings between Bollenbach and the Marriotts, because six years later Bill Marriott would welcome the deal-a-minute CFO back into his fold and ask him to fix problems that, ironically, Bollenbach's strategy had greatly contributed to before the 1986 tax act. The act greatly diminished the deductibility of losses from real estate depreciation and essentially ended what had been a thriving tax-shelter business on Wall Street. Wealthy doctors and dentists could no longer offset income with the depreciation embedded in real estate limited partnerships. So they stopped investing that way, and all of a sudden one of the biggest buyers of all those hotels that Marriott had been building disappeared.

Even after the 1986 tax act, Marriott went on developing hotels for a time. But by the late 1980s, it was clear that the industry had been overbuilt, and when the credit crunch of 1990 hit, Marriott was sitting on dozens of hotels, which had been built on speculation and for which no buyers were in sight. That year, the hotel industry racked up a loss of $5.7 billion, or about $1,800 per room. By 1991 new construction had virtually stopped. Marriott's stock, which had been riding the company's incredible 20 percent-a-year growth in earnings, was sailing along in the $40s. But over the next four years, it dropped to under $10 a share amid the worst commercial (and later residential) real estate bust in several generations. "By and large it was inventory built for sale, and Marriott was just stuck with it," Bollenbach said of those unsalable hotels. "The stock market absolutely hated what was going on. The stock was so low that Marriott was concerned the company might be taken over. There was even one overture from an Asian group. They said to Bill Marriott, jeez, maybe we could work a deal here and buy your company. Well, this was like asking to buy his children. He knew something needed to be done."

All the while, Bollenbach was engaged elsewhere. He was Holiday's CFO from 1986 to 1990. That hotel company had troubles of its own and a depressed stock price. When Donald Trump bought a stake and threatened to take over the company, Bollenbach—the guy in charge of the balance sheet—audaciously borrowed $2.6 billion and gave most of it to Holiday's stockholders in the form of a $65-a-share dividend. Trump quickly lost interest in what overnight had become a debt-burdened company. Bollenbach later sold the Holiday Inn chain—along with most of the company's debt—to British brewer Bass PLC for a respectable $2.2 billion. The remaining company was renamed Promus. In 1990, Bollenbach joined the Trump organization, where the Donald was himself having real estate troubles. Bollenbach persuaded banks to take Trump's stock and relieve the embattled developer of a $650 million personal debt.

Bollenbach would later work his magic at Disney and Hilton, where he became, if not exactly a household name, certainly a figure who commanded respect in the financial community. It was in February 1992, though, that Bollenbach returned to Marriott and began to hatch a plan to deliver the company from the ashes of the great real estate collapse. By then, he had become more intimate with the late 1980s real estate bust than most—having borrowed billions to build hotels in the go-go early 1980s, then warding off a takeover at the depressed hotel company Holiday, and then recapitalizing the close-to-insolvent Trump Organization. Bollenbach finished his work for Trump in 1991, about when Bill Marriott realized his company was in danger of being swallowed by anyone with an eye for long-term value and a few bucks in his pocket. Such people—blissfully, from Marriott's view—were scarce in those recession-racked years, though vulture investors like Chicago's Sam Zell (the grave dancer), Leon Black at Apollo, and Carl Icahn were on the hunt.

Bollenbach, who had cut his teeth with Marriott six years earlier, was by now a gunslinging CFO in need of a new assignment. "I actually approached Marriott one day and asked him if I could come home." Marriott could not have been more pleased. His stock had begun to recover as the worst of the real estate collapse appeared to be over. But it was still half where it had been a few years earlier. No one would buy his hotels, and he was carrying $3 billion in debt with little hope of working it off. Marriott figured that if anybody could get him out of this pickle, it was Bollenbach, who had helped him build many of the hotels in the first place. In February 1992, Bollenbach was hired as CFO and given free rein to devise a strategy for unloading the costly properties.

THAT'S GREAT, NOW SELL THE HOTELS

Bollenbach didn't need long to see that there was no market for the hotels. Institutions that once craved real estate in their portfolios were now disavowing the asset class for life. Some endowments and other conservatively run funds went so far as to write into their bylaws that they could not hold more than a small percentage of real estate. In retrospect, the wide loathing of real estate as an investment in the early 1990s was the perfect contrarian's signal. It would be years before real estate really took off again, starting in about 1995. But by 1992, things had pretty well bottomed. Bollenbach couldn't be sure of the impending turnaround at the time. But he knew what the hotels cost to build and that eventually they would be worth that amount—and then some. He decided not to sell.

Instead, he came up with a plan to refinance Marriott's crushing debt. The problem with much of the existing debt and the reason the stock market was so repulsed had to do with the nature of the debt, Bollenbach reasoned. There was a lot of floating-rate bank debt. Stockholders justifiably worried that interest rates would rise as the recession lifted and Marriott would be saddled with increasingly higher interest payments. Any recovery in the hotel business would be washed down the drain by the higher costs of borrowed money. So just a few months after he signed up, Bollenbach took a close look at Marriott's cash flow and reckoned that the cash from the hotels could easily service $1.5 billion or so of fixed-rate long-term debt. Once the long-term assets (the hotels) were matched with long-term liabilities (the debt), Marriott's woes would disappear, Bollenbach figured. So he set about refinancing some $900 million of variable-rate bank debt in two tranches, one for $500 million and the other for $400 million, and then made the rounds with the company's big shareholders and securities analysts. Bollenbach beamed as he walked them through the strategy. By securing a fixed rate that was covered by the income from the hotels, he explained, the hotels could simply be held—at little to no carrying cost—until their values rose again. To a financial mind like

Bollenbach's, it was the perfect argument, one that should have allayed all concerns.

But the shareholders had worries that Bollenbach knew nothing about. For starters, he was asking Wall Street to look at Marriott as an asset play, not an earnings story. That is, he was asking investors to hold the stock on the basis of the eventual recovery of real estate. It was a sound argument, given that the real estate market was obviously depressed and likely to recover at some point, and in the context of the new debt structure making the hotels pay for themselves. But asset plays were then a hard sell. Today, it's not unusual for heavily indebted companies with enormous assets—like Time Warner, Viacom, and many in the capital-intensive cable industry—to be valued on the basis of their assets and their ability to service the debt associated with those assets while the assets are given time to become more valuable. But it was an out-of-favor concept in the early 1990s, especially when the chief asset was real estate. Many money managers had lost money on their own homes, as well as in the real estate portfolios they managed. Real estate? Yeah. No way will I wait around for that to come back. Bollenbach was ahead of his time.

"With everyone, we'd go through this big story about how the markets were changing and all we'd have to do is hold the hotels for a while and everything would be just great," Bollenbach recalled. "They'd listen politely and write things down and nod their heads, and at the end of every story they'd say, 'So, OK, when are you going to sell the hotels?' It was clear that what we thought was a solution to the shareholder problem just wasn't a solution at all." The stock barely budged.

By April 1992, it was clear that another plan was needed. Bollenbach was pondering the issue one day and found himself musing that if he could just take all the dreaded hotels and put them in one little corner of the company, the rest would look good. Besides depressed real estate and onerous debt, Marriott owned two profitable food service companies and had an impressive store of long-term management contracts and franchise contracts. At some point, this musing gave way to a full-scale consideration of breaking the company into two in exactly that fashion. Bollenbach doesn't recall the exact moment that he devised the split, but it was only shortly after he had sold the final tranche of those long-term bonds to refinance the bank debt.

The timing would later become an issue because the bonds dived in value when the split was announced. Investors who had bought the bonds believing in Bollenbach's vision—the one he could not sell to the shareholders—turned and fought him bitterly when they saw his newest plan to improve the stock price. At the heart of a dozen or so lawsuits was the claim that Bollenbach knew he was going to split the company before he sold the bonds and that he did not disclose it to potential buyers.

HERE COMES THE JUDGE

Once the decision was made to explore a split, sometime that spring, Bollenbach and Marriott knew it would be an enormous undertaking. Marriott had always been a highly centralized company. This was to be no simple spin-off, in which a large company peels off one of its divisions with a separate management, separate facilities, and a separate set of books already in place. Bill Marriott ran his company like a family business. He was a micro manager. All decisions were made at headquarters in Bethesda, Maryland, outside Washington, D.C. "At any given Marriott hotel, in the kitchen there would be a picture of what ham and eggs look like," Bollenbach said. "Where the eggs sat on the plate, where the ham sat on the plate, where the parsley sat on the plate. And honestly, people would be terminated if they got inventive, you know, maybe changed the parsley and the ham to spruce things up. Put a banana on there, and you're out. It was that kind of culture."

Breaking apart such a tightly woven company could not be done quietly or quickly, yet it was important that word not get out because from the beginning, Bollenbach knew that his plan would inflame the bondholders. A swift negative reaction in the bond market might scuttle his deal before he ever got the chance to explain it. Amazingly, six months in the works and with dozens of top executives in the know, word did not leak until the day before the split was announced, October 5, 1992. Perhaps it did not because of the plan's pure audacity. No one believed the rumors. Or maybe it was because Sterling Colton, Marriott's authoritative general counsel who, along with Bill Marriott's father, had started the company as a nine-stool root-beer shop in 1927, started and ended every meeting with the stern admonition that any-one caught spilling the story would be regarded as a traitor during a war. So no one outside the company ever got word of the plan, and Marriott bonds traded like the investment-grade securities they'd always been.

Early on, Bollenbach knew he would need input from all the top executives in the company. And once they were clued in, they would spend much time jockeying for power and position in the postsplit companies. He didn't want that distraction. In perhaps his most daring and decisive move, he decided quickly who would run what after the split, and before he sought any input, he let everyone know exactly what his or her future role would be. "That put a badge on everybody," Bollenbach recalled. "You didn't have to worry what Mr. X was think-ing when he said let's put this asset over there. You didn't have to worry about whether they were doing that for the good of the com-pany or because it was a great asset and they had a personal interest in it. You knew they had a personal interest in it because you knew where they were going to be in the new company. It was healthy. It was good. By making clear all the biases, it made it easier for the groups to work together."

The logic was simple, pure, and effective. And exceedingly rare in corporate America, where it's far more common to pit one executive against another in a battle to the death with the survivor getting the promotion. In this case, the promotion came first. Bollenbach didn't want the competition to distract from the bigger issue of putting each hotel, each business, and each employee in the right spot to maximize the overall shareholder value. It has long been part of Bollenbach's modus operandi to delegate responsibility and to trust his executives.

Of course, even with the biases exposed, some assets were so valuable that no one wanted to back down. One such asset was a set of partnerships that gave Marriott a small stake in dozens of hotels that it had built and later sold to investment groups—all those doctors and lawyers who were looking for tax shelters before 1986. Marriott was their partner. For years it had routinely held back small equity positions in the properties it developed and then sold, a savvy play on the escalating value of real estate. Marriott was able to get most of its money out, so it could move on and develop the next property, retain the important management contract, and hold on to a sliver of the property itself.

As Bollenbach, Bill Marriott, and others weighed how to split the company in 1992, they all realized that the partnership stakes, though not worth much at that moment, would provide a windfall when hotel values recovered. Bollenbach, who was preordained as the CEO of Host Marriott—the bad Marriott, with all the hotels built on speculation and billions of dollars in debt—wanted the partnerships desperately. But so did the executives who would run the hotel management company to be called Marriott International.

To resolve such disputes, Bollenbach and Marriott had crafted another plan that proved invaluable. They had gone to Sterling Colton, who was nearing retirement and could be counted on to have only the company's best interest at heart, and asked him to serve as the ultimate arbiter of any dispute over how the assets were to be divvied. Colton agreed enthusiastically and became known simply as "the Judge." "We were trying to move somewhat fast," Bollenbach recalled. "Let me tell you there was lots of horse trading going on with the various assets. But when different groups couldn't decide on who would get what, you'd take it to the Judge and he'd say, 'Well, last week I gave you guys that. So this week I'll give these guys this.' And with Sterling, because he looks like the presence of God himself, there was never a question.

You just said, 'Well, that's that. Maybe I'll get the next one.'"

With the partnership stakes, it was Bollenbach's turn. They ended up in Host Marriott. But the Judge was partial to no one and dealt all the executives their share of setbacks.

Within Marriott, the split was widely viewed as an extraordinary step—but one that was needed. There were initial concerns about the certain hit that the bondholders would take when the split was announced. But the managers and the board generally agreed that the stockholders, who really owned the company, had suffered so long by then that their interests had to be front and center. There was a lone dissenter on the board, though. Harvard business ethics professor Thomas Piper, a longtime board member, couldn't endorse the split. He thought it was grossly unfair to the bondholders, and when the day finally came to vote on the matter, he resigned. It was not an easy decision. Piper loved his role as the board's moral guide. His office was always littered with stacks of research on business ethics. It was more than a hobby; it was an avocation. Twice Bollenbach visited him on campus in Cambridge to try to persuade him that the split was best. But Piper would not give.

"Fairness should always be a concern," Bollenbach said. "In a non-business environment, a kind of simple rough notion of fairness, I think he was right. It was not fair to the bondholders, and we later did things for the bondholders because of that. But the overriding issue in a corporation is that if fairness and the good of the shareholders conflict, your first duty is to the shareholders. It's an ethical dilemma, and I happen to come down on the side that your first duty is to the owners. There are other duties. But they are secondary to that."

Bollenbach, Marriott, Colton, and other executives made a big effort to persuade the ethics professor to change his tune. They flew him to Washington for one final attempt before they officially sealed the deal. It wasn't all out of empathy, of course. Bollenbach knew that the bondholders would be livid when they saw what he was doing. Clearly, it wouldn't look good to have someone on his own board so upset with the move that he felt he had to resign. Still, better that Piper resign than remain on the board and vote against the split, Bollenbach thought. So in a hotel room near Washington National Airport in early October 1992, Bollenbach said good-bye to Piper. He hasn't spoken to the ethics professor since.

"I always thought he didn't have his ethics figured out right," Bollenbach now muses. "It seemed to me that the correct ethical position was if he thought this was wrong, he should have stayed on the board and voted against it. I don't know where the ethics were in quitting."

SELL NOW, SUE LATER

By the time Piper resigned, the Marriott split had been six months in the planning, and Bollenbach was ready to publicly announce the split and then hold on tight while the markets reacted. Technically, the plan was for Marriott Corp. to pay the shareholders a special dividend that amounted to one share in a new company to be called Marriott International for every one share they owned of the old Marriott. Marriott International would have the company's 734 hotel and motel contracts and its 3,000 corporate and institutional cafeteria-management agreements and operate a growing number of retirement communities. The company would have $7.4 billion in annual revenue and only $20 million of long-term debt. The old Marriott, to be called Host Marriott, would have $1.7 billion in annual revenue and operate airport and toll-road concessions and own 141 lodging properties and 16 retirement communities. It would be saddled with $2.9 billion of long-term debt and act as a general or limited partner in a number of ventures, including the valuable partnership stakes that the Judge had given Bollenbach in a prominent internal dispute months earlier.

The press release had already been drafted. But one huge outstanding issue remained to the last minute. It had to do with the bonds. Bollenbach's bankers at Merrill Lynch and James D. Wolfensohn were squeamish about endorsing the deal because they thought that

Marriott's bondholders needed some security, some assurance that if the new Host Marriott, which was to be responsible for virtually all the company's debt, ran into operational trouble, it had an easy source of capital to tap to stay current on its interest payments. The bankers were insisting that Good Marriott—Marriott International—extend Bad Marriott—Host Marriott—a line of credit that could be activated without notice but that Host Marriott would have to pay for in an arm's-length, or fair-market, arrangement. "By now, I was wholly committed to Host Marriott and really believed it didn't need a line of credit because it generated sufficient cash flow to cover the interest payments," Bollenbach said. "So there was a tremendous amount of debate over how big the line of credit should be. I didn't think we needed it, and I didn't want to pay for it."

Over the weekend leading to the Monday, October 5, announcement, Bollenbach and his bankers at Wolfensohn haggled for hours over this issue. The bankers insisted on $600 million, which would cost Bollenbach's Host Marriott $12 million a year, or they would not render a favorable opinion of the deal, something that Bollenbach needed to sell the deal to Marriott's board of directors. Bollenbach insisted on half that amount. At one point, Bollenbach told the bankers from Wolfensohn that if they needed $600 million, he wouldn't do the deal. It was a bluff, and a poor one at that. Wolfensohn is a venerable firm. Its bankers have been through thousands of high-stakes negotiations, and James Wolfensohn, the founder who later became president of the World Bank, was keeping an eye on this groundbreaking transaction. He knew that Bollenbach wasn't going to blow six months of work over a relatively tiny issue, especially given that Bollenbach knew full well that the bondholders were getting the short end of the deal and deserved some protection.

"Glen Lewy, the senior Wolfensohn banker on the deal, absolutely insisted on $600 million," Bollenbach said. "I said, 'Look, Glen, if you can't give me a fairness opinion with a line of credit below $600 million, I'm not going to do this deal.'"

"So don't do it," Lewy shot back.

"Well, I immediately chickened out, and that became the line of credit," Bollenbach said. But he added with great satisfaction: "By the way, that credit line was never, ever drawn."

With the line of credit decided, Bollenbach formally announced the split as planned on that Monday. But the deal was anything but sealed. That day in the markets Bollenbach got what he had hoped for from the stock traders: Marriott's shares surged 12 percent to nearly $20. But the bond traders gave him what he had most feared: Prices weakened as credit-rating agencies put the bonds on their watch list for a possible downgrade. Within days, the bonds had lost 30 percent of their market value. It was a far bigger hit than Bollenbach, who suspected there would be a negative reaction, ever envisioned. In his worst dreams, Bollenbach thought the bonds might drop 10 percent and slowly trade higher as he made the rounds to explain the deal and to explain that the hotels had an ample cash flow to service the debt and even if they didn't, the line of credit, now much larger than seemed necessary, would give the company more than the operating room it would need.

Instead, the bonds traded down sharply. The most severe price erosion lasted but a day or two, after which the bonds did indeed trade higher as the bondholders grew somewhat more comfortable with the financials of the new Marriotts. But on Wall Street a few days is an eternity. Many institutions sold their bonds at deeply depressed prices, and even those who hung on didn't see a full recovery right away. The bonds ended up, on average, about 10 percent cheaper than before the deal was announced. On $1.5 billion of long-term bonds, that comes to $150 million of lost value—and it was no laughing matter.

SEND ME DEAD FLOWERS

Bollenbach certainly wasn't laughing. But neither was he crying, because the stock was moving higher and he thought that a 10 percent haircut on the bonds was both acceptable and perfectly legal—and above all else the right thing to do for the true owners of the company, the shareholders. Bollenbach had seen the market fallout. But at this point, he was still woefully unprepared for the firestorm that would ensue. A bondholders' revolt was in the works that ultimately would force the deal-making CFO to rethink his coup and come close to abandoning the deal.

On a basic level, Bollenbach found the bondholders' complaints absurd. Written into any corporate bond are "covenants," which amount to the rules by which the bond issuer must abide. His bond covenants were skimpy, omitting some routine items, such as "event-risk" rules that might have allowed the bondholders to redeem their bonds at face value if certain material events—like a restructuring—occurred. To compensate for the skimpy covenants, which meant a greater risk to the investors, Marriott had to pay a slightly higher interest rate. It was all spelled out, clearly, at least to Bollenbach, who had the authority to slice and dice Marriott's assets in the manner he had proposed. To Bollenbach, it was strictly a contractual issue. Was he allowed to split the company or not? If so, the bondholders didn't have a leg to stand on. But what he quickly found out was that many of the bondholders never read the bond indenture and, in fact, routinely failed to read such detailed information in many of the bonds they bought on behalf of their institutions.

In one exchange, Bollenbach recalled a woman who represented a big buyer of the Marriott bonds telling him: "You know you are going to ruin the bond market in the United States, Steve."

"How can that be?" Bollenbach quizzed her.

"Because you will force all of us to start reading these damn covenants," the woman complained. "We don't have time for that."

She was dead serious, and Bollenbach returned: "Well, you know, I think you probably make a million dollars a year, and you're telling me that you don't read these things? I think maybe it is you who will ruin the bond market in the United States."

That comment may have been a bit harsh, but Bollenbach has little patience for whining that comes from being unprepared or lazy. And at this point, he didn't yet know that the woman's rage was not isolated, that the bondholders as a group were determined to get satisfaction. "That was the whole conflict," Bollenbach recalled. "It was contractual. You could absolutely do what we did. There was no question about that, and it was later proven in court. The question was. Should you do it? Were the bondholders stakeholders who had some rights beyond what was in their contracts?"

In a sense, it was a rhetorical question because Bollenbach could not afford to alienate all Wall Street. In his mind, his duty was to the shareholders. The only thing he owed the bondholders was to live by the terms in the covenants. But he was still a young man at only fifty, and he knew that he would be selling more bonds for Marriott or some other giant corporation in the future. He certainly wanted to make sure that there would be buyers. So early on he knew he'd have to do something. He just wasn't sure what. The answer would come later at the suggestion of Henry Kravis, a disinterested party in this case but a deal maker so widely respected on Wall Street that he's been called King Henry. Bollenbach would seek out Kravis and in a simple, brief exchange, Kravis would advise him that the bondholders' fury could be assuaged only one way—short of canceling the entire deal: raise the interest rate on their bonds. It's axiomatic that on Wall Street they will sell their young for a few basis points. In the end, that's how Bollenbach pushed the deal through. But before he came to that point, he would first be taken to the brink of despair.

In the days that followed the announcement, the bondholders, when they weren't busy selling their Marriott bonds, were going back to read the bond covenants that they had ignored in the first place. Most came to the same conclusion as Bollenbach: The split was permitted. But this didn't mean that it was right or that they would have to take it sitting down. The biggest bondholders were among the largest institutions in the country—the Boston-based mutual fund behemoth Fidelity, whose bond funds that were held by Main Street investors across the United States had taken a hit; Minneapolis-based IDS Financial Services, another bond-fund purveyor; and the outspoken managers at CalPERS

(California Pension Equity Retirement System), who are well known for taking an activist role in companies in which their investments have not fared well. These and other giants of Wall Street were suddenly knocking on Bollenbach's and Marriott's doors demanding to be heard. "Just outraged, just absolutely outraged," Bollenbach said. "They were threatening lawsuits, making it personal, saying, 'I lost money. You tricked me. You're the reason I lost money, and now you've got it because all that value was transferred to the stockholders.'"

The bondholders got no immediate satisfaction. Bollenbach was convinced he was on solid legal ground and happy as ever to see the stock taking off. That, after all, was what he had been hired to do. But then it got ugly. In the ensuing weeks, the influential bondholders, all with contacts in the press, began to put out angry, mean-spirited messages that scared Bollenbach, Marriott, Sterling Colton, and other top Marriott brass. Marriott, especially, was wounded. For years he had run among the power elite in Washington, D.C., and he was a prominent person in the Mormon religion. Suddenly people were calling him names, accusing him of robbing one set of investors to enrich another. "They called him a sleazebag in the paper," Bollenbach recalled. "People who normally called him sir were calling him a sleazebag in the press. Their attacks were vicious. But they really knew how to get results because Bill Marriott just couldn't take that."

And it went beyond name-calling. At one point, the lawyer for a group of bondholders sent Bollenbach a bouquet of dead flowers. But Bollenbach's moment of deepest despair came when he realized that the bondholders, who by now were also filing lawsuits, were beginning to persuade their friends on Wall Street to blacklist Marriott. The big bond investors, valued clients of every major firm on Wall Street, started to pull the plug on any business with Marriott's bankers, which included the giant Merrill Lynch. Bollenbach feared he'd never be able to borrow money on Wall Street again. In late October a unit of First Chicago Corp., which had been a trustee for Marriott's publicly traded bonds, resigned.

Bollenbach's fear of being ostracized was driven home the following month, when mighty Merrill Lynch, which had eagerly sought a role in the groundbreaking transaction, recanted on the fairness opinion it had rendered. It was a terrible blow and was a direct result of the pressure that the bond buyers were putting on Merrill Lynch's sales force. Some big clients were boycotting Merrill Lynch, suggesting that the firm had duped them into buying the bonds without full disclosure. There may have been a boycott, but if anyone was feeling duped it was Merrill Lynch's own trading desk, which had bought and held some $20 million of Marriott bonds before the announcement. The traders took a beating along with their clients when the bond prices plunged. Merrill denied that the pressure led it to recant but did not offer any other explanation.

Bollenbach still bristles at the way Merrill Lynch treated him. "They were committed to us," he says. "They had given our board a fairness opinion. They were going to get paid $1.5 million. They had begged to be part of the deal. And now the other side of the Merrill Lynch house that made money selling bonds said, 'My god, you're killing us.' The irony is that they had begged to be in this deal. We already had a fairness opinion from Wolfensohn. We only needed that one. But Merrill Lynch bankers came and met with Bill Marriott and myself at a hotel opening in Philadelphia. I think they flew down in a helicopter to the groundbreaking ceremony to beg to get into this deal. And I'll always regret it. But the argument they made and that I accepted was that they were our traditional bankers and that if we really wanted to convince our board of the deal, we would need the stamp of approval from Merrill Lynch. Like a jerk, I thought, OK."

Later, when the bondholders started to scream, Merrill Lynch found itself in a tough spot. The firm's bankers tried for weeks to get Marriott's permission to give back the fee and rescind its opinion that the split was fair. Bollenbach would have loved to let them resign the account and take back his money, but by then he had come to realize that the bondholders would spin such a development into a major defeat. They'd use it as a rallying cry to put even more pressure on Marriott and its bankers and possibly kill the deal. So he refused. Bollenbach told Merrill Lynch that it had rendered a fairness opinion and had been paid for its work. It would not be allowed to resign the account.

The negotiations with Merrill Lynch went on for weeks, each time with higher-ranking executives, until Bill Marriott and Bollenbach finally met in a suite in the Marriott Marquis in New York with Merrill Lynch's CEO Dan Tully and David Komansky, its head of bond sales and trading, who would later become CEO. The Merrill Lynch bankers had caved in to the pressure from their bond-buying clients. "We're here to resign the account unless you pay us some more money and rebalance the debt between Host Marriott and Marriott International," the Merrill Lynch contingent began.

"I don't think we're going to do that," Bollenbach said in a stare-down with Komansky, who had been doing most of the talking for Merrill Lynch. "But if we do, how do I know you guys will stick with us?"

"You don't," Komansky answered.

"Thank you, Dave. I think we're done here."

The Merrill Lynch representatives later contacted Bollenbach, saying that they had gone over the numbers one more time and decided that the split wasn't fair after all and that they would have to go public with that view—unless, of course, Marriott would prefer that they resign the assignment and go away quietly. "We said, well, OK, in that case you can resign," Bollenbach said. That was on November 17, 1992, "and was really when the thing started a feeding frenzy among the bond-holders and became real news in the press."

HENRY KRAVIS, A BOND SWAP, AND A DEAL

And, of course, there were the lawsuits. The bondholders who went back to read the covenants saw pretty clearly that Bollenbach and Marriott had the freedom to shuffle assets in the manner proposed, but what galled them was that the company had sold hundreds of millions of dollars of bonds in the spring of 1992 without notifying them that such a draconian restructuring was being considered. The basic allegation was that Bollenbach had devised the split and then sold the bonds, and that this amounted to a fraud on bondholders, who were not fully informed. The allegation was not implausible on the surface. Even Bollenbach conceded that the timing was close, that the notion of a split first popped into his head just days after the final bond sale. Ultimately, the suits would be resolved quietly and with small-enough settlements for Bollenbach to claim a total victory. At that time, though, the Marriott brass was pinned in a bunker, trying to decide whether to advance or retreat.

Bill Marriott and Sterling Colton decided the deal had to be canceled, and they told Bollenbach so during a Saturday meeting in late October 1992, about three weeks after the split was formally announced. Bollenbach knows the value of a safe retreat as well as anyone. In later years he would back away from the Circus Circus deal and even the mother of all hotel-gaming takeovers that he wanted for a time so desperately: ITT Corp., which he lost to Barry Sternlicht's Starwood Lodging. But at this meeting he was incredulous: The retreat would not be a safe one; it would be under heavy fire, and he laid it out succinctly for his two teammates: "Hey, you think these suits by the bondholders are tough? What do you think the stockholders are going to do when you call off this deal and their stock gets cut in half?"

Oh, yeah. This was going to be a thornier problem than they'd realized. Bollenbach had gotten them into it, and it was clear they were looking to him to get them out of it. It was at this moment of despair that Bollenbach decided to cold-call Henry Kravis, the master of leveraged buyouts, who was well acquainted with piles of debt and an expert in assuaging angry bondholders. "Henry, when will this all end?" Bollenbach asked. "When the bonds trade back up," he replied.

It wasn't rocket science, by any means. And Bollenbach knew that raising the value of the bonds was the answer, too. But in that three-minute conversation with Kravis, it all kind of sank in. He must raise the interest rate on Marriott's outstanding bonds. And for good measure, he would bump the line of credit to $630 million, shift $450 million of debt from Host Marriott to Marriott International, and cut Host Marriott's debt from $2.9 billion to $2.1 billion before the split. Legally, he was not required to do so, and strictly speaking no one could force him to do it. But if Bollenbach wanted the nightmare to end, and he clearly did, he would have to buy off the bondholders. He did so on March 11, 1993. The biggest move was to swap $400 million of notes paying 9.5 or 10 percent for notes paying 10.5 or 11 percent. The cost to Marriott was about $100 million. But just like that, the bonds traded back up and the big bondholders stopped complaining. It would be years before all the lawsuits were settled, but with the bonds trading higher and the bond buyers no longer screaming in the press about their mistreatment, the suits faded to the background, and Bollenbach and company went on with the painstaking activity of notifying every hotel owner and business partner of what was going on while awaiting a tax ruling from the IRS that would let the deal go through. On July 23, 1993, some 85 percent of the shareholders who voted formally approved the split. At that point, Marriott's stock was trading at nearly $28—up from $15.50 a year earlier. The Marriott family, whom Bollenbach worked for and who owned 25 million shares, had made more than $300 million. The split was completed on October 8, 1993—eighteen months after the idea first popped into Bollenbach's head.

Host Marriott, the debt-laden real estate company run by the debt master Bollenbach, began trading at $6 a share. Marriott International, the Good Marriott with the valuable management contracts and minimal debt, began trading in the low $20s. The split was such a resounding success that Host Marriott later split and Marriott International spun off various properties. The value of all these pieces five years after the split was about $120 a share, a 360 percent increase that has left few doubters.

The losers in this deal included all those who sold their bonds shortly after the announcement and the lawyers who battled with Bollenbach over the bond suits and ultimately settled for fairly small amounts. Marriott's shareholders were the clear winners, but the bondholders won, too, because despite all the worry, they never missed an interest payment. No one won bigger than Bollenbach, though. His reputation took a giant leap forward with this deal, which also landed him as CEO of Host Marriott, a company that he went on to build into a giant in its own right. Bollenbach said that ending up as CEO of the Bad Marriott was never really a driving motive. It just made sense. He had been hired to deal with the hotels and the debt. He had liberated the shareholders from those assets, so who was better qualified to run them?

And run them he did. Bollenbach knew all along that the hotels were worth more than the market was willing to value them at. It had been the central argument in his initial plan: hold on until the values come back. He was now free to execute that plan. Only Bollenbach wasn't content simply to hang on. He was so convinced that the real estate values would recover that he went out and bought even more hotels, selling both stocks and bonds to raise the money to buy billions of dollars worth of real estate at a time no one wanted to own it. He could never have done that at the old Marriott. But his new Bad Marriott had an entirely different class of shareholder, one that understood how an asset-play works. Most shareholders understand earnings. With Bollenbach's company, you had to understand cash flow. He had plenty of it from his hotels. Meanwhile he was buying hotels cheaper than the cost of building them.

Host Marriott's shares began to rise almost immediately after Bollenbach hit the road to find investors who understood this little-understood dynamic. And as the stock rose, it became all that much easier for him to buy hotels, using his higher stock as currency. The success of Host Marriott after the Marriott split was a vindication of his initial plan, though clearly the old Marriott would not have fared as well with the plan because the reluctant shareholders would never have endorsed buying more properties when owning any properties at all was the perceived problem. Perhaps the cleanest illustration of how well Host Marriott performed was its 1998 sale of the Marriott in New York directly behind the Waldorf on Lexington Avenue. "It's the old Halloran House, and one of the best buys I ever made," Bollenbach says. "They sold it for $145 million, just four years after we had bought it for $55 million. So we made some phenomenal buys."

And how. Here are some excerpts from my conversation with the treasurer for hire, otherwise known as Stephen Bollenbach:

Question: *To what do you attribute the success of Host Marriott, which you ran after the split of Marriott Corp.?*

Answer: I think that it needed a change of shareholders. I think you needed a set of shareholders who would focus on cash flow and not earnings per share. And also I don't believe that the old combined Marriott, which viewed its problem as owning too much real estate, would have ever gotten in the market and bought real estate, bought hotels. And Host did. Host bought billions of dollars worth of hotels that are worth significantly more than it paid for them. Host is now a huge company.

Question: *Now, Host has split up, as have numerous companies. What's with all this splitting up? It's been quite a trend in the 1990s even while mergers have hit record levels. What's the place in history of the Marriott split, given what's followed?*

Answer: Well before the Marriott split, from the 1960s and 1970s, people believed that there was value in conglomerates. The notion was that if you had a smart management, they could run any kind of business, and if you just put everything together, it would give some sort of security to shareholders.

Say it's the old ITT [Bollenbach bid for what was left of that conglomerate in 1998 but lost to Barry Sternlicht's Starwood Lodging]. When the defense business was down, their bread company would be up. By the time you got into the 1980s, I think people realized that all you're doing is putting together a portfolio of companies, and the shareholders can make their own portfolio. If you want to own the Hartford Insurance company [part of ITT], but you don't want to own the bread company, then you're not going to buy ITT. But if you want to own a bread company, you go buy a bread company; if you want to own an insurance company, you can own an insurance company. So the fashion became, and I think it's right, to break up the conglomerates. So as the companies broke up, what happened is shareholders could then say, "Well, this is great, because— again, picking on ITT—I really do want to own the Hartford, but I couldn't buy it before because I didn't want to own the other stuff that was in there."

Question: *So why does this deal, the split of Marriott, stand out in your career?*
Answer: I guess for me, personally, it stands out because it was a really complex deal to do. It was really a bright idea. It was a new thought, and it was a difficult management process to get it done, and I get a big ego stroke out of that.

Question: *OK, it was a bright idea. But we just said that breaking up companies was nothing new.*
Answer: Oh, but not like this. Breaking up companies was nothing new, but this wasn't so much the breakup of the company; it was finding a way to dispose of hotel real estate in a market that just hated hotel real estate.

Question: *The bondholders' concerns that this kind of thing would happen over and over again, where the debt was lumped over here and the good stuff over there, that never really came to be?*

Answer: No, no, no.

Question: *Regarding the lawsuits, much has been made about evidence disappearing that might have shown that you had hatched the split before the last bonds were sold.*

Answer: Yeah, yeah, yeah. We had literally a roomful, just boxes and boxes and boxes, of information that we were required to give to the plaintiffs under discovery, and as a practice I just have never been one to keep files. But I had this file on this entire deal that was probably twenty pieces of paper, a single file, and I gave it to the lawyers, and it got lost. And this became a big deal. I mean there's a cartoon in the *Washington Post* that shows this little truck driving down the street and this box flying off the back and, you know, the bondholder says, "Well, here was the smoking gun." And it was as if these were the Nixon tapes, and it simply got lost.

Question: *Did you ever find the file?*

Answer: Nope. But I believe it was there in that roomful of documents. I used to tell the lawyers that if somebody would look carefully, they'd find it, but I don't think they ever believed me. I don't think my own lawyers believed me.

Question: *When did you figure out that you were pretty good at doing deals?*

Answer: It probably goes back to when I was in my late twenties and early thirties. I worked for a man named Daniel K. Ludwig, who was one of the richest men in the world. And he was interested in buying savings and loan associations across the United States. And so I traveled around for him and probably bought twenty-five companies in a period of three or four years. That's a lot of stuff, and so it was a good education.

Question: *Is there anything that stands out as when you said to yourself, you know, I could make a living doing this?*

Answer: Yeah, sure. A lot of times I've thought—and then backed away from it—that instead of running companies, I ought to be a banker. But I personally enjoy a broader job than just doing deals. Now, I'm recognized as someone who does transactions, but I think that's a little bit incorrect because I probably spent 10 percent of my time doing transactions and 90 percent running the company.

Question: *But when someone hires you today they're getting a deal maker. They expect deals.*

Answer: They're getting two things. A deal maker, and I've been the CEO of four different companies, so they're getting somebody who knows how to be the chief executive, too.

Question: *What's the deal that got away? The one you wished you'd done?*

Answer: That's easy. ITT. No contest. I mean, it was ours. We should have had it.

Question: *How did it get away?*

Answer: Bad luck. Truly bad luck. One of the things that still rankles me is that we figured if Starwood was going to come into the deal—as the rumors had it—it would be on the next Monday after all the rumors started. So Monday came and went. And I thought, *Phew, it didn't come. Great.* The following Monday they came, and the Monday after that was the Monday that the market dropped five hundred. If Starwood had come in on that day, they would have been laughed out of town. Their stock would have tanked like everybody else's. So bad luck, wrong day. A week later, wrong day.

Question: *So Starwood won out of pure luck?*

Answer: They had an unbelievably hot stock at the time. It's just dumb luck. If you ask anybody who won, they'd say, "Well, Starwood. They got ITT and you didn't." But I'd say, "Let's see." When they announced the deal, their stock was $60; today it's much lower. We were $26, and now we're $33 [Hilton was back in the $20s as of this writing]. In what sense did they win? They're down; we're up.

Question: *Could you have done anything to lock up that deal?*

Answer: I don't think so. The standard criticism is that had we offered a higher price at the outset, the CEO of ITT, Rand Araskog, would have been pressured into negotiating with us, and we would have gotten the deal. I think that's a shallow and uninformed view. If you look at what Rand Araskog was prepared to do to stay independent, you see that the only way he was going to be stopped is if we sued him in federal court. He was going to break up the company into three crummy little companies without a shareholder vote. If that's your mind-set, I promise you that another 10 or 20 percent in the stock price doesn't make you do what's in the shareholders' best interest.

chapter six

Gary Wilson

Other People's Money

LONG BEFORE STEPHEN BOLLENBACH, THERE was Gary Wilson. Bollenbach, through his cunning split of Marriott, formally elevated the status of chief financial officer from that of admired bean counter to CEO-in-waiting. But it was Wilson who made it possible. Wilson preceded Bollenbach as chief financial officer (CFO) at both Marriott and Disney and hired Bollenbach as Marriott's treasurer in the early 1980s. He was Bollenbach's mentor, nurturing his desire to buy, shuffle, and sell; feeding his knack for creative finance; and instilling in him a vocation for building shareholder value. These traits all blossomed in Bollenbach after the two parted company in 1985, and since then, the student has in some ways outdone the teacher. Wilson is openly admiring of Bollenbach's hallmark deal at Marriott, one that boosted shareholder returns and Bollenbach's career. "We did all kinds of things when I was there," Wilson said. "But Steve came along and did the Big Bang. That's to his credit." Still, whereas Bollenbach leveraged his deal-making prowess into merely a higher title (CEO of Host Marriott and later Hilton Hotels), Wilson dealt his way to a far more lucrative land, that hallowed destination known as principal.

Wilson became an owner and, as such, now gets to exercise his management muscle as often as he likes; the CEO reports to him. He enjoys greater freedom in running his company and allocating personal time. And being an owner has brought him wealth beyond almost anyone's expectations—save, perhaps, only his own. Think of Wilson's career as a prequel to the Bollenbach story. Wilson now is approaching the twilight of his career. It's not a footrace. But if it were, the younger Bollenbach might still have time to pass Wilson in lifetime riches, achievement, and fame—apt measurements of success on Wall Street. It matters little, though. Both are modern legends of finance.

Fittingly, the mentor nailed his most important deal slightly ahead of the pupil. While Bollenbach was a CFO kicking around ways to recapitalize Holiday Corp. and fend off would-be raiders, including Donald Trump in 1989—four years before he would rejoin Marriott and make his mark splitting the company in two—Gary Wilson was putting the final touches on the last big leveraged buyout of the greed decade. Everything Wilson had done in his career, if not in his life, pointed in one direction, and this would be the end of his journey: He and his longtime friend and frequent partner Alfred Checchi would buy struggling Northwest Airlines for $3.65 billion. It was a historic deal in many respects. It truly was the last big LBO of the 1980s, coming just ahead of the 1990–91 recession and punctuating the wildest period on Wall Street since the roaring 1920s. It was the fulfillment of Wilson's childhood ambition to own and run a big company one day. It would fulfill, in short order, another of his childhood goals: to be rich almost beyond measure.

The Northwest deal was a rare, daring LBO of a so-called cyclical business—one that is subject to the ups and downs of the economy. LBO artists typically target noncyclical companies, prizing their steady cash flow in good times and bad. Reliable cash flow is the key to staying current on the interest payments that accompany mountains of borrowed money. It's why KKR, for example, has long been enamored of retailers and food companies (Safeway Stores and RJR Nabisco); why Forstmann Little & Co., profiled in the next chapter, has gone for retailers (Department 56) and beverage companies (Dr. Pepper); and why Clayton Dubilier & Rice (profiled in chapter 7) targeted food company Arnold Foods and lawn-products company O. M. Scott. When the economy sinks, you still eat and drink and, yes, fertilize the lawn. But Wilson and Checchi proved that an LBO can work with a big cyclical company as well, even when the economy sours.

The Northwest deal also stands out as a rare takeover by outsiders in the airline industry. Before Wilson and Checchi launched their audacious takeover effort, the only industry experience they had was Wilson's brief tenure as a Northwest director and his dealings with airline food service executives while heading that part of Marriott's operations in the 1980s. Make no mistake. The airline industry is a tough one. It has minted hard-nosed CEOs like Bob Crandall at American Airlines, innovative entrepreneurs like Frank Lorenzo at Continental Airlines, profiteers like Carl Icahn at TWA, and brilliant renegades like Herb Kelleher at Southwest. It was no small thing for Wilson to step into this viciously competitive camp and plan to make not just money, but a fortune, and in the process change the culture of an entire industry and challenge its core business model.

Wilson did those things. And he did them with remarkably little at stake in terms of personal wealth—yet with remarkably successful results on that same score. Wilson and Checchi were 50-50 partners in the Northwest LBO. Together, they invested $40 million of their own money and wound up with 25 percent of a company bought for ninety times that amount. They took the company public in 1994 for $13 a share. The stock topped $60 early in 1998, giving their combined stake of 23 million shares a value of nearly $1.4 billion, placing each among the wealthiest Americans. As deals go, they don't get much better than this one. The list of billion-dollar winners is a short one, for sure.

Wilson, like Bollenbach, did hundreds of smaller deals while in the hotel business at Marriott and before then as a deal-maker-in-study, working for a small merchant bank owned by Al Checchi's uncle, Vincent. He's done only a few monsters, and nothing else like the Northwest deal. He's less a deal maker than a corporate strategist. At Marriott, he jump-started the company's growth by starting the company down the path of developing hotels, then selling them to tax-sheltered limited partnerships, and collecting a management fee for running the properties. At Disney, Wilson expanded the use of limited partnerships to fund movies, and in one deal, he saved Disney millions in borrowing costs by pledging the future royalties from Tokyo Disneyland as collateral on a $723 million bank loan. He also pioneered the use of Eurobonds and yen-denominated debt at Disney, to say nothing of piecing together the complex $2.6 billion deal to fund Euro Disneyland in France. But it was all just a warm-up for Northwest, a company that Wilson says he'll stay with the rest of his life. And why not? He's living the dream. If he gets the mega-deal bug again, there's still plenty to be done on behalf of this baby. His latest efforts have been in the area of forming alliances with other airlines, a strategy that has greatly boosted revenues at Northwest in recent years. There's just no reason for him to sell out and try again. He's done what he set out to do and is content.

That's a rare quality in a deal maker. Most of them are sharks that have to keep moving, keep feeding. For this book, I met Wilson at his New York City apartment on Manhattan's posh East Side, at Sixty-first Street and Park Avenue. He's lanky, well dressed, a tad eccentric, and wholly confident. He favors double-breasted suits and revels in stardom. He makes no apologies for his lifelong ambition to be rich and flinches not the slightest when asked about his wealth. He's quite comfortable with it. "I started with nothing from a small town in Ohio," he said. "As a kid, you dream about things. I always wanted to be rich and own something."

Now he does. Lots of things. Wilson lives on a multimillion-dollar estate in the Holmby Hills section of Los Angeles. He has a beach house in Malibu and keeps an apartment in the Minneapolis–St. Paul, Minnestoa, area—home to Northwest Airlines. He enjoys traveling the world. In a follow-up call, I spoke with him while he was on a yacht touring the waters near Greece. His New York apartment is bright and cheery—decorated by his decorator wife, Barbera Thornhill, an interior architect who did London's top-rated Halcyon Hotel. With its light-hued, textured wallpaper, it stands in contrast to the distinctly masculine dark-wood surroundings of most Wall Street power offices. I found Wilson to be enthusiastic, congenial, and exceedingly patient. He is, though, all business, smiling but generally tossing aside attempts at levity to return to the topic at hand. I should note that in many ways the careers of Wilson and Checchi are inseparable. The two have known each other for thirty years, and the Northwest deal was a pure collaboration. I did not speak to Checchi, choosing instead to focus on Wilson, who was the strategic mind behind the deal. That's not meant as a slight. Checchi, now more interested in politics than business, deserves much credit, and Wilson is the first to say so. The key decisions in this deal were made jointly. In the context of this book, though, I had to choose one over the other, and it was the strategist, Wilson, who won out. "But," Wilson notes, "the Northwest deal would not have been done without Al."

BUILDING A PAPER ROUTE

Gary Lee Wilson was born on January 1, 1940, on a farm in Alliance, Ohio. His father, Elvin, worked the presses at a local print shop and then, in his forties, bought and operated a competing print shop in the same town. He employed fewer than a dozen people. His mother, the former Fern Donaldson, was a homemaker and raised young Wilson and his younger brother, Hugh (now on the faculty at Texas A&M), with traditional Midwest family values. It was an unspectacular middle-class, blue-collar existence—one that would leave Wilson sensitive to labor issues as an owner-manager later in life. With no TV at home, Wilson would travel the world through books and stamp collecting. He managed at an early age to trade stamps for a profit. By the time he was eight, Wilson had started gathering corn from the fields near his house and selling it on the side of the road. At ten, he took on a paper route, and by the time he finished high school, he had two other carriers working for him and had built the route to two hundred customers, the largest route in Alliance.

Wilson graduated from Alliance public high school an A student and number two in his class. He lettered in track and football. The town was a hotbed of football talent, its most famous alumnus being Lenny Dawson, a standout quarterback for the Kansas City Chiefs in the 1960s. A dozen students from Wilson's class of 1958 went to major colleges on full football scholarships. Wilson, a running back, was one of them. He was accepted at Duke University and played in the 1961 Cotton Bowl. At Duke, Wilson's grades fell off slightly, but he graduated in 1962 with a degree in accounting and went on to earn an MBA from Wharton in December 1963. He's now in a second marriage and had a baby in 1998. He has two grown sons from the first marriage: Derek, who works at Salomon Smith Barney; and Christopher, who is an aspiring actor.

Fresh out of business school, Wilson made his first big career decision when he turned down an offer to join the distinguished consulting firm McKinsey & Co. and went instead with a small entrepreneurial firm in Washington, D.C., run by Al Checchi's uncle. It was an international economic consulting practice. But Uncle Vince, a wheeler-dealer in his own right, was fond of dabbling in overseas investments. In the early 1960s, Wilson hadn't yet met his future friend and partner, Al Checchi, who, eight years younger, was still in high school. But he took to the spirited and daring Uncle Vince quickly and eagerly accepted an assignment to live overseas, helping manage a company in the Philippines that Uncle Vince had invested in. Wilson made his mark quickly. He began as CFO of what was basically an agricultural concern with several big sugar mills. But he quickly moved to the operating side, taking on the additional role of chief operating officer and reshaping the company by selling one of the sugar mills and buying a construction company. "That's where I learned strategy," Wilson recalled. "We took this company and converted it from a sugar business, where there was a lot of government control, to a construction business, which was just starting to become very important."

Wilson, always looking to be on the fast track, worried about staying too long in Manila. So after five years, he returned to the United States. By then, he had met the younger Checchi and cemented a bond that sprang from their common love of football and their common desire to cut deals and get rich. Wilson hired Al Checchi one summer, and the two worked on deals from sporting goods to helicopter companies. Al went back to school in the fall, and in 1974 Wilson moved on to bigger things. He was hired as the treasurer of Marriott, a fast-growing hospitality company with a big interest in food services and at the time only a modest interest in hotels. Wilson, who would later become CFO and hire Checchi as the treasurer straight out of business school, might never have landed the job but for the fact that he already lived in Washington. That was Marriott's home base, and this famously frugal company didn't want to pay the relocation expenses needed to hire talent from another city. So the job went to the hometown applicant, Wilson.

"A WHOLE DIFFERENT KETTLE OF FISH"

Like Bollenbach, Wilson made his mark at Marriott. It was a brutally tough environment. Marriott had been one of the elite "Nifty-Fifty" stocks that practically every institutional investor favored in the early 1970s bull market. The stock had run up dramatically in those years but by 1974 was taking a severe pounding as the stock market suffered its worst decline since the Great Depression. Bill Marriott needed a solution, and his new treasurer gave it to him. That's when Wilson persuaded the company to focus on hotel development, and from 1975 to 1980 Marriott's earnings tripled. Wilson was named CFO in 1978. But he was still just a hired gun who longed to own his own company. He began pressing for his own business in the early 1980s.

It boggles the mind to recall that in the early 1980s, Disney Co., now a model of corporate success, was a floundering, unfocused, mismanaged company. By 1984, raiders, including Saul Steinberg and Irwin Jacobs, were circling the entertainment company with designs on breaking it up for big profits. Wilson was also interested, but for another reason. He thought that Disney's theme parks would go well with Marriott's hotels and that he would be the person to run that company. He urged Bill Marriott to get in on the bidding, but Marriott balked, saying it was too big a deal for his company to swallow. In the end, Disney fended off the raiders by selling a 25 percent stake of the company to Texas investor Sid Bass, where, ironically, Al Checchi had gone to work.

Wilson's next big shot came hard on the heels of the Disney disappointment. In the summer of 1984, Wilson had lined up Bill Marriott and Sid Bass to back him in a $1.2 billion bid for the government-run railroad company Consolidated Rail Corp., or Conrail, which the government was looking to divest. "It was all financed, and I was going to own a piece of it and run the company," Wilson said. But a competing rail company, Norfolk & Southern, outbid Wilson's group, and the dream was again temporarily vanquished. Ultimately, losing to Norfolk & Southern didn't matter. The government switched gears later that year and sold the company to public shareholders in the biggest IPO (initial public offering) ever to that point, raising $1.6 billion in 1987. Still, his disappointment was palpable, and Wilson grew determined to find opportunities away from Marriott. His buddy Al Checchi paved the way for his next move. After Bass gained control of Disney, the company hired Michael Eisner as CEO and gave him the responsibility of fixing the slumbering giant. Checchi introduced Eisner to Wilson, and by the following year, Wilson was brought on as CFO of Disney, where he eventually would become the highest-paid CFO in the country.

The new assignment couldn't tarnish Wilson's desire to run his own show, though. And by 1989 it was clear that Wilson would go no higher at Disney than CFO for many years to come. The president, Frank Wells, decided that he would not retire as early as planned, and heir-apparent Wilson began to hunt for other opportunities. This time, though, there was a difference: He was already rich. The famous Eisner turnaround at Disney was well under way by then, and Wilson was worth about $100 million in Disney stock and stock options. For the first time, he had a cache of money all his own. The next time a deal that he liked came his way, there would be no one telling him to forget it because it was too big or too expensive. This was a turning point for Wilson. The deals he had missed with Marriott in 1984 fed his desire to be an owner more than ever.

Back at Marriott in the early 1980s, when Wilson had run the in-flight catering division, he met Steve Rothmeier, the president of and heir-apparent at Northwest Airlines. The two became friends, and in 1987, when Wilson was looking for new direction in his career, Rothmeier (named Northwest CEO in 1985) asked the Disney CFO to sit on Northwest's board of directors. It was a fateful request. Wilson had never served on a board outside his own company but decided this was the time to branch out.

Founded in 1926, Northwest was one of the earliest commercial air-lines and focused its routes across the northern part of the country. It was one of only two (the other being Pan American Airways) that won the right to pick up passengers in Japan in an unusual "Fifth Freedom" pact with that country. This right gave Northwest a huge advantage over other international carriers and led it to establish many routes to Asia—routes that would become highly prized in later years as that region's growth exploded. Under federal regulation for forty years, Northwest enjoyed steady growth but was generally seen as an average airline with spotty service. Its reputation for conservative management and contentious labor relations was a legend in the industry. CEO Donald Nyrop ruled during much of the post–World War II period and was a famous penny-pincher who shunned new management tech-niques. Between 1962 and 1982, Northwest's unions went out on strike seven times. The pilots were out 93 days one time and 103 days another. The company avoided debt, and because it owned its own planes, rather than leased them, had one of the oldest fleets in the air by the 1980s. That situation changed somewhat after Rothmeier became CEO. For example, Rothmeier began to lease planes and aggressively modernize the fleet. But a decade after regulation ended, the culture of warring with unions and sloppy service persisted.

Wilson caught a glimpse of the war at an early board meeting, which he nearly missed because his Northwest flight was canceled. When he arrived, what he heard at the board meeting disturbed him even more. "I had spent most of my career in great operating cultures at Marriott and Disney," Wilson said. "This was a whole different kettle of fish. You sat around the boardroom listening to management figure out how they were going to screw people. This bothered me to no end. At Marriott and Disney, the employees were treated as the most important things ever." It was a culture clash that would never be reconciled. Rothmeier's contentious manner of dealing with the unions sickened Wilson. After a year on the board, he hadn't yet thought about buying Northwest, though he had had fleeting moments of such an ambition. More pragmatically, he was thinking about quitting the board. Then, in the summer of 1988, those sparks of ambition ignited into full-flame interest. One of Rothmeier's schemes to ace out the unions in a labor dispute backfired magnificently, and it opened the gate for Wilson to walk through.

STOP ALL CONVERSATIONS

To this day, Wilson can't figure out why Rothmeier did it. But that summer Rothmeier asked Wilson if he knew anyone who might have an interest in buying the company. Wilson's instincts told him that the CEO didn't expect a positive reply—that he was just trying to whip up a story that he could take back to the unions and somehow use to threaten them. And it might have worked. By that time, around the country buyouts were held in about the same esteem as the devil in church. The threat of a buyout, with its inherent promise of layoffs, cost cutting, and asset sales, might indeed have been enough to make the unions toe the line in pending contract negotiations. But there was interest, and not just the passing interest that Rothmeier might have wanted to stir a few rumors and give him some meat for the next negotiating session. There was genuine interest. This was Gary Wilson's shot, the one he had been building toward all his life. Rothmeier didn't know it, but he had just asked an eleven-year-old boy if he'd like to play for the New York Yankees.

Wilson had just one problem. He was CFO of Disney and couldn't take a lead role in anything that big and consuming if it had nothing to do with Disney. Indeed, when Wilson's role in the Northwest buyout surfaced publicly, Eisner became quietly irate, and Wilson would later resign the CFO post to become cochairman of Northwest. Wilson was willing to take that risk, though. He was becoming consumed with the idea of owning Northwest. When Rothmeier and Northwest's CFO John Edwardson (who later moved to United Airlines) visited Wilson at his home in Los Angeles and laid out the financials one afternoon. Wilson had that too-good-to-be-true glow. Here was a company that he thought was grossly mismanaged. The secret to running an airline in the deregulated environment after 1978 was to emphasize service, and part of that emphasis was to keep the employees happy. Yet Rothmeier's team continued to fight the unions at every turn. And Rothmeier had failed miserably in integrating Northwest with Republic Airlines, which he had bought in 1986 for $884 million. By the summer of 1987, flight delays, double bookings, and lost luggage were standard on Northwest flights and prompted passengers to start referring to the airline as "Northworst." Mechanics and baggage handlers conducted an unofficial slowdown that year, and the nation's fourth biggest airline ranked first in customers' complaints. An infusion of the Marriott/Disney culture would work wonders, Wilson believed.

Perhaps best of all, Northwest was carrying little debt—an incredible financial position for a company of its size and in a capital-intensive industry. Thus Wilson could borrow hundreds of millions of dollars to buy the airline and not be any more burdened by interest payments than most airlines were already. Meanwhile, the company's assets were first-rate. Northwest owned its own jets and held lucrative routes to Asia, the growth region of the world. So with the grin of a Cheshire cat, Wilson called on his old friend Al Checchi, who lived literally just across the street. The two conferred, and Checchi agreed that Northwest just might be the steal of a lifetime. They resolved to make the company theirs if humanly possible.

Step one for Wilson was a visit with his lawyer, Robert Friedman, managing partner at Simpson Thacher & Bartlett. This would be a ticklish matter, a board member making a bid for the company. The standard procedure in any takeover of this type is to buy just under 5 percent of the company's stock before you announce a bid. That way, if other bidders surface and win, you still make a bundle on the stock you bought before the bidding war started. It wasn't just selfish profiteering; it was common sense because serious bidders incur millions of dollars in costs. This is one way to cover those costs in a failed effort. Wilson was both encouraged and discouraged by his lawyer's counsel. Friedman told him that his position on the board set him up for charges of trading in illegal inside information. He advised his client to stop all conversations with Rothmeier and to resign from the board if he intended to proceed. Resigning was no problem. Wilson had had it with Rothmeier's hardball tactics long ago. But the potential for charges of insider trading was worrisome. Partly to allay concerns on that front, Wilson decided that he would buy Northwest only in a friendly, board-approved transaction.

"MARVIN DAVIS JUST BID FOR THE COMPANY"

As early as September that year, rumors had begun to surface that there might be a bid for the airline. That month Northwest, whose stock was slow to bounce back from the October 1987 stock market crash, failed to negotiate a widely expected deal to unload $350 million of Japanese real estate, prompting analysts to take a hard look at the company. The analysts generally found an asset-rich company with good earnings and low debt, yet severely undervalued in the stock market—a recipe for raider pie. An analyst at Morgan Stanley speculated that the stock, then trading in the $40s, might be worth $100 a share on a breakup basis. During a ten-day period in late October, the stock soared nearly 20 percent to the high $50s. Into that fray Wilson jumped. He resigned from the Northwest board and, on November 21, 1988, drew up the papers to form a partnership called Wings Holdings, which he seeded with $20 million, and then quickly began to build a 4.9 percent stake in the company (at 5 percent you must publicly disclose the investment). The founding partners were Wilson, Checchi, and longtime friend Fred Malek, who had been head of Marriott's hotel division.

It wasn't that easy, of course. The partners were wealthy and had solid credentials. But Northwest had a market value of $1.5 billion, and they would need to pay a hefty premium over that amount. Secretly, they hoped to get the company for $85 a share, or $2.5 billion. That was real money, even for a couple of wunderkinder who had struck gold helping Michael Eisner turn around Disney. As Wilson and Checchi pondered the pile of money they would need, they recalled a conversation they had some months earlier at the Winter Olympics in Calgary, Canada. It was with John Elliott, CEO of Elders IXL, the largest company in Australia and owner of Fosters Brewing, the dominant wool and agricultural-supply businesses, and a $10 billion merchant bank. Elliott had hit it off with the pair and suggested that they might do a deal together some day. So Checchi gave him a call. Lo and behold, the Aussie was in favor and jumped on board.

By mid-January 1989 rumors were flying again. The stock hit a new high of $59.125 on January 18, and any number of usual suspects were reportedly circling Northwest, including Donald Trump, Japan Air Lines, Saul Steinberg, Carl Icahn, raider Jay Pritzker, Coniston Partners, and Pan American. There was no mention of Wilson and Checchi, though, who had just finished buying their 4.9 percent stake at a cost of $75 million. It was time for them to move. On January 20, Wilson called Rothmeier to tell him that he had amassed a large stake in the company and would like to talk about a buyout. Rothmeier, who Wilson believed didn't expect things ever to get this far, was cool. But he reported the call to the full board, and a special meeting was called on February 22. The board debated how to respond and then informed Wilson that it would not negotiate with him unless he agreed to certain conditions. Among the conditions was the deal-breaking requirement that he not sell his 4.9 percent stake for at least two years and not buy any more stock while he negotiated. Such onerous and potentially costly conditions could only be meant to put off Wilson, which they did. For a month there was no correspondence.

Unsure how to proceed, Wilson thought he needed to make a more formal overture, but he wanted to be careful not to put Northwest "in play," Wall Street parlance for starting a bidding war, which would surely alienate the board. Besides, he didn't want any competing bidders if he could help it. So on March 23 he sent the board a carefully crafted letter. It assured the board that his group was in for the long term and that the partners had a history of building value everywhere they had been. The letter further said that Wilson would preserve the airline as it was. Headquarters would remain in the Twin Cities. No hubs would be changed. There would be no gutting, no large-scale layoffs or asset sales. It also said that Wilson was willing to work closely with the labor unions to try to end years of animosity. In Wilson's view, the wording was just vague enough that he thought the board did not have to disclose the letter to the shareholders, and he pointedly said so by stating in the letter that it "did not constitute an offer or proposal" to acquire the airline and nothing in it would "require public disclosure."

Even if the board had been impressed, it wouldn't have mattered. At a special board meeting four days later, First Boston, an investment bank that had been retained several months earlier to advise the company on its options, rendered its opinion that Wilson's group did not have the financial wherewithal to be considered a viable buyer, and the board voted not to pursue the matter. It might have all ended there, but for a colossal misstep by Northwest. The board put out a press release that was intended to discourage other bidders, but this was not the effect. True, it announced that it had adopted several proved "poison pill" provisions, including a shareholder rights plan, which, in the event of a takeover, would trigger a special dividend that would make any deal prohibitively expensive. It also announced a new executive compensation plan that would unlock "golden parachutes" in the event of a change in control. Such plans are lucrative to management, resulting in huge immediate bonuses. But they are costly to a buyer.

Finally, and fatally, the board disclosed that an unnamed party had acquired 4.9 percent of the company's stock and "proposed possible acquisition options." That was the bell ringer. The rule of the day on Wall Street was that if one bidder showed up, invited or not, others were free to follow, and a bidding war often ensued. It was free-form capitalism at its best. In those days, takeovers were mainly financial plays. Buyers hoped to create value quickly by selling assets or taking some other action. The thinking was that if one bidder saw an opportunity, it must be in there somewhere. Scores of analysts would look at the company, and the bids followed. Announcing that you had received an informal takeover proposal, one that did not need to be disclosed, was pure insanity. The board, in effect, put the company in play itself.

In this case, nothing happened right away. In fact, rebuffed and crestfallen, Wilson had already begun to sell his Northwest stock, soothed only somewhat by the gain he had recorded. He sold nearly 1 million shares at a profit of $25 million. "Then, a few weeks later," Wilson said, "I'll never forget this. I was at a party in Washington, and Al called and said, 'You'll never guess what happened. Marvin Davis just bid for the company.'" Davis was a high-profile corporate raider that the board wanted nothing to do with. On March 30, he suddenly and brashly announced that he would pay $90 a share for Northwest, a 50 percent premium over recent prices. He, too, was rebuffed. But by now rumors were flying of serious interest by at least a half dozen potential acquirers, including a group led by Rothmeier and funded by KKR. For the first time, Wilson's name surfaced as well. Wall Street traders were buying the stock in a frenzy, and it was clear that the board would have to do something. No deal would send the stock spinning lower and create grounds for shareholders' lawsuits. It had become a losing battle for the board, and on April 17 it announced that it would explore its alternatives, including a possible sale of the company. Three days later Davis commenced his tender offer at $90 a share.

ANOTHER DOLLAR, AND IT'S YOURS

For Wilson, this was all sweet music. It meant that his deal was still alive. He and his partners huddled. At $90 a share, Davis had offered more than the group wanted to pay initially. It would need help if it was going to go head to head with the likes of Davis. And who knew who else might join the fray? Ultimately, Pan Am, KKR, and Forstmann Little would surface as players. Wilson, who has a penchant for sticking with his friends, added an old chum from his days at Vince Checchi's consulting firm: Richard Blum, a prominent West Coast investor best known as the husband of San Francisco's dynamic mayor at the time, Diane Feinstein. The last critical partner to join was KLM Royal Dutch Airlines, which had been seeking a U.S. ally and saw this as a perfect chance to gain ground in the U.S. market. The latecomers paid dearly for their entry into this team. Whereas the original partners received 45 percent of the equity in Wings for $40 million, Blum got 10 percent for $100 million and KLM got 20 percent for $400 million.

That was the nature of the game. The early partners had invested a lot of sweat, and as their prospects for succeeding advanced, the cost of entry went up. That irked the management at KLM to no end, but they paid up anyway. The arrangement later severely strained relations between Wilson and KLM president Peter Bouw, and KLM sold its holding to Northwest in 1997.

With so many sharks swimming in the water, Northwest's board members came back to Wilson's group for in-depth talks. Wilson, at least, was the devil they knew. And Wilson's group was increasingly seen as the most friendly to labor and the least likely to gut the company for a quick profit. The group got a key endorsement from the machinists' spokesman, Guy Cook, who said the union looked favorably upon Checchi's and Wilson's past dealings with unions. Meanwhile, the stock was flying. It shot past Davis's price of $90, and by late April was trading near $100. So pressed, on May 4 the board announced that it would enter talks with Wilson and an undisclosed number of other suitors. A couple of weeks later, it set a deadline of May 30 for the final bids. This had turned into a full-fledged pressure cooker. As the stock price barreled higher, Wilson kept going back to his banks for more money, and they kept agreeing to give it to him. "By that time the banks were in deal mode," he said. "They were anxious to get this one." When the appointed hour arrived on May 30, Wilson and Checchi proffered their bid of $115 a share, or $3.4 billion. It was more than double the market value of the company when this all had started and considerably higher than the $85 a share the group first considered. But if the banks were willing, so was Wilson. And, boy, were the banks willing. Bankers Trust agreed to lend $500 million itself and was "highly confident" that it could syndicate the rest of the $2.9 billion in bank debt that it had committed to finance the deal.

After submitting the bid, Wilson's group was upbeat for several days. Word was trickling out about other bids, none of which were as high as $115. Wilson's confidence grew. But on June 5 the Northwest board threw him a curveball. In essence, it said that it could not decide who to sell the company to and announced that there would another round of bidding with a June 16 deadline. Wilson was rightfully upset. But ever the pragmatist with his eye on the prize, he reasoned that he had come too far to walk away now. He would have made tens of millions more just by selling his stock. But he was never just after quick profits, and this was the time to prove it. Ten days later, Wilson submitted his revised bid of $120 a share. As it turned out, that was $5 more than the next highest bid. But in a savvy move, the Northwest board approached Wilson and told him that even though he had the highest bid, there were other considerations that could push the deal to others. If, however, he was willing to give them one more ante—a so-called closeout bid that would ensure that the shareholders got top dollar without further delay or expense—they would shut down the auction immediately.

Wilson turned to his son, Derek, who had been working with him on the deal as a junior analyst, and asked, "What do you think, Derek, should we give them another buck?"

"Yeah, why not?" Derek Wilson returned. And with that, Wilson went to $121 a share, a closeout price that sealed his greatest deal. That last $1-a-share ante cost a total of $30 million but was insignificant, given how far they had already come from that $85-a-share target. In the wee hours of June 18, 1989, Wilson and Checchi entered into a definitive merger pact with Northwest. Some obstacles still remained before they could close the deal. Bankers Trust might fail to syndicate the loan. KLM's presence meant that the U.S. government had to sign off. With such things in mind, Wilson pressed for a quick closing, a measured strategy to head off any opposition before it could gain momentum. He opened his partnership's books to Northwest's unions, a tactic that built trust and advanced critical contract negotiations. The federal government wasn't happy about KLM's large position—it had 25 percent ownership though only 5 percent of the voting shares. But the feds approved the deal, stipulating that KLM reduce its stake over the next twelve months. When Bankers Trust lined up its loan syndicate at midsummer, everything was in place. On August 4, 1989, Wilson and Checchi climbed into the cockpit at Northwest.

SAVING THE DEAL

That, as they say, was the easy part. At this point, most deal makers would be happy with their fee and quickly look to unload parts or all of the company to strategic buyers at higher prices. But Wilson really was in it for the long run. And unfortunately for him, the short run was about to turn ugly and put his resolve to the test. In December 1989 he left his post at Disney to become cochairman with Checchi at Northwest and to devote all his time to it. Just seven months later, though, the stock market peaked, beginning a slow slide through the fall of 1990 and essentially announcing the start of a brutal recession. Worse, Saddam Hussein invaded Kuwait that summer and ignited what would become the Persian Gulf War. So on the heels of some halcyon years for the industry in the late 1980s came the worst three-year period in the history of commercial aviation. From 1990 to 1992, the industry lost $13 billion—more than it had ever earned. Northwest's contribution? Net losses of $1.7 billion. "It was a depression, really," Wilson recalled. "The Gulf War just killed us. Fuel is a huge part of our costs, and oil prices went way up. And the war made passengers feel insecure. They didn't want to fly, especially to Asia. They were afraid of sabotage. It was just a disaster."

Wilson and Rothmeier had a falling out soon after the LBO. So by the time economic troubles set in, a whole new management team was in place, headed by the former Marriott executive John Dasburg. Drastic times called for drastic measures, and as part of their plan to save the airline in the early 1990s, Wilson and his management team abandoned the industry's standard practice, which Wilson called "ubiquity at any cost." That strategy was designed to buy market share and maintain as many routes as possible no matter how much money they lost. Northwest would change that strategy by eliminating its money losers to focus on the profitable routes, content to maximize earnings at the expense of building a go-anywhere franchise. "In 1991 and 1992 we started getting statements that showed us what each route was making, and it became very clear to us that the strategy of ubiquity was not economic," Wilson said. "We were the first to do that. Now, 98 percent of our flights run through our hubs."

To fill in the gaps that such a plan inevitably would leave, the company embarked on a strategy of forming alliances with other carriers. Done properly, such alliances allow a Northwest passenger to connect with partner airlines on a single-ticket seamless trip anywhere in world. Northwest has been a pioneer in such efforts. It reached the first such deal with KLM shortly after the LBO, and despite a nasty falling out with KLM management over other issues, managed to sign a ten-year alliance with the airline in 1997, after Bouw's departure. That's how profitable, powerful, and popular the alliance system has proved to be. Through it, Northwest and KLM built their market share over the Atlantic Ocean from 7 percent in 1991 to 12 percent a few years later. Those routes were providing 30 percent of KLM's profits. Other airlines have been playing catch-up to this break-the-mold strategy in the past few years.

These changes did not have an immediate impact, though. At the time, Northwest was the fourth largest airline in the industry and suffering mightily from all its newly heaped LBO debt and the crushing economic downturn. A price war, launched by industry heavyweight American Airlines, hammered revenues, and in 1992 Wilson's baby and his dream of ownership were hurtling toward bankruptcy. By then, the slow simmer inside KLM's Peter Bouw had heated to a full boil over the original sweetheart terms that Wilson cut for himself and his Wings partnership. KLM had put up ten times as much money as Wilson's group yet had half as much equity. Even though those figures were disclosed at the time of his investment, he felt abused. "And when he smelled blood in the water, he basically tried to take us over," Wilson said.

KLM, which had invested 25 percent of the original equity, said it would inject $500 million in fresh capital. But the terms made it clear that Bouw was trying to hijack the airline. Even though foreign companies are restricted by federal law from owning more than 25 percent of a U.S. carrier, there are more liberal rules pertaining to the number of seats on the board. KLM wanted broader board representation. It also wanted the right to accumulate 51 percent of the voting shares, assuming the government would make an exception—not so far-fetched in this case, given that a bailout was needed to save the airline. Wilson and Checchi reluctantly signed on. But then Bouw, seeing a chance really to nail them, belatedly added a slew of other conditions that eventually reared up and bit him in the back. For example, he wanted KLM to have options that would let it buy shares, including some of

Wilson and Cheechi's, at steep discounts, and he wanted Wilson and Checchi to resign as cochairmen.

In response, Wilson began to work on Northwest's bailout plan and settled on one that would capitalize on his team's core strengths. Wilson would negotiate $250 million in emergency loans from banks and suppliers, including Bankers Trust, General Electric and United Technologies, and would then get the banks to defer more than $1 billion in principal payments. The master stroke, though, was in leveraging his goodwill with the unions. Wilson persuaded six unions to give Northwest a total of $886 million in concessions over thirty-nine months in exchange for 26 percent of the company's voting stock. That agreement reduced the ownership stake of Wilson and Checchi to about 25 percent from 45 percent. But when the unions finally agreed to the terms in July 1993—with Northwest's bankruptcy lawyers camped on the courthouse steps—Wilson had held on to the company and saved his deal.

Wilson and KLM's Bouw would continue to do battle for years, but the fight for control of Northwest was over at that moment. The recession lifted, and by 1994 the airline industry was back on its feet. Northwest earned $393 million in 1995, $573 million in 1996, and $583 million in 1997. Long-term debt and capital leases had been cut to $2.5 billion from $8.7 billion in 1994. Then, in 1997 Bouw left KLM, and Northwest formally severed the financial partnership agreement by buying back the KLM stake at, ironically, a huge profit to KLM. Today, Northwest is the fourth biggest airline in the country, and the largest in the world if you include Continental, which Northwest purchased voting control of in 1998.

It's hard to find any losers, though Pan Am probably was one. It had been interested in merging with Northwest and ultimately failed as a going business. Had it bought Northwest, it would have had the assets to recharge. Other bidders could be viewed as losers, too, though they actually made money. The way the stock rose during the bidding process, any bidders who took even a small position were able to more than cover their expenses. Still, by not going the extra mile, they gave up a windfall in gains.

The winners were many. Wilson and Checchi, for sure. They're still grinning. Their partners and lenders all did well. Even the unions, which gave concessions in the 1993 restructuring, have done well. By 1996, the average pilot, whose annual salary dropped from $80,000 to $68,000 in the givebacks, had more than doubled those lost wages in the form of capital gains on his or her stock.

The nagging question is why other bidders stopped so far short of Wilson's closeout $121-a-share bid. Wilson said he was willing to go as far as the banks would let him. Certainly, other banks were just as eager to back other bidders. Even the astute, slightly cocky Wilson fumbled for an answer on that one. It certainly helped that he had a reputation for building value and long-term commitments and that he communicated that interest well to influential union leaders who were concerned about the slash-and-burn tactics of other buyers in the 1980s. But it really came down to the fact that Wilson was there early and chose his partners well.

Those things allowed him to be in the deal cheaply. Wilson had long been known for his prowess in working with other people's money, or OPM. But this one topped them all. Being there early meant that he had to do most of the legwork, but that sweat equity gave him an enormous financial edge. Latecomers to his group would have to pony up much more than he for their piece of the equity. And in choosing KLM as the final major piece in the financing puzzle, he landed an operating partner with a strategic need to be involved. That need translated into a willingness to pay a healthy premium. The result was that Wilson had little of his own at stake. More so than competing bidders, he quite simply could afford to overpay and have the deal go bust. It was OPM. That's why he was willing to go as high as the banks would let him, and that's why he won the bid.

Here is a brief question-and-answer session with Wilson, the strategist, deal maker, and master of OPM:

Question:: *What is the ideal deal for you?*

Answer: I perform best when I'm in a corporation doing transactions within the corporation to create shareholder value. I'm not going out like Carl Icahn buying companies and selling off the pieces and then going to the next company. That's not my bag. My bag is to create value by growing a real industrial enterprise. At Marriott, to give you the numbers, we started out with a market value of $200 million in 1974, and when I left in 1985, that value was about $5 billion, and we had become one of the biggest hotel companies in the world.

Question: *It's perhaps an underappreciated aspect of your career that you once ran the in-flight food service operation at Marriott. You were the guy behind that famous airplane food, right?*

Answer: Well, yes. But we did it all under spec. Our kitchens catered to the specifications of the airlines. You can't blame the taste on us.

Question: *Why do you think Steve Rothmeier first approached you to buy Northwest?*

Answer: I'm not sure that even he knows. I believe it all had to do with labor. They were trying to find some strategy to work on labor. To this day, I do not know what that strategy was, but dealing with labor is what precipitated everything at Northwest. I think he just wanted to use it as a bluff of some sort.

Question: *How did Michael Eisner feel about your involvement with Northwest while you still worked for Disney? And why didn't you resign first?*

Answer: I didn't quit because I was in the middle of the Euro Disneyland financing, which was very complex. It was the biggest equity offering ever done in Europe [October 1989]. Even though I told Michael what I was doing, he didn't really think it would happen. And then when it did happen, it got lots of publicity. He was very sensitive to that, which he should be. All during the fall of 1988 and spring of 1989, I'm worrying about who's going to get Northwest while we're financing Euro Disneyland. I did my job. We did great financing Euro Disneyland. But Eisner was not happy. He simply didn't want his CFO involved in some other LBO, and in hindsight I can understand that. I resigned from my executive role at Disney at the end of 1989.

Question: *Was there a point at which you wished you hadn't gotten into the Northwest deal?*

Answer: No. As bad as things got, we were never losing our shirts. We didn't have that much tied up in the deal. But the thing that was at risk was our reputation. If this thing had gone under, we would not be on anyone's radar screen anymore, and we came within hours of bankruptcy in the summer of 1993. But I never regretted doing the deal because you have to be in the game to win.

Question: *You're known as a deal maker, and for years there's been speculation on when you would sell out Northwest and move on. Did you or do you ever plan to do that?*

Answer: Here's the point. We've never sold anything. In the Philippines I spent five years building a sugar company into a construction company. At Marriott we built the greatest hotel company from nothing, and Bill Marriott will tell you that it was our creativity that got him the hotels he wanted to manage. At Disney, I played a key role in the turnaround by doing Euro Disneyland and all the other financings of films and things that created value. And now we've done the same thing at Northwest. So I've done it four times. This is what I call deal making—building shareholder value. As I told you at the outset, this was my goal when I was a kid. I now own a major piece of an airline. We run it well, and I am creating value for myself and other shareholders.

Question: *What impact has your deal had on the airline industry?*

Answer: We have been a strategic leader in this industry since we bought Northwest, and I think our competitors would tell us that. As I said, ubiquity had been the name of the game in the 1980s, and when we got into trouble in 1991, we were part of that crowd. We didn't know enough to know that was the wrong strategy. When we figured out where we were making money and where we were losing money, we shrank back to our hubs—back to Detroit, Minneapolis, Memphis, Tokyo, and Amsterdam. That's where we had strength. Ninety-eight percent of our flights now flow through our hubs. In the 1980s, about 80 percent ran through the hubs. We had a lot of losing routes in those days. We simply reallocated aircraft to profitable routes, which was one of the keys to our success. It was a whole new strategy for the industry, one that others copied.

Question: *And now your push is in strategic alliances with other airlines?*

Answer: Oh yes, because with the aeropolitical world that we live in, it is impossible to merge with other carriers because of government regulation and union issues. But you don't need to merge with them. You can get most of the synergies from an alliance, where you're coordinating schedules and feeding people more effectively through your hub and your partner's hub. Strong alliances are virtual mergers. It's taken three or four years, but the industry is now following that.

Question: *What's the deal that got away from you?*

Answer: The deal we should have done was Marriott buying Disney. That was it. But it wasn't my company. It was Bill Marriott's. Bill's a conservative guy. He's done well without Disney, but if he'd bought Disney, it would have blown him off the charts. This is a deal that would have guaranteed Marriott continued 20 percent growth a year for years, and that was a strategic goal. It was a company that needed operating management, which Marriott was very good at. It was in the hotel and theme-park business, which we understood. We didn't understand movies, but we did understand merchandising—all the things that Disney was in. In hindsight, we would not have gotten all the value out of Disney that Eisner did, because he is a unique executive. We would not have done as well in animated films, which is where a lot of the value was created. But we would have increased prices and built hotels at the parks. The old Disney management didn't want to own hotels. Dumb. These hotels had 95 percent occupancy, and yet they wouldn't build them. Marriott would have done that. We would have captured maybe two-thirds of the value that Eisner created. That's definitely the deal that got away—for Bill Marriott.

Question: *What was the key to your finally offering $121 a share for Northwest? What did you see that let you get that far when no one else would?*

Answer: That the banks would lend us the money. It's as simple as that. You have to understand that you are living this deal twenty-four hours a day. You really want it. When the bid goes up, you go back to the bankers, and they are into it, too. They've got big fees, big things out there. The point is that we did pay a high price for this company. We did it because the banks would lend us the money. Now, one thing we knew going in, and what saved our ass when we got into trouble, was that we wanted bank financing. No junk bonds. This was not luck. We knew that if we ran into trouble, we didn't want to have to deal with a bunch of bondholders. We could deal with one group. I learned that in the Philippines. My boss told me that if you owe a bank a little, you're a creditor; if you owe it a lot, you're a partner. And he was right. Until we got the banks out—and they got every dime—they were our partners.

Question: *So you had no particular edge?*

Answer: We had a plan for dealing with this company, and I truly think that we were the only ones capable of doing it properly. Marvin [Davis] is not an operator. KKR didn't know who it was going to put in to run it. We had our team all lined up. And with what happened in the industry afterward, Northwest was fortunate that we ended up buying the company. The management in place could not have survived the airline depression. They would have had to merge, and Minneapolis might have lost its hub. What gives me the most satisfaction is that we were able to take a company that probably was not going to survive on its own, employing 35,000 people, to one that is now employing 50,000, and if you include Continental [Northwest owns a controlling interest], you've got 100,000 and possibly the largest airline

in the world. And we're moving strong into the next century. That's what gives me a kick. We were able to turn Northwest into a player even in a depression. We came from the jaws of death. It's one of the great turnarounds in American business; at least, I'm not sure that I can think of one that was greater.

chapter seven

Ted Forstmann

Master of the LBO

LBOS: *LEVERAGED BUYOUTS. IN THE 1960S,* they were scarce and small and went by the name "bootstrap," a reference to the struggling companies typically involved—companies that needed to be pulled up by their heels. In the 1970s, raging inflation provided the backdrop for a small band of ingenious money men to expand and exploit them and—almost mindlessly—mint fortunes with annual investment gains of 100 percent or more. The value of hard assets was rising at a rate higher than prevailing interest rates, so pioneers like Ted Forstmann—"Teddy," to his friends—and Joe Rice, whom you'll meet in the next chapter, invested in companies whose values stood a reasonable chance of rising in tandem with inflation. Thus, they earned back their interest expenses simply by being owners. The companies' earnings were a bonus, providing outsized returns.

In the 1980s, inflation receded and changed the nature of the LBO game. But returns remained high as these pioneers and others who flocked to the field bought billions of dollars of corporate assets that were grossly undervalued in the stock market. Traders and money managers were still shell-shocked from the previous decade of runaway inflation and tepid economic growth. So stock prices were down and bargains abounded. The strategy was to borrow to the hilt—up to 90 percent of the cost of buying a company—to get control and then bust up the company, selling the pieces for windfall profits. The phrase "The parts are worth more than the whole" could be heard in planning rooms all over Wall Street. All over the country, LBO artists—unfairly, in many cases—were lumped together with more villainous corporate raiders and blamed for the gutting and occasional destruction of companies with deep roots in America's communities. The LBO, looking so mysterious and sounding so exotic, came to embody everything evil about the so-called greed decade: hostile takeovers; ruthless job cutting; devastated cultures; crushing debt; and, of course, obscene profits.

In the 1990s, though, LBOs earned back the respect they had lost. First, a recession early in the decade demonstrated that many of the jobs lost to LBO-fueled mergers in the 1980s would have disappeared anyway in the rough economy of 1990–92. Later, takeovers and job slashing became common sights on the U.S. business scene. In the 1990s, it wasn't just "financial engineers" who were willing to slice and dice companies in the name of profit; big corporations were doing it, too, and in breathtaking numbers. Why? CEOs came to realize that merging with similar companies and then eliminating duplicate jobs and operations was the quickest way to lower their costs and become formidable competitors in the global economy and thus raise their stock price. The biggest employers in the land—from IBM and Sears to Merck and Boeing—embraced takeovers and cost cutting as a wholesome strategy, removing much of the tarnish from those tactics.

In this environment, the LBO guys found they often could not compete for takeovers with deep-pocketed corporate behemoths that had seen their stock prices double or triple in the 1990s bull market. Remember, those soaring stock prices gave publicly traded companies inflated currencies with which to go shopping for takeovers. Stock swaps ruled. Cash acquisitions were strictly stone-age. So rather than compete with the giants, LBO experts—with only their hard cash and sharp minds—changed their modus operandi again. These are the chameleons of Wall Street, always adapting their color to one that lets them exploit the greatest profit potential. They became buyers not so much of whole companies, but of unwanted divisions that could, with a little doctoring, stand alone as whole companies—divisions cast off by newly merged companies that were seeking to pare down to their core businesses.

It didn't hurt that, for the first time in twenty-five years, annual returns from LBOs had slipped from the obscene to merely the lush. In the last part of the 1990s, if an LBO returned 40 percent a year, it was a clear winner. That's hardly excessive, given the risks that LBO firms take. After all, the average investor in the late 1990s was able to earn close to 20 percent a year just by owning passive stock-index funds. And there were generally fewer LBOs in the spotlight than during the previous decade. So by the late 1990s, the LBO artist's public relations problems, which had endured during most of the 1980s, had pretty much disappeared.

It was in this friendlier period for LBOs—friendlier in the PR sense, not the economic sense—that Teddy Forstmann bagged his best deal: the 1990 acquisition of business-jet builder Gulfstream Aerospace Corp. Forstmann, founder and managing partner at Forstmann Little & Co., was among the first to ply his trade back in the 1970s. Joe Rice, a founding partner at the LBO firm Clayton & Dubilier (Rice's name was later added to the letterhead, and it became Clayton, Dubilier & Rice), was right there as well. Jerome Kohlberg, Henry Kravis, and George Roberts (put them together and you get the infamous KKR) came along about the same time, and then scores of copycats piled on.

Ultimately, KKR would become the most recognized name in LBOs. That firm's acquisition of RJR Nabisco in 1989, beautifully detailed in the defining 1980s story of greed, folly, and corporate high jinks, *Barbarians at the Gate,* by Bryan Burrough and John Helyar, forever fused the KKR name to the LBO business in a way that Forstmann and Rice never would. But while KKR was busy, as Kravis once said, "protecting the franchise" by lobbying hard for every big LBO in the market, Forstmann (and Rice, as you'll see in chapter 8) were being more selective and turning in dazzling results. KKR, of course, did quite well for itself, too. The $29 billion RJR Nabisco deal—at the time, the biggest takeover ever—is widely seen as a disappointment from the perspective of investment returns. But KKR has an enviable record. In fact, when asked about the deal that got away—the one they most

wished they had landed but didn't—both Forstmann and Rice immediately name Duracell, the battery maker that KKR bought in 1988 for
$1.8 billion and sold to Gillette in 1996 for $7 billion, a knockout by
anyone's definition.

The Gulfstream deal was Forstmann's personal TKO, not so much
because it made him a small fortune, but because it nearly failed and
would have dragged down his firm with it. Forstmann believes that no
other person on the planet could have saved Gulfstream from its low
ebb, a point that he admittedly played a role in bringing about. In
Forstmann's view, Gulfstream was a pair of transactions: the original
$850 million acquisition tended to mainly by Forstmann's partner,
William Brian Little, and then Forstmann's decision three years later—
after Little had left the firm—to step in as Gulfstream's acting CEO and
fix a deal that was rapidly turning sour.

The original purchase in 1990 was not Forstmann's finest hour. His
firm bought a struggling company in desperate need of capital investment, just ahead of a brutal recession and in the face of mounting competition. The 1993 decision was when Forstmann showed the savvy
and brute determination that have made him a Wall Street legend.
Forstmann's advisers, his confidants, and even his investors told him to
dump Gulfstream. They told him it was a hopeless loser and that he
should cut his losses and move on. Forstmann came close to doing just
that. But before he admitted failure, he wanted to take one last look—
from the fresh perspective of someone who might buy Gulfstream.
Buying good but mismanaged assets was, after all, the principal
province of an LBO artist. Did Gulfstream still have value and thus
promise? Did he, Teddy Forstmann, charter member of the LBO club,
still have the goods to get the job done? Yes on both counts, Forstmann
concluded. And to the astonishment of the LBO community and the
horror of his own investors, who openly worried that Teddy had lost
his touch, Forstmann elected to stay with Gulfstream.

From the brink of disaster in November 1993, Gulfstream roared
back to life under Forstmann. By October 1996, the business was so

hot that his firm was able to sell half of the company in an initial public offering of stock for about $1 billion—more than the purchase price plus subsequent investments. After another offering, this one for $800 million in stock, Forstmann's firm still owns 16.5 million Gulfstream shares (23 percent of the company), a stake worth $700 million. Measured from the point of deepest despair in 1993, the return to equity investors has been infinite because the company was all but worthless. Measured from his original purchase in 1990 (which is the only fair way to judge it), the deal has returned 43 percent annually to equity investors—or 13 times their original input. Forstmann's debt investors earned a respectable 25 percent a year. Forstmann's miracle turnaround at Gulfstream personally enriched him by tens of millions of dollars (he invests in his own deals, as well as takes a management fee), bringing his net worth to about $550 million. More critically, it cemented his reputation as an LBO master. Rolling up his sleeves at Gulfstream was a gamble that Ted Forstmann didn't have to take. The easy decision would have been to cut and run. But Forstmann was able to block out the naysayers and heed his own instincts. The reward was his best deal ever.

A DAILY GAME OF BRIDGE

I had not met Ted Forstmann before I started this book, but like a lot of Wall Street reporters, I guess, I felt as if I had known him for years. Forstmann is one of those ubiquitous Wall Street names; he pops up everywhere, often popping off about one of his passions. He has a highly public life off Wall Street, as a philanthropist who, in the midst of his career crisis with Gulfstream in 1993, visited war-torn Bosnia and donated $1 million to aid refugees, and as cochairman of George Bush's reelection committee in 1990. What he has enjoyed popping off about mostly, though, is junk bonds. He rails against them whenever he's given the chance and has penned numerous editorials on the subject for the *Wall Street Journal* and other publications, always lambasting junk bonds and anyone who touches them. Most notable among his targets are the junk-bond king Mike Milken and archrival Henry Kravis, whose firm was once the butt of a Forstmann joke that had Forstmann buying KKR for peanuts after a KKR investment in junk bonds forced the firm into bankruptcy.

I met with Forstmann at his office on the forty-fourth floor of the General Motors building in Manhattan in early March 1998. From his window, I could see to Queens and Shea Stadium. His office is decorated with inspiration. "When you're gruff, everybody hinders; when you're pleasant, everybody helps. Let's clear our path," reads one poster. "Admitting mistakes gets you higher respect. Excuses miss the mark," reads another. Forstmann is of average height and has dark heavy eyebrows; a field of silver hair; and penetrating, deep-set eyes. As you might expect, he's quick of mind. So quick, in fact, that he often fails to finish one thought before he moves to the next, sometimes leaving the interviewer confused about the point that he had intended to make. I found myself finishing sentences aloud just to make sure I was following him. Unlike Hugh McColl and Steve Bollenbach, who frequently digress but always bring their comments full circle, Forstmann rarely gets back to the original thought—unless prodded. He's a stream-of-conscious conversationalist, always eager to make the next point.

Forstmann and I met over lunch in his private dining area, a richly appointed room with a big circular wooden table at its center. Forstmann's private chef prepared pea soup, ham-and-Swiss sandwiches on rye, and an assortment of cookies and followed them with coffee and tea. Forstmann was open and forthcoming. He dwelled mostly on the second half of the Gulfstream story: the turnaround that he personally engineered after his firm had allowed the company to deteriorate badly in its first two and a half years as owner of the premier manufacturer of business jets. Forstmann is reluctant to place blame for the early troubles at Gulfstream on his former partner Brian Little, though that's probably where it belongs. Little had primary responsibility at the firm for Gulfstream in those years; Forstmann was busy with another company the firm had bought about the same time, the cable-TV equipment maker General Instrument. Ultimately, the mess at Gulfstream would so strain their partnership that Little would leave the firm, and that's when Forstmann stepped in to manage Gulfstream. Forstmann insists that Little, wealthy in his own right, simply tired of the Wall Street life and chose to pursue other interests. But the timing was such that a rift almost certainly took place.

Theodore Joseph Forstmann was born on February 13, 1940, one of six children and the second of four sons. His grandfather, Julius Forstmann Sr., founded Forstmann Woolens, a highly successful textile company later, handed down to Forstmann's father, Julius Jr. The family business allowed Ted and his siblings to grow up with plenty of money in the wealthy New York City suburb of Greenwich, Connecticut, where captains of industry often joined the Forstmanns for family dinners. Ted was an average student but a top athlete. By sixteen, he was a high-ranking amateur tennis player. Later, as a Yale undergraduate, he became an All-American hockey goalie. His love of sports, especially tennis, led him some years ago to organize the Huggie Bear pro-am tennis tournament played each September at a lavish summer home in the Hamptons on eastern Long Island. Forstmann plays every year. He also fancies putting up big money on who will win. At one tournament in the late 1980s, he bet $28,000 that the team of onetime top-twenty player Eric Fromm and amateur Steve Geller would beat the highly ranked Paul Annacone and onetime great Pancho Segura, then in his late sixties and thus considered an amateur. The Fromm-Geller team lost, and when Fromm later apologized to Forstmann, Teddy, who was having a good year in business and was feeling magnanimous, returned: "Eric, I closed two deals this week. I lost $28,000 on you, but I just sold Dr. Pepper for a $400 million profit. Don't worry about it."

That bit of generosity notwithstanding, Forstmann has always been a fierce competitor on the field. His tenacity was an outgrowth of a strained relationship with both his mother and his father. At one point, Ted gave up tennis because he felt his mother, Dorothy Sammis, pushed him too hard. All the Forstmann children were raised to be tough and aggressive and a little bit rude. Financially, the Forstmanns never wanted. But the family had some bumps along the way. In 1958—the same year that Grumman Aerospace introduced the first long-distance business jet—the Forstmann family business fell on hard times, and Teddy's father sold the company to J. P. Stevens. That's when it dawned on the kids that no family fortune was coming their way. They would have to earn their own riches.

After Yale, Forstmann held various jobs, including one teaching physical education at a reform school. He later enrolled at and earned a law degree from Columbia University, where he helped pay the way by betting large sums on his daily bridge game. After law school he worked for a time at the law firm Perkins Daniels McCormack and then at a few small investment banks, including Faherty & Smartwood, where he worked briefly with Henry Kravis. Then brother Nicholas and Brian Little convinced him to become part of a start-up investment firm. In 1978, Forstmann, Little & Co. was formed. Ted was the partner in charge of raising money, Nick was the partner in charge of numbers crunching, and Little was the partner in charge of deal strategy. Theirs was one of the first LBO firms on Wall Street.

Finance ran in the family blood. Nicholas Forstmann worked at Morgan Guaranty Trust for six years before he joined the eventual rival KKR. The older brother, J. Anthony Forstmann, was cofounder of the money-management firm Forstmann-Leff Associates. The Forstmann boys generally got along, though Teddy has said that his mother loved Anthony more, which soured the two brothers' relationship for years.

At his own firm, things began to click quickly for Teddy Forstmann. Speaking of those early years, he told *Forbes* magazine in July 1998 that "inflation was 14 percent and interest rates were 8 percent. You made 6 percent just doing a deal." His first deals were, of course, small. He acquired Kincaid Furniture Co. for $21 million and Union Ice Co. for $25 million. Others in the high-inflation years of 1978–83 included All-American Bottling Corp., Beverage Management, Unicom, Emb-

Rex Corp., and Topps Co. He held the companies three to five years and sold them for up to ten times what he had paid for them.

In the 1980s, Forstmann took on some larger deals—Dr Pepper Co., FL Industries, Sybron Corp., Grimes Aerospace Co., Lear Siegler, Pullman Co., and Moen. In the 1990s came General Instrument Corp., Aldila, Department 56, Thompson-Minwax Co., Ziff-Davis Publishing Co., CIDCO, Community Health Systems, and, of course, Gulfstream. In all, there have been twenty-three LBOs. In the nineteen years ending in December 1997, Forstmann's equity partners had invested $850 million, which rose to a value of $3.1 billion, a compound annual return of 55 percent. Forstmann's debt partners (he had a unique debt fund that I'll discuss later) had invested $4.7 billion, which rose to a value of $8.5 billion, a compound annual return of 20 percent.

HAIR-RAISING RIDE IN A BENTLEY

Long before Ted Forstmann decided to buy Gulfstream, he was a satisfied customer. The ultimate mogul's plaything, a Gulfstream jet allowed Forstmann to work and rest in leathery comfort while jetting from one company to another, from one investment partner to another, and from one philanthropic event to another anywhere in the world as he went about the business of deal making with the busy schedule of a head of state. "There's nothing like a Gulfstream," Forstmann said. "Like a Coke bottle, it has a timeless design. A Gulfstream looks and feels like a Gulfstream. The technology is very different today than it was years ago. But the basic Gulfstream look—the big windows, high tail, twin engines, sleek body design—hasn't changed all that much. There just isn't anything like it."

The original Gulfstream was a twin-engine turboprop, introduced by Grumman Aerospace in 1958, and was the first aircraft designed expressly for business use. The second generation, the G II, came along in 1966, followed by the G III in 1979, and the G IV in 1983. The latest reincarnation of the world's premier corporate jet—the G V—was the company's biggest gamble to date. It took flight in 1997 and capped Forstmann's heroic turnaround at the company. Gulfstream has gone through a number of wrenching changes in control. Grumman decided in 1978 to get out of the business-jet business and sold the line to Allen E. Paulson for $52 million. Paulson, an eccentric aerospace entrepreneur who had left home as a teenager, combined Gulfstream with two other plane manufacturers and sold the company in 1985 for the impressive sum of $637 million. The buyer was Chrysler Corp., which was looking for ways to invest its cash flow from car sales in a way that would make the company's overall profits less prone to cycles in the automobile business. It was an awful strategy, and by late 1989 as the car company was shutting down assembly plants, laying off workers, and searching for any possible way to conserve cash in what was to turn into a crushing recession. Lee Iacocca, the fabled car man who joined Chrysler in 1978 and revived it from near insolvency, put Gulfstream up for sale.

Forstmann knew instantly he wanted to be the buyer. It wasn't just that he liked the Gulfstream product. Teddy was by then highly successful and ran in elite circles—business, political, and entertainment. Aside from being friends with dozens of CEOs and being a popular figure in the Republican Party, he was close to numerous stars and musicians and was known to jam on keyboards with celebrity groups including the Nitty Gritty Dirt Band. In his circle were dozens of powerful figures who owned private aircraft, and every one of them who owned a Gulfstream swore by it. Here was a perfect company, he thought. It dominated its business, had a great product, and was being let go by a giant company that simply didn't have the time or resources to devote to it because its main business was cars—not jets. What's more, after an enviable string of successes in the 1980s, Forstmann was coming off his worst two deals: the car parts company Pullman and the glass company Lear Siegler, a pair of late-1980s deals in which he lost money. He needed a slam dunk like Gulfstream to get back on track. And as if that weren't enough inducement, this also was a time when the junk-bond market was in turmoil. Forstmann, who never used junk bonds, was being handed an opportunity to exploit his unique LBO structure.

The typical LBO formula calls for 60 percent to be financed by bank debt, which is secured by the assets in the company; 10 percent financed by equity, which is unsecured but carries potentially huge rewards; and 30 percent financed by subordinated debt, which carries a high interest rate but has little or no collateral. The subordinated debt is the critical third tier of the financing of most deals, and in most cases, LBO artists turn to the market for publicly traded junk bonds to fill that need. But Forstmann has had his own pool of subordinated debt since 1982, funded by investors who are willing to take the third-tier risks in any Forstmann deal. That's the pool that has returned 20 percent annually over nineteen years—an actual return far higher than the promised return of junk bonds even though they carried coupon rates in the high teens throughout much of the 1980s. This unique fund gave Forstmann easy access to subordinated debt when others who counted on junk bonds were having difficulty. Everything, it seemed, was aligned perfectly, and Gulfstream appeared certain to be a classic Forstmann winner. So Teddy went after it full throttle.

Iacocca had hired the Wall Street powerhouse Credit Suisse First Boston to unburden his company of Gulfstream. As a top deal maker, Forstmann naturally was in on the first round of solicitations, which aroused more interest than Forstmann had expected. Others, it was quickly apparent, saw some of the same virtues that Teddy saw and wanted the easy money, too. The bankers let Forstmann know that some dozen groups had signaled their intention to bid, including a cash-rich Japanese outfit that would need no subordinated debt and the franchise-protecting KKR, which always managed to find a way. It seemed that Forstmann would need more of an edge than his unusual debt fund if he was to land this deal. It was one that everyone wanted and appeared headed for an auction—the gut-wrenching process in which bidders evaluate what a company is worth and how much others are likely to pay and then offer something in between.

Forstmann hates auctions. In fact, he refuses to participate in them. It's one of his many idiosyncrasies and probably best illustrates the value of standing by your own principles in business and investing. In the late 1980s, auctions drove the price of many deals so high that companies in many LBOs collapsed or investors earned only pitiful returns because the high price required too much borrowed money. RJR, the big KKR disappointment, was in that pitiful-returns category. Forstmann made a point of walking away anytime a company was put up for public bidding, and because of that practice, he did only a handful of deals in the wild and woolly late 1980s, years in which LBO returns suffered mightily because of the high prices being paid. The late 1980s were tough on Forstmann as well. They gave him Lear Siegler and Pullman. But the period would have been worse had Forstmann changed his style to do deals that weren't right for him.

In the Gulfstream case, Forstmann thought, the way to land the deal before it went to auction was to reach the management and convince it that Forstmann Little was uniquely suited to running this company. Others, of course, thought the same thing. In the LBO business, company management often is retained to run day-to-day operations while the money men monitor the results and focus on the big picture. But management in this case was the elusive Allen Paulson, the seventy-two-year-old entrepreneur who had sold Gulfstream to Chrysler at an incredible profit five years earlier and stayed on to run the company for Iacocca. Paulson was nowhere near Chrysler's Detroit headquarters. Nor was he in Savannah, Georgia, the world headquarters of Gulfstream. He had decided to wait out the bidding process at his home in Palm Springs, California, and was taking no calls. Needing an edge, Forstmann hatched a plan to press his well-connected friends in business and Hollywood— all customers or, at least, potential customers of Gulfstream—to get through to Paulson. And it played out quickly. The self-made aerospace multimillionaire heard enough about Forstmann to agree to meet with him in Palm Springs. Paulson's chauffeur would pick Forstmann up at the airport, the Gulfstream executive told the money man from New York.

This was just days after the initial solicitation from First Boston, and Forstmann hopped a jet immediately. With a deal in the air, you don't ask too many questions. You just go. Forstmann wasn't even sure how he'd find Paulson's driver at the airport. That, however, proved to be an easy task. Paulson had sent a vintage Bentley convertible. But more to the point, its top was jammed half shut, half open. "This story is wacky from the very beginning," Forstmann said of his Gulfstream experience and the ride out to Paulson's estate. "This crazy butler is driving this Bentley with the top half up, all over the road. I have an associate who's hanging on to the seat for dear life as this thing is careening down the highway, about thirty minutes to Paulson's house."

Once they were inside, though, the hair-raising ride was quickly forgotten and soon paid dividends. Paulson liked Forstmann. As the two men spoke, Paulson suggested that he'd like to stay on as management and even invest some of his own millions in the deal. He also told Forstmann that Chrysler had added $40 million in annual costs that could be easily taken out and that instead of selling the typical twenty-five jets a year, he could probably goose that to thirty-five or forty. "Well, here's the guy who really built this company, and he's telling us all of this good news," Forstmann recalled. "We did some quick runs and said, 'Oh, my God, look at this. It's incredible.'" The TKO that Forstmann so desperately needed was there for the taking. It would be a typical deal: buy it, cut some costs, sell some more planes, improve profits, and sell it back to the public via an IPO in three to five years. Forstmann could barely contain his enthusiasm. He also knew that Paulson, who was close to Iacocca, would be just the grease he needed to squeeze in for an audience with Chairman Lee ahead of his competitors. That meeting was key because Forstmann simply would not be involved in the coming auction. He needed the Chrysler chief to cut a deal before things went that far. In all, the entire Palm Springs meeting lasted about three hours, and by the time Forstmann and his seat-hugging associate were back in New York, they had Paulson on board and were ready to push for a meeting with Iacocca.

THE HARD PART NO ONE KNEW ABOUT

Like clockwork, Paulson made the call that Forstmann had counted on and got Iacocca's ear. Iacocca was interested. But if he was going to call off the potentially lucrative auction, he would need three things from Forstmann and Paulson: the full price, complete assurance of the financing, and a rapid close. On the first point, Forstmann was being given a chance to exploit an unusual philosophy of his, one that few other deal makers buy into; on the latter two points, he was being handed a chance to exploit the competitive edge that his unique debt fund gave to him. These were the factors that got him the deal.

On the issue of price, Forstmann looked at Iacocca and told him to go ahead and name it. "What will it take?" Forstmann asked. "If I've got the money, we'll do it." Not that Forstmann truly would pay any number he could afford. But as long as the price is in the ballpark, Teddy is not one to haggle over the last few million dollars on a deal of this size. On this point, Forstmann can easily work himself into a rant.

"Any number of wonderful deal guys will tell you how important price is when you're buying a company," Teddy started. "But I will guarantee you that it's not that important. I guarantee you, OK? Now, should you pay three times what a company is worth? No. Or twice? No. But I guarantee you that price is not even one of the three most important things in acquiring a company—although the next hundred people you talk to will tell you that it is the most important and how they never overpay for anything even as they're overpaying for everything. But I will tell you that it's not that important. You buy the wrong business at 25 percent less than you should pay for it, and you take a little longer to go broke. You buy the right business at 25 percent more than you should pay, and you make five times your money instead of six. So you pick. Which one would you rather have?"

No. Price would not be the issue. This was a good company.

On points two and three, giving Iacocca confidence in the financing and assuring him of an early close, it was mainly a matter of explaining to the chairman Forstmann's unusual subordinated debt fund, which made him so different from KKR and others. With the junk-bond market foundering. Forstmann was pretty much the only one who could get third-tier financing anytime he wanted. Among the many aspects of the Gulfstream deal that Forstmann now finds so satisfying is that his debt fund proved invaluable—sweet vindication for the man who so publicly denounced junk-bond financing throughout the 1980s but lost deal after deal to those who used the high-risk bonds. Forstmann's debt fund meant that the money was ready for deployment. But even more critical, in terms of closing quickly, was having Paulson on board. Paulson had been running Gulfstream continuously for a dozen years and was investing his own money in the deal. With him, there would be no need for extensive due diligence. Paulson certainly knew where the bones were buried. As a team, Forstmann figured, they would be able to fly faster than any jets the two would later build together.

These factors and Forstmann's tireless devotion to circumnavigating the impending auction led to an agreement with Chrysler before anyone else submitted a formal bid. In February 1990, Forstmann agreed to pay Chrysler $850 million (Iacocca had wanted $25 million more; Forstmann does negotiate price at least a little). Manufacturer's Hanover put up $450 million in secured senior debt. Forstmann Little put up $300 million in subordinated, unsecured debt and the biggest chunk of the $100 million equity investment. Paulson put up the smaller chunk of the equity. He was named chairman and CEO of Gulfstream and owned 32 percent of the company. Forstmann Little owned the other 68 percent. It was supposed to be just another LBO. Cut some costs. Sell a few more jets. But it wouldn't work that way. The hard part was just beginning, and no one knew it.

FACE TO FACE WITH DISASTER

Not long after Forstmann completed the deal for Gulfstream in March 1990, he landed another big company: cable equipment maker General Instrument for $1.75 billion. That was in August 1990, and it was an important deal for a couple of reasons. The General Instrument purchase cost more than twice that of Gulfstream, and the company had more apparent problems at the outset. So Forstmann quickly focused his attention on that company and left the oversight of Gulfstream to his partner Little and longtime Gulfstream chief Allen Paulson. The General Instrument deal also proved to be a home run relatively quickly. Forstmann's equity investors eventually would earn nine times their investment in that deal. Success was clear almost from the start, providing a much-needed winner on the heels of two soured deals and one (Gulfstream) that was going bad fast. Making a quick success of General Instrument not only helped preserve Forstmann's reputation amid what remains his only real slump in deals in nineteen years but allowed him to refocus on Gulfstream when he finally realized the company's crisis state in 1993.

In the early years, Forstmann clearly had good reason for losing sight of the goings-on at Gulfstream. But that didn't make the troubles there any more palatable or less threatening. While he was diverted, his firm completely missed the fast-emerging competition from Montreal-based Bombardier, which in 1986 bought Canadair, maker of the Challenger corporate jet, and later added Learjet, de Havilland, and Short Brothers. By 1990, this was a well-capitalized competitor, something Gulfstream hadn't seen in its first thirty years of operation and, under CEO Paulson, chose to ignore. Other business-jet makers were gaining ground, too, including Dassault Aviation of France, maker of the Falcon corporate jet.

There was also the question of capital investment. In selling the division, Iacocca had said that the company would need billions of dollars in investment over five years to remain competitive. The company needed to be transformed from an old-line manufacturer, in which quality was more important than efficiency, to one that had to weed out costs and compete on price as well as performance. Chairman Lee, a car guy, wasn't up to spending that kind of time and money on jets.

Finally, the late 1980s were seen as a period of corporate excess. A backlash was developing across the land over richly paid CEOs jetting around the world in luxury paid for by shareholders. That sentiment and the deep recession of 1990 caused orders for jets to sag badly. By the end of 1990, firm orders for the G IV had slipped from 29 to 21, devastating news for a company that was planning to sell 35 or 40 jets a year.

Without grasping just how wrong things were in 1990, Forstmann still could see that he had a serious management problem—and it was the last thing he expected in view of the management's credentials. Allen Paulson, recall, had invested some $30 million of his own money and had nurtured this company from infancy. But Forstmann started to suspect that he just wasn't up to the job anymore. And the problem was compounded by the fact that most of his top managers had been with the company most of their careers and weren't much younger than Paulson. "Everybody was very old," Forstmann said. "Allen's people were the nicest guys going, but they were chronologically really old, sixty-nine, seventy-two, seventy-three, like that. There was a plantation mentality at the place. Nobody ever left." That was fine when Gulfstream was the only game in town, before the 1980s. But this old guard was evidently in denial about what was going on around it. Seeing that, Forstmann pushed Paulson in late 1990 to name a successor. Paulson reluctantly agreed, but then took months to do so.

Among Paulson, Forstmann, and Little, it was like the Keystone cops hiring a new chief at Gulfstream. The elderly Paulson suggested three people, none of whom passed muster at Forstmann Little. So Teddy's firm hired an executive-search consultant, which found three candidates whom no one liked. Out of desperation, they finally chose one of the three and offered him the job. But the candidate had seen enough and declined. Finally, eight months into the search for a younger manager, in May 1991, the search firm put forward a candidate whom everyone accepted: William C. Lowe, aged fifty, a marketing pro from IBM and Xerox. Lowe was named president with the understanding that he soon would replace Paulson as CEO. "He said all the right things and he really seemed to want the job," Forstmann said. "I think we all said, 'Well, thank God.'" But Lowe was not the answer.

Looking back, Forstmann can hardly believe he hired Lowe. "We were absolutely desperate," Forstmann said. "Despite everything I was doing on other fronts, I knew that the Gulfstream situation was not correct and that we needed professionals in there to run the company. I didn't know a fraction of what I knew a year later. But I knew that things were not right. But Lowe was not the right guy to run Gulfstream. He tried to spend his way to success, which you can sometimes do at big companies—not here. At the end of Lowe's tenure, we were selling fewer planes and had increased costs by $40 million a year. That's a recipe for disaster. Paulson was calling me and saying, 'Do you see what that stupid sonofabitch is doing?'"

Paulson wanted Lowe out almost as soon as he started. But Forstmann, also disillusioned by Paulson's performance, told the CEO to be patient. "Allen, you've got to give him his rope, give him a chance," Forstmann told Paulson. After all, it was Paulson who had told Forstmann that he could sell more jets than they had sold under Chrysler's wing. Wrong. And when Forstmann specifically asked Paulson about the competition—before he bought Gulfstream— Paulson told them there was none. Wrong again. "In a nutshell, we bought a company with a great product and management that were really nice people but quite old, and the world had changed underneath them. I must say, Allen, sorry that you didn't know that. You really didn't. You were oblivious to the competition, which had arrived. The name was Challenger."

Ultimately, Lowe won the power struggle. Both he and Forstmann were against developing a supersonic business jet, which was Paulson's pet project. And after investors balked at a planned $100 million stock offering of Gulfstream early in 1992, an embarrassed Paulson stepped back from active management. The canceled IPO was a huge setback and pointed up the deep troubles at Gulfstream, which posted a net loss of $49.7 million in 1991 and was on its way to another loss of $49.6 million in 1992. In retrospect, though, Forstmann calls it a blessing. The projections and statements in the IPO offering materials turned out to be far too rosy and could have been deemed grossly misleading. "It could easily have turned into a legal liability if those shares had been sold," Forstmann said. "Certainly there would have been moral culpability, at least the way I run my life." In the fall of 1992, Forstmann bought Paulson's stake in Gulfstream for $50 million, and the aerospace entrepreneur stepped down, though he remained on the board.

Now firmly under Lowe, Gulfstream laid plans for a new long-distance jet, one that would fly hundreds of miles farther than the G IV without refueling and ultimately prove to be the company's salvation. Bombardier was also considering an ultra-long-distance business jet. With one eye on Bombardier, in September 1992 Forstmann and Lowe decided that they could not risk being second in the market with such a product and committed to the G V, a sleek new corporate jet that would cost $35 million fully loaded (up from $26.5 million for the G IV) and fly 6,500 miles (up from about 4,000 for the G IV). With that commitment went any hope of reviving the IPO plans for years. The G V would take hundreds of millions of dollars and at least four years to develop. But by committing to it a year ahead of Bombardier, Forstmann got a critical leg up.

With a new longer-term strategy, he injected $250 million from his subordinated debt fund to replace some bank debt and buy out Paulson. Meanwhile, Lowe was on a spending spree, partly to start work on the G V but also to market the G IV, which was the company's current hot product and a cash cow. At this time, the G V was seen as crucial to the company's long-term dominance, but fiscal restraint was called for to survive in the near term. Forstmann knew it, yet as costs soared he looked the other way, assured by Lowe that the company was enjoying a banner year. At a board meeting in early December 1992, Lowe told the board he was on track to sell twenty-eight and maybe thirty G IVs by the year's end—not the thirty-five or forty that Paulson had spoken of before Forstmann entered the deal, but a number high enough in that tough economy to bring smiles to the directors' faces. But just three weeks later, at the year's end, the final tally was only twenty-six. Forstmann was incensed that his CEO could miss the mark he had set a few days earlier. The shortfall represented up to $100 million in lost revenue, enough to ruin the year. "At that point I knew we were in the soup," Forstmann said. "He gave us this news at a board meeting, and I remember the look on George Shultz's [Shultz, a director was the former secretary of state.] We knew we were in trouble with this guy. He had the slick Morgan Stanleyish presentation, but the job wasn't getting done."

Forstmann had overlooked many things while he assumed that business was turning up—not the least of which was that one of Lowe's financial executives had fallen into personal financial distress, which does little to build confidence. And at one point, Lowe commissioned his consultant wife to do a study for Gulfstream. "It wasn't a lot of money; it was the idea that was so grotesque," Forstmann said of that cozy arrangement. In this case, Forstmann's style hurt him. A delegator who inherently trusts the executives around him and a person who doesn't mind losses and initially paying too much if the business is sound, he stayed with Lowe too long.

Early in 1993, though, Forstmann had seen enough and hired the well-known New York headhunter Gerry Roche, chairman of Heidrick & Struggles, to find a replacement for Lowe, and fast. Roche delivered Fred A. Breidenbach, a career executive at General Electric. It wasn't easy getting Breidenbach to sign up. Fortunately for Forstmann, though, even a veteran who was schooled in GE's vaunted management ways was unable to spot the severity of Gulfstream's problems at a glance. So in April 1993, Breidenbach became president and chief operating officer of Gulfstream. Within days, he began to regret it. Upon initial inspection he found that the company was in danger of running out of cash just a few months down the road and that its weak financial position put it dangerously close to violating covenants on $400 million of bank debt. If the banks chose to foreclose, Forstmann's equity and debt investors would suffer horrible losses in the eventual liquidation of the company at fire-sale prices.

At this point, Forstmann knew it was time to get involved personally. Brian Little wouldn't officially leave the partnership for several more months—in the fall of 1993—but by that summer, Forstmann was the partner in charge of Gulfstream. He moved quickly, giving Breidenbach the authority to hire another GE executive, Chris A. Davis, as chief financial officer and sent a Forstmann Little partner, Sandra Horbach, to Savannah to go through Gulfstream's books line by line. What Horbach found appalled Forstmann. The company was operating essentially without a budget. If people wanted to spend more than was budgeted, they'd simply spend it and change the sales forecast to justify the expense. That's not how Lowe saw it. In a 1997 interview with *Business Week,* he said, "The company was just not funded properly, given the fact that we had decided to build a new airplane."

Nevertheless, the summer of 1993 was a busy one. Finally, Forstmann had the management he needed to start reducing costs. The banks granted covenant waivers to give the company time to shape up. The new team reduced head count by 750 employees and won price concessions from major suppliers. The team quickly managed to cut costs by $50 million a year, or 13 percent. But the company still wasn't selling enough jets to turn profitable. Including a $200 million restructuring charge, Gulfstream would lose a total of $275 million in 1993. By November that year, Forstmann, fed up, officially ousted Lowe and named himself chairman and de facto CEO of Gulfstream. He would have taken the CEO title outright except that he believed that the CEO should live near the headquarters in Savannah. It was then, November 1993, that Forstmann fully confronted the mess before him for the first time.

"GET OUT OF THIS MESS, WILL YOU?"

Forstmann briefly thought about selling. Bankers told him he might get $200 million or perhaps $300 million for the company, which would leave him with a $600 million loss on the deal. Allen Paulson, still convinced that he could sell thirty-five jets a year and cut costs, resurfaced, saying he'd be a buyer. "I said, I've got two words for you, Allen, and the first one begins with F." Then Forstmann reflected on the pain of taking that $600 million loss. "I became convinced that it would be the end of Forstmann Little," he said. "And I thought that would be the most unfair, ridiculous result. If it wasn't the end of this place, it certainly would be a terrible blot on my reputation. And, you know, I'm the guy who went around saying that if you're careful about these deals, they should all work, and I meant it. And it was just wrong for the employees; they were all going to lose their jobs. I used to carry on about junk bonds and how they made people lose their jobs. Now here we were about to get the same result without using junk bonds."

After Forstmann had looked deep into his soul, he went back to Sandra Horbach, who had pored over every line in Gulfstream's corporate books that summer. "If we didn't already own this company, would we buy it?" he asked her. "We most definitely would," she said after some reflection. "This thing is fixable." That's all Teddy needed to hear. He wasn't about to let his firm sink, his philosophy die, his employees suffer—not if the thing was fixable. He rolled up his sleeves and vowed to restore Gulfstream to its former glory.

To say that Forstmann's friends, advisers, and investors were incredulous is a bit like calling the *Titanic* a raft. "You're going to do this with your net worth and your reputation?" his longtime lawyer and friend Steve Fraidin asked. "Over my dead body, you will. I won't let you."

"Steve, don't talk to me like that," Forstmann responded. "I'm doing it."

Later, Forstmann went to have lunch with one of his biggest investors, a person with whom he's a had a long relationship of mutual respect, Dale Frey at GE. "Teddy, I'm glad you came up to see me," Frey started. "I wanted to talk to you about this goddamn Gulfstream. Get out of this mess, will you? Just get out."

"But Dale, I'll take a $600 million hit," Forstmann protested.

"Fine," was the GE executive's response. "How much money have you made for us over the years? I don't want you screwing around with this loser. Go out and find the next deal."

After lunch, on the way out the door, Frey revisited the subject. "So, we're going to dump this thing, right?"

Silence.

"You're not going to dump this thing are you, Teddy?"

"No, I'm not. I'm going to run it myself."

"I give you hundreds of millions of dollars, and that's exactly what I told you not to do, isn't it?"

"I know, Dale," Forstmann returned. "I know. But I have to do it."

"Well," the GE executive said in a resigned tone of voice. "I guess that's why we give you money in the first place. Get out of here and get to it."

Not all his investors were so gracious or forgiving. A small group—four in all—of Forstmann's faithful twenty-five or so big investors banded together to lobby Forstmann quietly to dump Gulfstream. He calls them "the cabal." The group let Forstmann know that it felt he had lost the touch. By then, Pullman and Lear Siegler were proved losers, and so, apparently, was Gulfstream. The cabal was convinced that Teddy, hugely successful and rich and with so many outside interests, simply wanted to hang on to Gulfstream as a status symbol, that he was not up to running it.

But Forstmann was ready for them. For one thing, he had made them and their predecessors and bosses millions over the previous fifteen years; for another, he didn't really need their permission anyway. When you give Ted Forstmann money to invest, he gets full discretion on how to invest it. "I don't have to report to you, or talk to you, or have meetings with you," he told the cabal. "No, I do not want an advisory counsel. If you knew what I know, you'd be doing what I do. And so I don't want your advice. I don't need it. I don't want it."

Those remarks didn't sit well with a bunch of stuffy Wall Street money men. But they had no choice in the matter. Forstmann was intent on running Gulfstream and rewriting a history that had gone ugly on his watch.

A UNIQUELY POWERFUL SALES FORCE

With Breidenbach on the operations side, Forstmann had already cut costs by $50 million a year. The next step was to convert $469 million of subordinated debt to preferred stock. Doing so cut the annual interest expense by $38 million and was the chief sticking point with investors in the Forstmann Little debt fund, who wanted to own bonds, not preferred stock. But saving nearly $90 million a year is what gave Forstmann the operating room he needed to keep the banks off his back and start developing the G V, which by now was considered the company's only hope. Orders for the G IV weren't coming in fast enough and, in fact, Gulfstream had seven of the jets sitting unspoken for at the Savannah assembly plant. No buyers in sight.

Forstmann overhauled the sales operation, hiring William Boisture from British Aerospace Corp. The sales strategy quickly changed. No longer would Gulfstream pitch its jets to corporate pilots, figuring they would be the best salesmen inside the companies to convince the executives that the Gulfstream was the jet for them. From now on, they would go straight to the CEOs. Of course, no mere salesman can reach captains of industry. That's why the pilots previously had been the focal point. Forstmann wrestled with this issue and eventually landed on what my have been his most brilliant idea in the Gulfstream turnaround. He reassembled the board of directors and put together a special advisory panel, coming up with a virtual Who's Who of industry, government, and Hollywood. Everyone, including Forstmann, had easy access to many of the three hundred to five hundred likely buyers of the G IV, which later proved still to have some life in it, and the new G V. They would become Gulfstream's sales force. The board included Shultz, the former secretary of state; Colin Powell, the former general and chairman of the Joint Chiefs of Staff; Drew Lewis, former secretary of transportation; Michael Ovitz, the Hollywood mogul and onetime Disney executive; and Charlotte Beers, the dynamic chairperson of the ad company Ogilvy and Mather Worldwide.

Did they enjoy being salespeople? Of course, they were much more than that, and it's not as though they made a lot of specific calls and visits to present their pitches to high-powered CEOs. The pitches were more casual, at dinner parties, charitable events, and the like. But, yes. They signed on willingly. Some of them—those in private industry— had invested with Forstmann over the years and felt indebted to him. Others enjoyed the prestige of being associated with Gulfstream, the premier corporate jet. And there were stock options. As the business turned around and the stock rose, these directors made millions of dollars. One particularly effective pitch came from Robert S. Strauss, former ambassador to Russia. In 1994, he phoned Walter Mondale, then ambassador to Japan, and the pitch helped Gulfstream win a lucrative contract for five G IVs with the Japanese air force.

Forstmann shook up Gulfstream's advertising, taking a lead role in writing the slogans and even some copy lines, giving it a more in-your-face tone. He offered rebates to anyone who would cancel an order for Bombardier's Global Express, his main competitor. By the end of 1994, after just one year with his sleeves rolled up, Forstmann had Gulfstream back on track. The company bounced back from three consecutive years of losses to post a $24 million profit. And with a rebounding economy and soaring stock market to help, orders for both the G IV and the G V were on the upswing. Continuing that momentum, in 1995 Forstmann hired Bombardier's master jet salesman, and a top executive, Bryan T. Moss, who became vice chairman of Gulfstream. The firm delivered 26 jets in 1995 and had a net income of $29 million, 27 jets in 1996 and had net income of $47 million, and 51 jets in 1997 and had a net income of $243 million, and it was on track to deliver 61 jets and post even higher earnings in 1998. By the end of 1998, Gulfstream had 135 jets on back order representing more than $4.3 billion in value, and couldn't make them fast enough.

Forstmann's crowning achievement at Gulfstream came with the company's 1996 IPO, the largest that year. He sold 43 million shares at $24 each, a deal that locked in solid returns for his investors and still staked them to a big chunk of the company. To turn Gulfstream around, not only Forstmann had taken the risk of investing millions in the G V to give the company a long-term future, he became part adman, part salesman, part executive, and part cheerleader. Under his watch, Gulfstream for the first time developed an active market in used jets, manufactured and sold not just its newest model but the slightly cheaper previous model as well, initiated a time-share program for smaller companies that wanted access to corporate jets, dramatically lowered the production time from sixty-seven to thirty days, and increased from 70 percent to 95 percent the share of jets that it sold fully loaded, compared with "green," a state in which the jets are packed off to others for the high-margin job of furnishing the cabins.

By the end of 1998, Forstmann was spending far less of his own time at Gulfstream—maybe 25 percent in all. He was weighing the sale of more shares to the public. And why not? The stock was sailing along in the $50s, more than double the IPO price and the ultimate evidence of a job well done. Forstmann is, after all, a deal maker. But he takes enormous satisfaction in Gulfstream's results and was in no hurry to exit completely. He has been a lifetime bachelor, and this deal was his baby. It was the one in which he proved everyone wrong and, at the same time, earned his place in Wall Street history.

This unusual odyssey produced no real losers, not in the financial sense, except perhaps the cabal of dissenting institutional investors whose lack of faith proved embarrassing. But even the cabal rode Forstmann's turnaround to gains because they were locked into the deal. Bombardier was a loser. Losing its savvy executive, Bryan Moss, was a blow. But in a more shattering turn, Bombardier and Dassault might today be the dominant corporate jet builders had Forstmann not stepped up and rebuilt Gulfstream out of gritty determination.

Forstmann and his investors, of course, were the big winners, along with all the employees of Gulfstream. But so, too, was the LBO industry, which at the time needed to be seen as something more than a group of rich Wall Streeters taking anything they could grab. Forstmann proved that the best money men are capable of more than plundering and pillaging. They can work hard and save a company that might otherwise go bust.

Here is a brief question-and-answer session with Teddy Forstmann, the man who rolled up his sleeves and turned a disaster into something special:

Question: *What do you think sets you apart from other deal makers?*

Answer: Let's put it this way. They're interested in doing transactions for fees. I'm not interested in transactions; I'm interested in creating value, and the transaction is just a piece of it. For most deal makers, the transaction is actually the end of the deal. For me, it's just the beginning. Every time we do a deal, I have another chance to make an ass of myself.

Question: *You've mentioned that Pullman Companies was your worst deal ever, and one of only two losers. What did you do wrong there?*

Answer: I violated my principles by buying it. I bought it because it was cheap. We sat around and said, "Well, we can sell off this and we can sell off that." There was a very definite rationale. But in hindsight and being real honest, they didn't have a core business that I really wanted to own. No dominant business that we could build. That's an inviolable principle of mine, and I violated it. It was cheap, six times the cash flow. But when the economy turned down and the junk-bond boys couldn't buy any of the stuff we wanted to sell, it just didn't work.

Question: *How did you get into this business?*

Answer: It was simple, really. The macroeconomic environment of the 1970s meant that you could borrow money. There was an arbitrage—and I guarantee there are very few out there who'll understand what I'm talking about. There were deal makers. But the environment was such that there was an arbitrage between what you borrowed money at and what you had to pay it back at because interest rates were lower than the inflation rate. So you could borrow money and pay it back in cigar wrappers. Finding a predictable cash flow was the thing, and I was right time after time. I just couldn't pass it up.

Question: *What would you say is the most imaginative aspect of what you do? The thing that really puts your stamp on a deal?*

Answer: After four years of doing LBOs in a conventional way, I grew to understand that the most important component of the capital structure was the subordinated debt. There's always equity around to try to make five or ten times your money, and there are always banks, the senior lenders. But this middle tier was tough. I think Mike Milken recognized the same thing. He just went about it in a different way. Before junk bonds, you had to go to insurance companies to get subordinated debt. Well, I said, I'm going to get my own because I don't want to go to insurance companies and I don't want to use junk bonds. Since 1982, we've had our own debt fund, as well as an equity fund.

Question: *Why would anyone invest in your subordinated debt yielding single digits when junk bonds serving the same purpose were yielding double digits?*

Answer: Junk bonds were high-yield but often no-return. You got yield and paper and promises and bullshit. High yield is wonderful as it takes the company down the drain into bankruptcy. Ours were low-yield but high-return. The debt fund compounded over sixteen years has returned 20 percent a year. That's high yield as it should be properly understood.

Question: *Why do you regard Gulfstream as your best deal?*

Answer: Do you have children? You say you love them all, but don't you have a special feeling for the one who struggles more than the others, especially when that kid is now playing quarterback for Notre Dame? That's Gulfstream.

Question: *What have you learned about deal making over the years?*

Answer: I've got to tell you, having done this twenty-three times, you never know everything. It's absolutely impossible. You never ever know everything going in. You've got to know the big things and the directional things, and you rarely get pleasant surprises. It's just part of doing deals. The one thing I do not know is that I'll ever do another deal because if I don't find what I want, I'm not going to do it.

Question: *How did Gulfstream change you?*

Answer: Not at all. I mean I learned some things—the rhythms of running a company are different from running my firm. And there are all those personnel issues, which I hate. They never end.

Question: *Teddy, you're an LBO guy, yet you've been running Gulfstream for five years. Isn't it time to get out and move on? Is there some part of you that doesn't want to let go?*

Answer: Sure. But it's not a part of me that's big enough to keep me from doing the right thing. There is definitely a part of me that is attached to Gulfstream. We just got the Collier award. It's the most prestigious thing you could possibly get—for technological excellence on the G V. The so-called competition says that we have no technology. Well, this award—the first winner was Orville Wright; others were Chuck Yeager and John Glenn—for a guy who didn't know anything about running a company, that's pretty neat stuff. And I'm telling you that at one point we didn't have the money to pay the bank interest.

Question: *When did you recognize that you were good at LBOs?*

Answer: I should tell you that I'm a guy whose parents didn't exactly build him up when he was a kid and inspire confidence. And so, the answer is going to seem strange. But I would say I knew in my heart that I was good at this about three or four months ago [late winter 1998] when Gulfstream's stock started going up.

Question: *Could anyone else have turned Gulfstream around?*

Answer: No. I don't think so. Boy, that's going to look bad in print. But I really don't think so. Could anyone else have turned IBM around like Lou Gerstner? Probably not. There are certain horses that do well on certain tracks. This track really fits this horse.

chapter eight

Joe Rice

LBOs with a Twist

DESPITE MANY SIMILARITIES IN THEIR BACKGROUNDS, Joe Rice could not be more different from Ted Forstmann. Both men grew up fairly well off in the northern suburbs of New York City, where a career in finance—on Wall Street, if you're good enough—is presented early and often to youngsters as the ticket to great riches. Both are lawyers turned investors. Both spotted the profits inherent in leveraged buyouts, or LBOs, well ahead of the pack. And while Forstmann takes great pride in creating long-term value, Rice emphasizes long-term values. For Rice the buyout process is not simply about earning extraordinary returns. It's also a romantic quest that permits him to back entrepreneurs with dreams. He bristles noticeably when lumped in with Wall Street's multitude of run-of-the-mill deal makers, a class that includes those who want nothing more than a transaction fee, a quick dress-up or bust-up of a company, and a fast sale for immediate gain. In a 1991 interview with Alison Leigh Cowan of the *New York Times,* Rice drew the line in concise terms: "Simon wouldn't know a buyout if it came along and bit him," he said of William E. Simon, the former treasury secretary whose 1982 buyout of Gibson Greetings was a huge financial success and put Simon's Wesray Capital on the LBO map. Another noted LBO firm, one formed that year, was Jack Nash and Leon Levy's Odyssey Partners, which earned only slightly more respect from Rice. "Odyssey is not in the buyout business," Rice told the *Times.* "The people who are in the buyout business are KKR, Forstmann Little, and us—then you start to run out of names."

Indeed, Rice had identified the Big Three of LBOs. But even in that rarefied class, there are distinct differences. KKR, as I've noted, is the 800-pound gorilla, fighting for every LBO of size. The firm's philosophy is to do more deals, gain a bigger share of the market, and brand itself as the preeminent name in buyouts. It has succeeded nicely, even though its overall returns are thought to be lower than the returns generated by Forstmann's and Rice's firms, where they do only one or two deals a year. Forstmann shuns junk bonds; KKR does not, and neither does Rice (even though his partners haven't always been enamored). Rice personally shuns the spotlight, preferring to share credit with his partners; Forstmann does not, and neither does Henry Kravis.

There is a defining story about Joe Rice, one that even he doesn't know if it's true—but one certainly rooted in fact. It has to do with IBM's decision to sell its huge office-products division to Rice's firm without so much as talking to any other potential buyers. The year was 1990, and the economy and the junk-bond market were falling on rough times. KKR had just completed its buyout of RJR Nabisco, the deal that set the standard for the size of deals and spawned the best-selling *Barbarians,* a book that detailed the chaotic two-month bidding process for the company. The bidding started at $75 a share and ended up at $109. Virtually every major brokerage, law, and public relations (R) firm on Wall Street lusted for a piece of the deal and the more than $200 million in fees it would generate. As the story goes, John F. Akers, the IBM chief who was weighing his options as he considered how to spin off his office-products division—and other divisions down the road—turned to *Barbarians* for a glimpse of the people and firms he might end up dealing with. It was a vastly different world that he saw. After reading the book, he dropped it on the desk of one of the IBM point men for the coming spin-off and instructed him to read it, too. The IBM executive asked why. "Because I won't work with anyone in that book," Akers sternly instructed.

To understand why, you'd need a lesson in IBM's culture and then you'd have to read the book. IBM was a prim and proper, conservative, thorough, and highly revered corporate icon. The 1980s were not exactly the deal community's finest hour. It was a period, and RJR was a deal that defined the period, when Wall Street had almost totally lost touch with the concept of building relationships and putting the client first. It was a mega-greedfest, in which everyone was a gunslinger. All parties were looking out for number one. Period. Akers, who had just arrived at the momentous decision to begin restructuring IBM through a series of spin-offs (for which he would need the gamut of investment bankers, LBO firms, lawyers, and PR people), must have been distraught, indeed, and he leafed through the book taking note of the financial wild west that he was about to enter.

As it happens, the boutique LBO firm Clayton & Dubilier, the firm that Joe Rice helped found and that would add his name to the letterhead in 1992, was not mentioned in the book. Chasing high-profile deals, bidding as part of a frenzy, proceeding without the full faith and confidence of management and the board—those things are not in sync with Clayton, Dubilier & Rice's culture. Rice and his partners had no interest in RJR Nabisco. They weren't involved. But both KKR, which won the bid, and Forstmann, Little, which sought to preempt the bid by convincing RJR Nabisco of the special merits of its debt fund, were in it neck-deep. So among the Big Three, that left just Rice's firm as an option for Akers. The story may be exaggerated. Rice can't recall when or where he first heard it. But he's dead sure that his firm's reputation for integrity, always working in partnership with the selling company, and looking to build long-term value without draconian cost cuts and layoffs—anathema on Wall Street at the time—is what led Akers to his door and landed him his greatest deal.

NO PUBLICITY, PLEASE

In his career, Rice has bought and sold more than forty companies—the last twenty-nine of them with Clayton Dubilier & Rice, the firm he founded along with Martin Dubilier and Eugene Clayton in 1978. Those twenty-nine deals had total equity investments of $2.5 billion, which after fees has returned $3.8 billion, to its investors, in eighteen fully realized transactions, a gross average annual gain of 45 percent. In percentage terms, the firm's best deal was the 1984 buyout of Arnold Foods, a company sold a couple of years later and a deal that generated a compound return to equity investors of 237 percent. CD&R has had only one clunker: medical supplies company Kendall International, which developed problems and then took four years to fix and unload. Among the firm's many winners were Stanley Interiors Co. and Kux Manufacturing Co. in 1978–79; in the 1980s, WGM Safety Corp., Harris Graphics Corp. (the first LBO that ever used junk bonds sold by Drexel Burnham Lambert), Nevamar Corp., Pilliod Cabinet Co., Uniroyal, O. M. Scott & Sons Co., and Uniroyal Goodrich Tire Co.; and in the 1990s, Van Kampen Merritt Co., Remington Arms Co., Allison Engine Co., Wesco Distribution, American Capital Management & Research, Kraft Foodservice, North American Van Lines, and Kinko's.

The best, though, was the IBM spin-off, which CD&R named Lexmark International. It wasn't so much a spin-off as a carve-out. Lexmark was the part of IBM that made and sold typewriters; computer keyboards and printers; and accessories like typewriter ribbons, correction tape, and ink cartridges. It was a tremendously complicated deal, and that's one of the reasons it stands out in Rice's mind. As Forstmann believes that no one else could have turned around Gulfstream, Rice believes that no other firm could have successfully carved out and nurtured Lexmark. In those days, IBM was highly centralized. Office products was a concept, not a functioning unit with stand-alone balance sheet and management. It was a product line that borrowed sales, marketing, and administrative support from the same staff that was lording over mainframes and personal computers. Rice's firm had to carve out all the critical components of a business from within IBM's ranks and resources—and the territorial managers and lawyers at IBM had to sign off on it all. In the end, Lexmark and IBM required some seventy detailed contractual agreements, each one exhaustively negotiated.

Rice is also proud of the fact that IBM chose CD&R to do the deal. He considered it a ringing endorsement of the style and culture and values, that he wanted to promote. This was no ordinary deal for IBM. The company, reeling from the trend in business toward networked PCs and away from Big Blue's powerful mainframes, was just beginning a massive restructuring in which it would cut its workforce by more than 100,000. The spin-off of its office-products division was to be the first of a dozen or so planned divestitures. So, like a communist nation converting to capitalism and selling its state-owned businesses to the public, it had much at stake with the first sale. That sale had to go well. Otherwise no one could be counted on to buy its divested divisions in the future, and all its plans would need to be revamped.

Furthermore, the LBO business was in disrepute, and like Forstmann, Rice felt unfairly grouped with the quick-buck, pillage-and-plunder crowd. This deal with mighty IBM would show the world that he was different. "Drexel Burnham Lambert had come under scrutiny," Rice said. "There was a congressional investigation of buyouts. Everyone in Washington was questioning them. This deal was a watershed event in the sense that here was a premier company in the United States that was using the buyout as a part of its new corporate strategy. We all felt that this particular transaction legitimized the whole process in a way that it had not been legitimized previously."

And, of course, the deal was a resounding financial success. Rice's firm paid $1.6 billion for Lexmark in March 1991. The deal included $205 million of equity from his investors; another $185 million of equity from pension-fund managers at General Motors, AT&T, and others; about $85 million of preferred stock; another $150 million in junk bonds; and the bulk—roughly $1 billion—in bank loans. After just one year on its own, Lexmark was ahead of schedule paying off the bank debt, which by the end of 1996 had all but disappeared. In a series of stock offerings starting with Lexmark's IPO on November 15, 1995, and ending with a stock sale in March 1998, CD&R sold its entire stake in the company for $877 million. That sale produced a gain of $672 million, of which CD&R took its usual 20 percent cut. Rice's share of that cut came to about $17 million, bringing his estimated net worth to between $40 million and $60 million.

Yet the deal was more about reputation and execution than about money. To appreciate that fact, you probably have to spend some time with Rice, an impeccably groomed, reserved, patient man with thin gray hair, known for his colorful shirts and ties and ubiquitous suspenders. Rice is a spokesman for the buyout industry. He's testified before Congress on LBOs and defended them publicly in televised debates and at industry conferences. I have had a casual acquaintance with Rice since my early days on Wall Street. He's a willing interviewee on the subject of buyouts, and I spoke with him by phone a handful of times in the late 1980s when his industry was so much in the news. For this book, I met Rice at his nine-room brownstone on East Sixty-third Street in Manhattan. He has four fabulously decorated floors, including a large drawing room with French doors leading to a small, ground-level garden terrace—a peaceful setup not often found in the heart of New York City.

It was March 1998, and Rice had just completed the sale of the last of the Lexmark stock. We sat across a small table, with the sun streaming in from the terrace. As ever, Rice was buttoned down, patient, and eager to explain the LBO world. When my tape-recorder batteries went dead, he graciously paused and then went off to the kitchen to find some new ones. Rice is probably the least well-known deal maker in this book, but that is by design. He's one of the architects of the LBO industry and because of his success could easily command more attention. But, as he said, "Around here, you keep your head down and keep plugging away. If you go out and seek the limelight, chances are something bad will happen. Henry [Kravis] has gotten publicity I would just never want."

EARLY LINKS TO KKR

Joseph Lee Rice III was born in Brooklyn, New York, on February 24, 1932. He is the eldest of three siblings and so much older than the others that he essentially was brought up as an only child. His brother, who is ten years younger, is in a computer-related business in Colorado. His sister, whom he remains close to, is twelve years younger and is a teacher in Scarsdale, New York. The Rice family moved from Brooklyn to the tony Westchester County suburb of Scarsdale when Joe was an infant and later to the more laid-back, rural outpost of Katonah some twenty miles farther north in Westchester County. His father, Joseph L. Rice Jr., was a successful businessman who cut his teeth in the electric utility trade and became chairman and CEO of Allegheny Power Co.

Young Rice was a sports fanatic. He played football and basketball and competed in track at Katonah and, later, Trinity Pawling high schools. He studied political science at Williams College in Massachusetts and was captain of the cross-country track team. He graduated with honors in 1954, then joined the U.S. Marines for a three-year stint. In the Marines, Rice was a lieutenant who commanded a rifle platoon and trained officer candidates. He then enrolled in Harvard Law School and graduated in 1960. His first job was as a lawyer for the general practice group at Sullivan & Cromwell, where he worked until 1966. While at Sullivan & Cromwell, though, Rice was exposed to the fledgling buyout world, when LBOs were small and infrequent and known as "bootstrap" deals. In 1965, Rice was tapped to represent Laird, a small brokerage firm, that had been building a bootstrap business. Rice was so captivated by the process that he asked the firm to hire him full time. He recalls one deal in particular. Laird paid $3 million for Ben Pearson Co., an archery-equipment company in Pine Bluff, Arkansas. It had $20 million in annual sales and was run by ex-McKinsey consultants Merle Bunta and Steve Hinchilfte. "They set up two young managers as entrepreneurs," Rice recalled. "It was just so creative." Ben Pearson grew into a major leisure-time corporation.

After learning the deal business at Laird, Rice moved in 1968 to the investment banking side of the retail brokerage McDonnell & Co., which ran afoul of securities rules a year later, and then left to found Gibbons, Green & Rice, a boutique investment firm that would specialize in private equity investments. In the early 1970s, his eventual partners, Gene Clayton and Martin "Dubie" Dubilier, were building their own practice as turnaround consultants. Dubie, a former ITT executive who got a patent at age twelve for inventing rustproof tracks for toy rail-roads, was a master operator who had helped save one of Jerome Kohlberg's early buyouts, Sterndent Corp. That was while Kohlberg was cohead of corporate finance at Bear Stearns—not yet hooked up with Henry Kravis and George Roberts. After KKR was formed in 1976, Dubie and Clayton were often called upon to help KKR evaluate deals. But they quickly decided that they wanted to be principals. That was where the real opportunities lie. The two sought a partner with expertise in finance to complement their operating prowess. That person was Joe Rice, and the three, along with operating executive Bill Welch, formed what is now Clayton, Dubilier & Rice in 1978.

Clayton retired in 1985, and Dubilier died in 1991. Rice has ele-vated senior partners to replace them, but the firm's philosophy of matching operating skills with financial know-how has never changed. Among CD&R's twenty professionals today about half have extensive experience running industrial companies: B. Charles Ames, formerly CEO of Reliance Electric; Leon J. Hendrix, formerly chief operating officer at Reliance; Chuck Piper, formerly CEO of GE Lighting Europe; Jim Rodgers, formerly senior vice president and member of the execu-tive council at GE; and Ned Lautenbach, formerly group executive of worldwide sales and service at IBM.

FIVE STEPS TO SUCCESS

By 1989, when IBM began to shop secretly for a buyer for what would become Lexmark, CD&R had established a solid reputation and was on every investment banker's list of potential buyers for just about any com-pany or division in the United States. CD&R is mainly interested in deals under $3 billion, reasoning that the 30 percent to 50 percent annualized gains it shoots for come more easily on smaller investments. In the heavy-deal days of the late 1980s, Rice received three hundred to four hundred "books" a year—a book being the financial information on companies looking for buyers. Perusing the paperwork, Rice usually whittled the list down to twenty-four or so, and would then send representatives—one finance expert and one operations expert—to visit the managers of each of those companies or divisions. Two such visits a month yielded the two or three deals a year in which Rice would participate. Selectivity has long been Rice's calling card, allowing him to handpick deals that are just right for his firm and capture the most out of each deal.

When Rice's team arrives on site, it takes about a day to look over the company, focusing mainly on the quality and commitment of top managers. Rice's priority is to assess the managers' ideas for improving the business, their appetite for cutting costs, and their willingness to work hard alongside CD&R's partners. Once the management has passed those tests, Rice looks at the business itself. CD&R has three basic criteria for cutting a deal: The business must be large enough to compete without cost disadvantages, it must have good long-term prospects, and the price must be in line with proved historical earnings power and likely future growth.

On this last point—the price issue—Rice has a notably different philosophy from Teddy Forstmann. He hates to overpay. But Rice readily agrees with Forstmann that paying a bit too much for a good company is better than buying a bad company dirt cheap. He's even illustrated his willingness to pay big premiums on occasion. In 1986, CD&R paid $200 million for the venerable O. M. Scott, the lawn-and-garden products concern founded in 1868 and then a unit of ITT Corp. The price was an unusually high multiple of ten times cash flow. At first, Rice balked. But the CD&R partners with hands-on management experience—a distinguishing characteristic among LBO firms—convinced Rice and the numbers crunchers that the deal was a good one even at that high multiple. They were sure that a few operational changes would cut costs and build the business, quickly dropping the multiple to just five or six times cash flow. So convinced, Rice paid the premium. When the company was in 1993, CD&R's equity investors had realized an average annual return of 46 percent.

Rice has a five-point plan for getting results. And the points go a long ways toward explaining why IBM, when it got serious about divesting office products, went first and only to Rice in April 1990. These are his basic tenets of investing:

- Build for the long term. Sacrifice short-term results if additional investment is likely to produce better long-term gains. Crucial to any successful deal, Rice says, is building the newly acquired company through better technology, product development, research, and marketing.

- Transform managers into owners. Rice insists that the managers take meaningful equity stakes in the companies his firm buys. Ownership turns them into cost-conscious, fast-acting entrepreneurs with a strong sense of accountability and a nose for only prudent risk taking.

- Do only friendly deals. No hostile takeovers for Rice. He wants not only division managers on his side but the parent company's managers as well. In his view, no deal is successful unless the seller and the buyer benefit.

- Be flexible on the financial structure. Rice is willing to defer to the seller. Parent companies that are divesting divisions usually have special tax, accounting, and personnel issues. Part of doing friendly deals is to keep the parent companies happy, and to do so, Rice offers the sellers a menu of options—from his firm's buying companies outright to partnering with the sellers or entering into long-term supply contracts with the sellers.

- Instill his values. He wants the management at new acquisitions to share his firm's values, which center on hard work, common sense, integrity, and reasonable expectations. Shared values create an environment in which it is easy to communicate, and one with little need for exhaustive checks and balances.

In April 1990, CD&R had fairly demonstrated all these qualities and proved the effectiveness of its philosophy, which was to mix financial expertise with hands-on management know-how. That month, the Lexmark "book," prepared at IBM's request by Lehman Brothers and J. P. Morgan, landed on Rice's desk. No one else got a peek. "In many respects, we were the only independent organization they could turn to," Rice said. "What they could have done was to sell this set of products to a competitor like Hitachi or Panasonic. But they didn't want to do that because it would have opened channels of distribution [the critical, proprietary pipeline to store shelves and direct customers]. Once you let competitors enter the channel of distribution, they start pumping a whole bunch of other products through the channel. You don't want that. So IBM needed someone who could manage the channel the way they wanted it managed and, in addition, build the business. That was us."

"KEY TO THE WHOLE TRANSACTION"

Rice had misgivings. He had never worked with IBM but knew of its highly centralized management structure. In a way, it was the same tightly interwoven structure that had been in place at Marriott Corp. and that presented Stephen Bollenbach with the unusually tough challenge of splitting that company into two. But Marriott was managed that way for a specific reason. It was a family-owned business, and Bill Marriott, who controlled the stock, wanted firm control over every aspect of the company. At IBM, the centralized structure served a curious ancillary purpose apart from anything having to do with Akers's effective running of the company.

The structure was an intentional impediment to long-standing governmental efforts to force IBM to break up. It may be a distant memory today, but in the 1960s and 1970s, IBM was as dominant in computers as Microsoft (which the government is now seeking to dismantle) has been in computer operating systems in the 1990s. It may well be that governmental trustbusters would have succeeded in forcing IBM to break up had the task been simpler—that is, if IBM had clearly defined divisions with separate managements, budgets, balance sheets, and sales forces that could have easily been pulled out.

Ironically, what the government never could get done, the market-place handled with the lightning efficiency of a supercomputer. In the late 1980s, technology shifted from mainframes to PCs. IBM, which was arrogant and slow to respond, began to fall behind the times. That's when Akers, as a matter of survival, decided to start busting up the company on his own. The idea was to cut costs dramatically and refocus and reinvigorate the lumbering giant. It would prove a Herculean task, one that Akers ultimately wasn't up to, though he bought enough time to survive long enough for successors (most notably, Lou Gerstner) to come along and get the job done. Rice knew that peeling the office-products division away from IBM would be a difficult assignment. But complicated, friendly deals were his forte, part of what set him apart and, in fact, the aspect of his reputation that brought Akers to his doorstep. So he and Dubilier and the partners at CD&R studied the Lexmark book carefully.

Martin Dubilier and Don Gogel were the most excited. From an operating standpoint, Lexmark offered all kinds of possibilities. It was primarily in the typewriter business, manufacturing a cash cow known as the IBM Selectric, the Cadillac of electric typewriters found in nearly every office in the world. The obvious challenge was to funnel the cash from that business, which was dying, into development of something with good long-term prospects. In this case, that something would be computer printers, a market IBM's office-products division had already targeted, though its misplaced focus at the time was on low-end dot matrix printers. Dubie wanted to roll up his sleeves and get started with the transition right away.

Rice was more keenly aware of the bookkeeping hassles involved in carving Lexmark out of IBM. But his partners' enthusiasm was catching, and the firm soon began working with IBM to see just how Lexmark might be put together. There was a single starting point: IBM couldn't document it, but it said that the office-products division would have annual pretax profits of $223 million. The challenge, then, was to assign the proper level of manpower; marketing; financial resources; and, most important, contractual relationships to ensure a future revenue stream that would produce such profits. What would it take? No one really knew. That's the job that lay ahead for Rice's firm. In laying out $1.6 billion for Lexmark, he would need to be sure that he got enough infrastructure from IBM to support a business that had no formal track record and no dedicated staff or budget.

As an example of how difficult it would be to break out Lexmark, consider that most of the sales of IBM's printers—the future growth of the company—were part of larger orders for computers and gadgets that Lexmark was not going to make. On its own, Lexmark might well be able to build new clients and prosper over time. That was part of the plan and, indeed, it would enjoy quick success on that front. But at least initially, it would have no sales except those to or through IBM. Extensive agreements would be needed to ensure that IBM did not find another source to fill those printer orders.

Extensive agreements would be needed to ensure other relationships, too, and that's why there were seventy separate contracts between IBM and Lexmark when the deal was finally done. There were supply agreements, in which IBM could not go outside Lexmark for five years to purchase any of the products that Lexmark made—either for internal use or for use as components in products that IBM sold. There were various transition agreements, in which IBM would take on certain administrative tasks until it was clear what level of support Lexmark would need to operate on its own. There was a critical bonus program, in which IBM agreed to pay $23 million in incentives to induce a sales staff to quit Big Blue and join Lexmark. There was an agreement for IBM, in which the pension plan was overfunded, to transfer to Lexmark a proportional share of the overfunding ($65 million). And IBM ended up agreeing to give Lexmark royalty-free licenses on all patents and trademarks needed to run its business. IBM also took the responsibility for $100 million in future medical benefits for Lexmark employees.

Each contract was painstakingly (and occasionally heatedly) negotiated. In one case, Rice recalled asking IBM's lawyers for a "representation"—essentially a guarantee—and the IBM lawyers did not want to give it to him. It concerned certain sales figures, which had never been recorded as distinct line items or fully audited. Nobody could be absolutely certain that the numbers were accurate, and the IBM lawyers were rightly concerned that IBM might be making promises it could not keep. But Rice would not back down. He wanted IBM to take on the risk of accuracy.

"Goddamn it," the lead IBM lawyer finally yelled. "Why do you want this representation? You've seen the books. You know as much as we do."

With one hand on his wallet, Rice shot back: "Because I am going to give you $1.6 billion for this goddamned business, and you ought to stand behind what you've said this business is."

Eventually, Rice got his representation, but not before sweat poured off his brow and he'd strained relations with the point people at IBM—Jim Forese, the man closest to Akers; and Greg Fleming, one of IBM's principal negotiators. As nasty as that scene was, no contract was more bitterly contested than Lexmark's right to keep putting the IBM name on products that it built. The IBM name and, indeed, all Big Blue's intellectual property—its patents and trademarks—were the company's most closely guarded assets. IBM's lawyers, accustomed to protecting those assets at any length for decades, would not easily be persuaded to allow Lexmark the right to slap the IBM logo on things built outside the company. "They viewed themselves as keepers of the Holy Grail," Rice joked. But for Rice, the intellectual property was a potential deal breaker, especially as it related to the Selectric. The typewriter business, being supplanted by word processors, was declining fast but would remain highly profitable for years. "We said you have got to give us this logo," Rice noted. "It was really the key to the whole transaction. We did not want to accelerate the downward slope of the typewriter business and felt the logo was integral to continued success in that business."

From the moment Rice and his team looked at the deal, they had identified a clear strategy for moving foward: run what was left of the typewriter business for cash and reinvest in computer printers for long-term growth. The strategy worked miracles. Today, Lexmark is a thriving printer manufacturer with about 12 percent of the market, up from 5 percent in 1990. Those share gains have come largely at the expense of mighty Hewlett-Packard, long the dominant company in that business and still with some 60 percent of the market. Lexmark might never have gotten off the ground had the downward slope in typewriter sales accelerated unexpectedly in those early years and robbed the company of research and marketing funds.

A SCARE, THEN A DEAL

By early spring 1990, Rice was pretty sure that the deal would get done, mainly because it became clear that Akers would make it happen no matter what. Even though office products was a pimple on the back of his giant computer company, the IBM chief had far more at stake than Rice did. Because this was the first part of a long strategy to restructure the company, Akers took a personal interest and interceded whenever CD&R and the various point men at Big Blue could not reach agreement. "It was clear to everybody that this had to be a cooperative effort," Rice said. "We went at this as a big partnership. I mean, we'd all done enough deals to know what was reasonable and what wasn't. And if people go to the table and say they're going to get a deal done, they can get it done without unduly subjecting themselves to risk. But you have to go at it with that partnership mind-set, and that is where Akers was the key figure. There were innumerable items where we were stonewalled at levels well below him. But he's the one who really wanted this to work. He had to be reasonable, and he was."

That spring, as Rice, Dubilier, and CD&R's other partners, including Don Gogel, who was a lead negotiator for CD&R, considered how to set up Lexmark, they instinctively focused on management. "We decided it would be silly for us to try to bring in someone from outside," Rice said. "The IBM culture is so peculiar that we knew we had to stay inside and pick someone who IBM would feel was right for the job. As it turns out, their first choice for CEO and ours was the same man," a thirty-two-year veteran of IBM named Marvin L. Mann. The second most important slot went to Paul J. Curlander, head of product development and later named president, who ultimately replaced Mann as the CEO. Mann was left to flush out the rest of the top management, and the manner in which he did so demonstrated clearly that he was on board with CD&R's style. Rather than create a deep organizational chart so that he was far removed from important managers who would report to executives several rungs below him, Mann opted for a horizontal approach. Key managers would report directly to him or just a rung or two below him. That approach gave the managers, who were also stockholders, easier access to the boss and empowered them to think for themselves—as entrepreneurs. They were owners now. It was the CD&R way.

With management in place, the key area to address was a sales force. IBM's vast army of salespeople was adept at selling sprawling mainframes and complete computer systems. Somehow, Lexmark would have to find two hundred or so who wanted to sell nothing but typewriters, ribbons, keyboards, printers, and ink cartridges. It was a huge potential stumbling block, one that was presented to the IBM negotiators. They readily agreed that Lexmark could not be considered a company without a dedicated sales staff, and to create one they offered the following incentive: $25,000 to sign up with Lexmark, $25,000 after one year with Lexmark, and another $25,000 one year after that. Money is a wonderful inducement. In short order, Lexmark had its sales team.

By July 1990, the negotiations, though tedious and exhaustive, had gotten far enough along that word leaked and newspapers began reporting that IBM was prepared to spin off its office-products line.

Even though a final agreement was still eight months away, a deal was announced on August 1, 1990, in Lexington, Kentucky, the home of the largest of Lexmark's three factories, which happened to be the city's largest employer, and home to four thousand of its six thousand workers. The other plants were in Boulder, Colorado, and Boigny, France. IBM said it was setting up the division as a stand-alone company and announced that Mann, who formerly had managed the Lexington factory, would be the CEO. The company also announced that it intended to sell Lexmark by the year's end to CD&R for about $2.3 billion. How did it choose the name Lexmark? To the chagrin of its faithful employment base in Lexington, the moniker had nothing to do with their hometown. *Lex* came from the word *lexicon*, which means words, and *mark* described what the company's products do: mark words.

The August 1 announcement between Rice and IBM was by no means binding. It was, in effect, a formal agreement to work out any remaining differences and then close the deal as soon as possible. In October 1990, with a recession just starting and the stock market reaching its lowest point in months, it became clear that four high-speed printers—the 4224, 4234, 3812, and 3816—and the plants where they were made did not fit with the business plan because they were typically paired with large business computers. Lexmark would focus on printers to be used with PCs.

Eliminating these printers from the deal served a useful purpose beyond simply not burdening Lexmark with assets that it couldn't use. It brought the price tag down considerably, to below $2 billion, and alleviated the mounting concern about loading the company with too much debt. The sinking economy was making everyone nervous, not the least J. P. Morgan, which led a group of banks that put up $1 billion for the buyout. Partly because of the weak economy and partly because IBM was looking for unusually conservative financing anyway, it became clear that the common debt-to-equity ratios of 8 or 9 to 1 in the 1980s LBOs would not fly in this deal. The ratio would have to be more like 3 or 4 to 1.

Negotiations bogged down as Rice questioned many of IBM's assumptions about the business, particularly in Europe. Only 50 percent of the sales that IBM said took place were verifiable. "There was no way to audit them because of the way IBM kept its books," Rice said. "So we went back and counted units sold in the United States, then the number of printers sold offshore. We calculated the gross margins on those sales and added them all up. That's a whole bunch of jumps. Lexmark had $1.8 billion in annual sales. So almost $1 billion of it you had to just kind of piece together." But by the first week of January 1991, most of the kinks had been worked out, and, to the relief of everyone involved, CD&R was able to announce that he had a firm financing deal with J. P. Morgan for $1.1 billion in loans and with Equitable Life Assurance Society for $150 million in subordinated, or junk, debt, yielding 14.5 percent and $85 million in preferred stock with two large pension funds. IBM, which had wanted a 20 percent equity stake, would keep only 10 percent. CD&R and its investors would own 53 percent of the equity, and institutional investors and management would own the other 37 percent.

From there, things progressed quickly. There was one minor tremor in February 1991, when J. P. Morgan said it was having trouble syndicating to other banks its loan to CD&R. The banks questioned "aggressive" projections for growth in the laser printer market. They were the same projections that had led Martin Dubilier to be so excited in the first place and that allowed him to convince Rice that the price was acceptable. But bankers are not operations guys, and they had a hard time seeing past the historical numbers. They lacked Dubie's eye for what could be fixed and how it would generate significantly greater growth. They certainly weren't willing to make the leaps that Rice accepted in estimating $1 billion in unprovable sales. J. P. Morgan might not have been in the deal had it not had a long and lucrative relationship with IBM. In any event, J. P. Morgan's difficulty syndicating the loan was of no consequence to IBM or Rice. The bank had already committed to lending the money. It was a cloud, one that reminded everyone of how tough the economy was becoming. But it could not stop the deal, and in time Morgan did syndicate the loan to five other banks. On March 27, 1991, the sale was finally consummated. Lexmark was truly a stand-alone company, and the difficult task of making it a winning investment was just beginning.

CULTURE SHOCK

By this time, much of the cost cutting that would be achieved through voluntary head-count reductions was already done. Remember, IBM had set up the freestanding division in August 1990. CD&R certainly was an architect of that division. But the firm wasn't yet in control, and the management there had to carry on. It couldn't hold its breath and wait for the deal to get done. The delays in obtaining financing caused by haggling over details ended up serving a useful purpose. IBM began to take the steps that Rice would have been taking if CD&R had been in control from the start. It cut the number of employees from six thousand to four thousand before Rice's team was on board, and that gave Lexmark an edge when CD&R finally landed the deal. Rice was able to avoid any nasty confrontations with his new employees at the outset. He was the good guy, not the bad guy. He was allowed to dwell on the improvements that would be made and thus win over the loyalty of the workers who would be critical in building the printer business.

The Lexmark team had clearly settled on the strategy of selling as many typewriters as it could and reinvesting in laser printers to be used with PCs in homes and offices. The typewriter business was declining about 10 percent a year, but it still had enough life to generate plenty of cash for research and development and a bigger marketing budget to support the sales of laser printers. However, it would not be an easy transition. For one thing, even though IBM had spent $350 million making the Lexington plant a model of automation, it was simply not geared up to produce printers in an efficient manner. The mistakes made there were vintage IBM arrogance. The entire plant was set up in assembly-line fashion, whereby all day long each worker would screw on the same part and then send the product further down the line. It was the old way. Bored assembly-line workers could hardly be blamed for numerous defects in workmanship. Big Blue was painfully slow to adapt, and that's ultimately what led to its fall from dominance. Modern factory management calls for smaller teams of workers to put together entire units, interchanging their jobs to help them stay alert and empowering them to suggest improvements. "We changed all the lines, took out a lot of the automation," Rice said. "IBM had really put its money in the wrong place." In the first year under CD&R's wing, defects at the plant shrank by 90 percent.

Lexmark stepped up product development. At IBM, it took three years to conceive and design a better printer. At Hewlett-Packard, the powerhouse printer that Lexmark would compete with, it took only eighteen months. "Chuck Ames [a CD&R partner] went back and said to the guys in Lexington that they have to get their product-development cycle down to fifteen months, or they would be out of business," Rice said. "And they did it. They became a very effective competitor against HP because they always got fresh product out just a little ahead of them."

Lexmark also changed the way printers were sold. At IBM, the strategy was to convince dealers that IBM's printers were a better mousetrap and hope that the dealers would then persuade their customers to buy IBM's products. But it wasn't working for Lexmark. Most customers asked for an HP printer without thinking. It was the dominant brand. There was no reason for dealers to argue. A sale is a sale. They simply ordered the HP printers. So the Lexmark team, aside from beefing up advertising, put together the first direct sales force in the history of printers. They went straight to the customers and sold them on the merits of Lexmark printers. "Now, even HP has a direct sales force," Rice said with satisfaction. The episode is strangely reminiscent of Ted Forstmann's pioneering of direct sales in the corporate-jet industry at about the same time. Forstmann bypassed the pilots, who for years had been counted upon to talk their CEO bosses into buying Gulfstreams, and went straight to the CEOs. It's that eye for structural change, the

ability to question long-held practices, that has made both men stand-
outs in the LBO world.

Finally, realizing that it could not compete with HP on all levels,
Lexmark developed a strategy of serving niche markets, designing spe-
cific printers for specific tasks. That means it offers fewer choices but,
Rice believes, better machines at better prices in its chosen markets.

Persuading ex-IBMers to sign on for wholesale change was not easy.
At first, few believed that they could compete without IBM's muscle
and financial safety net. But it didn't take long for the managers and
line workers alike to start to appreciate the advantages of working in a
small, entrepreneurial environment. In one case, a typewriter assembly
line was redesigned by the line workers and reduced assembly time
from eight hours to just one hour and fifteen minutes. Line workers
needing more parts found that they could simply pick up the phone
and order them, rather than wait for a bureaucratic centralized purchas-
ing department to do it for them. And for the first time, their bosses
shared financial results with them, which they found encouraging
because it was their ideas that were being put to the test.

Perhaps the biggest philosophical change at Lexmark was the elimi-
nation of the so-called contention system that was pervasive in IBM.
Under that system, staffers with different interests and ambitions would
battle each other for months so that top managers could be reasonably
certain that the decision was sound. That was not only a tough environment for workers to enjoy and be motivated in; it was costly in
terms of time. Many technology products are on the shelf for less than
a year. Such delays would keep Lexmark, and, in fact, did keep IBM,
hopelessly behind the competition. Early on, Mann knew he would
have to end any system that promotes infighting and the protection of
turf. That's why he adopted the flat organizational chart. Line workers
were only four rungs below him, whereas they had been nine rungs
below him at IBM and he had been four rungs below the IBM CEO.

A story in the *Wall Street Journal* one year after CD&R bought
Lexmark illustrates the many quick cultural awakenings among the

IBM staffers-turned-entrepreneurs at Lexmark. According to the article, among the incidents that first year were these:

- Roger Hopwood, Lexmark's manager of laser-printer production, asked a manager at one of his first weekly meetings a question he couldn't answer. At IBM, the manager would have taken months to study the matter and then report back. But Hopwood, signaling the new guard, said, "Fine, but I'm going to have these meetings every week, so I'll ask you again next week."

- When an engineer tried to cram new features into a printer and the product later flopped, the ex-IBMers' first inclination was to try to figure out who was responsible and take their pound of flesh. But the new culture, fostered by Rice and his partners, was less interested in affixing blame than saluting the engineer for taking a reasonable risk.

- At one point Hopwood was presented with a completed plan for a new laser-printer assembly line. He showed it to the line workers and said they would have to sign off on it and stressed that they shouldn't if they weren't totally satisfied. Getting the message, the line workers refused to OK it until design engineers solved some of their concerns.

- A worker asked Hopwood to OK a $26,000 purchase order for ionizing equipment. Hopwood declined, saying that he trusted the worker's judgment and that the worker should just go ahead and do what was necessary. A short time later, the worker came back to him and said that on second thought he needed only $6,000 worth of ionizing equipment. "If I'd challenged him, he would have said 'Oh, yeah, I need the $26,000,' and he could have proved it to me," Hopwood told the *Wall Street Journal*.

- Fridays were declared dress-down days, when all the blue-suit-wearing IBMers had to take off their ties. "I kind of walked in here without a tie that first day and felt ashamed," engineer Steve Olson told the *Wall Street Journal*. "I thought, 'Well, maybe I'll just sit in my office for a while, and maybe nobody will come by.' It was actually hard." In a lapse, Mann showed up one Friday in a full suit but quickly stripped off the tie and coat, winning the hearts of his employees.

- Achim Knust, the chief financial officer and one of the few outsiders brought in at a high level, couldn't stand all the charts and diagrams that the ex-IBMers brought to meetings. He banned all charts from weekly meetings so that the managers would stop wasting time preparing them.

- Lexmark managers went through file cabinets, discarding drawers and drawers of forms. The information needed to justify an engineering change was cut from fifty-eight items to twenty-four. When anyone tried to find out who needed all that information in the first place, "you couldn't find anyone who knew," Greg Survant, a manager in printer development, told the *Wall Street Journal*. "That's the crazy thing."

The cultural shifts had an immediate impact. At the end of 1991, just nine months after the creation of Lexmark, the company had worked off $300 million in debt way ahead of schedule, operating profits were 30 percent above the plan, and the company's net loss (losses are expected early in any LBO because of the hefty interest payments) was less than expected. Proving that its entrepreneurial culture was for real, Lexmark gave every employee in the United States a bonus equal to 2.5 times his or her weekly pay. The company has improved steadily since then and now employs 6,700 worldwide. It has added plants in Rosyth, Scotland; Juárez, Mexico; Orléans, France; and Sydney, Australia. It turned its first net profit in 1994 and posted earnings from operations of $243 million on revenues of over $3 billion in 1998. The company sold initial shares to the public on November 15, 1995, at $20 a share. As of early 1999, the stock had climbed to over $100.

Lexmark has truly been a winner for all involved. The deal enhanced Rice's reputation, allowing his firm to secure even bigger deals in the later 1990s, and it was a big step forward in removing the stain from an LBO industry that had gone haywire with greed in the 1980s. IBM, which would have stumbled all over its bureaucratic self in carving out Lexmark on its own, got the job done in a tough economic climate and was able to move on to further divestitures. Today, it is a healthy, happy giant of technology once again. And Lexington, Kentucky, once threatened with having the plant shut down and losing its largest employer, retained an important economic base. "It's just terrific," Rice said. "It really makes you feel like you've accomplished something."

Here is a brief series of questions and answers with Joe Rice, the mild-mannered capitalist in bright suspenders:

Question: *What has the Lexmark deal meant to you and your firm?*

Answer: There is no question, it was a defining event. In the development of any firm there are defining events. For us, there was one in 1983, when we bought a business from Harris Corp. [Harris Graphics]. It was the first divestiture that any big company had done by way of a leveraged buyout. There was O. M. Scott in 1986. That was a big deal at the time, more than $200 million. But in terms of creativity and the feeling that there was only one firm that could have done this, there is nothing like the Lexmark deal. In many respects, it epitomizes what the buyout business is all about: taking something that didn't exist and putting an entrepreneurial management in place and getting the new enterprise going. It feels great, just great.

Question: *Why couldn't anyone else have done this deal?*

Answer: We have the capacity within the firm to understand how the business world operates and what are the important parts of it. The extraction process, I suspect, others could have done. But in terms of building the organization, segmenting the market, shortening product development cycles, things like that, I'm not sure that anyone else in the buyout business would have done it.

Question: *What's the first thing you say to the line workers at a newly acquired company?*

Answer: Well, you're always concerned about how the people in the workforce are going to take the change. And you try to make the change as seamless as possible. You go in and you say, in the Lexmark case, "Look, it's going to be run by former IBM employees. We are going to do everything we can to make it successful. It's adequately capitalized. There is no reason to believe it shouldn't be a tremendously successful venture," and you just hope the folks believe it. The truth is, in the case with people working at a plant, they don't have a lot of options. Most of them can't get sore and walk off, saying I'm not going to work for you. They have time and a whole lot of emotion invested in their job. In many respects, they have to stick around and see how it works out. Fortunately, this one worked out well. And with what happened to IBM later on [its declining fortunes], we looked very good to the workers who left IBM for Lexmark.

Question: *Why did you get involved in LBOs in the first place? Was it the money?*

Answer: No. Very truthfully, I don't think there was any real money in this business until the 1980s. Before that we all lived deal to deal. We'd charge a fee for doing a deal, and we'd take half of that fee and invest it in the deal itself. With the other half we'd pay taxes. For me, it's the excitement and romance of building something new that takes on a life of its own and rewards those involved both monetarily and intellectually.

Question: *What changed that in the 1980s?*

Answer: It was the advent of the managed pool of capital, the LBO funds. That's when we all started raising our own funds, which changed the dynamics of the business. First, it gives you access on a discretionary basis to a large pool of capital, so that you are not running out looking for investors for every deal. Second, you get paid to manage the capital, so you have a steady stream of income against which you can develop an organization with paid professionals on staff. [The conventional fee was 1.5 percent of assets, or $15 million a year on a $1 billion fund.] Then, the pools of capital started getting larger and so did the deals. That meant that our carried interest [CD&R's 20 percent of the investment gains] got bigger, too. That's when we started making some serious money.

Question: *When did you decide that you were pretty good at this game?*

Answer: It was Harris Graphics in 1983. It was a success and provided us with validation for our strategy. We build a different mousetrap here. I happen to think it's a better mousetrap.

Question: *Is that because of your focus on improving operations, not just cutting costs?*

Answer: Absolutely. At Lexmark, we created a fine, competitive company out of nothing. That company is now building products that are sold to people all over the world. It's employing people all over the world. This is what capitalism is all about.

Question: *When you first looked at IBM's office-products division and saw that it was basically a typewriter business, which was about to go the way of the buggy whip, why didn't you just turn tail and run?*

Answer: We knew the decline was going on. But we felt that, without question, IBM's key asset was that it had terrific people and a marvelous research capability. And those people felt the laser printer was the next generation of technology. We just felt that the trick was to run these cash-generating businesses in a manner that would support the development of the laser printer, and that's exactly what happened.

chapter nine

Henry Silverman

Agent of Change

HE'S PART ICAHN, PART MCCOLL, PART
Bollenbach, part Wilson, and part Huizenga—a lot of pieces that add
up to one thing: pure gold. To be sure, there is only one Henry
Silverman. He's a deal maker's deal maker, having done literally hundreds of transactions in his more than three decades on Wall Street.
He's raided companies for quick profit. He's built his own company
through acquisitions, including some daring high-priced stock swaps.
He's created value through financial innovation. He's successfully challenged the assumptions of an industry. He's exploited the best that
franchise companies have to offer. In short, he's done it all and paved a
few new roads along the way. Silverman has made his share of mistakes. But his style of deal making, like investing in general, is a game
of batting average. As long as he wins more than he loses—and knocks
a few out of the yard in the process—he'll be a success. And talk about
batting average. Joe DiMaggio should have hit with this kind of consis-
tency.

Silverman is the rare breed of businessman who can coddle, nurse,
and build an enterprise and then, on a moment's notice, emotionlessly
sell it to the highest bidder. In his view, everything is for sale. If someone came along with more money than he thought his company was
worth, he'd sell it in a heartbeat. That is the soul of a deal maker.
Create value, then realize it. But as you saw with Teddy Forstmann,
even cold-blooded, profit-minded wheeler-dealers develop soft spots.

In Forstmann's case, his soft spot made for a better deal at Gulfstream. Silverman, though, has no such soft underbelly for any deal in his portfolio. And for him, the ability to look at all his acquired assets from a detached view—essentially to mark to market with every glance—has been instrumental in pushing him to the top of his class.

Silverman applies three basic criteria to determine the greatness of a deal. First, of course, the deal has to have made lots of money. Second, it also must have been done against considerable odds—in the face of rampant skepticism. And last, it has to have hinged on some unique insight or somehow proved that an unpopular premise was correct. For Silverman, such a deal came about in 1996, the year he bought Avis Rent-A-Car from General Motors (GM) and the Avis employees for $805 million in cash and stock. Avis was a struggling number two to Hertz's number one, and, at the time, the woefully managed car-rental industry had left a twenty-year trail of tears up and down Wall Street. The biggest problem: Renting a car in the early 1990s cost about the same as it did in the early 1970s. Prices were flat, and nobody was making money at it. "You could rent a tuxedo and a car to go to the prom, and you'd pay more for the tuxedo," Silverman is fond of saying. "Yet the tuxedo cost $200 to make, and the car cost $18,000. That doesn't make sense."

The odd pricing both bothered and fascinated Silverman, and his natural curiosity took over. He began looking for an angle. A curious, questioning mind is a trait of many deal makers. In my conversation with Ted Forstmann, he spoke often of "challenging conventional wisdom," saying that his penchant for asking "dumb" questions helped make him a success. The same can be said of Silverman, who began looking at the car-rental industry when no one wanted to touch it. Ultimately, Silverman would conclude that economic forces were conspiring to change the business for good and that a rich mine of profits awaited anyone who could get in cheap and quick.

Silverman, who didn't get in quite as cheaply as he had hoped, did get in quick, and like clockwork, within a year of his purchase of Avis, rental rates were indeed heading higher—about 5 percent to 10 percent a year. Silverman goosed that trend by raising rates first. But there was no guarantee that Hertz, the industry leader, and others would follow his lead. If they hadn't followed it, the deal would have been a dud, and this chapter would be on another subject. That's the fine line between winning and losing in the deal game (and, it seems, in subject matter for the print media). That fine line reinforces what Gary Wilson said in chapter 6 and what every successful investor and deal maker knows: You have to be in the game to win. Wait for a guarantee, and you'll be the last one on line.

For Silverman, Avis was a calculated gamble that paid off big-time. When he bought the company, it was his first big foray outside hotels and real estate. Critics thundered their disapproval. Not only was Silverman buying a business he knew nothing about, it was one with a spotty history of profits. But Silverman outfoxed them all. He split Avis into two. One company would consist of Avis's 1,200 rental sites and 175,000-vehicle fleet, generating $2 billion in annual revenue. The other would be a franchising company, with the right to license the Avis name to franchisees for 4 percent of sales. That part would also have the function of a central office, handling reservations and marketing. The split allowed Silverman to recover his entire initial investment within two years and be left with a $100-million-a-year annuity. It was pure magic, and here's how it worked: In 1997, he sold to the public a 75 percent stake in the part of Avis that owned the locations and cars. The IPO raised more than $300 million. That didn't go to Silverman; it went to the company to buy more cars and open more locations. But the 25 percent interest that Silverman retained in this newly public company quickly grew to a market value of $400 million—or roughly half his purchase price. The Avis deal also created a tax loss worth about $200 million to Silverman. And as part of the deal, Silverman also got Avis's Wizard Communications data processing and reservation system, which now functions as a stand-alone business with a value of about $200 million.

Voilà! The deal was paid for. Meanwhile, there was the other part of the company—the franchising part—that Silverman still owned, with an estimated value of $2 billion. "If I said to you that I could work something out so that at the end of the day you'd pay nothing for a $100-million-a-year, endless annuity stream, I suspect you'd ask where to sign up," Silverman quipped. "This is 100 percent profit margin. There are virtually no costs associated with it. That's what makes this deal such a financial success."

In many ways, Silverman is the deal maker whom nobody knows. Stars like Sumner Redstone, the chief of cable and movie giant Viacom who is profiled in the next chapter; Sandy Weill at Citigroup; and notorious types like raider Carl Icahn are familiar names around the country. Silverman isn't. But there's not a deal guy on Wall Street who doesn't know and respect him. There isn't a financial expert in the country who hasn't heard his name, and consumers would be stunned by the number of ways he touches their lives. Silverman is the chairman and CEO of Cendant Corp., a marketing and franchising giant based in Parsippany, New Jersey. Cendant franchises more than 6,000 lodging properties in twenty-five countries with nearly 500,000 rooms under the names Days Inn, Ramada Inn, Howard Johnson, Super 8, Park Inn International, Villager Lodge, Knights Inn, Travelodge, and Wingate Inn. The company franchises 12,000 real estate offices that account for 25 percent of U.S. home sales under the names Century 21, ERA, and Coldwell Banker. Silverman also owns the largest vacation time-share exchange, Resort Condominiums International; and the leading name in corporate relocations, PHH, which also has a big name in the management of fleets of vehicles and residential mortgages. He owns Avis, the world's second biggest car-rental system with a 25 percent share of the market to Hertz's 29 percent. And in late 1997, Silverman added to his stable the giant direct-marketing firm CUC International, which sells memberships to clubs, such as Shoppers Advantage and Travelers Advantage. In all, CUC has 30 million members who pay annual dues to get discounts on a huge array of household products.

A COLOSSAL CLUNKER

The CUC deal, which prompted Silverman to change the company's name from HFS—formerly Hospitality Franchise Systems—to Cendant, was by far Silverman's biggest clunker. It wasn't because the synergies he envisioned weren't real, but because CUC, before Silverman merged with the company, had engaged in a massive accounting fraud by faking about $500 million in revenue and pretax profits over several years. The fraud was discovered just four months after Silverman took control, and the resulting scandal took an enormous toll on him. It knocked the stock of Cendant for a loop, from about $41 to $7. Because Silverman is one of his own biggest investors—he owns 1.5 million shares of Cendant and has options on 38 million more, totaling 4 percent of the company—his personal net worth fell by $1 billion—from $1.5 billion to $500 million. More than that, though, the scandal rocked Wall Street, where Silverman had been considered invincible. More than $20 billion in market value was wiped out overall, and angry shareholders responded by filing nearly one hundred lawsuits. The scandal ravaged Silverman's reputation, and dealing with it through the summer and fall of 1998 seemed to age him much as the "zippergate" sex scandal aged President Clinton at about the same time. The most-voiced criticism was that Silverman, veteran of hundreds of buyouts and professed believer in taking nothing for granted, should have known enough not to buy a company before he thoroughly examined its books.

I spoke with Silverman for this book shortly before the scandal came to light, and one of the themes he stressed was the importance of due diligence. In the Avis deal, he said, "I really did my homework. I went to talk to the automakers and spent more time in Detroit than the Detroit Pistons and Tigers and Lions." In a 1997 interview with a colleague of mine at *Time* magazine, he said, "Never assume. I am an absolute jerk about following up. I call people constantly. I drive people crazy. The biggest mistake a manager can make is to assume that something is done." Silverman is a brutally intelligent detail-oriented former tax attorney who demands monthly financial reports and daily cash-flow figures. He brings his subsidiary heads to New York each month to report on their businesses. His motto: Give me more, rather than not enough; I'll throw away what I don't need. Silverman has insisted repeatedly that there was no way he could have known about the fraud at the time he merged with CUC. It was so well concealed that not even CUC's auditors allege they could not detect it. Still, in the eyes of some, he is to blame.

The CUC fiasco, as nasty as it was, does little to diminish a brilliant deal-making career that stretches back to the early 1970s, when Silverman ran his own "bootstrap" firm and bought and sold the likes of Yoo Hoo Chocolate Beverage and the Delta Queen Steamboat Co. And by late 1998, with all the bad news out about the CUC transaction, Silverman's stock was again rising. At about $21, it was still down 50 percent from its high, but $21 still represented a twelvefold increase from the time Silverman's company first sold shares to the public in 1992 at a split-adjusted price of $1.66. That gain equates to an annual average return of 46 percent—not the 80 percent figure that had made his one of the top three stocks on Wall Street for a while, but still a convincing market beater at the low point of his career.

For what it's worth, Henry Silverman is a man who regards his reputation as more important than money. He is committed to fixing Cendant, though it won't be easy. If he succeeds in working through the CUC nightmare, he may finally develop a soft spot for one of his corporate children, the kind you get by rolling up your sleeves and fixing a deal gone terribly wrong. But it's much too early for even Silverman to know how he'd feel about CUC once Cendant is repaired. Having survived the CUC debacle, though, Silverman seems a sure bet to recover and rebuild. That's why as of fall 1998, analysts across Wall Street viewed the beaten-down shares of Cendant as one the best values in the market. Many predicted it would double in twelve months.

Cendant's headquarters may be in Parsippany, but the company is really run out of Silverman's beautifully decorated thirty-seventh floor office on New York's West Side, at Fifth Avenue and Fifty-seventh Street. I met him there in early April 1998. I've never met a more focused executive. He's sharp. He finishes every thought. He rarely digresses. He speaks clearly and gets his message across the first time. He's a communicator, a skill that should not be underrated and one that played a vital role in the early growth of his company. There is nothing that Wall Street values more than a clear, simple story. It must be a success story, of course. But simple is good. It's easy to evaluate. Silverman has long had the knack of making his company's complex strategy simple.

It's no small skill. One of the reasons the old conglomerates like ITT Corp. were busted up in the 1980s and 1990s was that their stock prices became cheap when confused analysts failed to grasp the corporate strategy. *Mr. CEO, exactly how does that bakery business meld with dog food and batteries?* An analyst might wonder. Unable to fathom the answer, he or she would give it a conservative rating or just move on to other, more easily understood, stocks. Without these important boosters, the stocks would drop, and then raiders would come along to buy the companies on the cheap and sell the parts for more than the price of the whole companies.

In some ways, Silverman's company resembles those conglomerates with disparate businesses. But in Silverman's vision, these businesses are not disparate, and his effectiveness in delivering that message to Wall Street helped make him a darling for years. What now seems fairly simple—that anything that can be franchised fits with Silverman's company—was not always an easy sell. Fortunately for Silverman, he became adept at answering tough questions early in his career. An October 1997 article in *Fortune* magazine made the point: "Consider whom he had to answer to in his highest profile venture before HFS, running the leveraged buyout fund at corporate raider Saul Steinberg's Reliance Group Holdings in the 1980s. Investors in the $120 million fund included a group assembled by Drexel Burnham Lambert junk bond king Michael Milken—among them Milken himself, Seema

Boesky (then wife of arbitrageur Ivan), financier Carl Lindner, and casino magnate Steve Wynn. 'It was like playing violin in front of Isaac Stern,' Silverman says."

Silverman is lean and nattily dressed. With slicked-back thinning and wavy hair, he has the appearance of the stereotypical Wall Street shark. His office, which overlooks Central Park and Trump Tower and looks down on the tree-covered rooftops of Fifth Avenue, is a tribute to testosterone. It's wood-paneled with wood chairs and a big circular wooden table in the boardroom, which is where he and I spoke. The office has wall-sized paintings of soldiers at war and ironworkers at work, statues of hunters on the hunt, and pictures of battleships and more soldiers. This is a battle-tested deal maker, and everything in his office suggests that the battlefield is where he enjoys being most. As with Hugh McColl, my greatest concern with Silverman was that he was putting deals together so quickly that he might have pulled off something even more impressive than Avis by the time this book went to press. My first scheduled interview, as was the case with McColl, was canceled when Silverman became engrossed in a new deal, this one to buy American Bankers Insurance. That deal collapsed when his stock sank in 1998. The CUC disaster means that Silverman will not have made any further big acquisitions through the first half of 1999. Indeed, by the end of 1998, he had adopted a whole new strategy: selling companies to raise money to pay down debt and buy back Cendant shares on the open market. He was expecting to get a total of $1.5 billion for a French publisher of classified advertisements and his educational software company, which publishes such titles as Davidson and Knowledge Adventure. He was also considering selling his vast real estate holdings in the United Kingdom. There, Cendant operates parking garages with some $1 billion worth of property that Silverman proposed to sell and lease back. Ever the deal maker, Silverman explained that his stock was hit so hard after the CUC deal that it was valued in the market at about half what the company would be worth if liquidated. To capture that value, he decided to start liquidating—as any outside investor would. My guess, though, is that this self-liquidation will end long before he gets to any core assets and that sometime in the year 2000, he will again be acquiring companies.

REALIZATION NUMBER 1

Henry Richard Silverman was born on August 2, 1940, in Brooklyn, New York, and his parents later moved to the northern suburbs of Westchester County. His father, Herbert, was the CEO of Talcott National Corp., a commercial finance firm in the 1960s and 1970s. Silverman graduated from Williams College with a degree in American civilization in 1961. He went on to the University of Pennsylvania law school, from which he graduated in 1964. He joined the navy reserves as an attorney, making the rank of lieutenant commander and avoiding a tour in Vietnam. He is married for the second time and has three daughters and two grandchildren. He lives on Manhattan's upper East Side and has a home in Bedford Hills, New York, near where he grew up. He plays a lot of tennis and has long had a fondness for Cuban cigars. In the 1980s he smoked Punch stogies, which were so scarce that he could get them only through a Lebanese arms-merchant friend, who had ties to the Cuban defense minister.

His first job out of school was as an assistant to Steve Ross, then in the early stages of assembling the empire that would become Time Warner. Silverman practiced law briefly and then went into investment banking, starting that career at White Weld & Co., which was later acquired by Merrill Lynch. He then ran and dismantled a minicon-glomerate called ITI Corp. before he started his own mergers firm in the 1970s. At his mergers firm, he'd raise money to buy one small company at a time, spruce up its business plan, and then sell it. With Saul Steinberg, he went into the bus-shelter business, which nearly blew up as they tried to get a New York City contract and became the subject of a grand-jury investigation. The two were never charged and went on to win contracts in Philadelphia, Miami, and other cities. Silverman's reputation in the buyout world grew rapidly. He had teamed up with heavyweights like Steinberg and the "grave dancer," Chicago investor Sam Zell, and earned their respect. That success led him to his job running Steinberg's buyout fund from 1983 to 1990. At that fund, he bought the Days Inn motel chain for $590 million, expanded it, took it public, made it private again, and finally sold it in 1989 for more than $700 million. In his years with Steinberg, the fund realized annual average returns of 39 percent.

It was at Days Inn that Silverman had what would become his career-guiding epiphany: Franchising was where the money was. At Days Inn, he said, he spent 90 percent of his time managing the sixty or so motels they owned, but 90 percent of the company's profit came from the franchising end. From then on, he resolved to seek to own just the names, not the bricks and mortar that came with most businesses. He's managed well with that strategy in hotels and rental cars. The final piece of the puzzle, he said, is airlines. If he could franchise an airline, he'd enjoy all the cross-marketing benefits of being in the three most important travel-related businesses. But for reasons that will become clear when I discuss Avis, he's had a difficult time devising a strategy to franchise airlines and has abandoned the idea for now.

Silverman left Steinberg's employ to join the high-profile investment banking firm Blackstone Group in 1990. He was a general partner and ran the firm's $850 million buyout fund before he left in late 1991. During his tenure there, the fund concluded over $2 billion in bank financing and completed four acquisitions, including Six Flags Corp. for $760 million in partnership with Time Warner. In 1990, he purchased the Ramada and Howard Johnson hotel franchise systems (no hotels, just hotel names) for $195 million to launch what he envisioned as a franchised-hotel empire, which he named Hospitality Franchise Systems—later shortened to HFS. In 1992, after Days Inn ran into problems and then entered into bankruptcy proceedings, he bought that franchise system as well for $305 million. He took this unusual company public in December 1992, installing himself as CEO. Even then, Silverman was little known outside the deal community, but his breakneck growth at HFS following the IPO would make him not just a Wall Street darling but a legend. When HFS went public, it had an annual net income of just $30 million. That income would grow to $600 million by the end of 1997 and $750 million before onetime charges in 1998.

Until Silverman bought Avis in October 1996, he was in only two businesses: hotel and real estate office franchising. Although the two businesses didn't have a lot in common, by the mid-1990s Wall Street had begun to appreciate Silverman's strategy of owning the names, not the buildings. But that appreciation didn't keep his critics quiet in July 1996, when he bought Avis against the wishes of his biggest shareholders and even some on his own board. The franchising story made sense, they agreed, but the car-rental business hadn't made any money in years. The critics thought that Silverman was going a deal too far. Silverman had an edge, though. By then he knew more about the industry than even Avis's managers, whom he quickly let go. "They were fighting the last fight, the one for market share," he said. "But the world was changing." He delights in having spotted that change ahead of the crowd. When I asked him why Avis was his favorite deal, he didn't skip a beat: "It was the one with the greatest amount of skepticism, and the fruit always tastes better when it is delivered after a bath of cynicism."

WHOSE DEBT IS IT, ANYWAY?

The first time Silverman recalls considering the car-rental industry was in 1995, when he was helping a couple of friends—Dan O'Connell and John Howard at the LBO firm Vestar—analyze National Car Rental, which they had been thinking about buying from GM. Ultimately, his buddies at Vestar decided not to buy the company. They couldn't get past the industry's inability to raise prices and figured that nothing was going to change that. Much later, Silverman would conclude something altogether different—that twenty years of soft pricing was about to give way to a period of sustained price increases in the car-rental business, and that change would be the basis for turning it into an attractive investment. But he hadn't come to that conclusion yet. He was just starting to look at an industry that he found infinitely fascinating.

What's so fascinating about renting cars? To Silverman, it was simple. It was a mismanaged industry that had long been operated by companies that were interested in the side benefits, not the core function of renting cars at a profit. Now, the business seemed ripe for change, and he wanted to be there first to profit from the shifting dynamics. Decades earlier the car-rental business had been a good one. But in the early 1980s, big corporations like Beatrice and Allegis came to understand that owning a rental fleet would make them eligible for valuable investment tax credits because of the fast depreciation of cars. Never mind making a profit on car rentals, their executives thought. If you just break even, the business is worth owning because the tax credits trim corporate tax bills and boost earnings. In that environment, the business was not carefully managed, and its profitability began to slip.

Then in 1986 a sweeping tax bill diminished the appeal of owning large fleets of vehicles for tax reasons, and the industry underwent a complete change in ownership. But the new buyers weren't any more interested in the core rental business than were the companies that were unloading them. This time, the buyers were Ford (Hertz, Budget), GM (Avis, National), and Chrysler (Dollar, Thrifty). For the Big Three, car-rental companies became a means of controlling inventories and stoking vehicle sales whenever and however they saw fit. "If Ford needed to sell fifteen thousand Tauruses in December so they could claim it was the biggest-selling car of the year, guess what, they'd get a big order from Hertz," Silverman said. "The problem for Hertz was that it just got fifteen thousand cars it didn't need, didn't want, and couldn't rent." Excess inventory at all the car-rental companies was a big factor in keeping rental prices down during this period.

Eventually, the car-rental companies screamed so loud that their corporate parents had to do something to let them make money. So the automakers began entering into "put back" agreements, in which they'd agree to buy cars back from their rental-company subsidiaries for an attractive, predetermined price. In some cases, the automakers actually bought the cars back for more than what the rental companies had paid. Eventually, the rental companies began to abuse the system. They'd accept cars, let them sit for six months, and then sell them back to the automakers at a profit. This wasn't a real business. There was no reason to worry about pricing. The backdrop for this crazy set of circumstances was that Japanese automakers had been gaining ground in the U.S. auto market. The Big Three were looking for ways to keep their factories running. Their strategy with the car-rental companies helped. They kept building cars and stuffing them down their rental subsidiaries. But such a game can never last.

By the early 1990s, this practice had created a glut of good-quality used cars that began to undermine new-car sales. So the automakers rethought their strategy. They had come full circle and decided that the rental companies had to be run as viable businesses, paying and receiving fair market price for their cars. It was the only way to get a true picture of the demand and run their companies accordingly. They would have to operate on a model that made sense—not merely as a tax loophole or as a gimmick for goosing sales. And once they decided to change, it was clear that they no longer had to own the rental companies, so they might as well sell them.

Enter Henry Silverman. When his buddies at Vestar chose not to buy National Car Rental from GM in 1995, he began to investigate how such a company might fit with his own company, HFS, in franchising hotels and real estate offices. Silverman thought about buying National Car and merging it into a shell company he had under the HFS wing. That shell company was National Gaming, a casino marketing company he bought in 1992 but became disillusioned with; he sold its assets in 1994 at a loss of $25 million. (Until CUC, that ranked as his worst deal.) What was left was a balance sheet with no debt and $50 million in cash. It wasn't enough. Silverman quickly dismissed that idea because National Car would have been a $300 million acquisition—

too big for Silverman's shell company. But he had missed his chance. National Car ended up in the hands of a management-led team. The car-rental business, though, was by then thick in his blood.

Silverman couldn't get over the fact that National Car had a net worth of only $30 million and that someone had lent it $2 billion to fund its fleet. Ordinarily such a modest-size company couldn't borrow $200 million, much less $2 billion. He thought about it long and hard, and even today isn't sure when the answer popped into his head. But the answer was that those cars were essentially financed with GM's credit. Because GM had long-term agreements to buy back cars at a stated price, the lenders knew that the vast majority of that $2 billion in car loans was at little risk. GM—not the small car-rental company— would have to default before the loans were uncollectible. The lenders needed to worry only about the car-rental company's ability to pay its interest expense during the six-month period that it owned each car. The repurchase agreements are what make the car-rental business different from the airline industry as far as a franchiser is concerned. American Airlines, TWA, and Northwest have no one to "put" their jets to after a set period. Therefore, like GM, they must have deep balance sheets to carry billions of dollars in debt.

With this realization, Silverman concluded that there was no reason why the rental fleet and all those rental locations—the hard assets— had to remain part of National if he were to buy it. There was no need for a big-company structure because the cars would continue to be financed on GM's credit as long as it continued to provide put-back agreements. The company had passed a critical Silverman test. It could be split: a stand-alone company rich in tangible assets and a franchise company with little more than its intellectual property to manage. In other words, no bricks and mortar, the way Silverman likes it. This was a radical view. To that point, there had been few franchised car-rental outlets. Those that did exist were typically associated with car dealerships. No one saw the potential in franchising on a massive scale. There were still serious stumbling blocks. One was that most car rentals are business-related. Giant international companies, such as IBM and Boeing, have global contracts and demand consistent service and pricing, whether their people are renting in Texas or Toledo. That's hard to guarantee with a franchise system, in which the franchisees own their own companies. But the big hurdle had been cleared, as far as Silverman was concerned.

"So my first epiphany," Silverman said, "is that we could, in fact, separate the business into franchisee and franchiser. But we didn't think National was worth what they wanted for it." Silverman had been thinking about paying $300 million in cash. The management-led team that had bought it wanted more, and they got it when Republic Industries (run by Wayne Huizenga) paid $600 million in stock.

INTERESTING PARANOIA

The critical decision had been made, though. Silverman was going to own a car-rental franchise system. He just didn't know which one. As he pondered the issue, he thought of Jack Welch, the highly regarded CEO of General Electric. Silverman has long been a fan of Welch's. (What executive isn't?) The GE chief is famous for his view that that he doesn't want to be in any business unless it's number one or number two in its industry. So Silverman decided to start at the top. Why not? The number-one rental-car company was Hertz, owned by Ford. Number two was Avis, owned by GM. As a starting point, Silverman wanted to test one of his earlier assumptions—that the fundamentals of the industry were changing, that the automakers no longer needed car-rental companies to help them manage their inventories and boost their sales. By this time, it was the mid-1990s, and the threat from Japanese automakers was receding. Japan was in a deep recession, and U.S. carmakers had largely responded to the challenge of quality and begun to build better cars. The U.S. cars were selling on their own. Silverman met with top executives at the Big Three, including Jack Smith at GM, and learned two things:

- The automakers were selling cars to their rental subsidiaries at fair-market prices and buying them back used at fair-market prices. In other words, the rental companies were able to buy, rent, and resell the cars to Detroit at prices that made sense (and money) for everyone.
- The automakers were selling about as many cars as they wanted to the rental companies. In other words, their business was good enough that they were no longer looking to goose sales through arbitrary rental-company purchases. The cars were good enough to compete without that kind of support.

The relationship between the automakers and the rental-car companies had become economic. "So there was no longer a strategic reason for them to own a car-rental business," Silverman said. "They didn't need a captive dumping ground anymore because they had size and price right where they wanted them to be. We heard this from very senior people at all the major automakers, and we also talked to some of the larger import sellers like Toyota and Nissan and a few others. Everybody was seeing it from the same handle. And therefore if it was no longer strategically important for the car manufacturers to own the fleet, they should be willing to sell it to people like us. I mean, if you don't need it, you've got to sell it."

That's pure Silverman. Either you need it or you don't. If you don't, get rid of it and let others run it. They'll do a better job. Meanwhile, you'll do a better job with the assets that are central to your own business.

So Silverman approached Ford about buying the cream of the car-rental industry, Hertz, which had annual revenue of $4 billion. The Ford executives listened. They didn't argue with Silverman's reasoning and even believed that a sale of Hertz was in their best interest. But in the auto world, the 1980s threat of Japanese dominance faded slowly. Ford worried that this important outlet for new cars would dry up, that Silverman, a known wheeler-dealer, might flip the company to another buyer that would no longer buy cars from Ford. Silverman offered a ten-year contract to ensure this would not happen. But Ford balked anyway. "We're not really concerned about you," a Ford executive told him. "What about Toyota? The Japanese have a very long-term view. Who's to say that ten years down the road they don't buy your company and put their own cars in there?"

Silverman is no stranger to management thinking. He evolved on the financial side of Wall Street, a gunslinging LBO type. But in his career he has run numerous companies, including Cendant, and even his familiarity with managers' views left him perplexed and unempathic upon hearing Ford's view. Ten years is an eternity. "That was interesting paranoia, to say the least," Silverman said. Ford did offer to sell him its lower-tier rental company, Budget. But that wasn't part of Silverman's vision. He would move on to number two, Avis, where success awaited.

THE ONLY FOOL IN TOWN ·

Avis's history is a microcosm of the industry. Founded in 1946 by Warren E. Avis, a U.S. Air Force officer, the company enjoyed heady growth early on. In the bustling post–World War II environment, people were getting out and about for the first time in years, and Avis recognized the value of linking air travel with rental cars. He opened the country's first airport car-rental counter at Willow Run Airport near Detroit. He came to dominate airport locations around the country and by 1948 was opening additional locations in the downtown areas of most cities. The company went through numerous changes in control, and in the 1980s ended up in the hands of Wesray Capital, the LBO firm run by William E. Simon and Ray Chambers. Wesray sold parts of the business to take out some profit after its purchase and then sold what was left—the U.S. operations, mainly—to GM and an Avis ESOP, or employee stock-ownership program. By the time Silverman was on the scene, GM owned 29 percent, and the ESOP owned 71 percent. The ESOP and GM were primed to unload Avis. GM had become convinced that car rentals were a management drain. More important, though, GM and the ESOP both knew that within the year, the ESOP, formed in 1987, would be ten years old—the point at which retirees could start selling their shares. Who would buy them? GM wanted to get out of the business. The ESOP needed cash to meet the redemptions. Neither was a likely buyer. They had to find someone else, and that's when Henry Silverman walked through their door.

His first step, as is typical in such deals, was quietly to contact the ratings agencies Standard & Poor's and Moody's, the powerful research firms that judge the creditworthiness of America's big companies. Their ratings determine the interest rate that companies must pay to borrow in the public debt market. "We got kind of a jolt there," Silverman recalled. "They all said that they might have to downgrade our debt because they felt we'd never be able to pull off splitting the company into two pieces. But I didn't agree, and I had talked to enough lenders who didn't agree. So we went ahead. But the ratings agencies were a level of significant skepticism."

Fortified by enough outside opinion, Silverman pressed on. He had already set the price: $500 million. It was agreeable to all sides. One question still bothered him, though. What if rental prices didn't rise? He was going to raise them at Avis, all right. But what if no one followed suit and he had to backtrack? The whole business of splitting the company and franchising all the locations would be just a pointless exercise in slicing and dicing. He needed higher rental rates to make the deal work. "That's really my second epiphany," Silverman said of his conviction that competitors would follow his lead. "I believed that if we bought Avis, we could be a catalyst for change in the industry. The most important premise, and the really big idea here, was my thinking that if carmakers didn't own these fleets of rental cars, then they would eventually get sold to entrepreneurs like us, and the one thing that hadn't happened in twenty years would occur, which is that people would start raising prices."

This was Silverman's big leap. For Avis to be a winner, the most fundamental aspects of the car-rental business would have to change. But he was so sure that the automakers were going to sell to entrepreneurs, that it was a leap he willingly took. "The only way people like us can make money is, we've got to raise prices," Silverman said. "And what I've learned is that if you are the agent of change, if you're a catalyst in an industry, if you're the first mover, you'll make a lot of money."

There were other considerations, too. Because his company was heavily in travel-related services, he felt he had some "comparative advantages" over others in the car-rental business. One of those advantages was the ability to rent Avis cars at his hotels and exploit other opportunities to cross-market services. "Money is not a comparative advantage," Silverman noted. "The world is awash in capital. Comparative advantage is what you do that someone else can't or doesn't. In our case, it was the fact that we were putting millions and millions of heads in beds every year throughout our hotel businesses, through our time-shares exchange business, and through a variety of other travel businesses that we were in. We could stimulate demand in Avis. You know, we couldn't fill up 200,000 cars every night—but maybe 5,000 that weren't being filled. That obviously had a very beneficial impact on the bottom line."

With these things in mind, Silverman set to negotiate with GM and the Avis ESOP. They were both motivated sellers, and the business was awful to boot. He was in a strong position to hold firm at $500 million, the price he originally set. But in a cruel twist of fate—cruel to Silverman, anyway—the rental business began to perk up early in 1996. The economy was strong. People were traveling. Businesses had removed their early 1990s moratoriums on travel expenses. The changing of the guard that Silverman was counting on was already beginning. In April 1997, Ford spun off Hertz in an IPO. In a matter of months, Wayne Huizenga would buy Alamo and National Car, and Budget, Dollar, and Thrifty would all go public. Moreover, in anticipation of taking ownership of Avis, Silverman had begun to lobby for price increases, and there were signs that he would get his way. "You'd think that we would have gotten a hell of a deal," Silverman said. "But we didn't. We actually cut a great deal with GM and management. But when you deal with an ESOP, everything has to be approved by the Department of Labor." That circumstance created a sort of moving target for Silverman. Just as he would get the ESOP trustee, U.S. Trust, to agree to a price, the business would perk up a little more and U.S. Trust would up its price.

"That was very hard to swallow," Silverman said. "You never like to feel that you made a deal and you end up paying more. But the other side of the coin is that we did see the business improving, and the good news about that is you really don't mind paying more if you're getting more." That's a familiar theme. It rings true with Teddy Forstmann, who said he'd rather overpay for a good company than underpay for a bad one. It's certainly true of Hugh McColl, who was taken to task for paying huge premiums to buy Boatmens Bancshares and Barnett Banks.

Even though the negotiations dragged on, the deal was never really in doubt. It was just a matter of price, and on July 1, 1996, Avis, GM, and Silverman announced the buyout of Avis, complete with plans to split Avis in two and spin off the part with cars and offices—the Avis assets—to Silverman's shareholders as a separate company within a year. His phone began to ring immediately. "What are you doing?" asked the manager of one large mutual fund. "You had a great business model here. Why would you possibly want to do this? No one can make money in car rentals." One especially outspoken firm was State Street Research in Boston. Analysts there, who perhaps had checked with the ratings agencies, didn't think Silverman would even succeed in splitting the company, much less pulling off the planned spin-off of Avis's hard assets within a year.

There were other doubters and hurdles as well. Just a day after he announced the deal on July 1, the International Brotherhood of Teamsters, the union representing 21 percent of Avis's fifteen thousand employees, said it had hired an investment bank to make sure that the employees, who owned the company but knew nothing of the sale beforehand, didn't get cheated. Ultimately, the Teamsters would have a problem with the lucrative pay packages for managers. But because the price had been negotiated higher and the average Avis employee would receive a healthy $35,000, that never became a big issue. Here's how the deal broke down: Silverman paid $500 million in cash and $305 million in stock. About $155 million went to the managers as a result of the stock and options they had been given over the previous ten years. GM got $300 million in cash and stock for an ownership interest that had cost it $135 million seven years earlier. The ESOP got $350 million in cash and stock.

A few weeks after the deal was announced, Silverman switched plans. Business was so good that he decided to sell Avis's hard assets in an IPO instead of spinning them off as a separate company to the shareholders. One of his next moves was to oust "market-share-oriented" management, which had the wrong mind-set for the new car-rental world that was evolving fast, a world in which profits and higher prices were the key to success. Underscoring that decision, Avis raised car-rental rates across the board in the fall of 1996. For four months no one followed suit, and Avis's volumes suffered. Silverman conceded that "it got a little lonely out there." But he hadn't come this far to run scared. His patience paid off. As other car-rental companies fell into the hands of entrepreneurial owners, the pricing firmed. By March 1997, Silverman noticed that car-rental ads weren't harping on price anymore, but on things like service, quality, and convenient locations. Sure enough, prices had nudged higher, vindicating his master plan.

"The secular trend is clearly for more price increases, and it will go on as long as these companies are publicly traded and need to report higher earnings," Silverman said. "The public understands that cars are way underpriced. Just to give you an idea, if you rent a Buick Regal from Avis at JFK in New York, it's going to cost you about $45 a day, but the functional equivalent of that car at Heathrow in London is going to cost you $140. Same car. Same day. That disconnect is there because people in this country were competing for market share and not raising prices for twenty years."

Silverman had to sidestep one more land mine before the Avis IPO. A franchisee in North Carolina was accused of racial discrimination. The incident got a lot of coverage, and later allegations included discrimination against Jews and Eskimos, as well as blacks. Ultimately, though, those were seen as franchisee problems, not the fault of Avis management, and the decks were cleared to go public at $17 a share in the fall of 1997.

It's an irony that the Avis deal, a $2 billion winner by Silverman's count, wasn't more noticeable in the press. Avis is a household brand name, and these kinds of winners don't come along often. Silverman's theory is that he had just been so busy doing deals that he didn't have time to get out and show people what a winner this one was. Cynics might conclude that he's doing so now because of his recent travails with CUC. But I'd note that he selected the Avis deal for this book before CUC blew up.

The Avis deal had no obvious losers. That's another trend you find among deals by great deal makers. Most great deals spring from insights that few others had. That means there's no one left saying shoulda, woulda, coulda. "No one else wanted Avis," Silverman said. "We were the only fools in town." As of fall 1998, Avis's shares were trading above $20. So buyers of the IPO have done all right. Cendant stock was clobbered, but for other reasons. You could argue that GM and the Avis ESOP sold cheap. But they didn't. They were able to add $300 million to their original deal. Besides, GM and the Avis employees were clueless about how to change the culture of this industry. That was Silverman's vision, and now he is enjoying the rewards.

Here's a brief question-and-answer session with Henry Silverman, the only "fool" in town:

Question: It seems incredible that no one ever thought of franchising a car-rental company the way you did.

Answer: Well, I think the bigger idea, frankly, was the premise that the automakers would sell off the car-rental companies to entrepreneurs. There was a lot of faith in this deal. Faith number one was that even if you could do the financing, if pricing didn't go up, so what? So you had a nonrecourse loan, but you still weren't making any money. There are two elements to every transaction: Can I do this? And should I do this? So, yes, I had solved the Can I do this? But I hadn't solved the Should I do this? And the should part was based on the premise that the industry would go from nonstrategic owners to entrepreneurs, and then that the entrepreneurs would be intelligent enough to follow us in raising prices. That was the bigger gamble, and it's been clearly validated.

Question: *You talk about car-rental prices rising. That's bad news for consumers. How long and how far will this trend go?*

Answer: Prices are up 5 percent to 10 percent from last year, and I think that will continue because we are still so far below an effective return on the investment in the cars. So I think we have many years of price increases coming. It may be 4 percent one year and 12 percent the next. But it will average more than inflation, forever.

Question: *What do you see as your place in the business world? What is it that you do that makes you successful and different?*

Answer: First, I only want to be in service businesses. You'll never see us buying a company that manufactures a product in a factory. That is definitely not a business that we're ever going to be in. We have no comparative advantages in that kind of business. And you'll never see us in technology. Basically we want to be service businesses where we can compete by being smarter and have better intellectual capital than somebody else. Not financial capital but intellectual capital.

Within the service sector, I look for businesses where I can change the way they are doing business and hopefully change it for the positive. So I guess if I had to characterize it, I would say that I'm an agent of change. That's what we are. And when you change or transform an industry, you will make incredible returns.

Question: Agent of change *is a term that might apply to a corporate raider?*
Answer: I suppose. But this is not about taking the costs out, which is really what we all did in the 1980s. You only take costs out once. You can't do it every year. You have to figure out how to grow revenue in year two, and growing revenues is really where you come up with various enhancements like cross-marketing. We've done a lot of things in this company that no one has ever done before.

Question: *Why did you become a deal maker?*
Answer: Well, I think I'm really more of a manager than a deal maker, but I've done both. In a profile on me in *Fortune* magazine, they said that I know a lot more about Wall Street than most CEOs and a lot more about managing a business than most guys on Wall Street. And I think that's true. I started out life as a lawyer, investment banker, and LBO guy. So I come from a financial discipline side. The management came later, but it's really both now. You know, it's very challenging to acquire a company, integrate it, and run it more efficiently than it was run before. This is what I do. I can't paint or sculpt. I'm not Picasso. So this is a way for me to exercise the creative energy that I have.

Question: *Is it the deal or making it work that most invigorates you?*
Answer: I tell the young men and women who work for me that there is nothing more ego-gratifying than buying a com-

pany with somebody else's money. But guess what? It's the shareholders' money, and that means a lot of it is mine. So I'm well past the ego gratification point. Now when people congratulate me on the latest transaction, I always tell them to congratulate me when we've executed the business plan. Meaning that any dope with a fountain pen can buy a business. It's what they do afterward that counts.

Question: *When would you say that you realized you're pretty good at this?*

Answer: Well, first of all, you're always learning. I don't think I know everything. You're always going to learn more and more as you go forward. So I don't think that a lightbulb went on one day when I was shaving or something and I suddenly said, "Hey, I'm pretty good at this." You know, looked at myself and blew kisses. I don't think that happens at all. I just think it's an accumulation of experience. I've been doing this for thirty-four years, and I think that, assuming your health is good and you don't lose your brain power, you just get a little better, incrementally, each year. It becomes easier to make decisions because you've made them before. Some were lousy, and hopefully you don't repeat them. Some were good. Hopefully you learned from both. Actually, you learn more from the bad decisions than you do from the good ones.

Question: *Was there a specific deal that you felt put you on the map?*

Answer: Well, I've been a very visible executive for twenty-five years. I guess if I had to choose one where people started saying, "Hey, this is interesting, unique," it was when we went from a pure hotel franchiser to franchising other things. Nobody had ever created a pure franchise company. So when we said we were going franchise outside the box of hotels and made it successful, that would have been the moment. And that was probably when we bought Century 21 in 1995.

Question: *What is the deal that got away?*

Answer: There were many. But, you know, some of the best deals are the ones you didn't do. We were convinced, for example, that we needed a second brand in rental cars to go along with Avis. We've always done multiple brands, in hotels, real estate, and so forth. We worked on both Alamo and National Car. But at the end of the day, I felt they were overpriced. Both ended up being purchased by my pal Wayne Huizenga. We also passed on Value Rent-A-Car, which Wayne bought. He bought everything that we didn't.

Question: *How about deals that you wish you had done but for some reason didn't?*

Answer: Well, I'll tell you a story. The most I ever learned was from a deal that got away. It was my very first transaction as a principal. I was buying a company in upstate New York back in the early 1970s. It was in the catalog-showroom business, like a Service Merchandise or Best Buy. It had a great little niche in Buffalo, Rochester, Syracuse. I had worked out the entire transaction with the sellers, but I didn't have the money. I would have to raise the money to do this, and I told them that. I was brought up to always tell the truth, and I do. But they looked at me and said, "What do you mean you don't have the money?" And I said, "Well, that's the way these bootstrap deals work. You make the deal, and then you go around and get the money." And they said "Uh-uh, we don't give free options to anybody. We're going to sell this business to somebody who has the money," and they did. It broke my heart.

Question: *What was it that you learned from that experience?*

Answer: There was a second episode just like that one about six months later. In an excess of honesty, I told them that I would have to go out and raise the money, and they said, "Have a good life." And what I learned from those experiences is that honesty is a great virtue, but not having the money to do a deal is not something you need to tell anybody. Yes, if someone would ask me, I'd tell them, but from then on I would never volunteer it. And you know what? No one ever asked me the question. Sellers will assume you have the capital to execute the transaction. You don't have to say a thing. That was a valuable lesson to learn as a young whippersnapper.

chapter ten

Sumner Redstone

The Vision Thing

NEGOTIATE. SPEND ANY TIME AT ALL AROUND people who cut deals for a living, and you'll hear that word, oh, about every other sentence. You'll also gain a keen appreciation for what it really means. The dictionary says: "To deal or bargain with another, as in the preparation of a treaty or contract." But that doesn't begin to capture the flavor of the word on Wall Street, where a deal maker's definition might go something like this: "To beat, pummel, and trample, otherwise coerce, trump, outlast, and outwit, frustrate, or aggravate into submission, any foe, with the express intent of persuading that foe to put his wealth in your name." That's really what this deal thing is all about. Putting his wealth in your name. Getting the other guy to give more than he wanted. It's called winning, and nobody plays to lose. Negotiating skills often make the difference. They are a part of every deal maker's arsenal, and the great ones have them to spare.

Effective negotiating skills are difficult to define or describe. They come in infinite variety and may be unique to a certain personality. But one thing is certain: You know them when you see them. When Carl Icahn tells a precariously financed newspaper publisher, before an interview, that he's been buying his bonds—that's negotiating without peer. Icahn, as I pointed out in chapter 1, is one of the best. He's relentless and almost brutish. Sumner Redstone, on the other hand, is more refined but no less persistent and effective. Like Hugh McColl, the tireless banker, Redstone thinks nothing of keeping the parties in a deal locked up in a room for hours, wearing them down until they reach terms. Because of his mastery of the art of give and take, his chain of movie theaters today buys films cheaper than any company in the world. In 1998, he sold book publisher Simon & Schuster for $4.6 billion—a mere $600 million more than most observers thought it was worth. He also negotiated a dreamy deal to unload Madison Square Garden for $1.1 billion—about $400 million more than expected. "Deal making *is* negotiating," Redstone said. "I consider it a critical skill. A lot of it is natural, although law school for me, and being president of the debating club, helped a great deal. I feel that being a good negotiator gives me a competitive edge."

In his long career, Redstone has had plenty of opportunities to hone his negotiating talents. He has inked literally hundreds of transactions, starting with his theater-by-theater expansion in the 1950s and 1960s to his knockout mega-deals in the 1990s for Wayne Huizenga's Blockbuster Entertainment ($8 billion) and then Martin Davis's Paramount Communications ($10 billion). He calls Paramount "the deal of the century." He bought the company in 1994, attracted by its filmmaking capacity and deep film library. But Paramount came with a treasure chest of assets, many of which Redstone later sold—among them Madison Square Garden and Simon & Schuster. By mid-1998, he had recovered nearly the full $10 billion purchase price and still owned the movie studio and film library, assets that probably have a value of $3 billion to $4 billion. It's the same kind of home run that Henry Silverman hit with Avis, when he sold assets to recover most of his acquisition costs and was still left with a $2 billion piece of the action—the piece that he most wanted from the start.

Given all that, I was surprised that Redstone chose to talk to me about another deal, one from a few years earlier, his 1987 acquisition of the cable company Viacom. The truth is that Redstone talked a lot about Paramount anyway. It was as if he couldn't help himself. Having just sold the last of the noncore Paramount assets, he was in the mood to crow. And why not? The deal was a huge winner, made especially sweet by the fact that legions of doubters had gagged over the hefty price tag. It put Redstone in the camp with Teddy Forstmann, Hugh McColl, and Henry Silverman. He'd rather overpay for a good business than underpay for a bad one. Redstone has been criticized often in his career for overpaying. But the deals keep on working. In the Paramount case, even Redstone concedes that he paid $2 billion more than he wanted, driven there during a long and acrimonious bidding war against his onetime friend Barry Diller. The three years following the deal, Viacom's stock barely budged. By early 1998, though, the stock was moving. The market's fears had been eradicated; Redstone was vindicated.

Sometimes, Redstone noted, it's the little deal that sets up the big deal that makes everything possible. And in that framework, his $3.4 billion (not so little, really) acquisition of Viacom rates as his greatest deal ever. "Without Viacom, there would be no Paramount," Redstone said flatly. And to be sure, the Viacom deal was no slam dunk. Redstone showed dogged determination in raising his bid four times against a management team with the inside track, a group that raised its bid six times. At the time, Redstone was a wealthy but relatively unknown investor from Boston. He had built a four-hundred-screen movie-theater miniempire called National Amusements. He also had success speculating in Hollywood stocks. At various times he owned 5 percent of 20th Century Fox, 10 percent of Columbia Pictures, 8 percent of MGM/UA Home Entertainment, and a small stake in Orion Pictures. All in all, he made about $65 million on those deals. But he never went all the way and bought a big company.

Viacom would change that. It would capture his soul and lead him to risk virtually all the assets of National Amusements in his quest to own the company—which, once won, would vault him into the major leagues of deal making. In targeting Viacom, Redstone displayed uncanny vision as to how the media and entertainment industry would evolve. Wall Street was valuing the company on the basis of its hard assets—its cable systems wired to 840,000 households and its TV and radio stations. But Redstone, who cut his teeth in the movie-theater business, knew how scarce really good programming was and that the demand for good programming would only grow as technology made home entertainment more accessible. Viacom had syndication rights to such hits at *The Honeymooners* and *The Cosby Show*. More important, it had two pay-TV channels and the fledgling MTV and Nickelodeon channels. Those channels were barely on the map at the time, but they were what caught his eye. He had more than an inkling that they would become critical, and time has proved him correct. Today, the MTV networks alone are in more than 300 million households in eight-five countries and generate $1.5 billion in annual revenue. That part of Viacom, by itself, justifies the price that Redstone paid for the entire company.

The first time I met Sumner Redstone was in the fall of 1993 while I was attending a high-profile charity event in Washington, D.C. The Paramount drama was well under way by then, and Redstone's rival, Barry Diller, was also attending. Clearly, the two had committed to being there long before they locked horns over Paramount—or one or the other would have declined. The ugly battle over Paramount had so strained their relationship that being in the same place at the same time was a Chinese water torture for both. So neither stayed long. But I'll never forget how they each moved about the giant ballroom in separate places, hordes of scrambling journalists tagging along. They reminded me of a pair of tornadoes bouncing through the same trailer park, their blustery force naturally repelling one another so that they never hit the same spot together. I got only a handshake and a nod that night. My distinct impression, though, was that Sumner Redstone, a late bloomer on the national business stage, was relishing his time in the spotlight. Or maybe he just knew that he was going to win.

Since then, I've had only limited dealings with Redstone. In 1998, I interviewed him in his office for a story for *Time* magazine about the turnaround at the video rental-king Blockbuster, which suffered declining same-store revenue in 1997. For this book, we met in that same office—on the fifty-second floor of Viacom's world headquarters near

Times Square. Redstone has a stunning panoramic view of the Hudson River and lower Manhattan. His palatial quarters are decorated with dozens of family photos, including those of two grown children (both lawyers) and five grandchildren who know him as "Grumpy," as well as photos of him with various politicians and movie stars, such as Paul Newman, Gregory Peck, Julie Andrews, and Harry Truman. Redstone, who will turn eighty in 2003, was soft-spoken, gracious, and generous with his time as we spoke one hot and muggy late-June early afternoon. That's when I heard all about the Viacom saga—with a dose of Paramount thrown in.

"IF YOU WANT A LOUSY MEAL, ORDER FOR YOURSELF"

Sumner Murray Redstone was born on May 27, 1923, in a tenement on Boston's West End, a low-income neighborhood razed in the 1950s urban renewal push. He and his younger brother, Edward, were the two children of Michael Rothstein and Belle Ostrovsky, both of whom had emigrated to Boston from Germany. His father, who changed the family name, started out as a linoleum salesman from the back of a truck, then went into liquor sales and eventually owned two nightclubs before, in the 1930s, opening one of the first drive-in theaters in the United States, founding what would become National Amusements. His first big-screen theater was the Valley Stream Drive-in on Sunrise Highway on New York's Long Island. Area college students used to work their way through school there, hawking their wares at a flea market on the drive-in lot during weekend daylight hours. Redstone's father later bought several more drive-ins, and that's about where the company stood when Sumner joined the family business in the 1950s.

Young Redstone was an inspired student. His father had felt that everything in life came tough, and he prepared his boys to meet that challenge. They were raised in a strict but loving household, one in which the homework always got done. Sumner made it into the famous Boston Latin School, one of the country's toughest high schools. The school accepts only the cream of Boston's students and then flunks half of them out. But Redstone soared while he was there, graduating at the top of his class in 1940. From there, Redstone said, Harvard seemed like kindergarten, and he graduated in just two and a half years. He was then chosen for an elite intelligence team that broke Japanese military codes during World War II. Redstone earned two army commendations for his work.

After the war, Redstone enrolled in Harvard Law School, which he helped pay for by buying and selling pots and pans that the army and navy were no longer using. At Harvard, his memorable teachers included Archibald Cox and Dean Erwin Griswold, who later recalled giving Redstone the only A in his tax class. Redstone worked in the law for seven years, as a law secretary for the U.S. Court of Appeals, as a special assistant to the U.S. attorney general, and then in private practice as a partner in the Washington, D.C., law firm Ford, Bergson Adams, Borkland & Redstone. In 1954, though, he returned to the family business to help his father and brother Edward. Redstone took charge quickly even though he was not named president until 1967. His brother left the company in 1972. In the early years at his father's company, Redstone transformed it from a sleepy mom-and-pop drive-in-theater chain to a growing company with 250 indoor movie houses. The number would reach 400 by the time Redstone bought Viacom in 1987 and some 1,200 in the 1990s. Redstone helped invent the "multiplex" theater grouping of a dozen or more and owns a trademark on the name. Unlike a lot of theater chains that are built on leased ground, Redstone always bought the land under his theaters, and as real estate values soared in the 1970s and 1980s, all that land developed into a vital, strong asset base for his company, National Amusements, which was based in Dedham, Massachusetts.

Through it all, Redstone, who now has a personal net worth of $6.4 billion, has maintained a quaint, frugal lifestyle. He still lives in the modest three-bedroom house he bought in Newton, Massachusetts, in the 1950s, though he spends most of his time now in New York City, where he keeps a suite on the thirty-second floor of the Carlyle Hotel. Redstone is comfortable being in charge. He regularly advises his lawyers on the law. At restaurants he's been known to order for others and, if rebuffed, throws up his hands and says, "OK. If you want a lousy meal, you can order for yourself."

One of the defining moments in his life occurred in Boston's Copley Plaza in 1979. He was staying there when the hotel went up in flames. Redstone survived by climbing onto a third-story window ledge and hanging on with just his right hand while searing flames shot through the window. More than 40 percent of his body was burned. He was supposed to die. But after sixty hours of painful skin grafts he was still ticking. Today, his right hand is badly mangled—its tendons gone, its pinky finger cut off at the first joint. Redstone, who loves to play tennis, has to strap his racket to a glove because of the old injury. The fire story is probably the one most often told of Redstone. Journalists have written, for example, that it was a sign of his tenacity, which carries over into his business dealings. He is tenacious, for sure. But Redstone plays down any conclusions drawn from surviving the fire. He was fighting for his life, he says. It's that simple and it's something anyone would have done in that situation.

THE PEASANT FROM BOSTON

Redstone's earliest recollection of Viacom was in late 1985, when, drawn by the company's unusual set of assets, he began to nibble at its stock with no intention other than to own it as an investment. Then, in 1986, Carl Icahn amassed a 17 percent interest in the company and unofficially kicked off what would become a classic bid-'em-up 1980s-style corporate free-for-all. Redstone had built National Amusements into a big theater chain. "But I recognized that the real growth was not in movie exhibition," Redstone said. "Exhibition is still a good business. But the number of people that go to movies today is not that much different than it was twenty or thirty years ago. And I saw, without really understanding the assets of Viacom, that it was a sleeping giant. I could see that the businesses they were in were cutting-edge as far as growth for the future."

In those days, Viacom was principally an operator of cable systems with five TV and eight radio stations and a handful of shows and movies that it syndicated. It had been spun off by CBS in 1971, when the Federal Communications Commission ruled that the networks could not syndicate their own programming. In 1985, Viacom purchased the fledgling MTV and Nickelodeon channels from Warner Communications for about $500 million. It was a steal that would not become apparent for years. Icahn and most of Wall Street focused on the hard assets, the cable systems. But running a theater chain gave Redstone an unusual vantage point. He realized how tough it was to get good movies in his houses and keep filling their seats. So, somewhat ahead of his time, Redstone was more taken by the potential for MTV and Nickelodeon and other programming assets like Lifetime, Showtime, and the Movie Channel, which Viacom also owned. He was one of the original "content" visionaries, believing that the suppliers of programming would one day become more valuable in the market than the companies that delivered the programs over their wires. That vision is what led him to buy Paramount a few years later in another hotly contested bidding war. Adding a movie studio would let Redstone expand on the programming assets he was buying with Viacom.

Visions of content as king were with Redstone when Icahn announced in May 1986 that he had acquired 17 percent of Viacom and offered to pay $1.5 billion for the entire company. Wall Street was highly suspicious of Icahn. The raider had pulled this kind of stunt before, and most believed that he really just wanted to be paid to go away. Still, Viacom's board couldn't afford to sit on its hands. It began building takeover defenses, one of which was filing for a debt offering that included highly restrictive covenants limiting its ability to issue more debt or to sell assets. Those covenants had the effect of making the company more difficult to buy on borrowed money, which was the model for takeovers of the day. Viacom also registered the sale of additional shares and warrants in a manner that would greatly dilute Icahn's stake. That spring, Viacom's board also sounded out prospective "White Knights," or friendly investors who, if asked, would buy the company just to keep Icahn from getting it. Hallmark Cards was one company that had been approached. So was Shamrock Holdings, the investment concern owned by Roy E. Disney. The White Knight search also took the board to Dedham, Massachusetts, where it thought that National Amusements, run by Sumner Redstone, might have an interest.

It did, of course. Redstone began adding shares in small amounts in the spring and summer of 1986. At that time, he had no real designs on buying the company outright. Like everybody else, Redstone figured that Icahn would be bought out and that no White Knight would ever be needed. But he liked the assets and thought the stock was a good long-term bet. It was the same kind of play he had made in other media stocks, including Columbia Pictures and Fox. In fact, Viacom did buy out Icahn in June 1986. To get back the 17 percent stake that Icahn had collected, Viacom paid the raider $220 million and gave him $10 million of commercial airtime on its channels, and stock warrants on 5 million Viacom shares valued at about $30 million. Redstone kept buying, though. By July 1986, he had bought 6.4 percent of Viacom, and by early September, he had raised his stake to 8.7 percent.

On September 16, the Viacom managers dropped a bombshell. With Icahn only recently gone and this Boston man named Redstone lapping up every available share, the managers, led by CEO Terrence A. Elkes, proposed to buy the company themselves. They were willing to pay $37 a share in cash and another $3.50 in preferred stock for a total bid of $40.50—a $5-a-share premium over the stock's latest closing price and a total of $2.7 billion, including the assumption of $500 million in debt. Redstone wasn't happy. "I didn't intend to be a minority investor in somebody else's company," he recalled. "That wasn't the way I did things. And I was turned off by what they offered for the company and the kind of financial structure they were going to have. It would have meant that they'd have to liquidate the company, sell its best pieces. There was no way they could have operated Viacom the way they had proposed. That's really the moment I started thinking that I'd be more than a passive investor."

Redstone said that he felt compelled to act because this company, which he saw as a diamond in the rough, would have been taken apart under the management proposal. He had the option of selling his stock at a huge gain by then. But he also had his theory about the value of good programming, and increasingly he was falling in love with the way Viacom fit into the big picture. The multiplex concept that he pioneered had boosted the theater business for a while in the 1970s. "But when you get all done with it, what really mattered was what was on those screens," Redstone recalled. No. He would not stand back and simply make a buck. "Them going for the company was the biggest favor anybody did for me," Redstone said. "If they hadn't done it, who knows what would have happened. But when they went for it is really when they lost the company." Within days, Redstone went back into the market and bought more shares, taking his stake up to 9.9 percent.

Sumner wasn't the only investor who was thinking about Viacom. The Capital Group, a Los Angeles-based passive-investment firm whose media investments are run by the influential Gordon Crawford, had built a 9.6 percent stake. The investing triumvirate known as Coniston Partners—Keith Gollust, Augustus Oliver, and Paul Tierney—was hanging around with a 12.4 percent position. The well-known media analyst Paul Kagan put out a report saying that the company's breakup value was a full $10 a share higher than the management bid. That report set the "fair" price at $51 a share, underscoring the rapidly increasing value of broadcast and cable properties on Wall Street in the mid-1980s. There were rumors that Coca-Cola would make a bid of $45 and that Warner Communications was interested as well. Put it all together, and it wasn't tough to figure that Viacom would not be bought on the first bid. The price in the market had already shot past the management bid. There was no mistaking the tea leaves: Wall Street was preparing for a shoot-out. Nothing unusual there. By fall of 1986, bidding wars were so common you almost failed to notice them. That year was smack in the middle of the 1980s merger mania, and it was a busier year for takeovers than any before it. Some $228 billion in deals were announced. That figure would be eclipsed in 1988, and there'd be another record in 1989, but then the trend would melt, along with the junk-bond market, in the fall of 1989.

Although Redstone was fast concluding that he would bid for the company, he relished being "that peasant from Boston," whom not a great deal was known about and who few believed would really go after Viacom. "Not to be arrogant," Redstone said. "But they totally underestimated us. Management didn't take us seriously at all, and even the analysts were telling everybody that we were just in it to sell." With that kind of natural cover, Redstone was able to keep his poker face. On September 30, 1986, he applied to the Federal Trade Commission and U.S. Department of Justice for permission to buy up to 25 percent of Viacom and said that he might acquire additional shares. Still, few took him seriously. Asking for permission to buy more stock is required before you take that action, but there is no requirement that you follow through. Therefore, it can be a cheap way to keep heat on a company. That's the play traders thought Redstone was making in an effort to raise the stock price and sell out at a fat profit.

PARTNERS, WHO NEEDS 'EM?

Such interpretations finally began to crack a week later when, on October 7, Redstone reached an agreement to buy 2.9 million shares of the Coniston block for $43 each, giving him 18.4 percent of Viacom and making him the largest single shareholder in the company. "That was really a critical point," Redstone said. "I remember it very well. I went to meet with the Coniston partners, and things went fairly smoothly. They said to me,'Look, you're in this for the company; we're in it for the money, so let's make a deal.'" And they did. "At that point," Redstone continued, "I remember feeling like we were a real contender; people were saying, yeah, they are for real. And remember that management had very little stock, and we had this big position. It just gave us such an edge."

The same day that Redstone announced his new ownership level, he got another boost. The Viacom board, which had already rejected as inadequate management's initial bid of $40.50 a share, rejected a sweetened bid of $44 ($35 in cash and $9 in preferred stock). Viacom's outside directors, who held eight of twelve board seats, made up the "special committee" in charge of ensuring that any takeover was done at the best price possible. The group had hired venerable Goldman Sachs & Co. to render a fairness opinion, and that opinion stated simply that the bid was "outside the range of fairness." Redstone would later clash with the committee, which he calls the "nonspecial" committee, accusing its members of tipping off management to his offers. But for the moment, this nonspecial committee was doing him a favor. The rejection of the management's bid was a slap that suggested that management was trying to get the company on the cheap. The committee was practically advertising for someone to step up with a better bid.

The rejection of the management bid worked for Redstone in another way, too: It delayed an approval process that typically takes several months and in so doing precluded the deal from closing by the year's end. That's important because Viacom's managers had planned to sell assets to finance their takeover, and certain tax advantages would be severely curtailed after the end of 1986, a year of tax reform. The diminished benefits of future asset sales probably kept management from bidding more in the end. Management had another problem as well. It misapplied with the FCC for the transfer of broadcast licenses, a further delay that promised to push any deal into the new year. And to make matters worse, that fall an insider-trading scandal broke on Wall Street. Arbitrageur Ivan Boesky and investment bankers Marty Seigel and Dennis Levine and others were accused of tipping one another off to takeover bids, sometimes exchanging suitcases of cash in dark alleys for information. Drexel Burnham Lambert, the powerhouse junk-bond firm that was financing the management bid, was at the center of the scandal. It cast a cloud over that bid.

The board's move worked. It got another bid, all right—from

Viacom management. On October 16, the management sweetened its offer a second time. The price was still $44 a share. But the cash portion in this third bid was hiked by $2 to $37, and the new bid contained an unusual provision to give back 20 percent of the company to the selling shareholders after the deal was completed. In essence, management was now bidding for 80 percent of the company, not 100 percent. That amounted to a significantly higher bid and came with a financing package backed by an elite Wall Street group, including such blue-chip firms as Donaldson Lufkin & Jenrette, First Boston, and the Equitable, as well as Drexel. The board swiftly accepted it.

Sensing that his moment might soon pass, Redstone hurriedly met with the nonspecial committee the same day. He was told that the board was no longer soliciting offers. But three days later, on a Monday, Redstone made it clear that he would not resign from the battle, which hadn't even really begun. He announced that he was considering a competing bid and that he might take on one or more partners to put together a superior financing package. The rumored partners included Disney, Time, Coca-Cola, Gulf & Western, and MCA. Redstone met with cable-industry executive Charles Dolan, but nothing came of it. He also began initial inquiries into financing. He was determined to do the deal without junk bonds—a determination that he thought would give him an edge with the board in the scandal-filled environment. It would also keep his interest costs down. So he spent months lining up banks, and all the while Wall Street waited eagerly and wondered. A month later, Redstone still had not bid, but on December 3, 1986, he disclosed that he had bought more stock and now owned 19.6 percent of the company and that he was seeking regulatory permission to buy up to 49.9 percent.

One reason for the inaction was that Viacom represented a huge acquisition for Redstone. He was already sixty-three, an age that has many men thinking about a daily round of golf in Florida. Redstone was not cut out for timely retirement, though, and was looking to make a big splash on the national scene. Everything in his bones told him that Viacom was the company, and now was the time. But topping management's $3 billion bid would require bold steps and basically require that he mortgage National Amusements to get it done. Even for a wheeler-dealer like Redstone, such a gamble had to be weighed carefully. Today, Redstone says he'd never risk his company like that again—in pursuit of a single acquisition. Back then, though, National Amusements was a private company, and he didn't have the fiduciary duty that he now has to public stockholders. Back then, too, he still needed a monster deal to put him on the map.

There was also the question of partners. Redstone thought that it might make sense to spread the risk around by taking on equity partners. Partners, of course, would limit his upside as well, of which he felt there was plenty. Not sure how to proceed in the latter days of 1986, he decided to seek the counsel of a businessman and superstar deal maker in his own right, Laurence Tisch, who runs Loew's Corp. and at the time had just taken over the CBS network. On a visit to California, Redstone found Tisch in the lobby of a Beverly Hills hotel. A lot of people had compared Redstone to Tisch in the early phases of the Viacom battle, pointing to the fact that Redstone had acquired a large stake and was willing to run the business if he managed to buy it. "Listen, Sumner, what you don't want is partners," Tisch advised. "You've been running your own show too long to take on partners. Just get the company."

"MEET ONCE MORE AND END IT"

The words of the wily Tisch rang instantly true, and Redstone drove any notion of sharing the risks—or the rewards—of Viacom from his mind forever. And he moved forward. On February 2, 1987, he launched a competing bid. It was for the 80.4 percent of Viacom that he did not already own and totaled $44.75 a share—topping management's bid by 75 cents. Redstone had set up a separate subsidiary to make the purchase, called Arsenal Holdings. His offer included more cash ($37.50 as opposed to $37) and more preferred stock ($7.25 as opposed to $7). Like the management's offer, he proposed to kick back 20 percent of the new company to existing shareholders. But in a slick move, he proposed to capitalize the new company with more equity than management and bank debt instead of more expensive junk bonds. If his nominally higher offer didn't sway the board, then maybe his superior financing package would.

Certainly, Wall Street noticed. Traders who specialized in takeover stocks, so-called arbitrageurs, figured that the 20 percent kickback in Redstone's new Viacom was worth $4.50 a share (making the bid worth $49.25), while a similar stake in the new Viacom that the managers proposed was worth only $3 a share (making their bid worth $47). The main reason for the difference was that Redstone proposed putting in $400 million of equity—an enormous sum for his National Amusements, but one that gave him a clear edge over the thin $81 million equity proposed by management. Meanwhile, the thinking on Wall Street was that the bank debt, instead of junk bonds, would lower Viacom's interest bill by tens of millions of dollars every year—enough to make it a sounder company, which, in turn, would mean that the preferred stock being offered as part of the takeover package might be more secure and thus trade higher.

Redstone believed that he had them one-upped at every turn, and he made sure the board knew it. He also chided the board for being duped into accepting the management's lowball offer in the first place. In a strongly worded letter to Allan R. Johnson, chairman of the special committee, he wrote, "As you know, National Amusements began investing in Viacom shares more than a year ago in the belief that such shares would be a sound long-term investment. Unfortunately, National Amusements' desire to remain as a long-term investor in an independent Viacom, which we believe would have been in the interest of all shareholders, was frustrated by your management's attempt to acquire Viacom itself. This attempt was made notwithstanding the fact that your chief executive officer, a major participant in the management buyout group, previously was quoted as saying that Viacom is 'not interested in being taken over and would fiercely resist it.' Evidently, that meant only that Viacom management was committed to frustrate any takeover of the company except one undertaken by the management of the company."

Redstone was baiting the board and recognized that his inflammatory remarks might alienate the members and shove them deeper down the pockets of the management. But he couldn't help himself. He accused the board of "breach of fiduciary duty" by adopting takeover defenses that entrenched the management. He criticized its buyout of the Icahn stake nearly a year earlier as setting the precedent for paying "greenmail," so called because it was akin to blackmail—benefiting one shareholder at the expense of others. Finally, he took issue with the board's agreeing to "break-up" fees of $30 million in the merger agreement with management. That was the sum it would have to pay the managers if their deal did not go through for some reason. It was "almost as much as Viacom had earned in any year in its history," Redstone wrote in the letter.

It was not the last time he would clash with the board. In the coming month, an all-out bidding war would erupt, and Redstone would accuse the board of tipping his bids to management so it could quickly counter them. "That special committee was as married to management as if they had been part of the team," Redstone recalled. "It was just nonsense. They kept tipping management to our bids. Finally, I had to have a conversation with Allan Johnson about it. I mean, my lawyers and our bankers were not too excited about what I did. But I called Johnson and told him, 'Allan, I just want you to know that there is not enough money in the world to protect you and your associates from the claims that I'm going to bring against you for breaching your fiduciary duty." It was classic Redstone. Not only was he acting against the wishes of his highly paid advisers, heeding only his own instincts, but he was threatening litigation, which is one of his famous calling cards. The thing about being litigious, though, is that people take you seriously if they think you have a point, and from then on the special committee kept everything on the up-and-up.

That showdown was still a month away, however, and in the hours following his initial bid, Redstone didn't see it coming. He was confident that he would prevail. He had the higher offer, more cash, and better financing. He just could not imagine any grounds for the board to reject his bid. But the first sign of trouble came soon. Management started openly questioning how long it would take Redstone to get regulatory approvals to take control of Viacom's five TV channels and eight radio stations. It was already well on its way to getting the needed nod from the Federal Communications Commission. Redstone would have to start fresh, and the process could delay his acquisition by months. Redstone quickly countered that he could always put the broadcast properties into a trust, pending the needed approvals. But it was too late. The board had found the chink in his armor that Redstone believes it so wanted to uncover. On February 10, citing the possibility of costly delays, the board rejected his bid and said it would stick with management's.

Redstone was devastated. He had many options, of course. The stock he had accumulated was worth far more than he had paid. He could have accepted defeat and walked away tens of millions of dollars better off. But he was serious about programming being the key to the future of broadcast entertainment, and he couldn't bear to lose a company that he thought was well positioned to serve as a base for building a world-class entertainment company. By February 17, he had persuaded the committee to open Viacom's books so that he, the largest shareholder, could better evaluate the management bid that had the board's blessing. Redstone agreed not to buy any more Viacom shares unless he did so through a tender offer for at least 50 percent of the outstanding shares.

On February 23, Redstone delivered a new bid. This one raised the cash portion from $37.50 to $40.50 a share and included $6 of preferred stock. At $46.50 a share, it was $1.75 over his initial bid, and when you figured in the 20 percent equity stake that current shareholders would retain, the value came to about $51 a share. More important, though, Redstone defused the timing issue. In a letter to committee chairman Allan Johnson, he emphasized that he was on track for all needed regulatory approvals and could close the deal by April 30. Furthermore, he said that if he could not close by that date, he would begin accruing interest to all shareholders at a rate of 8 percent per year based on the $40.50 per share in cash that he was offering. He demanded a response by February 25.

But no response came, and Redstone worried that the managers and the board were cozying up to one another again. Sure enough, on February 26, management came out with a new bid that was increased about as much as Redstone had increased his bid. It would pay $38.50 in cash, up from $37, and $8 in preferred stock, up from $7. That and the remaining 20 percent interest to be held over by the shareholders were valued at about $49 a share. It was less than Redstone's offer, but because management already had a merger agreement that would cost the company $30 million if it was broken, it was necessary for Redstone to have a decisively better bid if he was going to prevail. So on March 2, Redstone again raised his bid—upping the cash portion to $42 and the preferred stock to $7.50. Management countered with a 50-cent hike in its offer, an increase in the preferred-stock portion of the financing package. The 50-cent hike sent Redstone through the roof. Even before that bid, he had become certain that the board was tipping management to his bids. He said as much in a letter to the special committee on March 2.

"We would like to make a few observations about the process that has been followed by the special committee, even though this letter is not the proper forum to express our views fully," Redstone wrote to the chairman, Allan Johnson. "There is something inherently wrong in a process which involves delaying a third-party bidder, particularly a major shareholder in the company, in order to give the company's management the opportunity to learn the contents of the offer and to respond not by making a superior offer but rather an inferior offer. Were it not for our perseverance in the face of almost every management entrenchment device devised to date, the members of management would have bought the company for themselves at a significantly lower price than that currently offered.

"After expressly representing that it was making its 'final' offer on Feb. 26, the management increased its offer after being given sufficient time to learn the contents of our offer. Even then, the management made a competing offer that had a lower value than ours. The management must have the sense that it need not have the best offer in order to win."

When the management trumped his new bid that very day with its own 50-cent raise, Redstone called Johnson and threatened to sue him and the entire committee. "Evidently," Redstone said, "he must have felt uncomfortable with what he had been doing because he said to me, 'What do you want us to do?'" Redstone asked the board to meet one more time to consider both bids and then end it.

THE AMAZING VALUE OF STOCK WARRANTS

The meeting was held just a day later, on March 3. It lasted all night and entailed eleventh-hour bids from both sides. The management ultimately would offer to kick back as much as 45 percent of the new company to the existing shareholders. But it just didn't have the flexibility it needed to raise the all-important cash part of the bid, and at 4 A.M. on March 4, the board finally endorsed Redstone's takeover proposal. That proposal had grown to $42.75 a share in cash, $7.75 in preferred stock, and a 20 percent kickback in the newly formed acquiring company. An exhausted but energized Redstone joked: "This could add ten years to my life," and it probably did. Even then, Redstone said he heard people sniping behind his back about his age: "Who's this sixty-three-year-old guy? He should be just taking it easy somewhere, having a good time." What they didn't know then and what is still true today is that this *was* Redstone's idea of having a good time, and it has kept him young of mind. The merger agreement was signed at 6:30 A.M. It valued Viacom at $3.4 billion and required Redstone to put in $130 million in cash. That amount, plus the nearly 20 percent of

Viacom that he already owned, brought his equity in the deal to $500 million. He got $2.3 billion from bank loans, $175 million in deferred interest debentures from Merrill Lynch, and $400 million from the sale of options and warrants of Viacom stock kicked back to the old shareholders, who retained a 20 percent stake in the company. Because Redstone was a 20 percent owner before the deal, his part of the kickback provision brought his ownership to 84 percent, leaving 16 percent in the hands of public shareholders.

In the weeks following the March 4 agreement, Redstone remained focused on closing the deal within sixty days so as not to trigger the interest payments that he had pledged as part of the merger agreement. In early April, Tisch's advice notwithstanding, he talked to cable TV executive John Malone at Tele-Communications about an investment in Viacom. When word of that conversation leaked, it fostered a mild panic on Wall Street, which became worried that Redstone was having trouble lining up the bank loans he had been counting on. Among the fears was that he might be forced to reduce personnel and strip the company through asset sales of some of its key properties—exactly what he had promised not to do during the takeover battle. Redstone recalled intense pressure from some of the banks to auction off pieces of the company. "And guess what they wanted me to sell?" Redstone quizzed. "Yeah. MTV. The MTV Networks, which are probably the strongest growth engine in the entire entertainment industry today. Can you believe it? The banks were in a position to sort of force the issue. But I just said no. That's why they're bankers. I mean in the same year that they wanted us to sell MTV, we launched MTV International, which now has well over 300 million subscribers."

On April 28, two months of exhaustive salesmanship finally paid off. Redstone announced that Citibank had committed $600 million in bank loans to go along with a $600 million commitment from BankAmerica. That left only $1 billion to finance, and with the two heavyweight banks on board, there was no longer any doubt that they'd find a syndicate of banks to take on the remaining risk. By then, too, Redstone had almost all the regulatory approvals he would need and was looking forward to the June 3 shareholders' meeting, where the deal was formally ratified.

Like so many successful deals, this one had a slew of winners. Redstone made good on his word not to gut the company, though he eventually sold two cable TV systems to cut his debt load. But the prime assets of Viacom, as he saw them, went untouched, and when he united MTV and Nickelodeon with Paramount Studios in 1994, he created a model entertainment company for the twenty-first century. He's got cable viewers, he owns programming through his syndication and TV production operations, and he has a major film studio. The upshot is that Redstone's company can now make profitable feature films starring, say, the Rugrats (a popular Nickelodeon program) for around $10 million—an amazingly small budget in today's Hollywood. Viacom's shareholders have benefited from his leadership, and the stock has recently taken flight after some rough years. Of course, Redstone was himself a huge winner. The 99 million shares of Viacom that he owns today give him a 28 percent stake in the company (but with 67 percent of the voting shares), good for a net worth of more than $8 billion—up from $500 million when he took over Viacom.

Some curious other winners included the raider Carl Icahn. Not only was Icahn paid a premium price for his 17 percent stake in Viacom in 1986, but as part of his deal to go away, he was given 5 million warrants to buy Viacom shares at $31. In effect, every time Redstone raised his bid for the company by $1 a share, it put $5 million in Icahn's pocket. In all, Icahn's warrants, valued at about $30 million when granted, paid him $110 million. Another warrant holder was Steven J. Ross, then the CEO of Warner Communications. Ross made a habit of insisting on warrants as part of the sale price whenever he departed with a Warner asset. Selling his interest in MTV and Nickelodeon to Viacom in 1985, Ross got, in addition to $500 million,

1.25 million warrants to buy the stock at $37.50 and 3.25 million warrants to buy it at $35. At the time of Redstone's takeover, those were worth $70 million and made for a sweet kicker.

The clear losers were Viacom's top managers, who failed at several turns to lock up the deal and lock out Redstone. Their first two bids were seen as obscenely low by the board, which seemed at least initially to take great pleasure in rejecting them. And when the bidders failed to fill out the correct form for broadcast license transfers, and in so doing pushed the deal into the next calendar year when stiffer tax laws applied, they really shot themselves in the foot. By July 1987—just four months after Redstone bought the company—the top managers were ousted. Redstone installed himself as chairman and hired the respected Coca-Cola executive, Frank J. Biondi, as CEO. Redstone recalled one particularly galling episode with former CEO Terry Elkes, shortly after Redstone won the bid. He met with Elkes, who had led the losing takeover effort on behalf of the management, and was looking to be filled in on some aspect of the company's operations. "I guess Elkes didn't know me very well," Redstone said. "He said to me that there was really no point in my attending the staff meetings. He said, in fact, that it might be better if I didn't. Can you believe that? I had just won the goddamn company. He just didn't see the daylight." Never, ever, tell a man who just paid $3.4 billion and mortgaged his life to do it not to get involved.

By August, Biondi and Redstone had cleaned house; what was left of the old managers had been replaced. Not that they went away poor. Elkes had some 436,000 shares worth $23 million and was given a "golden parachute" worth another $2 million. Other top executives left with pay packages ranging from $2 million to $12 million. But these amounts were nothing next to the value that Redstone has created at Viacom, enriching not just himself but his public shareholders.

Another loser was Coniston Partners. Of course, they made millions when they sold out their position to Redstone at $43 a share. But that was $10 below the eventual price. They left a lot on the table. "They were very smart, very successful people," Redstone said. "But they made a mistake. They should have gone for it."

Here is a series of questions and answers with Sumner Redstone, the tenacious seventy-something negotiator who is a regular viewer of MTV and has a soft spot for *Beavis and Butthead*:

Question: Are there any deals that you wished you had done, but didn't for some reason?

Answer: Not really. The thing we always needed to do from my perspective was acquire a movie studio. And that was a tough one to get done, but, of course, we ended up buying Paramount. We worked for years on that deal. I used to meet with Martin Davis off and on, and he wanted to sell but it never went anywhere. I just think that emotionally he was unequipped to make that deal. I always thought maybe that would be the deal that got away. But it did finally happen, even if it was a struggle.

Question: Given the success of the Paramount deal, what is it that makes Viacom so much more special?

Answer: Well, because Viacom was the start of it all, and what Viacom had, above everything else, was the MTV networks. They were in their incipient stages of growth without a single subscriber overseas. MTV was considered a fad, and the banks wanted us to sell it. But Viacom had what would become the most powerful growth engine in our industry, and I saw its value.

Question: What exactly did you see?

Answer: I can't tell you that I saw how it would ultimately be manifested. But from the first day, I had a vision of creating a giant software company. We didn't have Paramount yet, so I can't say that I saw us making Nickelodeon shows into full-length feature films, as we did with *Rugrats*. But everything that followed was consistent with my vision. People talk about vision all the time, and when something goes wrong, as it did for us for a while with Blockbuster, they say you didn't have vision. But we've had unclouded vision about where we were going from day one. And that was, as I say, to create the preeminent software-driven media company in the world. That was our vision, and I think we are there. It's hard to understand because a lot of what we do is instinctive. That doesn't mean guesswork. It means all your experience in your life going into a computer which is your mind and coming out with, "Yeah, do it." That's not guesswork. It's instinct, and instinctively, I saw that the software of Viacom was going to drive the company.

Question: What's your favorite deal story?

Answer: It was during the Paramount battle. I had gone out to an Italian restaurant in New York, Scalinatella, and there was a big snowstorm. And I'm walking and I step into a snowbank and lose my shoe. Well, you know, New Yorkers get such a bad rap, when they're really very friendly and helpful. All of a sudden, all these people are looking for my shoe. Somebody even runs out and gets a shovel. So finally some guy who was working his ass off finds my shoe and hands it to me. And I said, "You know, I don't know you. Tell me why you've been out here looking for my shoe." And he says, "'Listen,' I just want to make sure you're healthy after you take over Paramount." And what's interesting about that is that it showed that even though we didn't have the press on our side—they were all for Barry Diller—we did have the people. We had the waiters.

Question: Did you ever worry that you were betting the ranch to get Viacom? Did you ever think you wouldn't win?

Answer: No and no. I just knew it was right. And that's not arrogance. I was so strong in my view that this was the thing to do, that it was going to create a whole new world for National Amusements, that I just refused to lose. Now, you might say, was there a limit? Yes. But it was higher than my opponents'. I was in a stronger position than they were, and I knew it, and that was the key.

Question: What did you learn from the Viacom experience?

Answer: This was my first real big deal, and I figured out pretty quickly that I was just a peasant on Wall Street, that I was on my own with my advisers and that they were just looking out for themselves. I'll tell you another story to that point. It was late one night at the Carlyle Hotel, and we were trying to decide how to proceed in the Viacom battle. Well, there's this banker from BankAmerica who just disappears for about two hours right in the middle of this meeting. When he finally showed up, I asked where he had been. His wife had called. She had a flat tire, and he went out to fix it. That's unbelievable. We had all these people here trying to decide if we should spend $3 billion, and he goes to change a tire. I said to him, "You know, there are automobile repair services that you can send to take care of things like that."

Question: Any other stories from the Viacom deal?

Answer: Just one, a little thing. I don't even remember where we were, but it was a meeting where management was trying to bring us into their deal and we weren't interested. So this hotshot banker working for Elkes says, "Listen, for every

move Sumner has, we have an anecdote." It was so funny. I
mean, I'm sure he does have plenty of anecdotes, but what
he meant was antidote. And he didn't have enough of those.

Question: When did you know that you were good at doing deals?

Answer: I don't know that I'd put it that way. Let's just say that I had
a lot of experience. I started with a couple of drive-ins, not
even an indoor theater, and I just started building this chain.
Unlike my competitors, I didn't go into shopping centers on
leases. I did it the hard way. I bought the land and went to
zoning-board and planning-board meetings and built our
theaters. In the course of time, I came to know the film
companies very well and came to negotiate a lot with them.
We used to fight to get first-run films when they were favor-
ing some of the bigger circuits. I did some hard negotiating
and even some litigating. It was a struggle, but I ended up
negotiating some great deals. Those days were like a training ground for me, and I guess sometime around then I realized that I was pretty good at it.

Question: Why did you buy the property instead of leasing?

Answer: That was very important because the real estate was a hedge
against the business itself. And when it appreciated, it gave
us a big asset that other people didn't have.

Question: What is the secret to negotiating a deal?

Answer: First, you have to be articulate, say what you want. Second,
you have to be of very logical and rational mind because
nobody is going to deal with you unless you make sense.
Third, you have to know what you want and go out and get
it. You have to be persistent and not waver, and you cannot
be dissuaded. You have to keep negotiating. When we sold
Simon & Schuster, we did more negotiating after the bids

were in than before. It was big money. We worked with each
bidder to elicit the best price we could. Fortunately, the people we sold to have done well. We got everything we
wanted and they still did well, which is good. That's the
way I like it because we have ongoing relationships and we
may want them to bid again. So the best kind of deal is one
that works out well for both sides, and if there's an edge,
you naturally want it. But you want it to work for both
sides.

Question: *Tell me what kind of opposition you faced when you decided to bid
for Viacom and when it became clear that you were paying a price
that everyone thought was too high?.*

Answer: We bet the ranch, that's for sure. But I could afford to from
one perspective because I didn't have any public shareholders. On the other hand, if I was wrong, it would have sunk
National. But I knew that I was not wrong. I was totally
confident that this enormous risk would pay off. It was
much the same with Paramount. People that I had the greatest respect for would come to a meeting and say, "Look,
Sumner, you know we're not telling you what to do," and
then they'd give me a whole case for not doing it. I said,
"You know, you are making valid arguments. I hear you and
I understand how you feel. But we're going for it." You have
to see that you are right and not be deterred. Even my
father, who I was very close to, told me I was making a mistake in going for Viacom. He said, "Sumner, everything is
going great. You have a great company. You're making
money. Why do it?" He later died before he had a chance to
see the results we've had here. We'd never risk Viacom the
way I risked National. But we still take big risks.

WANTED MAN

WANTED MAN

THE FORGOTTEN STORY OF
AN AMERICAN OUTLAW

TAMSIN SPARGO

BLOOMSBURY

Published by Bloomsbury Publishing, New York and London
Distributed to the trade by Holtzbrinck Publishers

All papers used by Bloomsbury Publishing are natural, recyclable products made from wood grown in well-managed forests. The manufacturing processes conform to the environmental regulations of the country of origin.

Library of Congress Cataloging-in-Publication Data

Spargo, Tamsin.
Wanted man : the forgotten story of an American outlaw / Tamsin Spargo.—1st U.S. ed.
p. cm.
ISBN 1-58234-228-8
1. Perry, Oliver Curtis, 1866–1930. 2. Brigands and robbers—New York (State)—Biography. 3. Train robberies—New York (State)—History—19th century. I. Title.

HV6653.P47S65 2004
364.15′52′092—dc22
[B]
2004050150

First U.S. Edition 2004

1 3 5 7 9 10 8 6 4 2

Typeset by Hewer Text Ltd, Edinburgh
Printed in the United States of America
by Quebecor World Fairfield

CONTENTS

(Reproduced from the collection of the Library of Congress)

I AM STANDING at a photocopier in the Library of Congress, scanning the room. The readers sit hunched over documents, pencil in hand. Nobody is interested in what anyone else is doing. Each is locked into his or her own world and time. There are no briefcases or bags, diaries or mobile phones. The personal clutter that connects us to the outside world has been taken away at the door, to be stowed in a locker until we leave. We may have arrived with a laptop or a leaky ballpoint, but now we each have only a pencil, some lined paper and a numbered locker key. I am number thirty-five.

One of my fellow researchers protested that he felt like a new inmate being admitted to prison. I have to confess that I quite like it. It's liberating and reassuring all at once, almost a return to childhood, or my childhood at least, when someone else held the keys and the purse strings, leaving me free to play. Here you don't have to worry about losing anything except, perhaps, a sense of time.

But today security is on my mind. On the ceiling small video cameras are fixed at regular intervals. I try to work out what areas they cover.

I hope I look calmer than I feel. How do I do this? Do I 'accidentally' drop the photograph on the floor with some other papers, then palm it into my trouser pocket? If I keep close to the photocopier it may work. But what if they search your pockets when you leave?

I didn't check because, when I walked into the library, I had absolutely no intention of stealing. I was a respectable academic on her way to view a newly donated archive. Barely twenty minutes later, I'm contemplating theft and my body is telling me that this isn't idle day-dreaming. My heart is beating fast, my palms are sweating. Then, just as I realize that the clichés are true, I know that I won't do it.

I finish my photocopying, return the documents to the librarian, reclaim my belongings and leave. As I pass through security at the main entrance I notice they don't check pockets.

Half an hour later, I'm sitting in a café, despondent, as if I've failed a test. I hadn't wanted to steal a unique manuscript or even a rare book, just a cheaply produced nineteenth-century tintype photograph. And it probably wouldn't have been missed. There were a dozen others in the folder where I found it. The archive was not yet catalogued, and I had been allowed access as a special favour. Why had I stopped? Was it fear of being caught? Or of what I would do with the photograph if I got away with it?

It wouldn't have been my first theft, although it would only have been my second. As a child I stole an eraser from the village shop as a dare, egged on by bolder girls. It wasn't the eraser I wanted, of course, but their approval. When I got home, I was so racked with guilt that I buried it in the part of the garden we called the wilderness. I felt hot flashes of shame every time I entered the shop, and whenever I saw those girls. I had passed the initiation test, but I would never be part of the 'gang'. Now, although I had never wanted a material object as much as I wanted the photograph, my nerve had failed.

I first saw the photograph in a 1950s coffee-table book about the Wild West. Since childhood, I have had a special relationship with the American West. Like many children who grew up in the 1950s and 1960s, I believed the world of cowboys and indians, ranchers and outlaws was not only real but current. Forty years ago, every other television programme seemed to be a Western, and the world of *The Virginian* appeared every bit as real as the English countryside. It seemed a place of safety, its moral certitudes as snug as its log cabins and wigwams. I moved on to *The High Chaparral*, and later, with my friends, debated the relative charms of Hannibal Heyes and Kid Curry. Our adolescent West was wilder, freer and full of passionate possibilities. Men on horseback rode through our dreams as, we were sure, they would one day ride into our lives.

I had a special connection. The characters from films and television were figures in my own family history, as real to me as my grandparents. And I was sure that I too would one day live in this world of legendary men and women. While my friends tried to gallop bareback and carved 'Pete Duel RIP' into their desks, I dreamed about what I was sure was my own manifest destiny. My father, nearly sixty when I was born, was raised on a farm in Cornwall, but the stories he told me at bedtime transported me to a more alluring family home. In the late nineteenth century, many of the Spargo men had gone west to America to seek their fortune. A cousin found a new life as one of the 'muckrakers', writers who exposed the suffering and corruption beneath the gilded surface of American society. An uncle worked as a carpenter for Buffalo Bill and stayed in the New York hotel run by Colonel Tom Thumb. The kitchen table on which I wrote my homework was made by a man who had built a shooting range for Annie Oakley. My own grandfather worked in a

3

hospital in New York where he met Sitting Bull, before returning to Cornwall to raise cattle and a family.

As I grew up, so did my passion for the West. I rushed to the cinema to see *Butch Cassidy and the Sundance Kid*, *Willie Boy*, even *Little Big Man*, and scanned the shelves of second-hand bookshops for faded coffee-table books about the world of chuck-wagons. I knew, deep down, that my West was mythical, that when Uncle William worked for Buffalo Bill, he was building the scenery for a dream. But myths, and dreams, when we believe in them, even with our fingers crossed, do shape our lives. What I was looking for in the history of the West was not the truth, but a way back to the lost world of possibilities – of security, of freedom and of passion – of my own childhood.

Many books on the West are full of photographs: formal portraits of lawmen, mug shots of convicts, and chilling pictures of dead outlaws held up for the camera by their killers. In most, the eyes of the living men and women seem as dead as the deceased. They gaze into a middle distance, for ever out of our reach. But there are exceptions. The man in the photograph I wanted is one.

His collar is slightly too tight and his hair roughly cropped. He is unshaven, his face is bruised, and although his eyes seem troubled, one corner of his mouth is lifting towards a smile. Although the photograph was taken over a hundred years ago, he looks shockingly modern. He looks alive. His name is Oliver Curtis Perry and from the moment I first saw his face, I was in the grip of a powerful obsession that was not in the least academic. I wanted his picture not for my files but for my bedside.

When I saw Oliver Perry's photograph, I fell, unknowingly, for a doubly wanted man. The photograph was originally carried in the pocket of Pinkerton detectives in a nationwide manhunt. To

4

those who wanted to bring him to justice, he was a remarkable, ruthless criminal, but to many of his fellow Americans he was a romantic, daring outlaw. This man occupied the dreams and fantasies of a generation.

I was only the latest in a long line of women, and men, who had fallen for Oliver Perry. Yet today, apart from sketches of brief moments in his life, he is a forgotten man, his story lost. What drew so many people to him in his lifetime? Was it the same challenging, wounded look that compelled me so long after his death? And why, unlike other outlaws, has he been almost completely excised from history?

Years after I stopped believing that I would ride off into the sunset with an outlaw lover, I had found myself face to face with him. The photograph transported me from my adult world of history into an adolescent romance, and I wanted it like young girls want pictures of their film-star idols. When my nerve failed, I found myself back in the real world, alone.

Because he was an outlaw and I was an academic, stealing his photograph would have somehow connected us. Leaving it in the folder felt like a betrayal, a confirmation that we were separated by more than time.

I kept tracking him across New York State and beyond, in detective agency archives, in prison records and newspapers of his day, even unearthing his own writings, unread since his death. With his photograph always in my head, if not my pocket, I proved a better detective than I would be a thief.

In the end I discovered a man of greater complexity and power than the handsome outlaw I had been hunting. I found many clues to his appeal to the men and women of his day. I also found out the terrible reason why he had been forgotten.

New York

0   50 mls
0   50 kms

P.G.Cubbin, FBCart.S - Nov. 2003

CHAPTER I

Wild Western Ways
in the Empire State

I N M A R C H 1929 the thirty-first President of the United States
of America, Herbert Hoover, proclaimed: 'Ours is a land rich
in resources; stimulating in its glorious beauty; filled with millions
of happy homes; blessed with comfort and opportunity. In no
nation are the institutions of progress more advanced. In no
nation are the fruits of accomplishment more secure.' Just a few
months later, the stock market crashed and the happy nation
sank into depression and despair. In the hard years that followed
people would do almost anything to get by. On city streets men,
women and children queued for handouts and picked through
garbage to find food.

The city of Utica in central New York State's Mohawk valley was
as hard hit as any other. Once-booming businesses closed or laid off
most of their workers. Many Uticans who had come from other
lands, or from the surrounding countryside, searching for a better
life, moved on once more, in search now simply of work. Some
turned hobo, travelling along the railroad lines, risking the wrath of
the 'bulls' employed to keep the trains free of passengers who
would not or could not pay. An optimistic few, remembering tales
from their childhood, searched for better fortune nearer home.

Stories had been told about fantastic wealth, a robber's horde, buried in the Frankfort Hills, just outside the city, forty years before. So, armed with shovels and picks, Utica's Depression dreamers headed into the hills to dig. None succeeded, but their attempts to strike it rich in a world with no other hope echoed the actions of the man whose treasure they were seeking. Like them, he had hoped that one lucky break would transform his life of misfortune.

In the aftermath of the Civil War that convulsed the nation in the 1860s, America had entered an era of extraordinary economic growth. The technology of war, as ever, propelled the peacetime nation into a new age in which memories of loss mingled with hopes of gain. Steel, oil, copper, and the railroads needed to transport them, transformed the United States into one of the world's top three industrial powers. They also turned wartime speculators and profiteers into a new commercial aristocracy – J. Pierpont Morgan, John D. Rockefeller, Cornelius Vanderbilt, August Belmont – whose empires were centred on the Empire State. In New York City alone there were over a thousand millionaires by the 1890s. Their success seemed to be the ultimate fulfilment of an American dream, but real life for most Americans was in stark contrast.

Workers endured harsh, dangerous conditions, poor pay and no job security in industries that were almost entirely unregulated. Safety measures and decent wages were costly and, in a fiercely competitive free market, profit ruled. Exploited workers, in the mines and on the railroads, turned to desperate measures. Their strikes were, in turn, violently suppressed by hired strike breakers. Beneath the gilded surface of the age something very much like class war was simmering. Among the immigrants who

8

arrived daily from the Old World were radicals, socialists and anarchists, determined, in different ways, to forge a better society. Their arguments found a growing working-class audience. Middle-class liberals, meanwhile, feared that the great industrialists were corrupting the system by routinely manipulating politicians for their own ends. In some circles a new name was found for them: 'the robber barons'.

In this competitive world, the fantasy of making it big fuelled a million schemes that fed on people's dreams. Every day a golden new business opportunity was advertised to take the citizen's dollar. Some were stranger than others. In Portland, Oregon a stock company was established to breed black domestic cats for fur. The company announced that an island would be purchased so that the stock could be isolated from other cats and live on fish. Prospective investors were assured that there were millions to be made in cats. For every dollar there was a waiting speculator. The spirit of the age was distilled by one commentator: 'Get money – honestly if you can, but at any rate get money!'

In New York State the post-war era had brought dramatic change. More and more people kept flooding into the state but the competition from more fertile agricultural lands in the west hit the upstate farmers hard. Rural workers soon began to give up and move to the towns to work in factories and mills. The booming cities of New York State were full of men and women, native-born and immigrant, who had grown up in close-knit communities but were now among strangers.

The landscape of the state still shows the effects of the industrial boom. The railroad travels north from New York City through the Hudson valley, then west along the Mohawk valley from Albany to Utica, and beyond to Rochester and Buffalo, tracing the ancient ways of the great rivers and the more recent routes of the industrial era. Cities are strung along the twin highways of water and rail, some named prosaically for their business, like Gloversville, others, like Amsterdam and Geneva, recalling the homes left behind by waves of immigrants. Still others speak of heroic identifications. The Empire State, even in its most mundane places, is overlaid with names from a classical mythology: Troy, Rome and Utica.

In 1891 Utica was a city of some standing, with new electric lights shining out across the dark surrounding hills. It was also the place where one of the most daring crimes in New York's history took place.

Late in the night of 29 September 1891 the New York Central 'American Express Special' set out from the state capital Albany on its long journey. The train, known to railroad buffs as 'the hottest of hotshots', travelled at top speed and carried no passengers. It was a vital link in the economic chain that connected businesses in the east and west of the nation, stopping to pick up freight along a route that finally led to Chicago. Like any freight train it was made up of cars owned by different companies. One of these was special. Outside, it looked just like any other, a wooden wagon with a solid door at each end and sliding panel doors with windows in the sides. But this was no ordinary freight car, carrying tinned goods or leather shoes.

It was owned by the American Express Company and was known by railroad workers as the 'money' car. It carried specie or cash from the United States Treasury for western banks, as well as bonds, jewellery and other valuables. Inside it was divided by crossways partitions into three compartments. In the central one, which held all the valuables in four large safes and numerous

10

sacks, travelled an American Express employee called, innocuously enough, a 'messenger'. His job was to deal with all the paperwork for the company, but he was also an armed guard. The American Express Special, as it was popularly known, was reported to carry loads worth up to a million dollars.

Few messengers expected to use their regulation revolvers, on the eastern leg of the journey at least. Robberies had been a hazard in the wilder west since the first recorded train robbery in 1865. These were violent crimes, with trains derailed or blown apart and trainmen forced to defend their basic livelihoods with their lives. The names of the western outlaw gangs, Reno, James, Younger, were already legendary. Their methods were brutal but their origins in civil war conflict attracted the sympathy of some ex-Confederates and many romantics. A few radicals believed they were no more ruthless than the respectable 'robber barons' of the east. Men who made money fast, legally or illegally, inevitably did so at someone else's expense. Was a fast, bloody death in a western street or on a railroad track so much worse than a lifetime of dangerous drudgery in a factory or on a train? Whatever their thoughts about the comparative morality of bosses and outlaws, most easterners were relieved to know that daring train robbers belonged in another world, far away from 'civilized' New York.

But that September night everything changed. 'Wild Western Ways in the Empire State' declared the *New York Herald* the following morning, while Joseph Pulitzer's *The World* seemed geographically affronted: 'A train held up right in the heart of the Empire State! And this on one of the most frequented roads in the Union – the New York Central! It seems almost incredible that such wild Western methods could be successfully practised in the centre of civilization without a trace being left as to the perpetrators of such a daring deed; yet such is a fact.'

The American Express Special was speeding though the 'burnt stone' canyon, a few miles east of the bright lights of Utica, when it suddenly ground to a halt. The trainmen, who travelled in the last car, jumped down to investigate and found that someone had cut through the air-brake hose at the rear of the money car. Inside they found Burt Moore, the messenger, dazed and gasping, 'I've been robbed.' The robbers had apparently disappeared in the pitch darkness of the canyon. Unable to see well enough to give chase, the crew travelled on to Utica to report the crime.

There the shocked messenger explained what had happened. He was working in the central section, with the end doors locked. The front partition door was open to make room for the freight, and sacks and parcels were piled high against the front car door because it would not be used on the journey. When the train approached Frankfort, he was crouched with his back to this door, checking the waybills that identified the sender, destination and recipient of all the freight. The train was travelling at full speed, engine roaring and cars clattering over the switches. Once or twice he thought he heard something and looked around but everything seemed in order, and his revolver was near at hand, on top of a trunk.

Suddenly he heard a louder noise, turned and saw a man pointing two guns at him. His face was completely covered by a red hood, except for slots through which his eyes flashed. 'It's money I'm after,' he shouted. 'Quick, we're getting near to Utica!'

Moore claimed that before he could react, a shot whistled past him, and the robber grabbed his revolver. The masked man made him unlock a safe, then emptied it, tossing aside bags of jewellery, and stuffed half a dozen canvas bags into a large bag he carried over his shoulder. Keeping his guns trained on Moore, he moved slowly towards the side door and opened it as if to jump. But the train was travelling too fast and he changed his mind, backing towards the front door. Slowly, he felt his way back through the piles of packages and, keeping one gun stretched in front, dropped the bag through a square hole in the door, then wriggled, one foot at a time, back through the hole and dropped out of sight. Moore assumed that he had swung down to cut the brake hose that ran underneath the cars, to stop the train and make his escape. Whatever he did, he disappeared without trace.

The car itself told the story of how the robber had entered it. Standing on the platform as the train sped noisily through the night, he had bored a small hole in the front door, to spy on the messenger, then made four more holes lower down, and sawn out a panel, about fifteen inches square. Then he had leaned through, pulled out a box to stand on, squeezed into the car and surprised the messenger. It was a devastatingly simple plan, brilliantly executed. Unlike his western predecessors, this man had worked alone, and had used skill rather than brute force. He had also chosen to rob a train in the busiest state in the Union.

The police immediately cabled American Express and the railroad company. The robbery was a real embarrassment to both – and a threat to future profits. They swiftly announced that the train had been carrying an unusually small amount of money, less than $20,000 in total, and that mostly bonds. While all those interviewed, including New York Central Railroad President Chauncy M. Depew, acknowledged it was 'a queer case', they immediately insisted that little could have been stolen. American Express announced that the robber had stolen less than $1,000, and one official, stretching credulity to breaking-point, argued that it was only $150. Newsmen were sceptical. One consulted an Albany banker who confirmed the general view that the train was more likely to have carried at least $100,000.

American Express lost no time in employing the Pinkerton Detective Agency to find the robber. The agency had, like the corporations it now worked for, been 'made' by the Civil War, when its agents worked undercover for the Union side, and was known for getting results by any means necessary. Now the 'Pinks', under the direction of Robert Pinkerton himself and the agency's New York manager, George Bangs, assembled in Utica. There they joined a throng of railroad detectives, local police and newsmen and started the painstaking process of searching the surrounding towns, villages and countryside. It was the biggest manhunt upstate New York had seen for many years.

The Pinkertons had years of experience in dealing with train robberies in the west, where a network of detectives, local sheriffs and informers had given them real success. But this was a challenge. The man they were after was clearly no ordinary robber. George Bangs, a man not easily impressed, wrote to William Pinkerton, 'The man who committed the train robbery here is one of the nerviest I ever heard of. There are few if any men who possess the daredevil courage to accomplish what this train robber did yesterday.' And as the days passed no trace of the robber came to light, nor any clue to his identity.

Then, five days after the crime, a couple of local men made an important discovery while picking ink-berries in Borden's Grove. This was a patch of scrubland near an abandoned distillery, some three miles east of Utica. They were about to call it a day and go home, when they spotted a lot of torn paper on the ground. On closer inspection, the paper turned out to be wrappers from money and bonds. Nearby were empty money envelopes, packages and jewellery boxes as well as large cotton bags with the marking 'Am. Ex. Co.'. Among the papers they found a waybill listing 'three diamond rings' and an envelope marked '$5,000'.

They bundled everything up and went to find a local reporter who immediately set off on the trail of the robber. Just behind the place where the wrappings had been found was a deep, overgrown ravine that ran south from the canal into the Frankfort Hills. Full of stubby trees and bushes, it offered ideal hiding places. The reporter drove along the road until he found what he was looking for: someone who had a story to tell.

Erving Vance, a farmer, was not an ideal witness. Until an apparently miraculous but mysterious 'cure', he had been totally blind. His sight had been only partially restored, however, and he had to rely on his ten-year-old son to help him on the farm. On the evening after the robbery, he had gone out to bring a horse into the barn for the night, taking his son with him. As he approached the barn he saw an object looming in the semi-darkness and assumed it was the horse, but the object said, 'Good evening.' 'Well, what do you want?' Vance had replied, startled. The stranger had answered that he was looking for Mr Rider's place. 'Holmes Rider?' asked the farmer. 'Yes,' came the answer.

Suspicious of anyone prowling around his farm, Vance had asked who he was. According to the farmer, at this point the man started to behave as if he was slightly drunk. He said he had been drinking with two friends, had fallen asleep on the road, and woken to find they had gone. As far as Vance could make out, the

15

man had said his name was Stevens or Stevenson, and he came from Little Falls, but had worked in Amsterdam for a time before that. He had seemed increasingly uneasy and anxious to leave. Told the way to Rider's farm, he started off in another direction until Vance called out. After some hesitation he changed his path and the farmer and son, who knew nothing about the train robbery, watched him disappear into the darkness.

Vance gave the reporter a description that, although lacking in detail because of his impaired vision, matched that of the train robber given by Burt Moore: about five feet nine, of rather slight build, with a small dark moustache. His son confirmed his story and other sightings followed. A bee hunter remembered seeing a man who kept his face hidden and who, if a local barber was to be believed, made his way back to Utica that evening, walked into the barber's shop and asked to have his moustache shaved off. The man's clothes, the barber said, were dusty and covered with 'stick tights' or burrs, and he clutched a newspaper-covered parcel. He had paid from a 'good roll of bills' and left. After that the trail went cold. But the reporter's search had uncovered two things about the robber. The fact that he had named a local farmer suggested that the robber might be a local man. The fact that he had coolly walked back into Utica, under the detectives' noses, confident that he would not be identified, showed that he was as daring as a wanted man as he had been as a robber.

The Borden's Grove find had also proved something else: that whatever American Express said, this had been a major robbery. Someone leaked the fact to a reporter that four more canvas bags and their contents had not been accounted for and the remaining empty bags were soon found on top of an eastbound freight car near Albany. Whatever the official line, the growing band of newspapermen in Utica knew they were on to a real story and the public were eager for the latest chapter.

If American Express was under pressure, the crew of the robbed train had reason to feel even more uncomfortable. Many people insisted that the robber must have had inside knowledge or help, and the police were searching for one suspect, an escaped convict, just because he had been a railroad worker. The most worried man was messenger Burt Moore. Although he had been in shock after the robbery, he had not been hurt. To some observers this was deeply suspicious. He was a powerfully built man who did not appear to have put up much of a fight. It was also rumoured that no evidence could be found that any shot had been fired in the car. Possibly Moore had invented the shooting because he was worried his employers would not think he had put up enough of a fight, but as time went on, some whispered that he had been in cahoots with the robber. Moore was anxious to show that he had done everything he could to protect his employer's goods, even claiming that he had managed to hide some money by kicking a sack of bills out of sight while the robber was distracted. His employers announced that they had total faith in him, but he had been immediately suspended from duty after the robbery and was under continual surveillance.

A week after the Borden's Grove find and nearly a fortnight after the robbery, American Express issued an official statement: 'We have got a pretty good clue to the robber and we are going to get him. It may take time, but we will run him down if we have to follow him to "Kingdom Come" . . . Watch us while we nab the robber.' So watch the people of New York did, for weeks on end. But still there was no arrest.

17

Pinkerton Detective Agency Flyer.

CHAPTER 2

'Probably now wearing diamonds'

WHILE THE people of New York wondered if the Pinkertons had finally met their match, the detectives believed they had found their man. They had started to follow a lead from one of the train's crew, Frank Stacy. He had caught a glimpse of the robber as he jumped from the train and thought he recognized him as a one-time colleague on the New York Central. For the first time, the wanted man had a name: Oliver Curtis Perry.

The Pinkertons at first revealed nothing to the police or the press. They started by targeting the suspect's relatives, particularly his aunt, a respectable woman called Mary Hamblin, who lived in the nearby city of Rome. Agents offered her $250, a substantial sum, for a photograph of her nephew but she refused to cooperate. Eventually they had a warrant issued against her and obtained a copy of the photograph for use in their circulars. These were sent all over the country, offering a huge reward of $1,000.

The circulars gave a description that echoed those given by Burt Moore and the local witnesses, but was clearly based on detailed knowledge of the suspect:

Oliver Curtis Perry is described as 26 years of age, 5 feet 6 to 7 inches in height, slight build, weighing about 130lbs, dark brown hair, small moustache, inclined to be sandy (probably now shaved off), brown eyes; high, white forehead, with wrinkles between eyes, giving his face a troubled and thoughtful expression; thin lips, rather long nose, slim white hand, with enlarged knuckles from hard work. Has a scar about three inches long on upper part of forehead, which is noticeable when his hat is off; also has scar on left arm and above right nipple. He is gentlemanly, polite and effeminate in manner, but acts nervous and uneasy; has a girlish voice, dresses in dark clothes, invariably wears gloves, and is noticeably particular about keeping his hands clean. Had gold open face watch, 14 karat, stemwinder, size 18, Samuel C. Tappen, Troy, N.Y., maker, name on dial and movement, nickel movement, case No. 14,608; also a gold watch chain. Also wears a ring, with stone on little finger of right hand, (probably now wearing diamonds).

The photograph shows a handsome man with dark eyes, gazing calmly past the photographer. He is dressed like a respectable gentleman but not a man of means. The fabric of his suit looks, on close inspection, to be coarse. He may, like many Americans of the period, have taken advantage of the cheap 'smart' clothes designed to make a hick pass without being mocked in the city, or a worker feel like a boss, if only on Sundays. But he was clearly a man of refined tastes: his cravat looks like silk and has a sprig of flowers on the knot. His hair is sleek and his moustache is slightly curled at the ends. A comment under the picture warns the viewer: 'The above likeness is a good one but flatters. His face is not so full and the lips are thinner.'

The flyers gave a wealth of detail about the robber's looks, but what about his character? Who was Oliver Perry? While the hunt continued, two wildly contrasting versions emerged as the press fed the public appetite for information on him. The Pinkertons declared that he was a clever but ruthless outlaw. According to them he was born, as many had suspected, in the Mohawk valley, and had a long record of crimes across the States. But for the past two years Perry had been working on the railroad and living quietly in Troy, a city near Albany, some of whose most upstanding citizens sprang to his defence. They insisted that Perry was a man of strong religious convictions who had seen the error of a wayward youth, and tried to keep to a steady path until this extraordinary allegation had been made. These were eminently respectable people, and their loyalty to the fugitive surprised the detectives. One, the City Missionary and Sunday School teacher, Miss Amelia Haswell, protected him even more ferociously than his aunt had done, destroying his photographs rather than have them used on reward posters. Oliver Perry clearly inspired strong passions.

The agents redoubled their efforts, with William A. Pinkerton himself leading investigations across the continent. Detectives searched hotels and brothels, Christian associations and saloons; they even arrested a man in Vermont and announced their hunt was over, only to discover it was a case of mistaken identity. Perry was not to be found. In the press speculation continued about whether or not he had worked entirely alone. The fact that he had been a railroad worker had explained his inside knowledge of trains but it was over two months since the robbery and Burt Moore had still not been allowed back to work. Could he have been an accomplice?

Then, in December, two strange things happened. First, a lawyer from Troy delivered a parcel of jewellery stolen in the robbery to American Express. The Pinkertons questioned Perry's religious friends, but revealed nothing to the press. Next, an astonishing letter, postmarked 'Guelph Ontario', arrived at the investigation headquarters. Its exact contents were not revealed, but it was signed 'Oliver Curtis Perry' and accompanied by a diamond-studded brooch from the Special, to prove its authenticity. Its writer made a full confession, and insisted that Burt Moore was totally innocent. Perry, it seemed, had recklessly revealed his whereabouts in order to prevent an injustice. Agents in Ontario were alerted, but again they failed to find him. To those of a romantic inclination the letter was an act of gallantry, designed to save a working man from more trouble, while others were amused by Perry's ability to tease the detectives.

New Year came, still there was no sign of an arrest, and still the robber's reputation grew. Anyone who had got away with a fortune as he had would have earned the secret admiration of all but the most determinedly upright: his robbery was quite simply astonishing. But there was something about Oliver Perry, sketchily as he had been drawn, that particularly caught the imagination of New Yorkers. The references to his troubled expression and nervous manner had suggested to some that this was a daredevil with a sensitive soul. The comments from the good people of Troy had, after all, painted a picture of a hard-working man and his letter had shown he was honourable. And, despite the Pinkertons' snide remark, everyone could see that he was handsome. Perry became the object of the day-dreams and fantasies of men, women and children: a man you might want to be, or be with, or become.

Soon rumours spread across the state that poor people were finding jewels and money on their doorsteps with notes from Perry giving his compliments. Although there was never any proof that these incidents actually occurred, they fed a mythology that was growing around the young robber. Handsome, boyish, clever and honourable, he now became for some people a latter-day Robin Hood, a worthy successor to Jesse James, an eastern outlaw to rival any the west could boast. Did he, like them, have a dramatic past to explain his criminal present? In the coming months and years, tall tales would be spun about what Perry did on the run: stories of romantic assignations with beautiful women, of cool conversations about the robbery with unsuspecting detectives, and of secret caches of loot left deep in the Utica Hills to be recovered one day. Whatever the truth about Oliver Perry might turn out to be, New York had fallen in love.

CHAPTER 3

Shades of Jesse James!

I T W A S 20 February 1892. The American Express Special was once again making its run with the extra-valuable Saturday load. In the money car, messenger Daniel McInerney settled down to his paperwork. In the early hours of the morning, as the train pulled out of Syracuse, where it had stopped to take on freight, a smartly dressed, bearded man leapt unseen on to the forward platform of the car in front of McInerney's. Once aboard, he removed his gold-framed spectacles and placed them in the inside pocket of his overcoat. Then he climbed on to the platform railing, grasped the edges of the two cars and hauled himself up on to the roof.

Crouching low and keeping to the middle, he ran along the roof to the other end and dropped down on to the rear platform. From there it was just a step to the front platform of the car he was interested in, the money car. The speed of the train, as it left the depot, had forced him to jump aboard the wrong car. The run along the roof had not been part of his plan but he had managed it without even taking off his hat.

Once safely on the platform, he removed the derby and, threading a cord through the sweatband, strapped it to the railing, with his valise. The man who had got away with a fortune from American Express was robbing the same train again just five months later.

From his satchel Perry took a red hood with eye and mouth holes, which he tied tightly around his neck. It was the same mask he had used last time. Why change a winning formula? He strapped his Colt .44 and cartridge belt across his overcoat. The revolver was cumbersome, with a seven-inch barrel and a bore you could put your finger in but it had an impact as big as its pull. He placed two smaller revolvers, Derringers, in his coat pockets, within easy reach in case he dropped the larger gun. Given what he was about to do, that was a distinct possibility.

He levered himself up once again, this time on to the roof of the money car. From his satchel he took a rope with a hook at one end and knots at intervals along its length. He attached the hook to the overhanging eave on one side of the car. Then, keeping the rope taut, he stretched it across the roof and dropped it over the other side. It slipped down beside the door. Unlike the solid end door, this had a glass window. Perry leaned down, listening for any sign that he had disturbed the messenger inside, then inched down the rope.

The train was now travelling at nearly fifty miles an hour. A slip would be fatal. Perry wrapped his legs around the rope, to leave his hands free. The wind was so strong that the rope was blown away from the car several times, once nearly crashing into a bridge as the train hurtled under it. Seeing it just in time, in the lights of the train, Perry grasped the roof ledge and pulled himself towards the train. He missed death by inches.

He had to move quickly as well as carefully. The biting wind was almost unendurable. Wearing only fine kid gloves, his hands were becoming numb. He slapped them against his sides to keep his circulation going, then made his move.

Half an hour after the train pulled out of Syracuse, Daniel McInerney was startled by the sound of breaking glass. Grabbing his gun, he turned to see a revolver poking through the smashed window in the door. Just as he caught a glimpse of a masked head framed in the window, a voice called out, 'Hands up!'

A split second later both men fired at once. A bullet hit McInerney's gun and sent it flying back over his shoulder, breaking his fingers and smashing his wrist as it flew. With his good hand, he grabbed the air-whistle cord above his head and pulled it hard. No whistle sounded. He pulled again. 'Let go of that rope, damn you!' shouted the stranger. McInerney kicked out wildly to extinguish the lamp, plunging the car into darkness. A shot rang out and a bullet grazed his temple.

Dazed by the blow, he could hear the intruder climbing into the car and struggled desperately to pull the cord again. This time a third shot hit him in the thigh and floored him. The whole exchange had taken only seconds.

Too shocked to register much pain, McInerney could feel blood oozing from his leg. Perry struck a match and lit some waybills. In the light of the burning papers McInerney caught the full effect of the red mask and the two heavy revolvers. 'Damn you!' shouted Perry. 'You tried to kill me.'

Perry ordered McInerney to light the lantern, unlock the safes and put the money on one side. 'There is no money,' McInerney replied. Taken aback, Perry demanded that the messenger open the packages he had pulled out on to the floor. Sure enough, there was no cash, only jewellery and silverware. This wasn't right. He only wanted ready money this time, not goods that had to be sold.

McInerney insisted that the money was being carried on another train. Perry didn't believe him and ordered him to start opening up the other packages.

Emil Laas, the conductor travelling in the rear car, thought he heard the air-whistle sound faintly. When he went to see if anything was wrong in the money car, he peered through a hole and saw the strange hooded figure. He signalled quickly to the engineer to slow down but the masked head emerged from the side window and shouted, 'God damn you, shove her ahead!' A bullet whizzed past and the conductor complied.

As the train steamed on, Perry was still trying to find the money, but he started to worry about McInerney who was losing a lot of blood and showing real pain now. 'Are you hurt much?' he asked. Then he leaned forward to examine the messenger's wounded face by the light of some burning waybills. But as he got close, he saw McInerney staring at him and pulled back. Even with the mask, he couldn't let the other man look too closely. It was too risky.

Then, as the train approached Port Byron, it started slowing down. The engine had been signalled to halt to let a coal train pass. As Laas jumped off and called for the station operator, McInerney appeared at the car door, swaying and mumbling incoherently. There was no sign of the masked man. He must, Laas thought, have jumped off the train before it had picked up speed.

In fact, as they slowed down at Port Byron Perry had silently swung up on to the car roof and packed the rope away in his satchel. Then he dropped off the train on the side away from the trainmen just before it stopped. He hid while the train was being searched and gathered his thoughts. A freight train, bound for

Syracuse, was pulling out. Reckoning that he would be expected to try to get away on the freight train, he decided on a different course of action. He stowed away his disguise and other gear in his valise, and put on his hat and eyeglasses. Then he climbed back aboard the Express just before it set off for the next stop, the village of Lyons, and hid between cars.

When the train arrived in Lyons, McInerney was carried off for medical attention and the train was backed up on the number two track to take on water. Even though a messenger was seriously, perhaps fatally, wounded, the train would have to continue on to its destination as it had in the last robbery. When profits might be lost, the demands of the business outweighed the needs of its employees. Perry, meanwhile, slipped off on the far side, away from the platform, and walked swiftly along the track. Keeping hidden behind stationary train cars, he made his way to the street running up to the station. Then, cool as can be, he sauntered on to the platform as if coming to buy a ticket or meet a passenger. But his disguise, so often his best weapon, now proved his undoing.

While his train was refuelled, Emil Laas was discussing the robbery with the other railroad men, when he had his second shock of the night. At the far end, leaning casually against the station building, he saw a well-dressed young man he had noticed at the depot in Syracuse earlier that night. He hadn't thought much of it at the time, but this didn't make sense. There was no way the man could have got to Lyons that quickly except on the Express. The man had to be the robber. He shouted to the others. They rushed at Perry, then stopped in their tracks when he levelled his revolvers at them and ordered them to stay away.

Keeping the guns trained on the men on the platform, Perry backed slowly across the tracks. A west-bound coal train was standing on track number three, waiting for the signal to pull out. He swiftly uncoupled the engine from the rest of the train. Then he climbed over the water tank and ordered the startled engineer and fireman off the cab at gunpoint. As the men on the platform looked on in disbelief, Perry pulled open the throttle like a seasoned engineer and gave four whistle blows to signal departure. Hearing the whistle, the flagman, unaware of the unfolding drama, signalled the okay and Perry's engine pulled out of the station. Laas and the others were momentarily stunned but swiftly set off after Perry in the uncoupled Express engine. One of the men had hastily grabbed a double-barrelled shotgun.

As they raced through the quiet of the early morning, the Express quickly gained ground on Perry's 'hog', as the older, slower freight engines were known. Near a bridge over the Erie Canal, halfway along the ten-mile stretch between Lyons and Newark to the west, Perry saw that he had no hope of out-running his pursuers. He slammed on the brakes, threw his engine into reverse, and built up speed until the engine hurtled backwards towards the Express. Perry was turning a race he couldn't win into a duel. Bullets flew as the engines chased and faced each other until, out of ammunition and reluctant to tackle Perry unarmed, the trainmen returned to Lyons. Behind them, their quarry-turned-opponent steamed away towards Newark.

But Perry had been too busy changing direction and shooting at his pursuers to keep the engine stoked, so the steam started to give out. He might have struggled into Newark but he knew that

The Engine Duel (*Utica Saturday Globe*).

the railroad men would have wired ahead and arranged a welcome party. So he abandoned the engine at Blue Cut, a couple of miles east, where he ordered a startled switchman to take the engine back to Lyons, and scrambled quickly up the embankment. When he reached the top, he looked around to see if anyone was watching, then set off into the countryside. Escape would not be easy. Heavy snowdrifts would make the going hard and the advancing daylight would help his pursuers.

By this time, the Rochester police force had been wired and were assembled at Rochester's Central station where they awaited the Express's arrival. McInerney was taken by ambulance to his parents' house, then, after questioning the crew, the policemen climbed aboard a specially requisitioned engine and set off on the thirty-five-minute run to Blue Cut. They telegraphed to Newark to have some local men meet them, but when they arrived at the Cut, no one was there. The crew of a passing

31

freight train claimed to have seen Perry a short distance further east, so the police set off in that direction.

After struggling through the snow for some minutes, Perry spotted a farmhouse. Samuel Goetzman was in his kitchen having breakfast when there was a knock at his door. The caller, his face blackened by soot and sweat, told the farmer that he was a Pinkerton detective. He said he was chasing three men who had just robbed a train down on the Central and made off to the hills to the north. In order to pursue them he needed to borrow a horse.

Goetzman's first inclination was to shut the door. But after a great deal of persuasion, he reluctantly took the stranger to his barn. The man demanded to know which was his best horse. Goetzman pointed to a black mare. She was actually his second-best, but there was no reason for the stranger to know that. He asked the detective how he could be sure the mare would be returned. Perry was starting to explain that if anything happened to the horse he could sue American Express for compensation, when the farmer's wife walked in on them. When she realized what was happening, she flatly instructed her husband not to lend the stranger the horse. The mare happened to be her favourite, and if her husband was stupid enough to trust a total stranger, she was not.

Caught between civic and marital obligations, Goetzman asked if the 'detective' would show him his papers. The man replied that he didn't have any, but that his name was Cross. When Goetzman shook his head and said he needed some proof, Perry finally lost his temper. He grabbed a bridle from a hook on the wall and started to put it on the mare. While Goetzman stared, his wife tried to snatch the bridle off the stranger. He pulled it free, fitted it, and started leading the mare out of the barn. If he was determined to have the horse, Mrs Goetzman was equally resolved that he should not. Shouting at her husband, she tried to wrest the reins from the so-called detective. Fearful of losing any more time, Perry changed tactics. He pulled a revolver from his belt and pointed it at the woman.

The move worked. Goetzman rushed to find a blanket and strapped it on the mare. Keeping up his pretence, Perry demanded to know which was the best road to cut off the robbers' escape. The farmer told him to ride to the Blue Cut and turn right. He watched as Perry rode off, then took off after him in his cutter, a type of sleigh. At Blue Cut he saw, by the tracks in the snow, that Perry had gone left instead of right. Convinced now that the stranger was no detective, Goetzman called the local watchman who joined the chase.

The police, meanwhile, had realized that they were on a wild goose chase and doubled back to Blue Cut. There they tried to find someone to lend them horses or a cutter, but the local farmers were wary of all strangers. The city lawmen were greeted with as much suspicion as the bogus detective. Eventually a farmer agreed to drive them and they set off south in the direction taken by Perry.

Perry himself rode hard through the icy morning, anxious to keep ahead of the men he knew would be following. The snow had arrived about ten weeks earlier and few had travelled these roads since, as bare rock giving way to deep snowdrifts made the way perilous for horse or man. Eventually, about four miles on, Goetzman's second-best horse began to tire. Perry pulled up at a farm owned by another immigrant farmer, a Swede by the name of Frederick Beal.

33

Beal was feeding his chickens when Perry rode into the yard. Assuming the stranger wanted to ride through his fields because the road was blocked with snow, Beal called out, 'You can't get through here, there's too much snow.'

'I don't intend to go through,' came the reply. 'I want one of your best horses, and one of the fastest, right off.'

Beal asked what he wanted it for. Perry told him that he needed a horse and cutter to go to the aid of some men who were hurt down on the railroad. Beal started to ask what had happened and who Perry was. Unwilling to go through a repeat performance of the Goetzman conversation, Perry reached for his gun and fired a warning shot. Beal hitched up the cutter. Perry grabbed the reins, turned the cutter around so fast that it nearly toppled over, and sped out of the yard.

Soon every farmer and lad in the area were chasing Perry along the narrow tracks, on horseback, in cutters, buggies and carts. Few knew about the train robbery, but horse theft was about the worst crime a man could commit in the eyes of a Wayne County farmer.

Each time the farmers began to gain on Perry, at an awkward corner or a deep drift of snow, a shot from his revolver would keep them at bay until he was out of danger. One young man, Charlie Burnett, earned a new reputation for daredevil courage. Fired up by the thrill of the chase, he determined to be the one to catch the thief. Twice he forced Perry to change direction by shouting to wagons coming towards them in the opposite direction to block the road, making the robber turn down smaller side roads. Finally, he managed to overtake him and, trying to overturn his cutter by barging his horse against Perry's, forced him to turn abruptly into a log road that ran into Benton's swamp.

34

The combination of snow and half-frozen swamp water forced Perry to abandon the cutter after a few hundred yards. He struggled on, wading through the swamp, until he reached a scrubby wooded area at the far edge. Keeping a safe distance between themselves and Perry's guns, his pursuers discussed their next move. Behind the vanguard of angry farmers, three more groups had been advancing. First were the Rochester police in their commandeered cutter. Second was a large posse from Lyons. Third were local Pinkerton agents. Altogether, more than fifty men were now crowded at the edge of Benton's swamp.

It was about 11 o'clock. Perry had been on the run for at least five hours. Exhausted, numb with cold and now soaked to the skin, he found a half-collapsed stone wall. Unable to walk any further, he crouched down behind it. His pursuers had split up to surround him. Just before midday, someone spotted Perry. Knowing that the posse would eventually close in on him, he had built up the loose stones from the wall into a sort of fortress. He knew that although he still had some ammunition, he could not win in any shoot-out with so many men. His only hope was to keep them at bay until nightfall and then try to creep away unseen. It was a long shot. There were hours to go before it would get dark, and he thought he heard someone in the posse call out a request to send to Lyons for long-distance rifles. For what felt like an age to everyone, there was a tense stand-off. No shots were fired and it seemed that both sides were playing a waiting game, to be decided by which arrived first, the long-distance rifles or nightfall.

'Is there an officer in the crowd?' It was Perry's voice from behind the barricade. 'I am,' shouted back Jeremiah Collins, the young deputy, known to everyone as Jerry. 'If you drop your gun

35

and come on unarmed I'll talk with you,' Perry replied, 'but if you try to play me any tricks it will go hard with you.'

Ignoring all the warnings that he would get himself shot, Deputy Collins laid down his gun and walked across the open swamp towards Perry's improvised fortress, his hands clasped behind his back. Perry kept his gun trained on the approaching Deputy. 'Stop and hold your hands in front of you where I can see them.' Collins did so and moved forward again until he was standing against the wall in front of Perry.

'Is the messenger alive?' was the first thing Perry said. In the car he had been genuinely concerned about McInerney, who was about the same age and build as him, no tough guy. His plan had been to 'get the drop' on him, shock him into surrendering his gun, not have a shoot-out. But now he needed to know for another reason. If McInerney was dead or dying and he was facing a murder charge, there might be little reason to give himself up.

Collins said the messenger was alive and asked Perry to point the muzzle of the gun away from him. Perry hesitated, then laid it on the wall.

'You might as well give in,' Collins said, 'the whole country is out after you and you are bound to be caught. Suppose you do kill a few people. It'll only be worse for you in the end.'

'If I give up,' replied Perry, 'it means spending all my life in prison. Liberty is sweet to me and I'll sell it dear.'

Then, hearing a noise behind him, he turned around to check, and at that moment Collins took his chance. He knocked the pistol off the wall into the snow and launched himself across the wall, grabbing Perry in a bear-hug. Perry struggled and managed to unbalance Collins. The two men fell to the ground fighting.

Eventually Collins pinned him down on his back. Perry kept struggling. His arms held down, he tried to bite Collins's face, but the Deputy had size on his side. The watching men, bolder now, moved in as Collins handcuffed his captive and prepared to take him back to jail. Slowly the crowd dispersed. Some returned to their farms and chores they had left undone. More followed the posse back to Lyons to witness the next scene in the drama.

Perry had done the unthinkable. After single-handedly robbing the American Express Special and evading capture for over four months he had, everyone assumed, got away with his crime and a fortune. Now he had risked everything, including his freedom, by trying to rob the very same train again. Why had he done it? This robbery had been as meticulously planned as the first but the decision to do it was extraordinary. Was he showing off, inviting capture, or both? What sort of man would be so bold, so rash? America's most wanted man had been captured, but just who was Oliver Perry?

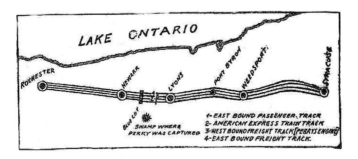

The scene of the robbery and chase

CHAPTER 4

'Woman's Mawkish Sentimentalism Again Manifests Itself'

T HE WAYNE County Jail in Lyons is an attractive building on the outside. Standing on Butternut Street, in the chocolate-box pretty centre of the village, it looks like a sturdy family house. Until not long ago it was just that, housing the sheriff and his family, as well as local wrongdoers in separate quarters. Today it

Wayne County Jail (From the collection of
the Wayne County Historical Society, Lyons, New York).

is a museum. The family quarters display civil war memorabilia, regional crafts and work by local schoolchildren, symbols of a close-knit community, past and present. On the ground floor a small room serves as office and shop. At the back of this is a stout door behind which is the one part of the jail that has no modern use: the cellblock.

When word spread that the captive was Oliver Curtis Perry, the notorious train robber, reporters, policemen, detectives, treasure hunters and curious members of the public descended on Lyons in droves. Almost as quickly, keen entrepreneurs started hawking a suspiciously large supply of bent bullets and shards of glass among the crowds as genuine souvenirs of the engine duel.

While the people of Lyons stood outside the jail hoping to catch a glimpse of the man the press now declared had 'outdone' Jesse James, inside a crowd of policemen, detectives and even reporters had been granted access to identify the suspect. When they placed the exhausted robber in one of the small cells, the lawmen knew they had a real catch. All they needed was a formal identification as the prisoner insisted he was called William Cross and came from New Mexico. Perry must have been exhausted and should have been overwhelmed, but he impressed everyone with his cool manner and dry wit. One railroad detective who had encountered him years before asked if he knew who he was. 'Yes,' replied Perry, to the amusement of onlookers and the annoyance of the detective, 'but I never knew any good of you.'

When Perry had been formally identified, he dropped the false name that he may have hoped was a last chance of evading charges for the first robbery. Calmly and without apparent concern, he confirmed that he was indeed Oliver Curtis Perry, the son of Oliver H. Perry, a contractor from Syracuse, and

40

confessed to the attempted robbery that day and to the successful robbery in 1891. Such was his apparent self-assurance that an agent for American Express who spoke with him in the jail told reporters, 'I never saw anyone who was so cool.' His coolness would be put to the test as he awaited his trial.

The jail itself was not daunting. Many prisoners preferred the regime of the county jail to the penitentiaries to which they might be sent after sentencing. The smaller jails had quite a homely atmosphere, and conditions, though tough, were rarely unduly harsh. Most prisoners were being held for minor offences, like drinking or fighting. Many knew their keepers. Like the lunatics in early Bedlams, however, the more infamous prisoners in jails were expected to be on display. Some guardians of law and order were happy to run their jails like sideshows, while others were more reluctant. But when more influential local citizens wanted to see the show, few sheriffs had the real power to refuse. The Wayne County Jail was no exception and soon Perry would have a stream of visitors. Among them were reporters with whom the young robber struck up a very special relationship.

Oliver Perry had a remarkable ability to make use of the press. From his earliest interviews in Lyons it is clear that he knew he was big news but also that he could manipulate public sentiment and spin a story for his own ends. Many years later he would quote President Theodore Roosevelt's comment that the quickest way to work for change was through the newspapers. Now he just seemed to have an almost instinctive understanding of how his gifts as a story-teller and talker might win him new friends. As he adjusted to his new situation, the man who had meticulously planned two robberies now embarked on a new project: to win over his audience. Public fascination with Perry had grown since his mysterious disappearance from Utica and he had followed the stories in the press that had fed this interest. Now he took the chance to tell his own tales. He started by explaining how he had evaded capture in Utica. His account pushed at the edge of credibility, especially an anecdote of hiding in a field where an unknowing farmer built up a corn stack around him, but the basic narrative made sense and fitted in with the witnesses' stories.

Perry clearly had an acute sense of his audience's tastes. The anecdotes he told with most relish were clearly designed to humiliate the Pinkertons. He claimed, laughing, that he had been under their noses all the time, and had even been out walking with agents who were holding the flyer with his photograph. Perry knew that many of the public would be on his side. The agents' work as strike breakers made them targets of radical condemnation but they were also despised by country people for their city arrogance and by others for their underhand tactics. When agents hurled a bomb into Jesse James's home, killing his young stepbrother and blowing off his mother's arm, their attack on the family affronted public decency and won sympathy for the outlaw. Perry made his own feelings clear: 'I hate Pinkerton men. I have nothing but contempt for them. They are nothing but the scum of cities, though I wish to except from this assertion some of the officers. I was working on the Fitchburg Railroad when, during the strike on the New York Central, Pinkerton men were employed, and though I probably only disliked them before I hate them since.' Local reporters were glad of a chance to mock the Pinkerton detectives for their failure to catch a man who had 'finally been landed by rural officers in a rural jail'.

Justice, meanwhile, moved swiftly. The first stage of Perry's arraignment took place the day after his arrest. In the afternoon of Monday, 23 February he was charged with two offences – shooting at an engine and assault in the second degree on the engineer of the freight train whose engine he stole. The main purpose was to enable the Wayne County lawmen to hold Perry until Daniel McInerney had recovered sufficiently to testify. Then Perry could be charged with breaking into an express car and assault with intent to kill.

The first hearing took place before Justice Theodore Fries and years later his grandson Theodore Harry Fries, nine years old at the time, recalled the scene. Word spread that Perry was being brought out, and as he was marched through the streets, hand-cuffed to Deputy Collins, people filled the sidewalks and leaned out of windows to catch a glimpse of him. Some even clambered on to rooftops to get a better view.

Amateur photography was the newest fad at the time and the local dentist set up his camera in the street, hoping to catch the desperado as he passed. In an age of slower shutter speeds, when newspapers still employed artists to illustrate their reports, it seems unlikely that this early paparazzo would have been suc-cessful. In any case Perry, much to the frustration of the crowd, had covered his face with a white handkerchief. Sharp observers noted that it was silk. The effect was tantalizing. All the crowd could see of the infamous Perry was his eyes.

Justice Fries's office was not large, so nearly all the furniture had to be removed to make room for the participants and spectators. Sheriff Thornton's party and the lawyers were forced to squeeze past dozens of people standing on the stairway leading to the office. Perry looked slightly pale and both he and Collins lost their hats in the scramble, but, as one reporter observed, he

43

was 'perfectly collected, his piercing eyes staring boldly into the faces which surged around him'.

Young Theodore Harry took refuge from the sea of legs, standing on top of a desk that was also a convenient vantage-point. In the rush and crush, coats were torn, hats trampled, and pictures on the wall broken. The room was so tightly packed that when Theodore Harry's grandfather felt faint in the middle of the hearing, he had to be passed over the heads of the crowd to the door. It was some time, his grandson recalled, before the elderly gentleman saw the funny side of his undignified exit.

Perry's response to being charged was both assured and surprising. 'I have no counsel and I want none,' answered Perry. 'I will argue my own case. I plead not guilty.' He had gained some control in jail by making a confession but that no longer suited his purpose. He kept up his new image of the witty performer, amusing the court by playing word-games and chopping logic with the witnesses just like a real lawyer. But he had a serious intention: pleading not guilty gave him a chance to try to undermine the charge of shooting with intent to kill, the most serious he faced. In his cross-examination, he asked the witnesses if they could swear that the shots he fired at the engine were aimed to kill. Both men admitted that they could not. Justice Fries decreed that there was, nevertheless, a case to be heard by the next Grand Jury.

If Perry was disappointed he made no sign but when he was escorted to the police court to face the next charge, the crowd began to annoy him and he muttered, 'I'll hire a hall and give an exhibition of myself. The people act like a lot of cattle or bronchos on a ranch out west.' There were clearly limits to the performer's patience.

Perry soon regained his composure and scored a few points cross-examining witnesses in the second hearing but was again held for Grand Jury trial on $3,000 bail. It was judged highly unlikely that anyone would stand such a high bail, but if someone did, the Lyons authorities were prepared. They announced that they would simply charge Perry on another count and take him back into custody. Perry would be in the Butternut Street jail for a long time: the regular Grand Jury hearing was many weeks away.

Standing quietly at the back of the courtroom while the witnesses were examined was a respectable-looking middle-aged man. He was Oliver H. Perry, the accused's father. As the hearing ended Perry walked up and kissed him, reassuring him that everything would be all right. Back in the jail, the two men talked through the grilled corridor door and the father asked if he could give Perry some oranges, his favourite fruit. It was a rare moment of intimacy for the man who had been performing for days.

When his father was searched, as a matter of routine on leaving the jail, nobody expected to find anything. But in the respectable builder's pocket was a pencil drawing of a key with a message in Perry's handwriting: 'make of very hard wood, be sure and not get it brittle, for it must be very tough and strong make it about the size of this drawing. Hole in key 3/8 of inch. make the key blade so thick as it is drawn above.' It was a guide to making a key to the corridor door.

The discovery of an escape plan was a real embarrassment. Perry had clearly been plotting escape from the moment he arrived in the jail, while he was charming reporters and playing the lawyer, and the Lyons men had suspected nothing. Pinkerton

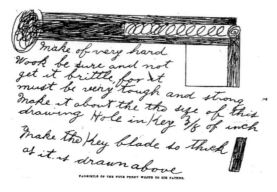

Perry's drawing.

detectives were still hanging around the jail, looking for evidence that the Lyons lawmen were incompetent. Now they seemed to have found it. Thornton reacted swiftly, calling in a local blacksmith who riveted heavy iron shackles linked by an eight-inch-long log chain round Perry's ankles.

Cool as he seemed on the surface, Perry was clearly determined to be free. Asked why he had tried to escape, he replied quite simply, 'Did you ever know a bird to be imprisoned and did not try to get free?' And when his plan was frustrated he took the chance to make fun of his keepers, commenting wryly, 'I think you ought to get a jail strong enough to hold me without this. I ain't very hard to hold.' Was this reaction, like his mockery of the detectives hunting him after the first robbery, just youthful bravado, or a symptom of the same reckless streak that had led to his arrest? It certainly made the lawmen even more determined to avoid further embarrassment. He went on to joke that shackles were often called 'Irish Charms'. But the officers noticed that when he walked these charms were slippery, as his feet, which were long and slim, looked as though they could slip through the shackles. They swiftly ordered the blacksmith to fit a new, tighter pair. Again Perry reacted with some swagger: 'I think these people must be afraid of me for they anchor me down as if I was a giant.'

46

Perry's escape attempt revealed his ability to conceal his real purposes. It also pointed to a complicated family history. Oliver H. Perry had vehemently insisted that he had no idea that the drawing had been slipped into his pocket. The lawmen had no proof that he was lying but some reason to doubt him. He seemed respectable enough, living and running his building business in a decent road in Syracuse, but he had had his own run-ins with the police, usually over scams to pay off debts. Eventually they released him without charge, but banned him from visiting his son again. Thornton and Collins pretended to Perry that his father had betrayed him and he seemed to believe them, complaining loudly about not being able to trust anyone. They were obviously trying to undermine his confidence, but was he just feigning anger and hurt to keep his father out of more trouble? Or was there, as some observers thought, a hint of real doubt and anxiety in his reaction? The lies both men told about their relationship made it hard to know.

When his father had first been questioned about Perry, he claimed not to have seen him for many years, after an earlier estrangement, but he was clearly lying. Neighbours testified that a man identical to Perry, going under the name of Mr Hopkins, had visited Oliver H. and his wife Sarah just before the recent robbery. They remembered him particularly because he had shown off a strange object: a pickled human ear. Perry adamantly denied visiting his family and, despite his scheme with the drawing of the key, and his show of anger at his supposed betrayal, seemed determined to protect his father from involvement in his current predicament. With his father banned from the jail, Oliver Perry kept in contact by writing, while his father began to give his own interviews to the press about the son from whom he had supposedly been estranged. Mrs Perry, a striking woman, visited the jail with clean clothes but did not stop to see her son. Her behaviour seemed as odd as her husband's was slippery. What mother, knowing her son was shackled in a cell, would not seek to comfort him?

Clean clothes would clearly have been welcome, even if they did not come with comfort, as the contents of Perry's valise revealed that he had a definite liking for the finer things in life. As well as the drawing of the key, Perry had given his father a ticket to reclaim a valise from storage. Detectives followed him back to Syracuse, impounded the case and took it back to Lyons for examination. Its contents were fascinating, offering proof of some of the known facts of Perry's past and tantalizing hints of others yet to be revealed.

An expensively bound Bible with many passages underlined and marked in red ink appeared to indicate that Perry had indeed shown religious inclinations, as the citizens of Troy had insisted after his first robbery. One underscored passage read: 'For the weapons of our warfare are not carnal but mighty through God even to the pulling down of strongholds' (Corinthians X: 11). The Bible also showed Perry's determination to conceal his identity. It had clearly been a gift and bore his name imprinted in gold letters on the cover. A date remained, 1891, but the name had been scratched out with a knife.

More religious cards and pamphlets were bundled together in a leather case, along with a red railroad flag and a long-blade butcher's knife, its blade spattered to the hilt with what one paper luridly called spots of 'blood rust', cartridges and tools for cleaning revolvers. Other items included the smoked-glass spectacles Perry wore as a disguise, some fine silk underwear, a pillbox with the place of purchase scratched off, a mouth organ, a buckskin bag containing Mexican coins and two pieces of gold wire, probably from broken jewellery, a Spanish–English phrase book, published in Mexico City, an 'indecent book in Spanish', that sat rather oddly with the religious reading matter, and a glass jar containing the severed ear of a black man.

The ear was final proof that the son had been visiting his family just before the robbery, but, although they were sheltering him, there was no evidence that they had been aware of his plans to rob the second train. The ear gave Perry a chance to display his rather dark sense of humour, as he teased reporters that he had killed the ear's original owner and had planned to send it to the detectives. He eventually revealed that it was a souvenir of a night-time visit to a dissecting room with some medical students he had lodged with while on the run.

The most intriguing find was a small collection of photographs, all of women. Two were in an expensive, Russian leather pocketbook. The third was in a frame. The photographs in the pocketbook were in sharp contrast to each other. One, a cabinet photograph taken in Wilmington, Delaware, was of what the papers called 'a coarse-faced woman'. The other, a tintype, showed a girl in her early teens. Entwined about it was a braid of jet-black hair. The framed photograph was of a plain-looking woman wearing spectacles. At the bottom of the picture, in Perry's handwriting, was the inscription, 'My Mother, December 21, 1891'. The woman in the photograph looked nothing like the Mrs Perry who had been seen in Lyons. Who were these women in Perry's life and where were they now as he sat shackled in his cell awaiting his trial?

If the mystery women had so far failed to appear, plenty of

others had flocked to Butternut Street to see the famous outlaw. Perry's reactions to being expected to 'perform' ranged from angry resistance to charm. When men were allowed into the cellblock to see him, he often turned his face to the wall or covered his face, telling Sheriff Thornton that for all he knew they might be Pinkerton detectives. He was much happier to see the dozens of female visitors, both young and old, many of whom brought gifts of books, flowers, fruit, candies and other treats. Among them was Mrs Goetzman who had apparently forgiven him for taking her favourite mare. While plenty of men expressed a grudging admiration for his daring, something made women in particular take to the young robber. Perhaps it was his looks and daredevilry, or the boyish charm that seemed to enrage the detectives. Whatever the attraction, here was a young man in trouble, a captive prodigal son who seemed to have no lover or mother ready to comfort him.

Not everyone approved. The Reverend Dr Ostrander, a local Presbyterian minister, roundly condemned the women of Lyons in his sermon for their wicked folly in gratifying the vanity of a criminal, and some reporters took their chance to reprimand the fairer sex whose appetite for news of Perry they kept feeding. One paper censoriously announced: 'Flowers for Perry: Woman's Mawkish Sentimentalism Again Manifests Itself', yet kept featuring Perry stories almost daily. 'The law,' Perry observed after the Reverend Ostrander's sermon, 'rigid as it is, is a great deal more charitable than some people's Christianity.'

Disapproving clerics and hypocritical reporters did little to stem public enthusiasm for Perry. While their parents could visit the jail, the local children busied themselves taking turns to play the robber or the lawman in noisy re-enactments. Or, as Theodore Harry Fries remembered, they crowded the sidewalk outside Ed Walter's second-hand store. There, in the window, was a large crayon drawing of the scene of Perry's capture, showing the robber at bay behind the brick wall, brandishing his guns. To the nine-year-old and his friends, the picture was as good as the movies would be to their own children, and Perry was a real-life hero and villain rolled into one.

CHAPTER 5
'I lived a wild life . . .'

IN THE weeks when everyone waited for the trial that would decide Oliver Perry's future the young robber started to reveal more about his past. In his cell in Lyons, smoking cigars provided by grateful reporters, he began spinning together fantasy and reality in stories that would enthral an eager public who wanted to know everything about Oliver Perry.

Shortly after Perry's arrest, his father had claimed that he and his son were related to Oliver Hazard Perry, naval hero of the War of Independence, and to August Belmont, the influential New York financier. For many, this was final confirmation that Oliver Curtis Perry was no ordinary thief. He already had good looks, intelligence, daring and a kind heart, if the rumours of gifts to the needy were to be believed. Now he had an illustrious lineage. But while his father was certainly named after Commodore Perry, the kinship, if any, was distant. Yet if Perry's lineage was not as illustrious as his father asserted, his life, according to his own stories, was as dramatic as his crimes.

Few of these 'revelations', some of which were undoubtedly inventions, can be verified now, without reliable records to distinguish fact from fiction. But they fascinated press and public alike, building a mythology around Perry that tapped into the fantasies of his age: of a Wild West that was swiftly being tamed, of Mexico, a land of passionate rebels and sensual delights, and of the fateful act that propelled an ordinary working man out of his unrewarding daily grind into the world of wealth. Perry evidently shared, and lived, some of these dreams. But he also knew their power.

Amidst the exaggerations and the fantasies were the bare bones of the story of a short but dramatic life. Perry described a boy from upstate New York who ran away to start a new life out west, as a ranch hand and cowboy. He said almost nothing about his childhood and gave few details of his western days, saying simply, 'It was a wild life and entering heartily into it I became wild and reckless.' Years later he would describe turning to crime with a gang of 'mates' in Texas and Nebraska, and hint that he had learned to rob trains in the west. But in 1892 he would only say that two or three years earlier he had tired of his wild life and decided to 'reform'.

In the hope of living a respectable life he returned to New York. There the wanderer settled in the city of Troy. One day he was encouraged by acquaintances to attend a prayer meeting at the Helping Hand mission, run by Miss Amelia Haswell, the woman who infuriated detectives by destroying Perry's photographs when he was on the run.

Amelia Haswell.

Amelia Haswell took a shine to him and he gradually trusted her enough to tell her about his troubled past and even began to call her 'Mother', the name inscribed on the photograph of her he carried in his valise. Convinced that he deserved a second chance, she helped him to get a job with a local railroad company, the Fitchburg, and even let him stay with her while he looked for lodgings. Perry started work as a brakeman, a dangerous job that involved running along the tops of cars on moving trains in order to reach the brakes between them. Later this skill would be a key to his daring robberies. But his church friends in Troy saw no signs of his future fall from grace. He made no secret of his 'sinful' youth, they said, but seemed to be genuinely trying to reform: he did not drink, would not tolerate swearing, joined the Railroad Young Men's Christian Association, and even asked to be excused from work on Sundays in order to attend services. He also showed early signs of his ability as a charismatic speaker to entertain and persuade an audience. Then he had been in demand at mission meetings, exhorting sinners to repent, while later he would charm the hardened men of the New York press and through them a growing band of supporters.

The Trojans were not the only ones to be convinced of Perry's sincerity. The Fitchburg line ran between Troy and North Adams in Massachusetts, through the newly built Hoosick tunnel. As a railroad worker, Perry lodged at both ends of the line and made a similar impression in both places. His North Adams landlady, Mrs Sutton, told the press that Perry was no trouble, and that another lodger, a young lady, had often played the organ and sung for him. He had given no hint of his criminal past, but his musical tastes might have offered a clue. His reading matter, Mrs Sutton recalled, was invariably devout, including a book, inscribed as a gift from Amelia Haswell, called *Precious Hymns for Times of Refreshing and Revival*. But his favourite song had been 'Seven Long Years I've Been in Prison'.

After about a year as a brakeman, Perry was seriously injured in an accident on the railroad. He was running along the top of a train when it entered the Hoosick tunnel and he was knocked on to the tracks, seriously injuring his back and fracturing his skull. When he was eventually discharged after a long stay in hospital, he was penniless and unemployed. Few jobs were held for injured employees and he received no sick pay. His church friends used their influence once again to find him a job, this time a less hazardous position on the New York Central passenger service between Albany and Syracuse, working inside the trains rather than on top of them. This meant a move to Albany, the state capital, where he worked until early May 1891 when he was given ten days' leave of absence for medical reasons. But at the end of that time, instead of returning to work, he handed in his notice and disappeared for some months. He never explained how or where he spent the summer months, but in mid-September he started work on the Central once more. Two weeks later he robbed the American Express Special.

Perry's explanations of his motivation in committing his first train robbery are an intriguing mixture of fact and fabulation. The immediate catalyst, he said, was a run-in with his trainmaster who had reprimanded him for a minor infringement of the company's uniform regulations. While being told off, he had, he said, experienced 'a feeling of rebellion which I was unable to overcome'. Clearly, being forced to conform and being rebuked by someone in authority had triggered more than normal levels of resentment. The young man who had lived a wild life out west was feeling increasingly trapped and exploited in the regulated world of the industrial east.

For a while he brooded on his situation, then saw a way of escaping it. 'As I stood there thinking I saw the express boxes being loaded upon the train and I thought of the wealth in those safes in the express car. I knew that my position meant drudgery and hard work for small pay all my life. I resolved to do something desperate, and naturally the safes in the express car were the first objects of my ambition.'

His resentment about his apparent lot in life may have been fuelled by a new influence. Amelia Haswell, who insisted on the sincerity of Perry's attempt to live a good Christian life up to that point, believed that he had been led astray in Albany by someone she called an 'Ingersoll man'. Robert Ingersoll was a free thinker whose radical views of subjects from equality to prison reform and atheism were popular with those campaigning against social and economic exploitation. As Perry's hostility towards the Pinkertons who had broken the Fitchburg strike had revealed, he held some views that might have been seen as radical. He told one reporter, 'When going through the country I used to compare my condition with that of the rich. . . . Remember, I didn't plunder from those who couldn't afford to be despoiled. Look on these hands. They are hard with honest toil and I would wear them to the bones at work before I would inflict a loss on anyone unable to sustain it. But I thought the American Express Company could sustain a little plucking and I set about it.'

Perry certainly resented being exploited but he was also quite capable of using the rhetoric of oppression to win public sympathy, and his claim not to have robbed the poor was at best naïve. It is, as ever in his interviews, hard to distinguish between truth and invention. Later he hinted that there had been another, far more personal, catalyst for his first train robbery.

'I wanted to settle down. I wanted to make a home. Of course, I had a reason for wanting to make that home. I wanted it to be as good as the homes I saw. I thought a great deal about it. I'd knocked about the world a good bit. I'd been earning my own living since I was eleven years old. I had never had a home of my own. I had never married, and I did not mean to marry until I thought I could make such a home as I'd thought about. I believed – I had reason to believe – that I should have the companion I wanted. I intended to go West and settle down and have a home. I intended to live a straight life and be an honest man. I'd been a wild boy, but I had come to the time when I was a man, when I would look my life over and think what I was going to make of it.' Realizing, he said, that an ordinary job would never pay enough, 'I thought this all over, and I saw the only way was a bold stroke, with big chances.' Tellingly, given his positively dangerous level of confidence, he added, 'I believed I was clever enough not to be found out.'

Perry only hinted at a romantic twist in his tale, and was always guarded in his references to it, but Amelia Haswell made it explicit. Towards the end of his time in the west, she said, he had worked for a time on a ranch in New Mexico where he had fallen in love with his employer's daughter and she with him. The young couple had gone riding together in his free hours and met in secret until her father found out, dismissed Perry and sent her away. Perry had resolved to prove he could be respectable and buy a decent home for them both. So he had moved back to New York, hoping to return for her when he had made enough money. According to Amelia Haswell, he 'could never speak of the girl without becoming nervous, and the tears would come into his eyes'.

But everything went wrong. Perry had already become disillusioned with the slow, small rewards of honest work when, sometime before the fall of 1891, he discovered that his 'sweetheart' was gravely ill and possibly dying. This, his friend assumed, was the reason for his leaving Albany in the summer months. In the early fall, Amelia Haswell received a letter from Perry that claimed he was enduring 'the greatest sorrow of my life' and was 'tempted almost beyond endurance'. She had been away on vacation when the letter arrived and by the time she had a chance to reply, her good counsel came too late. It was Perry's desperation to help his girl, Amelia Haswell believed, that made him take the greatest risk of his life and rob the express. Already convinced that he would never earn enough money honestly to match the gilded palaces of New York's robber barons, he now feared he would never be able to provide a modest home for his sweetheart. So he turned his railroading skills to his own, criminal, advantage. Then, evading capture in Utica, he made his way west, only to find that he was too late. His sweetheart had already died.

Perry told his own story of what happened next. 'I had the greatest disappointment a man can have. . . . So I never made that home and I never settled down. I was reckless then. The money was no good to me. I lived a wild life and I gambled the most of it away. I did not care what became of me, that is the truth.' A passing remark, possibly designed to test his audience's credulity, and certainly mischievous, led to a totally untrue story that Perry had tried to join up with the famous Mexican revolutionary Catarino Garza, struggling to overthrow the tyrannical President.

He certainly spent time in the border country where Garza fought, and then in Mexico, a country he loved: 'it is beautiful there – always summer . . . Everyone went promenading in the evening and there were bands of music and something going on all the time.' But Perry denied any involvement with Garza and talked instead about losing himself in his reckless life after the robbery and his sweetheart's death.

He insisted that he had never been a drinker, but admitted to having taken opium. His main diversion and vice, predictably in the light of his crimes, was gambling. Then, as Christmas approached, he decided to return to Troy. He was taking quite a risk, going back to one of the places where he was well known and where his friends were still being watched by the police and detectives. But it seems that Perry was tired of drifting, even in fine clothes, and wanted to see his 'Mother'.

On 22 December 1891 he turned up at Amelia Haswell's house and confessed the truth about his involvement in the robbery to her. She tried to persuade him to hand himself in, but he was afraid that his past record and the determination of American Express and the Pinkertons to make an example of him would guarantee a lengthy sentence in prison. He was particularly worried that he would end up in Clinton, the daunting institution in the far north-east of the state, known as 'Little Siberia'. In the end, he gave Amelia the jewellery to return to American Express, which she did, through a lawyer friend, and moved on.

If Amelia Haswell knew where he had gone, she said nothing. Her loyalty to Perry was extraordinary. She had not only destroyed her photographs of him when he was a wanted man, but had even called at the photographer's to ask that the glass negative be destroyed. In response, the detectives had her mail intercepted and kept her under almost constant surveillance from the first robbery and even while Perry was awaiting trial.

Perry spent the next two months in Canada, where he posted the letter exonerating Messenger Moore, and, sometime before the end of February, went to stay in Syracuse where he visited his family. There he decided on the biggest gamble of his life: robbing the American Express Special a second time. While he tried to explain the motivation for the first robbery at some length, Perry admitted that he committed the second on 'impulse', and to make money because 'I had lived a life that brought expensive tastes and unfitted me to go back to earning $2 a day.' As a wanted man, he must have had a stark choice: turn himself in and face a long prison sentence or live as an outlaw indefinitely. He clearly dreaded prison, so surrender was unthinkable. To live on the run cost money, to live even half-decently cost a great deal. Another robbery was the only solution, and why not try to repeat a success?

Perry's stories of his life up to the recent robbery made sensational reading in 1892 and throughout his life. Some parts were undoubtedly exaggerated, others made up. Over a century later it is not easy to establish the whole truth. Neither he nor Amelia Haswell ever named his doomed sweetheart and there is no documentary proof that she ever existed. But what respectable family would acknowledge that their daughter had planned to elope with a ranch hand, let alone one who became a notorious robber? The Pinkertons reported that Perry, as a man with a criminal record known to the eager agents, had been followed from Deming, New Mexico to Flagstaff and Tucson in Arizona in the summer of 1891, before the first robbery, and was seen in El Paso, Texas on 28 November, shortly afterwards. Was he just meeting up with old mates from his wilder days or was he travelling to find his sweetheart? There was one tangible clue to support the story: the photograph of the young girl, with the lock of dark hair wound around it, in Perry's wallet. Amelia Haswell said that both belonged to his sweetheart and had been carried by Perry since their meeting. She may have been naïve and the story certainly sounds like a romantic cliché designed to win sympathy, but it is possible to be too cynical. Some romances are true.

The stories of Perry's crimes, his tragic romance and shattered dreams made him an ever more appealing figure. Men and boys could imagine his wild cowboy days, as industrialization made the frontier seem more like a myth every day. Radicals and reformers could identify with the working man who had finally snapped under the weight of social and economic injustice. Romantics could feel for the sensitive but proud man, torn between right and wrong as he fought to build a life with the woman he loved. The man shackled in the Lyons cell was, if anything, even more alluring now than he had been as a handsome fugitive.

There were, of course, exceptions to the general enthusiasm, such as an anonymous letter sent to praise Deputy Collins and denounce Perry: 'I say most emphatically that if the Ladies will go to see this inhuman *Toad*, let them carry the *Cross Bones* and exhibit them, and for Dessert, paris green puddings, with strychnine flavoring, and to save the great vigilance of Watchmen, spike both feet solid to the floor, strip him naked, pack him in solid ice, smash of the hand he shot McInnery [*sic*] with, give him chop sticks in the other hand to eat with, shut out all light from his cell, and to add to the darkness shut the Nigger in with him, with a double barrelled shot gun, in this way you may rid yourselves of both.'

There was plenty of ammunition for less unhinged assaults on Perry's self-defined character, although the 'evidence' was as unreliable as that for his deeds of heroism and romance. Labourers' daughters and fine ladies alike claimed to have been engaged or even married to Perry, then deserted. He was accused of swindling businesses in Philadelphia, duping clergymen in Canada, robbing a traveller in California and, most seriously, of killing a Montana saloon keeper in a brawl. Perry roundly protested his innocence of all the charges and even found unexpected support from Pinkerton agents whose alleged sightings of the wanted man became useful alibis. He was never charged with any of the supposed crimes and such was the public interest in and support for him that the rumours simply added to his allure. A reporter conducted an opinion poll of local citizens and found that all but one would like to see Perry freed.

The Perry myth also had obvious commercial potential. In a bizarre realization of Perry's joke about making an 'exhibition' of himself, Robinson's Musee-Theater in Rochester boasted a new display: two figures of Oliver Curtis Perry in wax. One showed Perry in his famous train-robbing outfit, with hood and rope; the other depicted him 'as he would appear on the street'. Newspaper advertisements described the Musee-Theater's attractions:

In the curio hall the original Kawakamis, sword fencers and athletes from Japan, will be seen, their acts combining the three elements of curio, novelty and speciality. Mr. and Mrs. Kawakami will appear in the costumes of ancient Japanese

DESPERADO PERRY'S OUTLAW REGALIA.

Perry's train-robbing disguise as worn by Robinson's waxwork.

warfare. Miss Kate Koon, lightning artist, is announced to 'paint beautiful designs in two minutes'. The Hungarian gypsy band is there and there will be seen in wax a representation of Oliver C. Perry the daring train robber recently captured near Lyons.

Despite the exotic charms of these fellow attractions, it was the wax Perry that topped the bill. General admission to the Musee-Theater was 10 cents, with seats for shows from 15 cents and boxes at 25 cents. Doors were open from 1 p.m. to 10 o'clock at night.

When news of the exhibit reached Perry, he was not flattered. He hired a lawyer, through his Trojan friends, to demand that Robinson withdraw the exhibit or face an injunction. Displaying an extraordinarily canny sense of his value as a commodity, Perry calculated the price of his reputation as $10,000, the amount for which he threatened to sue Robinson. Robinson bullishly announced that new Perry figures would soon be exhibited in his Buffalo museum. However, in the next week's advertisement in Rochester, there was no sign of the Perry exhibit. The new star attraction was 'Prof. Dick's EDUCATED FLEAS. Flea Circus, Flea Actors, Flea Tricks'. Supporting the fleas, possibly in more ways than one, was Angola, 'the Only Living Gorilla in America'.

Perry's self-marketing was even more explicitly revealed in a letter he wrote to his father. He told him that he wanted him to have his possessions after his trial: 'I think you could take my clothes, satchel, revolvers, mask, hooks and rope, in fact all my things and sell them to some museum for a good round sum of money. I also will have some things sent to you in time that will make quite a collection. I have a large western hat cost $15.00, boots $12.00, two blankets, one saddle blanket and one bed blanket made by hand by the Indians, and a number of other things. I will have them sent to you just as soon as I think best. If you can consult some good lawyer and have him correspond with different Museum Managers and in that way perhaps you could get a good offer for the collection. I would not take less than $200.00 for the collection and I think you can get more.' The man who had risked everything in one last gamble may have lost but he was evidently determined to get some profit.

CHAPTER 6

'It's a long time to wait and I don't like the idea'

WHILE HE was working the press, performing to the gallery and protecting his interests, Perry had also been busy behind the scenes. Since his foiled escape attempt soon after his arrest, he had seemed more concerned with charming the public at large than rejoining them. But in fact he had been plotting escape all the time and when his efforts were discovered a different side of his personality came to light.

First, the Sheriff disturbed Perry as he was trying out a half-finished lead key in the corridor door, resembling the wooden one he had sketched. The key was confiscated and the jail was searched. At first, the lawmen assumed Perry was being helped by an outsider, but soon they discovered it was an 'inside job' when they found more escape 'tools' hidden in other cells: lead foil that could have been melted over a lamp to form the key, pieces of wire to use to turn it, a steel strip, taken from the sole of a boot and sharpened, and a small piece of paper on which was scrawled 'We want it right off'. Evidently Perry and some of his fellow prisoners had been in league and the construction of a key for the corridor door had been merely the first stage in a plan. All the men were questioned and their answers kept secret.

Perry, whose own cell held no suspicious items, watched the entire search impassively. But one by one his plans to secure his freedom began to unravel. More tools were discovered hidden in an enlarged rat hole and eventually even Perry's clothing came under suspicion. First, the sacking wrapped round his shackles to stop them rattling was removed and the leg irons fell to the floor. He had cut them in two, using a small saw concealed in his Bible, which the Sheriff had let him keep for spiritual comfort. Amelia Haswell's gift had evidently been customized in a manner of which the missionary can hardly have approved.

If the Sheriff had been more thoughtful than careful when he first took Perry into custody, he was now determined to see, quite literally, that he had no more tricks up his sleeve. Perry was ordered to strip. All his clothes, the same ones he had worn when he was arrested and had, to his evident discomfort, been wearing ever since, were carefully examined. Then the lining of his jacket was ripped open. Sewn into the collar and waistband was a total of $250 dollars in $50 dollar bills. He had hidden them after the Utica robbery in case of emergency. Perry seemed so prepared and so determined to escape that, according to a report, nobody in Lyons believed 'he will come to trial without at least one fierce dash for liberty'. But his options were fast running out.

The Sheriff had to resort to stiff measures to contain his apparently incorrigible prisoner. Perry was moved to a smaller cell, only six by four feet, with a solid door rather than open bars, making it gloomy as well as cramped. He was told he was to be kept in close confinement until the trial and would have no unsupervised contact with other prisoners or visitors. Instead of eating in the corridor with the other prisoners, he would be fed in his cell. His meals would be passed through the small hole in

Wayne County Jail cellblock (From the collection of
the Wayne County Historical Society, Lyons, New York).

the upper part of the cell door. A watchman was to be stationed
outside his door, day and night.

Up until this point Perry had impressed people with his
apparent nonchalance, but the discovery of what was clearly a
careful plot and of the money that he might use for bribes or to
get equipment began to depress him. The man who enjoyed
telling tales clearly depended on his real plans being kept hidden.
Being in jail had not been that depressing, while he had the ability
to work on his fellow prisoners as carefully as he charmed the
press, to build a team around him and plan each stage of the
escape. Now he was back to square one. Close confinement
meant he had no chance of working on a new plan. He was
also beginning to suffer some pain as the result of an injury,

almost certainly a rupture, incurred during the long chase on horseback. Was the apparently indomitable Perry beginning to show signs of strain? He had also been warned that the Grand Jury hearing might not be until mid- June, two months away. 'It's a long time to wait and I don't like the idea,' he admitted but he was still defiant about the trial: 'I will plead not guilty. My sentence will be none the lighter if I do not.' He might be unable to escape what now looked like his certain fate, but clearly had no intention of taking his punishment meekly.

The discovery of one after another of his tools and activities also pointed to an inescapable conclusion that began to eat away at Perry. Someone had betrayed him. Isolated in his tiny cell and seeing his plans systematically frustrated, he turned his mind to the question of his betrayer's identity. He eventually decided it was a tramp known as 'One Armed Ed', who did chores in the jail. Ed suffered a twisted remaining arm as a punishment when he passed Perry his food, but was an innocent man. It was revealed much later that the informer had been another, younger prisoner who received a reduced sentence as a reward.

The growing strain on Perry showed when visitors tried to get a glimpse of the notorious prisoner, but even under pressure he managed to turn an unwelcome reality to some advantage. Although he was no longer allowed unsupervised visits from friends, local people and reporters still called at the jail and asked to see him. But when the officers allowed them to take a look through the cell door, Perry demonstrated a new technique for dealing with them. While the visitor tried, or asked, to see his face, he would turn towards a looking-glass in his cell. By watching them watching him he was exerting the only control he could as a prisoner, allowing people to see only what he wanted them to see.

Other visitors to his cell got harsher treatment as he began to take out his frustration on the jailers who had resorted to tough measures to contain him. Deputy Collins found him trying to break his shackles by dropping one of the legs of his iron bedstead on them. When guards tried to stop him he started hurling some heavy earthenware cups, which he had hoarded after meals, at them. As a punishment and to prevent similar incidents, his wrists were shackled, although when Collins tried to fit the new restraints he only avoided being covered with the contents of Perry's lavatory bucket by threatening the prisoner with his revolver. Perry's days of sitting with a cigar entertaining his visitors were definitely over. Until his trial he would be involved in regular skirmishes with his keepers, especially Deputy Collins.

Collins, made impatient by Perry's slipperiness and impudence, was reportedly keen to strip him of all his comforts, putting him on bread and water and even giving him a good thrashing if necessary. Sheriff Thornton, a milder man who was much more sympathetic towards his prisoner, had gone out of his way to treat him well, even writing to a newspaper to deny a report that Perry had obtained weapons to attack, and even kill, Collins. As the public awaited Perry's trial, the contrasting attitudes and approaches of the two lawmen became the subject of heated debate in their own right.

To some, Thornton was a gentle, kindly man who treated his young prisoner with sensitivity, to others, an indulgent fool who was being duped by a devious criminal, while Collins was seen as tough but fair, or, as Perry certainly believed, a licensed bully. It was a conventional enough debate

Sheriff Walter Thornton.

about how to deal with criminals. But there was a particular twist to the story of Thornton versus Collins in the battle over Perry's treatment. Thornton was a Republican and stories about his apparent laxity versus the more effective approach of his Deputy appeared in the *Wayne Democratic Press*. The famous prisoner, who had used the press to win public support, had become a pawn in a game of local politics.

Deputy Sheriff
Jeremiah Collins.

Inside the jail, Perry was more concerned with getting some personal revenge on Deputy Collins for his punitive approach. He wrote a jail diary, now lost, that included an account of his arrest in the swamp that was clearly designed to undermine Collins's claim to the reward for his capture. He claimed that he offered to surrender if Collins shared the $1,000 reward equally with him, or let him walk away unharmed and surrender instead to the crowd. When Collins agreed to share the reward, Perry let himself be captured, feigning the fight that had given rise to such praise for the Deputy's courage. But once Perry was in custody, Collins had conveniently forgotten the deal. While Perry may have hoped to damage the Deputy's reputation, and the diary was conveniently leaked to the press, nobody seemed to believe his version.

The long wait for the trial continued and, without new incidents, the press turned to other news. The harsh winter had turned to a milder spring, and May Day workers' marches, which many had believed would bring bloody revolution to Europe and provoke radical unrest nearer home, turned out to be peaceful protests. Of greater interest to readers looking for dramatic stories was the sad tale of George Hamilton, 'the screaming boy' of Kentucky. The fourteen-year-old, a bright chap with a 'genius in mechanical affairs', had been struck down by terrible headaches that left him deaf and blind and unable to taste the food that kept him alive. All he could do, his body so twisted by pain that his head was bent back to his hips, was scream. His doctors could do nothing, and on 7 May the screams finally stopped. Some torments were worse than any prison sentence.

CHAPTER 7

His Career Ended!

P ERRY'S GRAND Jury hearing began, earlier than he had
been led to expect, on 17 May. Predictably, the Wayne
County Court House was filled to overflowing. Over the next
two days more than forty witnesses were called (although one
over-excited reporter gave a count of more than a hundred),
including the entire crews of both trains Perry was alleged to have
robbed, numerous detectives and members of the public. Before
testifying, Burt Moore and Daniel McInerney, now apparently
restored to health, called in at the jail to identify Perry as their
attacker. Although McInerney insisted in court that the incident

had not affected his mind, he was so
anxious while in the jail that he hid
behind Moore.

Almost as soon as the hearing started, a
shocking drama unfolded that distracted
press and public attention. One of the
witnesses for the prosecution was a
young New York City jeweller's store
porter called Albert Stanton, who had
been subpoenaed to appear to make a

Messenger Daniel
McInerney.

75

formal identification of items stolen in the Utica robbery. The day after he testified, apparently without incident, he set off for home by train. Towards the end of the long journey, just after four in the afternoon, he suddenly stood up, walked into the middle of the carriage and said, 'Well, I might as well do it now.' Then he took out a pocket-knife and cut his throat from ear to ear.

He left a wife and three children and no clue to his brutal suicide. Stanton's life, up to this point, had been unremarkable. His employer suggested that anxiety about testifying in such a high-profile trial might have tipped him into insanity: 'I believe that he fairly worried himself into suicide.'

While such anxiety might have been enough to disturb some-one who was mentally or emotionally fragile, it seems odd, if this was the reason, that Stanton did not kill himself on the way to the trial. The real reason for the suicide was never discovered. It may have been entirely unconnected to the trial. Whatever its catalyst, Albert Stanton's death was a sensational distraction from the hearing. It was also only the first of a series of tragedies to befall some of those whose lives became briefly entangled with Perry's.

Perry himself was formally arraigned on Thursday, 19 May. The large crowd, including a gallery full of women, was looking forward to a dramatic climax to Perry's time in Lyons and, indeed, his career. There had been much speculation about how he would plead, given his apparent determination after his long confinement to make a fight of it. A few days earlier he had been told that the District Attorney was subpoenaing his friend, Amelia Haswell, who had been bedridden by the strain of the detectives' constant pressure. The news that she would now have to make the long journey west strengthened Perry's resolve to force a trial and he engaged the services of a lawyer.

Just before he was called, the woman he called 'Mother' visited him in jail. The two spoke for a long time. Concerned about Perry's increasingly distressed and destructive behaviour, Amelia tried to persuade him that there was only one way to make the best of a hard situation, to take his punishment and trust in the Lord to protect him.

Perry was brought into court at five in the afternoon, heavily shackled and closely guarded. In a grey suit and with his moustache grown again, he looked as dashing as he had in his 'wanted' posters, but he was noticeably paler after months in jail. He spoke briefly with his attorney and was then asked to stand to hear the indictments against him.

The room was silent as the District Attorney read the indictments. The first was for burglary in the third degree, second offence, and robbery, first degree, second offence, both committed in Herkimer County on 30 September 1891. This indictment was for breaking into an express car and committing robbery by taking property in the care of Messenger Moore, to the amount of $5,000. The second was for burglary, first degree, second offence, assault, first degree, and attempt at robbery, first degree. This indictment was for breaking into the express car in Cayuga County, and attacking Messenger McInerney on 21 February 1892. The third was for assault in the first degree on Alexander McGilvery, the engineer of freight engine No. 511, whom Perry drove from his engine at gunpoint when trying to escape. The fourth and final indictment was for discharging firearms at a locomotive.

Most people expected Perry to put up a fight. But after each indictment was read, he spoke only one word: 'Guilty.' Amelia Haswell was convinced, and had convinced him, that this would encourage a merciful, lighter sentence. Perry may have taken her advice, but when he entered his plea his voice was almost inaudible. The realization that he was willingly committing himself to the incarceration he dreaded, and had fought so bitterly to avoid, must have been hard to bear. The District Attorney immediately asked that sentence be pronounced. The judge, William Rumsey, following the letter of the law, informed Perry that he was officially entitled to two days' respite before sentencing. The public strained to hear Perry's faltering reply: 'I have no reason as far as I am concerned.'

A *New York Herald* reporter commented that 'the whole scene was as businesslike and free from excitement as if the business before the Court were the argument of a technical motion involving a question of $10 costs'. But when Judge Rumsey pronounced his sentence it was clear that justice was not only swift but severe.

Perry was sentenced to five years for the first count of the first indictment, and twenty years on the second count, five years on the second indictment, ten years on the third indictment, and nine years and three months on the fourth indictment. The sentences were to be served as hard labour in Auburn prison and were to run, not as sentences often do today concurrently, but consecutively. In all he was to serve forty-nine years and three months. Even by the standards of the day, it was a harsh sentence.

'Half A Century Hard' was how one paper described it. If he survived, he would be released at the age of seventy-five in the almost unthinkable year of 1942. Perry listened to the sentence without any obvious show of emotion. One Lyons reporter interpreted his expression: 'Perry received his sentence as meekly as an erring child receives a mother's kind reproof. The bravado had left him. The wild western spirit had died away and the most noted desperado of the East, perhaps of the country, quailed before the verdict of grim justice.'

Swift calculations of the time Perry would serve, with reductions for 'good behaviour', were published, amounting to a term of twenty-nine years, four months and twenty-three days. In this case he would be released on 13 October 1921 at the age of fifty-six. But few who had witnessed, or read about, his escape attempts and refusal to knuckle down to life in jail believed his sentence would not be served in full. If he tried the same tricks in Auburn he would learn what the real penalties for insolence could be. A formality that followed his sentencing added a slightly chilling note to the hearing, as Perry's will was approved. In it he bequeathed his personal effects, including $300 cash and a diamond ring to his father, and his pistols to Sheriff Thornton.

Although he seemed to have been in a daze during the hearing, Perry swiftly rallied, laughing and talking as he returned to the jail, and set about preparing for the following day's move to Auburn. The prison's reputation was as fearsome as his was daring, but Oliver Perry was clearly determined to put on a show of defiance.

CHAPTER 8

Perry Dons the Stripes

THE PEOPLE of Lyons had one last chance to see Oliver
Perry before he disappeared into prison. As he was taken to
the station to catch the train to Auburn, he treated them to one
last display of celebrity behaviour, giving mementos to a small
group of people, including his lawyers and some newspaper
correspondents. Each lucky man or woman was presented with
a Mexican coin or piece of gold, a tiny share in Perry's exotic
adventures and ill-gotten gains.

When they reached the station, the crowd was so big it was
hard for the Sheriff and his men to get Perry through to the train.
Once they were in the car, the crowd surged forward to surround
it. Perry seemed tense and muttered about not being able to
breathe. Twenty minutes passed before the train finally pulled out
to make the journey east to Auburn.

The party soon had to change, at nearby Geneva, and this time
some of the crowd managed to get inside the train. One man,
apparently very drunk, lunged at Perry, shouting that he was
going to give him a good thrashing. Sheriff Thornton moved
swiftly to protect his prisoner. He had the man removed from the
car, then locked the door to prevent further incidents as the train

moved on. Perry relaxed a little and started reading a newspaper, commenting on the speculation about his possible release in 1921 for good behaviour: 'Boys, come over when I'm discharged and we'll all have an oyster supper.'

At the next stop, Waterloo, the crowd stayed on the platform, but a young lady who was leaving the train approached the party. Ignoring her mother's protests, she handed Perry a small bunch of lilies of the valley. He thanked her and placed the flowers in his buttonhole. But, although he was clearly still trying to maintain, or live up to, his romantic image, the constant attention, both aggressive and solicitous, was wearing him down. So at the next stop, when people asked to see the famous Perry, they were pointed not to him but to a guard in plain clothes. It was a simple ruse, but effective. After all, which man was handcuffed to which? It even fooled a newspaper correspondent who 'snapped' the wrong man and left contentedly to the cheers and laughter of the passengers 'in the know'.

The mood was still light as they continued to Aurelius. The conductor, making his rounds, asked Perry for his ticket. But after it had been punched earlier in the journey, Perry had given it to a bystander as a souvenir. So he jokingly suggested the conductor put him off the train. At Cayuga the train stopped for ten minutes for refreshments and Perry asked for some luncheon. Sheriff Thornton told him he would eat at Auburn but some other passengers went to buy him oranges. He ate two while plans were made for the imminent arrival in Auburn. As he saw the prison through the window, he was heard to mutter, 'I now have a home.'

The crowds hoping to see him enter his new home had been gathering since the early morning. Auburn had seen some des-

perate criminals but few as exciting as Perry. Men and women
had rushed to the station to meet each New York Central train,
hoping he would be aboard. Others waited outside the prison
gate. By noon both places were teeming. Perry and his escorts
finally arrived at the depot just before 1 o'clock. The crowd
watched him climb down from the train, handcuffed to one
guard, and escorted by another, then followed them out into
the street. But the 'prisoner' they followed was really a young
reporter from Lyons, and his 'guards' were other newsmen.

The real Perry and his party had waited for the decoys to draw
the crowd, then walked undisturbed to the ironically named
'Home' restaurant, where a good dinner was ordered for everyone.
Thornton meant to give Perry one last treat, but it was not a wise
move. As word spread about his whereabouts, people rushed to
stand outside the restaurant. When the time came to leave, the
Sheriff had to call the police to clear a path through the crowd.
Eventually they reached the imposing entrance to Auburn.

In its early days, reformers, government representatives and
experts, including Alexis de Tocqueville and Gustave de Beau-
mont, travelled from across the world to visit Auburn. Built in
1816, it was the home of the 'Auburn system', a once-
revolutionary penal regime at a time when the idea of reforming
prisoners was still new. This involved convicts sleeping in individual cells, instead of shared rooms as they had hitherto, and
working together in the day, but in total silence at all times. This
double isolation was idealistically designed to encourage them to
contemplate their own mistakes, without the corrupting influence
of other criminals, and, pragmatically, to make them easier to
manage by removing the possibility of plotting against the authorities. Although the men found ways of communicating,

Auburn Prison (Courtesy of Cayuga Museum).

a prisoner discovered talking at any time, unless responding to an officer's question, was subject to instant and severe punishment.

The Auburn regime was a modification of the even more extreme 'Pennsylvania system', which isolated prisoners in individual cells twenty-four hours a day, even for work. Auburn tried this in 1821, locking eighty prisoners in individual cells. The effects were dramatic. By the summer of 1823, it was found that total isolation had driven many of the men insane. When one cell door was opened, its occupant ran out and threw himself off the fourth-floor landing; another banged his head against the wall until he lost an eye. So Auburn decided to allow prisoners to work together, but in silence. Apart from being less obviously inhumane, this was also more economically practical. Prisoners locked in cells could only be employed in handicraft rather than more lucrative industrial production. In the nineteenth century prisons, with a slave labour force, had real economic potential.

By allowing 'congregate' labour, Auburn thrived. In 1892 it had a foundry as well as workshops producing goods from pearl buttons and furniture to brooms and boilers. It even, briefly, ran a silk factory. Commercial companies started to object to unfair competition from prison industries, and by 1895 New York's prisons would only be allowed to manufacture goods for their own use. But when Perry arrived, Auburn was, supposedly, an ideal blend of theory and practicality, a model society run according to the twin principles of industry and discipline.

Auburn created many of the features of prison life that swiftly became visual clichés, such as striped prison uniform and close-cropped hair to symbolize the convict's changed status. The prison also introduced a special walk, called 'lockstep', in which each prisoner shuffled along, holding the man in front, as they moved between cells and workshops or the dining hall. Lockstep, as the name suggests, turned men into a human chain. It also served as an abiding mark of their convict status. Years after they were released, when their hair had grown and uniform was a bad memory, ex-prisoners could be identified by the way they walked,

Prisoners in Lockstep (Courtesy of Cayuga Museum).

pushing their feet along as if still in lockstep. Auburn had recently shown its pioneering spirit yet again, and acquired a new notoriety, when, in 1890, William Kemmler became the first man in America to die in the electric chair.

Today Auburn's fearsome reputation has been eclipsed by the violent riots in neighbouring Attica, and its ivy-covered entrance makes the maximum-security prison look almost cosy. Yet inside the tension is still palpable. There may be a gym and a garden, as well as work and education, to occupy bodies and minds, but the men, mainly young African-Americans from downstate, are still obliged to walk in silence in the corridors so that the officers can be heard and no fights can be masked by inmates talking. Conversation in the yard is no longer forbidden, but the strangeness and strain of this male society are immediately apparent to a visitor. A

woman walking through the yard on a hot summer's day, un-
seasonably dressed in trousers and a long-sleeved shirt, is palpably
aware of the now hidden violence of these men's constraints.
Nothing is said, but hundreds of staring eyes speak clearly.

Perry walked through the gate into Auburn just after 2 o'clock.
Inside his new 'home', Mr and Mrs Perry were waiting. But
before anyone could speak, the Warden intervened: 'Bring that
man this way; he's my prisoner now.' He had not taken kindly to
waiting while his prisoner had been dining at leisure. Perry tried
to speak to his father but was hurried away. In the keepers' hall
his handcuffs were removed and then he was swiftly marched to
the barber's shop where he was stripped, dressed in prison
uniform, his hair clipped short and his moustache shaved.

When he was next seen by those who had escorted him from
Lyons, the change was shocking. He had arrived in a suit and hat
with the bunch of lilies of the valley still in his buttonhole, quite
the gentleman, if only in appearance. In a worn, stained uniform
he seemed to have been stripped of more than his smart clothing.
The process, called 'dressing in', was designed, as it is today, to
transform the criminal into a prisoner, to strip and shear away
individuality. It remains one of the most dramatic and symbolic
acts that marks the attempted reduction of a man to an inmate.

Although the Warden was keen to process him as quickly as
possible, Perry managed to do one last thing before he was taken
away. He turned to the Sheriff who had treated him with kindness
and made a small presentation. Perry was reduced to wearing 'the
stripes' but when he left Auburn, Walter Thornton was newly
adorned with Perry's gold collar stud and a pearl scarf pin. He
returned home to face accusations of 'bad taste' in giving Perry a
last good dinner, and a few months later died suddenly in his

sleep of a suspected heart attack. Deputy Collins fared much better, later becoming his county's best-known sheriff, remembered until his death for capturing Perry.

It was assumed that in Auburn Perry would disappear from public view. Reporters would find it less easy to interview the apparently ever-willing speaker in prison than in the County Jail, and he would have no easy way of addressing the public through them. But the mythologizing of Oliver Perry continued all the same. Just a day after he was sentenced, *The NY Central Train Robbery, Or, the Nerviest Outlaw Alive*, was published. Priced at 5 cents, it was Number 42 in the 'Nick Carter Library', subtitled 'The Best 5 Cent Library of Detective Stories'. The series was one of the most popular collections of pocket-sized 'dime novels' that offered easily concealed adventure to youngsters and their parents. The latest edition told the story of fictional detective Nick Carter's involvement in the downfall of the very real train robber. Framed by an imagined conversation between Nick Carter and Jerry Collins, totally inaccurate fantasies of Perry's outlaw life as a crack shot and hardened killer as well as debonair deceiver were interwoven with facts to create a character to match his western counterparts, Billy the Kid and Jesse James. In popular fiction, as well as public opinion, Perry had joined the outlaw elite.

The real Perry was in trouble just days after his arrival. It was not, this time, because of his attitude, arguing with his keepers or trying to escape, but it would still have a dramatic impact on his mood and on his future. He had been sent immediately to work in the foundry, but the heavy labour had caused the rupture that had only given him discomfort in Lyons to make him seriously ill. Unable to work, the man who hated confinement was locked up in his cell all day, except for mealtimes. It gave him plenty of time to think, to plot and also to brood.

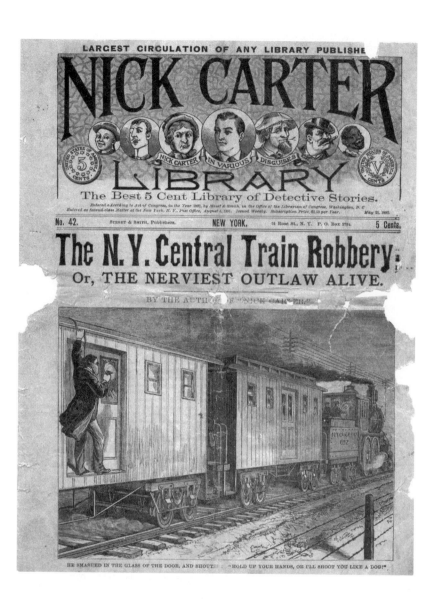

Nick Carter Library
(Courtesy of Onondaga Historical Association Museum
& Research Center, Syracuse, NY).

Just weeks later he was in real trouble after attacking a 'life man' called John Bender. The two men quarrelled at dinner and, to everyone's amazement, Perry produced two knives, threw one to Bender and challenged him to fight. When Principal Keeper James Shaw interfered, Perry surrendered. Whatever the ostensible reason for the fight, Perry had shown the other men what he was made of. Bender was an unpopular prisoner who regularly 'peached' on others, a good target for a new man who needed to show his mettle. All new prisoners have to prove themselves to avoid victimization. For a celebrity like Perry, as he was assessed by inmates and keepers, this was doubly important. His fame might easily make him a target for others. Also, as his time in Lyons had shown, he liked to win the support of those around him.

Perry paid a heavy price for his skirmish. His punishment, decided by Keeper Shaw, was nine nights in the dungeon. The dungeon cells were in the dimly lit basement, with bare stone walls and floors and no windows. When Perry was brought in, the first barred door would have clanged shut and then a second, solid oak door would have been locked, leaving him in total darkness. While he was effectively blinded, his other senses would, to make matters worse, have become more acute. The walls of the basement dungeons frequently ran with damp and crawled with vermin, although the bedbugs that plagued the normal cells would have been absent because there were no beds and no bedding. Prisoners sent to the dungeons were expected to sleep on the bare floor. They were also stripped of most of their clothing, supposedly to prevent suicide.

The cold would have been almost unbearable but any warmth would have intensified the stench rising from the uncovered bucket that served as a lavatory. And this dark, damp, cold and foul-smelling world was also silent. Regular cells in which prisoners were held in solitary confinement might allow precious whispered conversations when the guard was out of earshot, but in the dungeon the double doors sealed a man up as if he was in a tomb. The press frequently called any prison a 'living tomb', but the dungeon really merited the description. To the isolation that had driven men insane in the earlier experiment was added almost complete sensory deprivation. In the dungeon Perry would have been totally disoriented. The only way of telling day from night would have been when, once a day, the outer door opened and he would be given a piece of bread, weighing not more than two ounces. From a tin cup held by a guard he would have been able to drink two ounces of water. Then the door would shut and darkness would return for another twenty-four hours. Apart from occasional visits by a silent physician to check his pulse, this would be his only human contact.

Few prisoners' memories of the dungeon were recorded, but two accounts suggest its horrors. Alexander Berkman was a Russian-born anarchist, sentenced to twenty-two years in prison, shortly after Perry, for the attempted assassination of an industrialist. On his release, he recollected a spell in a dungeon in another prison that was nearly identical to the one Perry occupied in Auburn.

'Utterly forsaken! Cast into the stony bowels of the underground, the world of man receding, leaving no trace behind . . . Eagerly I strain my ear – only the ceaseless, fearful gnawing [of rats]. I clutch the bars in desperation – a hollow echo mocks the clanking iron. My hands tear violently at the door – "Ho, there! Any one here?" All is silent. Nameless terrors quiver in my mind, weaving nightmares of mortal dread and despair. Fear shapes convulsive thoughts: they rage in wild tempest, then calm, and again rush through time and space in a rapid succession of strangely familiar scenes, wakened in my slumbering consciousness.

'Exhausted and weary I droop against the wall. A slimy creeping on my face startles me in horror, and again I pace the cell. I feel cold and hungry. Am I forgotten? Three days must have passed, and more. Have they forgotten me?'

Berkman, a man of courage and intelligence, had been in the cell for only one day. The effects of a single night in the Auburn dungeon would form the climax to the reformer Thomas Mott Osborne's searing 1912 indictment, *Within Prison Walls*, based on time spent undercover as a prisoner. His description of how he felt when about to be released from the dungeon suggested the profound psychological damage such isolation could also cause: 'I find myself wondering why I am not ready to shout with joy, and I discover it is because I feel as if all power of emotion has been crushed out of me. It is not merely utter and hopeless fatigue; it is as if something had broken inside of me; as if I could never be joyous again . . .' Osborne's reaction was tempered by his knowledge that he would be released. The real victims of the dungeon, like Perry, would have had no such sense of control. A prisoner in the dungeon was stripped of all the simple features of human society; he was reduced to a blind, bare creature, sustained on a starvation diet, locked in a lonely world from which he might never escape.

In this world present fears or guilt about the past could be magnified to the point of inducing severe depression and even temporary psychosis. The nightmares and hallucinations of many prisoners would gradually become their reality. At the end of their punishment many appeared docile, but this was rarely contrition, whatever the authorities claimed. Exhausted and desperate men would say anything to get out, but even then the punishment was not over. Some prisoners were so disturbed they were declared insane, some attempted suicide or self-harm. Men from the dungeons were also condemned to seek out the shadows even when they were returned to the light. After days or weeks of gloom, even pale winter sunlight through a barred window could cause intense pain. For those trying to control unruly prisoners, the dungeon was also a double-edged weapon. It offered at best a deterrent and a temporary control; at its worst it turned the difficult into the truly dangerous. In the long hours and days of isolation, dislike and distrust of the system and its representatives often turned to implacable hatred.

The horrors of the dungeon were confirmed by the least liberal of commentators. At an 1892 meeting of the National Prison Association, it was condemned by those urging a return to corporal punishment. One physician declared that although public sentiment condemned the flogging and paddling (the beating of prisoners with a flat wooden or leather paddle) that had been the norm until outlawed by the state legislature, the dungeon, or dark cell, was far more damaging. Corporal punishment was widely viewed as 'a relic of the dark ages', he argued, but the dungeon was a 'refinement of torture': 'It is a system of punishment which strikes not only at the physical power, it is a mental and moral degradation. It is not the confinement which produces a seeming submission, but it is the starvation and you have only inflicted a punishment when you have deprived the body of its rightful supply and this cannot be done without injury.'

93

Perry appeared to have submitted when he was released after nine days, but the authorities took no chances. They placed him in a brick-built cell in the centre of a row in the basement and he was not returned to work. The men who occupied the cells either side of his spent each day in the prison workshops, but he was locked up alone, twenty-four hours a day. The cell had a wire grating in front of the bars to prevent anyone from slipping him a knife or other implement with which to attack or escape, and a keeper prevented communication when other prisoners filed past on their way to work or eat. The keepers themselves were under strict instruction not to speak with the prisoner. So the young man who thrived on conversation and story-telling was isolated yet again.

Whatever the adverse psychological effects of such continuing isolation and lack of stimulation might have been, the keepers were pleased with its results. Over the next few months they reported that Perry was quite docile, and there were suggestions that he might eventually be returned to hard labour. But once again, Perry deceived his keepers. The brutal regime of the dungeon had certainly had an impact on him, but it had not broken his spirit or his resolve. With nobody to talk to and nothing to distract him, he turned his mind to the one thing that he still wanted above everything else: freedom.

On 23 October Oliver Perry escaped. The day before, when a keeper delivered his supper just after 4 o'clock, he saw nothing unusual although he commented later that Perry seemed to be in good spirits. But when the prisoners returned from work an hour later, the man who occupied a neighbouring cell called out that there was a hole in the dividing wall. The keepers ran to inspect it and found a large hole in the twelve-inch-thick wall. Perry must have dug when the other men were at work and concealed the hole with a towel. To their surprise, the keepers saw Perry was in his cot, sleeping through the commotion. But when they shook him, they found that the sleeping convict was really a bundle of clothes. He had waited until the keeper left, after seeing the other prisoners off to work, then wriggled through the hole and walked out of the open door of the neighbouring cell into the corridor. During the day only one keeper patrolled the wing, so he had no trouble in evading him and getting out into the yard. There he could hide in an outhouse until darkness fell to cover his final escape over the perimeter wall. The alarm was sounded and hours went by while guards searched every inch of the prison but to no avail.

Some time later a keeper saw someone walking swiftly across the prison yard from the foundry towards the collar shop. He shouted to him to stop but the man started running. Assuming it was Perry, the keeper fired a shot from his Winchester over his head and brought him to a halt near the pearl button shop, where another keeper jumped out of the shadows and struck him on the head with a heavy night stick. The blow was so powerful that the night stick broke in two. Perry fell to the ground, unconscious and bleeding heavily, and was carried into the Keeper's Hall. His head wound was washed but not judged serious enough for dressing, and he was then sentenced to twenty-five nights in the dungeon, to begin immediately.

To the embarrassment of his keepers, the story was swiftly leaked to the press. How could a man kept under such close surveillance have managed to dupe them so thoroughly? It seemed to have been only his own haste that was Perry's undoing. If he had paused to conceal the hole in the neighbouring cell after climbing through it, his absence might not have been noticed until after lock-up time. Then the guards on the perimeter wall came off duty, and he would most likely have been able to scale it to freedom. The mistake was uncharacteristic of his usually careful planning – the rest of the preparations suggest that he was as meticulous as ever. He was almost certainly disturbed at the last minute.

His capture was as controversial as his escape was shocking. Although the keepers insisted they had warned Perry before knocking him down, anonymous sources claimed this was untrue. Although he had been judged fit for immediate punishment, all the reports stressed the severity of the blow that felled him and some claimed he might die. The most damning report was from an Englishman called Edgar Moulton who was visiting Auburn on behalf of the Prison Reform Society and claimed to have witnessed the capture: 'The assault on the prisoner seemed to me to be entirely uncalled for and unprovoked. I have visited the prisons of the czar. Much as they are to be condemned, I have never seen or heard of a single brutality which equalled the attack made on the prisoner in Auburn last Sunday.'

The prison authorities issued a denial, but Moulton's story struck a chord with a growing number of New Yorkers who feared that the closed worlds of the prisons concealed terrible abuses. Perry was now an object both of admiration, for his daring, and of pity, for his treatment. A local newspaper editor, defending the prison, feared that Perry would gain new admirers because of the escape and roundly denounced his supporters: 'Is it not about time that Oliver Curtis Perry be treated like the outlaw and desperado he is and not like a hero of the Jesse James stripe of a man?'

Perry was, in fact, doubly punished. As he faced the darkness, silence and starvation of the dungeon for over three weeks, he also knew that his failure had condemned him to serve many more years in prison. For the escape attempt he lost nine years, eleven months and four days of 'good time'. Even if he behaved like a lamb from now on, he would serve at least forty years. A calmer man might have realized that the real battle now was to survive and submit to the regime in the hope of a quieter life, however limited. But Perry was a fighter and was set on a course that would lead to continuous conflict with his keepers.

Over the next few months he was sentenced twice more to spells in the dungeon, for 'insolence and threats to Night Guard', then 'striking keeper, insolence and threats'. Just as he had become increasingly desperate and unruly in Lyons when he realized he could not escape, so now he made life as difficult for his keepers, and for himself, as he could. The perpetual conflict, punctuated by sensory deprivation and near-starvation that weakened his physical condition, took a heavy toll. Perry was not obviously broken, as so many others had been, but the damage had been done. His hostility to authority became ever more extreme and he lost any sense of perspective in his understanding of his own situation. Oliver Perry was under extreme psychological pressure.

There was, briefly, a glimmer of hope by the spring of 1893, when he was sent back to work in the foundry and found what he called 'a little gleam of happiness'. But one violent attack extinguished it. Perry had gradually become convinced that Principal Keeper James Shaw, who had first sent him to the dungeon and ordered most, if not all, of his subsequent punishments, had a serious grudge against him. He believed that Shaw, apart from singling him out for rebuke, was reducing his food rations out of spite. Shaw was a big man with a tough style and, although there is no evidence to suggest he was maliciously inclined towards his prisoner, Perry's fears were not unusual. In the crowded conditions of a prison, fears multiply like germs, and withholding or contaminating food, with saliva or worse, was, and is, an easy way of unofficially punishing a prisoner. A man who, like Perry, had been on starvation rations in the dungeon for long periods might well be particularly anxious about having his fair share of food. But Perry's fear turned to panic.

Isolated from anyone, friends or family, who might help him keep a sense of proportion, he decided that Shaw was out to kill him and resolved to fight back. So he got hold of a file from a workshop and hid it in his uniform until one day he broke ranks and lunged at Shaw. He was immediately overpowered by other keepers and dragged to a dungeon where he was blasted with a high-pressure fire hose until he was subdued. On 11 May 1893, he was judged guilty of 'threats to kill officer and refusal to come out of cell', and was returned to the dungeon. This time he was given a little longer than usual. His sentence was forty-four days, over six weeks.

When he emerged from this terrible punishment it was clear that he had suffered a total breakdown. The anxiety that Shaw was trying to starve him had been magnified into a total paranoia that his keepers had been bribed by a vengeful American Express to starve or poison him. In the isolation of the dungeon, the 'normal' prisoner's obsession with food had been fed by memories of the constant harassing of his family and friends by detectives. The story-teller had spun a new tale that made complete sense to his damaged mind and on his release from the dungeon he was determined to put a stop to the detectives' agents by any means he could.

Eventually, worried about his increasingly violent behaviour, the Warden called for a formal medical examination by Dr Conant Sawyer, the prison physician, and a specialist in 'brain diseases', Dr Frederick Sefton, who confirmed that Perry had 'hallucinations', evidence of an 'unsound mind'. Such was Perry's reputation as a would-be escaper that some observers insisted that he was feigning madness to get a transfer to a less secure institution. The authorities took no notice. On 27 December 1893, after twenty months in Auburn, Perry was officially declared insane and an order was drawn up to transfer him to the Matteawan Asylum for Insane Criminals.

CHAPTER 9
'God forgive us all . . .'

THE PERSONALITY traits and psychological characteristics that contributed to Perry's trauma were quite likely the same ones that had brought him to prison in the first place. In line with the thinking of the day, the doctor who certified him looked for mental illness in his family, citing the fact that his paternal grandmother had been insane. But if his family history had something to reveal, it was a troubled childhood, not a genetic inheritance, which would eventually lead Oliver Perry to the dungeon and despair.

The history has been hard to uncover. The lives of the nineteenth-century rural poor are often elusive. Sometimes names appear in census returns, in church or institutional records, but the lives behind the citations are rarely visible. Perry's boyhood was doubly obscured. When he was a wanted man in the 1890s, detectives had to overcome his family and friends' efforts to cover his traces, but within a matter of decades he was almost entirely expunged from his family's memory. No stories seem to have been told in the Perry family about their black sheep. Even more painfully, while many families have obscured the traces of a bad or mad relative after their deaths, Perry had been repeatedly disowned by his family since birth.

Perry told the same brief story of his early boyhood all his life. His parents, who lived on a farm, separated just a few years after his birth, when his mother left. He said he was born on 17 September, but gave the year as 1865 and 1866 in different accounts. His father, the outwardly respectable but slippery Oliver H. Perry, was a native New Yorker, one of thirteen children born to a farmer. In January 1865, at the age of nineteen, he married a fifteen-year-old called Mary Allen. She was the daughter of a widowed farmer who had married Oliver's own, equally young sister, Sarah Emily. They lived in what was known as the 'Irish Settlement', near a Mohawk Valley township named Ephratah after the biblical land of plenty. There, just over eight months later, Oliver Curtis Perry was born.

The only fact about his mother that Oliver Perry ever recalled was that when he was a very small boy she left him and his father and never came back. No one knows why she left or where she went. She simply disappeared from public, and private, records; she may have married again or, as some reports hinted, died soon afterwards, but she left no traces. Oliver H. Perry soon married again. His new wife, Sarah, was, like Mary and his sister, fifteen years old at the time of her marriage and first pregnancy. Blanche, Oliver's half-sister, was born in 1872.

When her own child was born, Sarah wanted a home of her own and insisted that there would be no place in it for her stepson. No reason was ever given. Perhaps she was insecure about her husband's feelings for his first wife and took it out on their son. In adulthood Perry would poignantly stress that his father had 'insisted' on keeping him, but in fact he offered little resistance to his wife's plan. Perry's grandmother looked after him for a while but when she died he had nobody to turn to. The little boy was effectively alone in the world.

102

A signpost still points the way to the Irish Settlement. When Perry was born it was a community of small farms worked mainly, as the name suggests, by those of Irish descent. The poor soil offered only a basic living, and when competition came from the opening up of western farmlands, many were forced to seek a second income at the nearby timber mills. Today the tarmac road soon dwindles to a dirt track, with woods thickening and closing in on either side. But there is no sign of farms or houses. All that remains of the settlement where dozens of families worked the land, and where Perry spent the first years of his life, is a few barely visible walls, none more than a few stones high, overgrown with ivy and brambles. Looking closer, it is possible to see the broken outlines of houses spaced alongside the road. Within a few decades, the Irish Settlement, a living community, had been reclaimed by the woods that once provided its timber. The speed with which human attempts to make a home can be undone, not by war or demolition but by the gradual, relentless reclamation of nature, is both surprising and moving.

The Irish Settlement today.

The wild wood, one of the most abiding and unsettling locations of childhood fantasies and terrors, is a fitting symbol of Perry's earliest years. In fairytales it is the testing ground for children who roam too far and find themselves alone and frightened by the unknown. Traditionally, in the end, lost children learn their lessons and return safely home to their family. In Perry's case, the wood has overwhelmed the home, as once the tangled relationships of his family left him lost and rejected. Unable to find a place where he felt at home, he would spend the rest of his childhood wandering.

His aunt Mary wrote about her family's guilt in a letter to a newspaper when Perry was awaiting trial: 'God forgive us all for our negligence in not taking care of him in his helplessness. . . . He was turned out on the charity of the world, when, if we had taken him in, all would have been well with him.' But none of his family would take him in, so before he was ten years old, he was almost certainly left in what was known as an 'orphan asylum', although he had both a father and a stepmother living. The impact on a little boy is hard to measure. Intriguingly, in the Depression years Louis Berg, whose *Confessions of a Prison Doctor* argued passionately for reform in the treatment of offenders and for an understanding of the impact of broken homes on young children, would call those who turned to crime because of being unwanted, 'stepchildren of society'.

Perry later referred to working on a farm from the age of eleven. He was probably left in an orphanage or refuge and 'adopted', as so many children were, to provide slave labour. Nobody is sure where Perry was left, although a newspaper report in 1892 identified a likely place in upstate New York where names he later supposedly used as aliases were popular. He soon ran away from his adopted home, as resentful of working for nothing as he would later be in prison.

By the summer of 1880 he had travelled to Minnesota and was staying with his aunt Mary. She and her husband Edward had moved from New York to the sparsely populated Otter Tail County where they farmed and ran a small general store in a village called Luce. His aunt described a sensitive, kind boy: 'He was naturally kind and tender-hearted, but, as I said before, circumstances made him what he is. He has been known to give his last ten cents to a little beggar girl . . . who was (as he thought) in more need than he was, although he had no place to lay his head.'

But by the age of fourteen he had left Minnesota. It is not clear whether he was sent away or left of his own accord. His aunt's sense of guilt may suggest that he was sent away, but he may have been simply restless and homesick. As he later commented, 'I was a headstrong boy, and have had a blot on my whole life.'

By the winter of 1881 he was back in upstate New York, sleeping rough. His father lived in a village called Amboy in Oswego County with his second family, including eight-year-old Blanche and a six-year-old son, Claude. Neighbours remembered his elder son visiting occasionally, but never staying long. Perry clearly wanted to belong, but his family's relative indifference and his own restlessness left him perpetually unsettled. His step-mother had made it clear he was not part of her family, and his father, with the responsibility of his new family, had little time for his first-born son.

Oliver Perry was forced to be a man when he was still a little boy and he had no reason to trust anyone. His mother had abandoned him, his grandmother had died, and what could he expect from a father whose love and protection were so unreliable? Little wonder that as a grown man he would have such troubled relationships and see betrayal even before it happened. Or that he would grow up determined to prove himself, to win the acceptance and admiration, if not affection, that he had been denied. Underneath the clever robber and slick self-inventor who charmed the press and public was a deeply insecure little boy.

Unwanted, he took to a life of what he later called 'roving'. He learned early how to handle a gun, as many country boys did. He travelled alone, around the Mohawk valley where he would one day hide from his pursuers, and further afield. To survive, he learned how to live by his wits, if not always within the law.

CHAPTER 10

A Bad Boy's Career

O NE COLD November day in 1881 Oliver Perry was arrested
in the city of Amsterdam in the eastern Mohawk valley. Two
boys had reported him to the police for stealing a new suit of
clothes from a man at the railroad depot. He was alone, homeless
and had to pay for shelter. He was held in the lock-up over the
weekend, tried, found guilty, and sentenced to an institution that
was called, with bitter irony, the Western House of Refuge.

It was located in Rochester, the city just south of Lake Ontario
where the adult Perry would one day appear in wax. Today the
gleaming new towers of Rochester's optical and photographic
industries dwarf its older buildings, creating an impression of
bland modernity and affluence. But right through its heart runs
the deep gorge of the Genessee River, a reminder of a rugged,
ancient landscape.

The House of Refuge was itself originally established as a
progressive institution, but by 1881 it was at best an overcrowded, ill-disciplined prison, at worst a hellish place where
young children were subjected to physical, psychological and
sexual abuse by their fellow inmates and, all too frequently, by
their keepers.

Newspaper reports from the years when Perry was an inmate make shocking reading. Time and again the Board of Managers, comprising eminent local citizens, condemned the institution. In 1883 it was denounced as 'brutal in the extreme', and a year later the *New York Times* noted that 'the most cruel and inhuman treatment has been inflicted upon the boys'. An official investigation found that brutality was widespread and possibly systematic. Witnesses reported beatings with rulers, paddles, strops and sticks, as well as a key used to twist children's noses and ears. Even when 'properly' administered, punishment was harsh. Children found guilty of rule-breaking, including whispering or failing to meet work targets, were punished by beating or starvation rations of bread and water. If Perry had experienced hardship as a roving boy, the privations in the Refuge were worse. One eleven-year-old boy was put on a bread-and-water diet for four weeks.

Boys who tried to escape or were insubordinate would be stripped and locked up in dark cells, not unlike the dungeons in Auburn, with boarded-up windows and a heavy door with a few ventilation holes. The existence of the rat-infested cells was initially concealed from the Board of Managers, but was eventually revealed by witnesses, including a boy who had been held in one for six months. An investigator who entered a dark cell had to leave immediately, driven out by the stench from the waste bucket that served as the boy's lavatory and would be emptied only once a day, if the keeper was diligent. In these dreadful cells boys slept naked, except for a blanket, on the floor. Conditions were little better in the regular dormitories, with open waste buckets and no lavatory paper. Unsurprisingly, the Board worried that boys were 'acquiring the most filthy personal habits without fault on their part'. Could this be why Perry was so fastidious in later life, when many reporters commented on his almost obsessive need to keep his hands clean?

There may have been another, more disturbing, trigger for his need to cleanse himself. Apart from the hard labour, locked fire-escapes, poor food, filth and summary punishments, the boys faced another threat: sexual abuse. One employee made extensive, albeit coyly worded, accusations of 'immoral practices' on the part not only of boys but also of their keepers. Perry, even as a grown man, was delicate in stature and looks, described by the Pinkertons as 'effeminate'. When he was admitted to the refuge he was small for his age. He was fifteen or even sixteen, depending on his real birth year, but as records show, he was only 4 feet 11¾ inches tall and weighed 91¾ pounds, and so a likely target for sexual predators. Years later, he would complain bitterly of how young men were systematically sexually abused by older convicts, but in his youth there was nobody to turn to. So he concentrated on gaining some weight and building up his strength. This was clearly designed to help him defend himself, to turn a slight boy who might be treated as a girl into a man. He certainly learned a style of fighting – scratching and biting – that would stay with him all his life. Whenever he felt overpowered, particularly by a bigger man, Oliver Perry would fight frantically, almost hysterically, like a little boy.

The exact nature of Perry's experiences in the House of Refuge will never be known but they certainly shaped his character and established a pattern of response to prison that would last a lifetime. He must have found the institution almost unendurable, even without the additional torments of punishment and abuse. Used to a life on the road that, despite its hardships, was free, the confinement alone would have been wretched. Living rough as a boy-man he had learned to conceal his vulnerability beneath a

tough, clever manner that seemed like impudence and brought
out the worst in his keepers. When chastised he resorted to
running away, as he had done as a child. Escape was almost a
compulsion for a boy who had no reason to believe that there was
any other way of learning to live within the rules in an unfair
system. In his desperate plotting to escape he demonstrated, even
at this early stage, two defining characteristics that would be seen
again and again in his adult life: the extraordinary intelligence
and ingenuity that would make his crimes and escapes so remarkable, and the charismatic charm that would allow him to
exert an almost mesmerizing influence over fellow prisoners,
hardened reporters and ordinary Americans.

His keepers, infuriated by his conduct, wanted him moved to
an adult prison. In 1883 one wrote to the Superintendent:

> The boy has always been a vulgar and low dispositioned boy,
> and of late his disregard of all advice makes me call your
> especial attention to his case. He has never cared for his studies
> and his whole general deportment has been low and vulgar. He
> is constantly reported for disorder, quarrelling, impudence and
> vulgar actions and language. . . . Lately he has been engaged in
> altering and picking locks and in attempting to escape till his
> example and acts are so bold and defiant that his removal from
> this institution is quite a necessity. Quite recently he secured
> false keys with which he let himself out of his dormitory in the
> night time and broke his way through the shop, stealing
> therefrom knives and weapons of defence but was unable to
> scale the walls. Certainly his low and vile disposition with no
> intention to reform exerts a very dangerous and pernicious
> influence over the other inmates.

Intriguingly, the expertise with making false keys that would emerge in Lyons seems to have been evident while he was still a boy.

To his keepers Perry was simply a bad lot, but an investigation into the institution revealed that some of his accusers were guilty of worse. One was dismissed for cruelty and incompetence, and another was reported by a witness to have given a newly admitted boy fifty strokes with a rattan cane. Yet another later became an officer in the police force and joined in the hunt for Perry after his second train robbery. After his capture Perry was anxious to show he had not intended to hurt anyone, but he made one exception. He swore publicly that if he had been able to get a clear shot at the ex-keeper he would have killed him.

The keepers' request to have Perry transferred was granted. On 7 March 1883 he was sent to the Monroe County penitentiary 'for correction during the pleasure of the Board of Managers for a period not exceeding two years'. There his behaviour followed the same pattern as in the Refuge, but one dramatic incident revealed a particular facet of his personality that would later become almost as defining as his need to escape.

When he arrived he was put to work as a heel trimmer in a workshop where convicts laboured for a shoe-making company. He struck up a relationship with the keeper in charge of the workshop, a man called Kelly, who felt sorry for a boy stuck in a men's prison and sometimes shared his lunch with Perry. But when Perry was transferred to work on a machine rather than with the trimming knife, he was discovered sabotaging it, presumably because he had hoped to use the knife in an escape attempt. Publicly reprimanded by Kelly, he grabbed up a skiving knife, used for trimming leather, and lunged at the keeper as he would later lunge at Shaw in Auburn.

111

When his punishment was complete, he was transferred to another workshop but took the chance, when sent to Kelly on an errand, to attack the man who had frustrated his plans. This time he created a diversion by shouting to the other prisoners to get out and creating a stampede. In the chaos he seemed torn between trying to escape and getting his own back on Kelly. When the panic subsided Kelly had a cut on his arm and Perry a stab wound in the stomach, described in official reports as accidentally self-inflicted. He was taken to the prison infirmary and then into solitary confinement for the remainder of his sentence.

When he left the penitentiary on 15 March 1885, at the age of nineteen, Perry had acquired a range of skills, in shoe-making, lock-picking, improvising weapons and fighting. He had learned that he could influence and manipulate others, but could also find himself at their mercy. An intelligent but volatile young man, he could be charming and aggressive by turns. He had entered the House of Refuge as an unruly boy who longed for affection and belonging but chafed against restrictions; three-and-a-half years later he left the penitentiary as a young man with a deep hatred of authority and confinement. And he had clearly decided that the best response to both was to fight, with whatever resources he had. He had also developed a pattern of behaviour that would mark the rest of his life and involved a series of men who might be seen as father figures.

The testimony of the Monroe keepers suggests that he forged a number of close relationships with keepers. These were men in authority whose approval and affection he craved but whom, ultimately, he could not trust and whose attempts to discipline him provoked his most extreme reactions. Another workshop overseer claimed, like Kelly, to have liked the difficult prisoner.

He told reporters that 'young Perry had a particular liking for me and would do almost anything to please me', and that the young man had come to his house for dinner after his release. It is quite possible that there was a sexual dimension to the relationships, and the men's descriptions of their relations with the young boy sound very like those given by men who 'groom' children as potential sexual partners. They may have been genuinely sympathetic, but, whatever their motives, Perry was almost certainly unconsciously trying to re-create his relationship with his own father. Later, in Lyons, the gentle Sheriff Thornton and tougher Deputy Collins embodied different aspects of the father, one offering support, the other punishment. His own father had alternately owned and disowned him, leaving his son locked in a perpetual battle with authority. Again and again, he would turn to a keeper, a lawman or a doctor for support and understanding, only to feel betrayed and abandoned. This would lead, in turn, to intolerably disruptive behaviour that ultimately would become self-destructive.

Oliver H. Perry was still ambivalent about his son. He claimed later that he tried to secure Perry's release from Monroe and although he had not fought for him in childhood, it seems he sometimes intervened in emergencies, as he would again in 1892, when he concealed his fugitive son and later tried to help him escape from jail. Like many badly behaved children, Perry must have unconsciously known that breaking the rules brought him the rewards of parental attention. As he grew up, did the same impulse lie behind the ever greater risks he took and the ever more daring crimes he committed?

Initially Perry tried to settle down to an honest life, getting a job as a clerk in a Rochester shoe store. The storekeeper remembered him as a pleasant-looking young man, a 'great talker' and a bit 'fly', although generally reliable. But he soon found the settled life difficult and after three or four months gave in his notice.

In the following spring he was in trouble again, this time for stealing from his own family. Together with some other men, he broke into his uncle's store in Minnesota and stole money from the till, some revolvers and clothes. The other men, who he said were army deserters, escaped but Perry, who stayed around assuming he would not be suspected, was followed, searched and arrested. He was sentenced to two years' hard labour in Stillwater prison. His sympathetic aunt believed that he had been harshly punished because he would not betray his 'pards', but he seemed unconcerned about betraying his own family's trust. Perhaps this was understandable, given his history. Anticipating the justification of his later robbery by condemning an exploitative system, he claimed he was just taking what was owed him for working for his uncle as a boy.

Stillwater was one of the mid-west's best-known prisons, but less for its tough regime than for its famous inmates. Here, the young man who would become the most famous train robber in the east encountered the west's most notorious living outlaws: Cole, Jim and Bob Younger who, with Frank and Jesse James, had terrorized the west in the aftermath of the Civil War, robbing trains and banks. Although Perry later remembered them, they do not seem to have impressed him much. All three were model prisoners, while Perry was as rebellious in Stillwater as he had been in Monroe.

He was released in the summer of 1888 when he was twenty-two. Then, probably fuelled by tales told by Stillwater inmates, he headed further west. The west may have been tamer in the late

1880s, but it was still a wild place where the rules of eastern society rarely applied. Here a man could move more freely, on cattle trails and railroads, and pick up casual jobs where few questions were asked, a definite help to an ex-prisoner and especially appealing to a young man who hated regulation. But the boundaries between legality and criminality, even between lawman and outlaw, were also less secure, and Perry almost certainly crossed the line.

He gave varying but always vague accounts of this period of his life, when he would have met his doomed sweetheart on a ranch in New Mexico. He certainly worked in the west, as a cowboy and ranch hand, and got into bad company. The Pinkertons believed that he learned the basics of train robbery at this time, and he later claimed to have been in a gang who operated in Texas, Nebraska and the Chicago area. He never gave any details, nor did the Pinkertons, and when he robbed the American Express Special he worked alone, using methods unlike those of any gang. It is possible that he was embellishing, just as others tried to pin unsolved crimes on him, but there may have been a gang whose story has been lost for ever. One thing is certain: in the precious months he spent in the west, Perry was a free man.

But sometime in 1888 or 1889 he decided to move back to New York. He later claimed, and Amelia Haswell believed, that this was because he had fallen in love and hoped to earn money to buy a home for his forbidden sweetheart. But there may have been another catalyst for his decision to end his roving life and settle down.

The Perry family clearly had a strained relationship with their wayward elder son. But as 1888 drew to a close, it was his half-sister Blanche who was in the news. Just before Christmas the

115

fifteen-year-old girl was shot dead on the snowy sidewalk outside her father's house by her estranged husband, William Crossley, who then turned the gun on himself. The couple had been childhood sweethearts, then fallen out when Crossley headed west to make a fortune but returned, broke, bitter and sure that his beautiful young wife had been unfaithful.

The murder and suicide made sensational news, especially as the funerals of husband and wife both took place on Boxing Day, with Blanche buried in the Perry family plot and William in the Crossley grave, facing each other in perpetual accusation across a narrow path in the same cemetery.

Perry was not listed as being present at his half-sister's funeral but he may well have been incognito, if he was still in trouble with the law. He may not have been in New York at the time, of course, but the date of Blanche's murder coincides intriguingly with the timing of his apparent decision to start life again in Troy after his western wildness. The coincidence certainly offers an alternative to the story of Perry's doomed New Mexican romance as the reason for his decision to return to New York. His choice of alias when arrested – William Cross, so near to William Crossley – was surely not a coincidence. Why would a young man adopt a version of the name of the killer of his own sister? Was it an act of revenge, or a sign of his guilt about his own strained relationship with his family? While he was waiting for his trial he wrote to his father: 'If anything should happen to me I want to be buried alongside of dear Blanchy.' It is hard at a distance to know if this and his other affectionate references to his little brother 'Claudy' were genuine signs of strong family feeling or displays of expected sentiment.

Intriguingly, if less attractively, Blanche may also have played another part in her stepbrother's life after her death. Descriptions of her striking dark looks resemble uncannily those of the girl in the photograph he carried and whom Amelia Haswell believed to be his dead sweetheart. Photographs and jewellery with locks of hair were popular mementos of dead relatives. It may have been a coincidence and Perry's sweetheart may have been real. But the similarity begs a probably unanswerable question. Faced with a struggle to win sympathy after his crimes had been discovered, and needing the support of his devout but romantic 'Mother', had the ever-resourceful Perry used his sister's image to spin a tale?

As ever, Perry is infuriatingly difficult to pin down, alternately crying out to be read, as he was by the Pinkertons, as a cynical manipulator of other people's naïve or idealistic beliefs, or, as he was by his Christian and liberal supporters, as a damaged boy whose kinder, more thoughtful nature was crushed by his in-ability to cope with a brutal system. In truth, he was probably both, the product of a troubled childhood and a brutal adoles-cence that would turn him into a daring but volatile rebel, capable of sensitivity but also of ruthlessness. His was a personality that would both lead him to prison and make him particularly vulnerable to its impact.

Whether affected by a forbidden romance or a family tragedy, by 1890 he had decided to try conformity, working on the railroad, becoming part of a community. But disillusionment with the poor rewards and petty restrictions of his new life had swiftly driven him to prove his ability and his worth as an outlaw. For a few months he had experienced the intoxicating excitement, unprecedented luxury and strange, hunted freedom of his life as a wanted man. Finally, in Auburn, confined and isolated, his highly strung nature had been stretched to breaking-point.

CHAPTER 11

'Came to Hell'

T HE MATTEAWAN Asylum for Insane Criminals, daunting as it sounds, offered Perry a glimmer of hope. Staying in Auburn would undoubtedly have doomed him to decline or possible suicide. In the asylum, much nearer Troy, it would be easier for Amelia Haswell and Perry's other old friends to visit him and offer some emotional support. Although breakdowns induced by the stress of isolation are traumatic, they are rarely permanent. In more stable and secure conditions, given a chance to build reliable relationships with other people, even those with extreme psychotic symptoms can recover and may never experience another episode.

On 28 December 1893, one day after he was declared insane, Perry, looking pale and thin, was escorted by three armed guards on the long train journey from Auburn to Matteawan. Word spread quickly among the passengers and soon the car he was in was crowded. But anyone expecting to see the famous showman put on an act, or to hear the ravings of a madman, was disappointed. Perry was unusually quiet as the journey took him back along the tracks of his robberies, through the landscape of his childhood, hugging the course of the Hudson River until,

119

the following morning, the guards escorted him through the crowds and into a carriage and headed for the asylum.

An imposing building on a hill just outside the small community of Beacon, Matteawan was New York State's institution for prisoners who had been certified insane after sentencing. It had been open for just over a year. On 25 April 1892 crowds of villagers had watched the first sixty prisoners arrive in chains. Newspapers of the time noted that while some were in straitjackets, others carried personal possessions including birdcages. They had all been held in the previous State Asylum for Insane Criminals, near Auburn prison, whose location was far from ideal, with incessant noise from nearby factories. The State Commissioner in Lunacy, Dr Carlos F. MacDonald, argued that the insane should be put to farm work in the open air, and campaigned for the foundation of a more suitable asylum. Eventually, the state legislature voted to pay for a new institution at Matteawan, whose rural location offered peace and fresh air. To many people, the insane were still objects of fear and scorn, the criminal insane even worse, so at its inception Matteawan must have seemed liberal indeed.

Local feelings were mixed. The asylum offered much-needed employment, but the idea of insane criminals breaking loose filled many with dread. Despite reassurances about security, within three months of the opening several 'patients' had escaped and there were persistent rumours about would-be escapees feigning insanity in order to get into, then out of, the hospital. Now a man who had publicly declared his intention not to serve his sentence, who had repeatedly shown he had the initiative and nerve to break out, and who had nearly escaped from Auburn, was arriving. Even in the Certificate of Lunacy the physician Conant

Sawyer had warned, 'he is a bad des-
perate man and you cannot be too care-
ful, or he may well escape from your
place'. The man in charge, Medical
Superintendent Dr Henry Allison, knew
he had something to prove.

Allison was an urbane New Englan-
der, born in Concord, New Hampshire
in 1851, who trained in medicine after
reading classics at Dartmouth College.

Dr Henry Allison.

He started his medical career at the Willard State Hospital in
Seneca County, New York before taking up a position at Auburn
and then at Matteawan. He had been warned by Auburn officials
that Perry would be troublesome, but laughed, 'I guess he'll get on
all right here.' Perry also seemed initially optimistic about the
hospital and its Superintendent. On arrival, he held out his hand
to Allison, saying, 'You are a man and a gentleman. I can tell it by
looking at you. I am glad to come here if you are in charge, for I
know you will treat me well. You have a kindly face; you have no
idea how different it is from those I have left. My God, I hope I
never have to go back there again, to be beaten and starved and
poisoned.'

He repeated his hopes to a reporter who was allowed to
interview him soon after his arrival. The newsman was shocked
at the change in Perry's looks since his trial, describing him as
pale and thin, with sunken cheeks and the hair at the back of his
head worn thin. But he thought that apart from insisting on his
persecution by Auburn officers, Perry seemed fairly rational as he
spoke of how friends would see his situation: 'Yes, I have a great
many friends outside, and I want them to hear that I'm all right.

Tell them I'm glad to be just where I am, too. They'll wonder at that, won't they? Don't think for a moment that I don't know where I am, young man. I'm in a lunatic asylum, but better far to be in an asylum, than in that cursed prison. . . . Perry in a madhouse. It makes me laugh to think of it. And my laugh is a treat to me. I thought I should never laugh again after I had been at Auburn for a time.'

Once more Perry hoped to make a good impression on a figure of authority and a fresh start in a new place, but while it was a relief from Auburn, the regime in Matteawan would not be to his liking. After an interview with Dr Allison, he was immediately sent to a cell on an isolation ward. The ward was in a separate building, connected to the main block by a long corridor. There the most unruly and dangerous inmates were held in separate cells where a system of sliding doors allowed guards to watch them, unseen, at any time of day or night. This enabled them not only to check for signs of normality in prisoners faking insanity but also to guard those prisoners who, like Perry, were most likely to attempt to escape. It is not difficult to imagine his reaction.

If this disheartened Perry, the Superintendent's views on insanity would have plunged him into total despair. Although the men and women in Matteawan were still convicts, they were called 'patients' in recognition of their illness. But these patients had little hope of being cured, even if their current condition was one that would today be judged temporary. Edward Meredith, committed two years earlier because of a 'delusion', like Perry's of being poisoned, had, exceptionally, been able to prove his sanity and won his freedom, but only after a lengthy court battle with the prison and hospital authorities. In practice few patients ever returned to complete their sentences in prison. As an alienist, a specialist in mental disorders, Henry Allison took his role in caring for individual patients seriously, but he recognized that his role was also to contain those who threatened the social order.

The closing decades of the nineteenth century may have seen great changes in the treatment of the insane generally, with increasingly professional psychiatric approaches adopted in purpose-built institutions, but insane criminals were, above all, a threat to be contained. Shortly after Perry arrived in Matteawan, Dr Allison addressed the American Medico-Psychological Association at its annual conference and his paper, 'Insanity among Criminals', was published in the Association's influential *Journal of Insanity*. In the article he described men with mental disturbance very much like Perry's and argued that even when they are 'no longer insane, in the strict meaning of the term', they are 'in a condition which is recognized as unsoundness of mind', 'not amenable to prison discipline and are incorrigible'. Such prisoners should, he argued, be kept in hospital for an 'indeterminate sentence'. He concluded that by committing the insane 'for life', the judiciary and medical professions would succeed in 'permanently ridding society of many dangerous and undesirable elements'.

So while a public still in love with his romantic past wondered if Perry was shamming, he and his friends must have feared that he was now condemned to perpetual imprisonment. His escape attempts had lost him his remission, but while his sentence had a time limit, he had hope. If he recovered psychologically, he could, one day, be free. But would the Superintendent ever judge him eligible? There are no available records to reveal Henry Allison's original assessment of Perry. But the patient made his feelings plain on his cell wall. Below his name and the date, he wrote, 'CAME TO HELL'.

CHAPTER 12

Lunatics on a Rampage

I N   A P R I L 1895 Perry took everyone by surprise once more. In the eighteen months since his transfer from Auburn he had been regularly treated for unruly behaviour but his overall condition seemed to improve. Amelia Haswell had welcomed the chance to visit him in the more conveniently located institution but was often told he was too ill to see her. When she did get to see him, he complained about his cell in the isolation ward, the behaviour of the keepers and doctors, and of being prevented from taking any exercise in the fresh air. Amelia complained to Dr Allison, but Perry decided to take more direct action.

Just after 11 o'clock on the night of 10 April a watchman on his usual round walked towards the isolation ward. Checking here was really a formality. The isolation ward was a prison within a prison, designed to prevent escapes. So its outer walls had a lining of sheet-iron between two layers of brick, its windows were secured by iron bars and galvanized wire shutters, and the ceilings had even been secured with stone flagging. The cells had been constructed just as carefully. The doors were made of two-inch-thick oak and each had two locks, specially designed so that they could only be turned from the outside. As a final security measure, the keepers who held the keys were bound by the strictest orders never to take them outside the prison. Any man who did so was risking instant dismissal.

The watchman walked briskly along the corridor to the only door into the isolation ward. On either side, just before the door, were rooms used by the ward attendants. As he passed by, both were quiet, as he expected. At this time of night most of the prison attendants were asleep. He unlocked the door, entered the ward and was about to start checking the cell doors when he heard someone calling him from a cell at the far end. It was Perry. The train robber, who was housed in one of six cells that stood at a right angle to those along the length of the ward, was a demanding patient. Only the day before he had complained about being disturbed by noise from workmen in the nearby chapel and had asked when he could expect some peace. He was told the work would finish in a couple of days.

'What's the matter in there?' called the watchman. Perry asked for water. As the watchman started to turn away, three men pounced. One grabbed his keys while the others held him down. Before he could cry out, someone placed a hand over his mouth. He was bundled into Perry's cell, then tied to the bed-frame with strips of torn sheet. One of the men stuffed his mouth with rags and his attackers rushed out of the cell.

While he struggled in Perry's cell, its former occupant, together with the watchman's other assailants, Patrick Maguire and John Quigley, and two other men, Frank Davis and Michael O'Donnell, whom they released en route, unlocked the ward door, then locked it again behind them. They crept past the attendants' rooms and down the corridor. At the far end were stairs to the prison chapel, one of a very few parts of the prison, outside the ward, with which these 'isolation' prisoners were familiar. They unlocked the doors at the foot and top of the stairs with the watchman's keys. In the darkness

THE INSANE PRISON AT MATTEAWAN.

A—ISOLATION WARD.
B—CORRIDOR THROUGH WHICH THE MEN PASSED.
C—CHAPEL.
D—WINDOW THROUGH WHICH THEY PASSED TO ROOF.

Matteawan State Hospital.

they could just discern what they were looking for. At one end of the room was a step-ladder, left by workmen repairing the ceiling. Maguire had seen it at a service he attended – to his keepers' amazement – in preparation for some patients' confirmation by the Bishop of Albany. He had told Perry, who complained about the noise, to discover how long the ladder would be in place. Now Perry and his companions climbed twenty-five feet to the top of the ladder, pulled themselves up through a small hatch in the ceiling, and disappeared.

They crawled on hands and knees along the dusty attic floor until they reached a dormer window. No one had thought it necessary to secure an attic window above a double-locked chapel. The glass was easily broken and the men slipped through the window and out on to guttering along the eaves, forty feet above the ground. They edged along the guttering to the front of the building, then shinned down a pair of iron drainpipes. Someone shouted 'Halt!' and a shot rang out. A watchman stationed outside had spotted them and fired in their direction. The men kept on running and the watchman rushed inside to raise the alarm.

127

Dr Allison ordered men to surround the building to prevent any further escapes. Inside, the whole asylum was in uproar, as keepers and prisoners woke to cries of 'Escape!' Keepers still half-asleep emerged from their rooms and ran along the corridors, but nobody knew who had escaped. Eventually, men ran to the isolation ward and discovered the truth.

Soon police officers, detectives and local inhabitants were on the lookout for the fugitive lunatics. The moon, appropriately enough, was full, and the bright light made the searchers optimistic. The men were all wearing the asylum uniform of grey pants and vests, grey coats and blue and white striped hickory shirts. While their uniform would be an obvious give-away, they had another, more immediate problem. The men held in the isolation ward of the asylum were judged too dangerous to be allowed to wear shoes. They were on the run in felt slippers or barefoot. Surely they could not get far? But despite an all-night search, no trace was found of the five men.

The following morning Allison took stock of the situation and prepared a statement for the press. Any escape was embarrassing, but this was particularly humiliating. Most of what had happened was pieced together easily enough. The men had obviously planned the escape after seeing the workmen's ladder in the chapel when attending Sunday service, and had used the watchman's keys to free their companions and then unlock the ward door. But one question remained unanswered. How had Perry and the others got out of their cells in the first place? Their fellow inmates were being interrogated, but if any were sane enough to give answers that made sense, they were not doing so.

The Superintendent candidly announced that the only explanation was that an asylum employee must have colluded in the escape.

Although he refused to speculate, the newspapers all reported that the watchman had been suspended from duty and was being questioned. To help in the hunt, Allison's Deputy, Dr Robert Lamb, supplied the police with recent photographs of the escapees. Lamb was a keen amateur photographer and had jumped at the chance of testing his skills by developing pictures from negatives in his own darkroom. The pictures were sent to the police in all major cities and to American Express, whose representative rushed to Matteawan. Perry may have been paranoid about the company persecuting him but he was not wrong about their continued interest. They still wanted their missing money and they were still determined he should suffer the full penalty for his crimes.

Little is known about Perry's fellow fugitives. Three were burglars whose 'insanity' had evidently not prevented them from joining Perry in planning and executing a very complicated escape: Davis, the oldest at forty-two, was serving twenty-five years for burglary; Maguire, known as 'Ugly Mac', was a forty-year-old housebreaker who had made several escape attempts in the past; O'Donnell was the youngest at twenty-five and had eleven years of a sentence for burglary left to serve. John Quigley was a rather different case. He had been in trouble since childhood and seems to have had a life of extraordinary misfortune that left him seriously disturbed. After a series of petty crimes, he shot and killed his mother in what the Coroner's jury decided was an accident. Soon afterwards, he was shot through the ear while being arrested for breaking into a woman's house and criminally assaulting her and was sentenced to fifteen years in Sing-Sing. There his behaviour resulted in a move to Matteawan where, like the others, he met the persuasive Perry and became involved in the escape.

While the hunt spread out across the surrounding countryside,

John Quigley.

everyone tried to work out where Perry would head. Most agreed he would make his way to a city and possibly seek out one of the wealthy and influential friends of whom he sometimes boasted.

Two days after the escape, on Good Friday, the first fugitive was caught: the pathetic and confused John Quigley who had been utterly unable to cope with life on the run. He was found by local men near an empty freight car, still in uniform, begging for food, and returned to Matteawan without a struggle.

His account of the escape, when interrogated, answered some questions. It also had many echoes of Perry's past escape plans, in Lyons and even Rochester. The keys the convicts used to open the cell doors had, he said, been made from prison spoons. In the isolation ward men judged too dangerous to go to the dining room ate with an iron spoon, as knives or forks could be used as weapons. Patrick Maguire, one of these men, had not only managed to hide two spoons but also, Quigley claimed, used his past experience as a jeweller to turn a thin strip of tempered steel inside the sole of his prison slipper into a saw. Then he transformed the malleable spoons into keys to fit the cell doors; although each cell had two locks, top and bottom, the same two keys would unlock any of the cells on the corridor. Quigley could not explain how Maguire had got the impressions of the locks but it was assumed that a prisoner allowed in the corridor had helped.

Maguire had then apparently slipped the key to the bottom lock through the small aperture in the cell door to one of these milder prisoners, Frank Davis, as he walked along the corridor. On the day

130

of the escape, Davis unlocked the bottom lock of Maguire's cell on his way to supper. When the watchman came to inspect the ward soon afterwards everything seemed quiet. Although he was officially supposed to check every single lock, he rarely did so. After he had gone, Maguire used his improvised saw to cut through two strands of the heavy wire mesh that covered the peephole in his cell door. This allowed him to bend down the mesh, stick his arm through and turn his key in the upper lock. He swung the door open quietly and crept to Davis's cell. Davis passed the other key through to Maguire who released him. Next they released

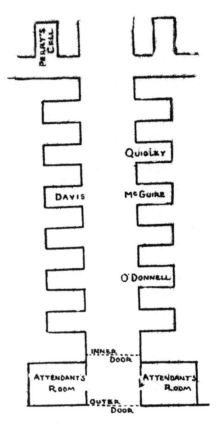

Isolation Block in Matteawan State Hospital.

Perry. Then all three returned to their own cells, pulled the doors to and waited for the watchman's next round.

While Quigley settled back into the relative security of confinement, it seemed that Perry had also returned to familiar territory. A number of storekeepers reported seeing him in Troy, a not unlikely place for him to seek sanctuary. The city's press was, on the whole, still sympathetic to Perry, one reporter summing up the general feeling that his recent escape proved that his 'courage, persistence

131

and ingenuity are qualities which would have made him successful in an honest career'. Sympathetic as Troy might be, sightings of Perry were also reported across the state in any place where a connection with his past could be made. A mysterious man in a sombrero appeared in several villages, leading to rumours that the expert in disguise had adopted a new image. A woman asking questions about him was assumed to be a past lover and a confused man even confessed to being Perry. Perry was everywhere and nowhere to be seen. As one editor succinctly explained, 'Oliver Curtis Perry is a criminal who in two senses is literally out of sight.'

In an attempt to hasten his capture Governor Levi P. Morton took the unusual and dramatic step of proclaiming that the State of New York would offer a $1,000 reward for his arrest. Together with the rewards offered by American Express, this put a bounty of $2,250 on Perry's head. The sum was quite astonishing. Dr Allison's generous annual salary was $3,000, and the reward was much more than most men could hope to earn in a year. In contrast, the reward for each of the other men was $250. Once again, railroad detectives, Pinkerton agents and the press rushed to outdo each other in the hunt for this most wanted man.

Patrick Maguire and Michael O'Donnell were captured soon after Quigley, about forty miles from the asylum. Like Quigley they were weakened by hunger and exposure in the cold spring nights. Now only Perry and Davis, who was regarded as the most dangerous of the other fugitives, were at large. A rumour spread that they might be travelling together, disguised as tramps. This made life even harder than usual for innocent men who were living on the road, some of whom were harassed and even arrested. But Frank Davis was caught alone, after five days on the run. He put up more of a fight than the others, running until shots were fired. Perhaps out of some sort of respect, or pity, his capturers plied him with whisky and took him back to Matteawan roaring drunk.

Now only Perry was free. Dr Allison announced that he was confident he would be back in custody within twenty-four hours. Sure enough, on 16 April a newspaper headline declared 'Perry Caught'. But the item continued 'Buying velvet capes at $6.50 and $7 at the New York Cloak and Fur Coats Store, No. 49 east Main Street, on easy payments of $1 or 50c weekly. No collectors.' As the initial fears about escaped lunatics subsided, and recollections of the earlier, charming Perry filled the papers, his capture had become a joke.

Perry's escape was remarkable, not just in his ingenuity in getting out of a specially designed double prison, but also because he was still officially considered a 'madman'. It was clear that Perry had planned the escape with as much intelligence and care as his earlier attempts and executed it with more success. And he had obviously built up strong enough relationships with the other men to earn, and return, their trust. Oliver Perry might be certified insane, but what was his real condition?

Patrick Maguire.

Michael O'Donnell.

Frank Davis.

As Perry appeared in 1895 before escape.

As Perry appeared in 1891 before conviction.

$2,250 REWARD.

ARREST
Train Robber

Oliver Curtis Perry, alias James Curtis Perry alias "Curt" Perry, alias Oliver Moore. Escaped from the State Hospital for Insane Criminals, Matteawan, N. Y., on the night of Wednesday, April 10th, 1895.

Handwriting.

Oliver Curtis Perry was convicted at Lyons, N. Y., on May 19th, 1892, for train robbery, sentenced to 49 years and 3 months in the State's Prison at Auburn and transferred December 28th, 1893, to the State Hospital for Insane Criminals at Matteawan.

DESCRIPTION.

Perry is described as follows: Age, 27; height, 5 feet 5½ inches; weight, 130 lbs.; hair, brown; eyes, brown; complexion, dark sallow (pasty); chin, round; smooth shaven, can raise small dark moustache; large Adam's apple.

Scars: { 1 right side of scalp, 2 on back, 1 left side of head.
{ 2 small ones on left thumb, 1 back of index finger (left hand).
{ 1 near wrist inside right hand, 1 large scar left forearm.
{ 1 large scar on throat just below Adam's apple.

Forehead, square and high; wrinkles between eyes gives his face troubled and thoughtful expression.

Perry may use any of the following names: Oliver, Curtis, Perry, Haswell, VanAllen, Havens, Hamlin, Allen, Gavens, James, James Curtis, James Perry, James Curtis Perry, Oliver Moore.

Perry is said to have been at one time a cattle herder (cowboy). Before his conviction for train robbery he was sentenced twice for burglary, and while in prison learned the shoemaker's trade; has also been a freight and passenger brakeman. He professes religion, and will try to impose on ministers and class leaders of churches, particularly Presbyterian.

Please search hotels and keep general lookout around railroad depots, saloons, gambling resorts, etc., and inquire of Yard or Train Masters for his having applied for employment, and of Railroad Trainmen for his having "beat" his way on freight or passenger trains. Also inquire of ministers, class leaders and at Young Men's Christian Association Rooms for trace of him. He is likely to be travelling as a tramp.

REWARDS.

$1,000 by the State of New York through proclamation of His Excellency Governor Levi P. Morton, issued April 13th, 1895.
$1,000 by the American Express Company.
$250 by Dr. H. E. Allison, Medical Superintendent Matteawan State Hospital, Fishkill Landing, New York.

The above rewards will be paid for the capture and return of said Oliver Curtis Perry to the Superintendent of the Matteawan State Hospital, Fishkill Landing, New York.

Send information (telegraphic or otherwise) to the nearest of the above-listed offices.

PINKERTON'S NATIONAL DETECTIVE AGENCY,
66 EXCHANGE PLACE, NEW YORK.

Or

H. S. JULIER,
GENERAL MANAGER, AMERICAN EXPRESS COMPANY,
65 BROADWAY, NEW YORK.

New York, April 16th, 1895.

1895 Reward poster (Reproduced from the collection of the Library of Congress).

CHAPTER 13

'A man always has hopes when he is free'

E DWARD CLIFFORD, a railroad detective, patrolled Weehawken on the New Jersey shoreline, across the Hudson River from New York City. In the early hours of the morning on the day after Frank Davis was caught he spotted a fire near the riverside railroad tracks. They were close to the palisades and cliffside where tramps often sheltered, so he decided to check them out. As he approached, he saw a group of men huddled over the fire and one standing alone, further away. The man's face was covered in dirt, but Clifford was suspicious. He walked away and called a police officer.

When Oliver Perry spotted the officer, he scrambled up the cliff to a narrow path on a ledge in the rock. He got about a hundred yards along it before losing his footing and falling on to the rocks below. His ankle badly sprained, he could barely walk and within minutes he was pinned to the ground.

Perry limped painfully as they walked him to the police station in Weehawken and reportedly begged, 'I'll do anything for you. I'll cut wood or do any honest work. Don't send me back there again.' But in custody, questioned by the Chief of Police, Simon Kelly, he insisted that he was a labourer who had fallen on hard times and did not want his family to know he was destitute. He was, in short, just one of the many tramps who hung around the industrial shoreline of the Hudson. He certainly looked the part. He was wearing a short black sack coat tucked into worn, torn trousers, held up by suspenders worn over the jacket, a battered hat and shoes split along the sides. In the pocket of the coat was an old newspaper but not a single cent.

If Perry's outfit resembled a parody of Dickens's Artful Dodger, his physical condition was no laughing matter. His face was pinched and weather-beaten and he had clearly had little to eat for some time. And when his shoes were removed, it was clear that the fall from the cliff was not the only reason for his halting gait. His feet were so badly swollen, blistered and cut that it was surprising he had managed to walk at all. They also seemed to have been badly burnt by lime, almost certainly from walking barefoot in brickyards near Matteawan.

His pathetic condition appeared to arouse Chief Kelly's sympathy. It is possible, of course, that the policeman was using his head rather than being all heart, hoping to gain his prisoner's trust. Whatever prompted him, he treated his prisoner with kindness. He sent out for breakfast, which Perry ate ravenously, and had his feet bathed and bandaged. But if Perry was exhausted and battered, he seemed, remarkably, to be displaying all his old coolness under pressure. When he was free he displayed an ability to make the best of even a bad situation as consistently as in prison he made it worse. As he had in Lyons, he initially resisted admitting his identity, but eventually, after a detective from the Mulberry Street police headquarters in New York City had arrived with a photograph, he called for Kelly and offered to give him a full confession.

Once again, Perry tried to take charge of the situation, rather than waiting to be pushed. It seems that he also had no illusions about Kelly's possible motives. The man who had once calculated the value of his own image knew exactly what rewards his reflected celebrity could bestow on someone else.

Kelly, who would soon become Mayor of Weehawken, wasted no time in displaying his famous prisoner. Outside, word of his capture had spread and hordes of people were arriving in the small town. Among them were reporters who had raced up from New York City, eager to get an interview and ready to reward the man who gave it and the man who allowed it. As soon as Perry's questioning ended, he was given a chair in the jail corridor and the waiting reporters were admitted. They had come prepared, remembering his taste for cigars as well as for attention. It was his first interview for three years.

Perry seemed relaxed, almost his old self, sometimes laughing as he recalled particular events, sometimes becoming more thoughtful, stroking his bruised feet and staring into the distance. The listening reporters, who had warned the public about this ruthless man's violent tendencies and claimed he would not be captured alive, waxed lyrical about his clear, frank gaze and fluent conversation. The interview itself, however, was not an entirely sedate exercise. Every few minutes policemen, brandishing clubs, rushed outside to drive crowds away from the windows where they were climbing on to one another's shoulders to catch a glimpse of Perry.

Inside, Perry described his first night on the run. 'I followed the east star. The moon rose early. But the moon travelled so fast that to follow it one goes around in a circle. I selected that star because I know it is a fixed star.' He had not lost his knack of appealing to

137

the press as one positively rhapsodic account of his journey revealed: 'This man of crime went forth under the stars, with the soft light of the moon bathing him in its splendour. . . . What thoughts, what fancies spread through his distorted mind no one knows.' The romantic vision of the vulnerable man blessed by the lights of heaven was not cluttered by facts. After giving them his best image, Perry flatly refused to provide any information about his first few days on the run, although he insisted, almost in tears, that he had not stolen anything and was ashamed of the way he looked in his ragged clothes.

He eventually said that he had made his way to New York City, refusing to say where he had stayed. Instead he told a long story of how he had been repeatedly turned away from charitable hospitals before eventually being given perfunctory treatment for his wounded feet. 'If I have a mania,' he commented, 'it is the exposing of the cruel manner in which unfortunates are treated in public institutions.' The statement was undoubtedly heartfelt but he would also, conveniently, strike a chord with the liberal New Yorkers who were beginning to protest about the treatment of the poor and needy and who might, in turn, be sympathetic to his own cause. It was the first hint that Perry might say something controversial about his experiences in the asylum or in prison.

He gave only a vague account of how he ended up on the Weehawken shoreline, and no reason for heading there, but hinted that he had been helped by a number of women who took pity on a stranger down on his luck. The Perry charm had clearly not deserted him even if his condition was less than glamorous. But for all his bravado, and whatever spin he might put on it after the event, his time on the run was not easy. Freedom meant everything to Perry, but it came at a price.

Touchingly, he seems to have been caught because he craved not only the warmth of the tramps' fire, but also their company; 'I was cold and the fire looked bright and cheerful. The company of the tramps, too, was not unwelcome, for I was lonesome.'

The man who had admitted to being lonely also seemed, underneath the swagger and wit, to be preoccupied and even rather frightened. When someone suggested he would have been caught eventually anyway, he replied thoughtfully, 'A man always has hopes when he is free, and I had a heavy, long sentence before me.' Then, *The World*'s man observed, 'this man of nerve paused, and his grey eyes seemed to be looking far away. They are fascinating eyes, that suggest sinister things.' Perry was clearly worried about returning to the asylum but, with characteristic bravado, issued a warning: 'If they abuse me as they have in the past I'll take any means to attract the attention of the world to myself. God knows I've suffered enough there already. I'm an American, and, although a criminal, I'm not a bad man.'

When Dr Lamb arrived to collect Perry, he was shocked to find that his patient had gone. He had been taken to the more secure Hudson County Jail in Jersey City to wait for requisition papers. Because Perry had crossed the state line between New York and New Jersey, extradition papers signed by the Governor of New York and countersigned by the Governor of New Jersey were needed before he could be sent back to Matteawan. Perry's threatened showdown with the asylum authorities might be delayed.

CHAPTER 14

Habeas Corpus

The World's illustration of Perry,
Clifford and Kelly after his capture
(Reproduced from the collection
of the Library of Congress).

PERRY DID not wait to be taken back to Matteawan before
speaking out about the abuse he claimed to have suffered
there. He spent a night sharing a cell on Murderers' Row with
Paul Genz, a man who had killed his wife and was convinced he
deserved to die. Determined not to be sent back to Matteawan
without a fight, Perry used an interview with some of the most
influential reporters in the state to launch a campaign against the
asylum's regime. Bathed, shaved and rested, he sat outside the cell
with his now customary cigar. His manner as he described his
experiences impressed his audience, and the *New York Times*

spoke for all the press when it noted that 'there was nothing in his appearance, manner, or conversation to indicate insanity'.

Perry's account of Matteawan made, and makes, disturbing reading. He described two methods of punishment used when men were unruly, often when keepers deliberately provoked a patient into 'giving a cross word, and then they begin'. The first was a brutal assault: 'One keeper will grasp a man's neck from behind, and, after the fashion of a garrotter, will compress his windpipe and shut off the air from his lungs. He is then thrown to the ground and held there by two men, while others kick him in the stomach and side with the side of their boots. This style of kicking is used so as not to leave marks and is called "hoofing". The blood gushes from the patient's mouth until he becomes insensible, and is carried to a room, where he lies for hours before recovering consciousness.' While these beatings generally took place at night and were inflicted illicitly by the keepers, the second form of punishment was administered by the physicians, as part of the legal 'treatment' of patients: 'The other punishment is the "black medicine", which as I understand, is a decoction of opiates. It makes the patient's mind active, so that he has delusions, but paralyses the body so that he cannot move. The effect lasts five or six hours, and sometimes three doses a day are given.'

He described the process of being drugged. 'I suppose I became excited, for the doctor said I had a delusion. After I had talked to Dr Lamb, four keepers . . . threw themselves upon me and knocked me down. While these men held me Dr Lamb injected some drug into my arm, and I became unconscious. When I recovered my senses the next day I was lying completely nude on the floor of my cell. I complained to Dr Daly about being drugged. I said I wanted exercise or work, anything to keep me occupied, and from brooding over my condition.' The drugs brought unconsciousness but also hallucinations, sometimes of terrifying creatures, sometimes, as Perry recalled with bitter humour, of more mundane things, as in an incident when the floor tiles seemed to turn into pieces of pie, his favourite dessert. Visions apart, his distrust of institutional food was exacerbated by his discovery that drugs were routinely added to it. Although he did not know whether this was on the orders of the medical staff, or was a practice adopted by the keepers to make their job easier, he had experienced similar symptoms after eating to those caused by injections.

He may have escaped from Matteawan because, having recovered from his breakdown, he was gripped by the compulsive need to get away. But, having been caught, he now started to campaign against the regime he had complained about to Amelia Haswell. Once again he demonstrated his remarkable ability to appeal to particular audiences. Just as he had worked the press and public in Lyons by constructing a romantic image of himself, so now he seemed to target sections of the press and the public who were already calling for reform of penal institutions. While his protests were undoubtedly heartfelt, he also began to use reformers' terminology and references to suit his own ends and turned every interview to the subject of this new campaign.

While some of the behaviour of both attendants and physicians may have been occasioned by the frustrations of dealing with the violently insane, some was undoubtedly the result of a relative indifference to their rights, as a growing number of New Yorkers had begun to argue. Asylums, like prisons, were closed worlds where brutality and cruelty could go unnoticed and complaints

by the victims unheard. Unusually, Perry, who had every reason
to be both angry and intemperate, and was still officially classed
as insane, offered a rational explanation for the regime. Middle-
class reformers regularly condemned the prison workers who
abused patients, seeing them as brutes, almost sub-human, without attempting to examine their place in an exploitative system
that showed them as little respect as they afforded their charges.
Perry was no friend of guards or keepers, but he did understand
the economic problem. The attendants were, he said, 'brutal,
ignorant fellows' but they were 'hired at $20 a month'. How, he
asked, could intelligent men be expected to apply for such posts?
Perry was ambitious in his target: he wanted to attack the whole
regime, not just the workers.

The press divided sharply over Perry's new role as a protestor.
While he was always good copy, most newspapers followed clear
party-political lines on issues like institutional reform. In an
intriguing contrast to his days in Lyons, when his treatment
by the Republican sheriff had been attacked by the Democrat
press, now it was the latter that called for Perry's allegations to be
investigated, and the Republican press that dismissed them. He
won some serious supporters from the respectable press.
Although his paper included a far from flattering phrenologist's
'reading' of Perry's head, the editor of the New York Times took
his new stance seriously. He reserved judgment on Perry's specific
claims, but called for an investigation solely on the basis that
Perry was evidently sane.

Henry Allison refuted Perry's charges, insisting that attendants
were never permitted to use unnecessary force, except in self-
defence. Perry, he claimed, was 'subject to uncontrollable man-
iacal excitement, during which he is extremely noisy and defiant,

144

so that he disturbs the whole ward, refuses to listen to reason, and is extremely threatening in language and manner . . .' He also denied that the ability of Perry and his companions' to plot the escape was proof of sanity: 'It is a trade with them, the same as the carpenter's trade or any other trade a man learns. They are criminals and it is their business to conspire.'

Inside the jail, Perry was proving very popular with his fellow prisoners, including the depressed Genz, who surprised everyone by washing and bandaging his new cellmate's feet. He and other inmates, including Thomas McLaren, who had murdered his mistress, and George Armstrong, a wealthy 'green-goods' man or confidence trickster, almost came to blows as they tried to outdo one another and the guards in looking after their famous companion. But while Perry enjoyed the attention, he seemed increasingly agitated. Repeatedly advised to sit so that his feet might heal, he kept standing up, as if unable to stay still. Bystanders noticed him pulling his weight off his feet by grasping the bars of the cell tightly behind him.

Although he was no longer in the grip of a debilitating breakdown, his behaviour suggests that he was still in a fragile condition, distressed by confinement and increasingly anxious about being sent back to an asylum whose keepers and doctors he had publicly denounced. He admitted to his cellmates that he was worried about retribution, and said that, if only he had the hidden fortune he was rumoured to have, he would do anything, pay anyone, even to delay his return. Given a chance, he told them, he would fight for his liberty 'inch by inch'.

Meanwhile, the battle over the reward for his capture had intensified. Chief Kelly called on Governor George Werts of New Jersey, on the day after Perry's arrival in Jersey City, to ask him

145

not to endorse the requisition papers until the reward had been paid to the Weehawken detective and policeman whose claims were being challenged by the former's boss. Werts agreed. Then a second man asked for a delay. But Alexander Simpson, a local lawyer, was not acting on behalf of any of the reward chasers. George Armstrong, the 'green-goods' man, had hired him to work for Perry. It seems an extraordinary act of generosity. Perhaps Perry had hinted that he could pay him back, perhaps Armstrong, like Kelly, hoped to make something from his association with the star criminal, or perhaps he just liked him.

The following day Perry was to appear in court, but there was a problem. His feet were so painful that he said he was unable to walk the 200 feet from the jail to the courthouse. So, followed by a large crowd, an under-sheriff and a constable made a basket of their hands and, with his arms around their necks, carried him to the courthouse, up two flights of stairs and into the hearing. It made a striking scene, emphasizing Perry's broken condition. Simpson immediately asked for a writ of habeas corpus. He had decided to challenge Perry's identification by exploiting the vagueness of the commitment papers. Justice Lippincott, following the letter of the law, agreed and ordered that Perry be held until proper evidence of his identity had been produced. While the move was exploiting a legal technicality, it offered Perry some hope of delaying his return to Matteawan and a chance to air his grievances in open court.

Henry Allison, who had assumed he would be taking Perry back to Matteawan, issued a statement to waiting reporters, insisting that Perry was both insane and 'untrustworthy', and went home. His mood can hardly have been improved by the atmosphere in the jail, where Perry was being treated like a hero.

Like so many celebrities today, Perry had even been commissioned by a newspaper to write his own story. *The World* printed his own version of his life and crimes, complete with a reproduction of his signature. Sub-headings provided a safe moral framework for the sensational story but the appeal was clearly the 'voice' of the star.

'I do not consider myself a great criminal or a cold-blooded desperado. Many a man who sits in his office in Wall Street is as much a robber as I am. It is simply a difference in methods . . . I had no ambition to be a dime-novel hero. . . . I did not want this notoriety. I am not proud of it.' He reiterated his allegations of institutional corruption and brutality and defended his friends, Frank Davis, 'a man who had forgotten more than I ever knew', and Amelia Haswell: 'She has been like a mother to me . . . They said she was something more to me than that, and tried to bring scandal on her good name . . . and I have been driven almost wild, knowing I was powerless to protect her and that she suffered through her friendship to me.'

Whatever his feelings for the missionary, he revealed that he could no longer claim to be a believer. 'I have received letters from religious friends, exhorting me to turn from evil and serve God in prison. I may disappoint them, because I can't see things quite as they do. Their religion is enough for their lives but I have had other experiences. I am not a fanatic like some. I can't believe everything I read in the Bible, nor that I have heard in churches. I do believe in the religion of doing right, however far I have been from living up to it.' Those who thought his religiosity was a clever ploy to manipulate gullible do-gooders must have been taken aback. Even a teller of tall tales may speak the truth. If Perry had rejected Christianity, he had clearly not replaced it, as

147

Amelia Haswell had feared, with a radical political creed, although he did joke, 'I do not know anything about Socialism or Anarchism, but I know that when a man takes it on himself to equalize unjustly distributed wealth by robbing express trains, he makes a mistake.'

He gave brief stories of both his train robberies, then turned to his own character. 'I realize that society will not tolerate men of the stamp I proved myself. I realize that when a man once steps outside the law, every hand is raised against him, and he is hunted down like a wild beast.' But, he continued, 'I don't think I have vicious instincts. I'm not any better than I might be and during my imprisonment I have been so brutalized by association with the most degraded men; I have been so knocked about, sworn at, drugged and beaten that I have lost, perhaps, a good share of what refinement I ever had.

'The newspapers have called me a "gentleman desperado" and have spoken of my hands and slender fingers, the hands of a man who has never done hard work. Right here I want to correct that. I am an uneducated country boy. I grew up without schooling. Whatever I have learned I have learned by experience . . .'

But if he was proud of his humble origins, he was also keen to show that he had good taste, even if it differed from that shown by those who followed his adventures so avidly. 'I enjoy a good book and I like to read American history. I never had any taste for sensational literature, dime novels and detective stories, even as a boy.' He complained that all he could get hold of at Matteawan were 'Irish newspapers of Nationalist proclivities', and expressed a particular liking for the works of Nathaniel Hawthorne. He claimed that his favourite was, appropriately enough, *The House of the Seven Gables*, which tells the story of a man released from a long and unjust prison sentence. He also revealed that the diary he kept in Lyons had been just the start of a writing habit that was becoming a passion. 'I used to spend some of my long nights of sleeplessness during my imprisonment making rhymes. I'm nothing of a poet, but I can jingle words, and in the long night watches it helped to pass the time when I could not sleep.'

Books duly started arriving at the jail for Perry, along with flowers, cigars, boxes of fruit and candies, sent or brought by well-wishers. 'Why, what a nice little fellow,' said one female visitor, 'he doesn't look bloodthirsty at all, does he?' Recovering from the indignities of dressing as a tramp, he regained his old sartorial style when a local clothier delivered a new suit to the jail. Perry promptly sent a note back, which the clothier published in the local newspapers. It read: 'Kind Sir, If clothes make the man and gentleman, then I am sure, for I feel more respectful [sic] since receiving your kind gift. May the success that follows all just men be with you. Yours, O.C. Perry. N.B. Please excuse the chirography, for the drugs have caused it.' In fact the $15 suit had been paid for by Chief Kelly, but the clothier saw his opportunity for some free publicity, while Perry evidently saw a chance to remind the public in his carefully worded postscript of the effects of the 'black medicine'.

This mutually beneficial relationship continued when Perry, clearly still aware of his 'market value', offered the clothier a deal. In return for a set of underclothes and a shirt he would sit for a photograph that the shopkeeper could use in future publicity. Astonishingly, the Sheriff did not object. Perry asked for three or four dozen copies of the picture, hoping to sell them as souvenirs to the men and women who visited the jail to see him. His fame was soon confirmed by a visit, staged by a newspaper, of one of

America's other most notorious criminals, George Bidwell, who, twenty-five years earlier, had stolen nearly $5 million from the Bank of England.

Perry's evident enjoyment of his renewed celebrity gradually began to worry even those editors who took his allegations of abuses at Matteawan seriously. His rather too adept manipulation of public feeling through the press was beginning to make him a less attractive figure to those who had sympathized with his situation. And the legal battles to keep him out of Matteawan were beginning to have a farcical aspect that threatened to make not only the asylum authorities but also the law look foolish.

Was Perry undermining his own case by enjoying his brief spell of pleasure and control too much? Could his desire for attention, admiration and the brief pleasures of winning a battle of wits be as compulsive as his need to escape? While the liberal press still called for an investigation, the conservative press bristled at his easy life in jail, condemning the 'rising tide of swash' caused by his 'hair-raising tales of Torquemada-like atrocities' and mocking his protestor's credentials as well as his popularity: 'if the people admire his type of citizenship, let him be canonized, pardoned by the Governor and sent to the State Senate as a Lexow Reformer'. Lexow had produced a shocking report on police corruption that was clearly not to the editor's liking. Even he stopped short of recommending one exasperated editor's solution to the problem of Perry: execution.

Ironically, it was Henry Allison who gave the liberal press the ammunition they needed to renew their attacks on the state's penal institutions through Perry's allegations. If he hoped to quash Perry's claims, he was badly misguided. He gave a detailed description of the use of drugs in Matteawan that merely supported Perry's case. He admitted that the drug hyoscin, with which Perry had been treated four or five times, caused drying of the body's mucous membranes and the tongue, and impaired vision, but said these side effects were easily counteracted by stimulants and caused no long-term damage. One reporter challenged Allison to say what the effects would have been on a man who 'was already thirsty and sane', arguing that such drugs should not be part of 'the modern enlightened method of treating insane patients'.

Dr Carlos MacDonald, President of the State Lunacy Commission, swiftly issued a vehement defence of the system, Matteawan and its Superintendent. His assessment of Perry was clear: 'Perry is a type of lunatic that is found in all criminal asylums in which desperate and criminal tendencies are interwoven with insanity. Such persons also have a morbid love of notoriety and enjoy immensely being the central figure of a public sensation or scandal. Such persons usually excite the sympathies of the morbid curiosity seekers who, actuated by maudlin sentiment, visit prisons and jails and bestow attention upon notorious criminals.' Those who agreed had ready evidence of Perry's impact on at least one such person. After the hearing he was visited by Amelia Haswell. 'There goes my best friend in the east,' he said as she left.

The legal process of extraditing Perry seemed to be spinning out almost indefinitely, much to his relief and the pleasure of the hotel and saloon keepers who were catering to the press. Writs and warrants piled up until eventually, after a week, Governor Werts stepped in and signed the requisition papers without waiting for Justice Lippincott's judgment. Relations between neighbouring states had to be protected. Lippincott tried to muster as much dignity as he could and announced that Perry would have his day in court.

When it came, the courtroom was crowded as everyone waited for the final act in the legal drama. Perry's lawyer made one last attempt to stop the extradition, insisting that as only sane men could testify in court, and as Perry could not be denied a hearing before being extradited, he would have to stay in New Jersey until he was either proved to be sane or had regained his sanity. But Lippincott was firm, in decision if not tone. 'I do not see, in view of the evidence, that I can do anything but refuse the defendant the discharge asked for, and order that he be remanded to the custody of the sheriff to await action on the requisition from the governor of New York.' The battle was over.

Perry was taken from the court, handcuffed to a keeper and still walking with difficulty. He was to be accompanied back to Matteawan by Dr Lamb and Chief Kelly. Suddenly, to everyone's amazement, he turned to his lawyer, swore and slapped him across the face. Perry was pulled away and the party moved on. Simpson said nothing. Instead he ran to the Justice's office to demand that a warrant be issued against Perry for assault and battery. Two police constables were given the warrant and set off to arrest and detain Perry. Perry had not lashed out in anger but was enacting a scripted final scene in the legal farce. He had been told by his lawyer to hit him so that he could be arrested and kept in New Jersey while new legal manoeuvres were planned.

But Dr Lamb was too fast this time. He quickly signed the receipt for his prisoner, had him bundled into a waiting coach and set off for the railroad station. Before the police could catch up to arrest Perry, the party had boarded the train and headed for New York.

It is not difficult to imagine what Perry must have felt as he returned to face the men he had accused of brutality. In Jersey City the public excitement about his case and the attention of press and sympathizers had once more kept some of his fears of being incarcerated at bay. Now the reality was all too apparent. But when the train pulled in to Fishkill landing he made a good show, handing out his photographs to the waiting crowd. Henry Allison announced that Perry would be placed in one of the general wards and would not be returned to solitary confinement unless his behaviour made it necessary.

He may privately have wondered how long it would be before Perry or one of his keepers forced another confrontation. But in June, two months after the arrest that had convinced so many that Perry was sane, Allison announced that he was sending him back to Auburn, 'free from any active mental disturbance'. The announcement sat rather oddly with Dr MacDonald's earlier confident assessment of Perry's lunacy but to those who had been impressed by Perry it was good news. His fellow fugitives had mixed fortunes. Frank Davis attempted suicide by hanging himself with a sheet and faced a lifetime in Matteawan. Patrick Maguire plotted another escape, before betraying the keeper who was helping him and earning a return to Sing-Sing to complete the four years of his sentence. John Quigley disappeared from public record.

On 2 July 1895 Perry made the long journey back to Auburn, this time overnight. He arrived at half past eight in the morning and was met by reporters who noted he was heavier than he had been before his transfer to Matteawan, but looked haggard and careworn. As he walked from the train he told reporters, 'I can see where I have erred in my life, and if I get my liberty again I will

153

lead an honest life.' He insisted publicly that he was glad to return to Auburn, conforming to his usual pattern of trying to win sympathy. Bizarrely, given his earlier paranoia about being poisoned, he even compared the prison rations favourably with those in Matteawan. But he also declared that he had no intention of working without pay. Although he maintained a cool front, his fear of retribution by keepers was soon revealed when he privately begged the Warden for a transfer to Clinton, the prison whose reputation was so tough it had deterred him in 1891 from giving himself up.

The Warden insisted that if he conducted himself properly, he would receive fair treatment. Then he was returned to his old cell in the basement. It was reported that he would not be made to work. He might have recovered from his last breakdown, but now the conditions, dictated by the authorities and self-imposed, for mental collapse were once more in place.

CHAPTER 15

A Missionary's Work

WHILE PERRY faced life in Auburn, the investigations into his escape from Matteawan took a sensational turn. Two suspected accomplices were identified. One, predictably, was a keeper. The other was the respectable Troy City missionary, Amelia Haswell.

Amelia Haswell was the daughter of an English naval captain who moved to New York State to raise his family on a farm. She was born in 1849 and dedicated her whole life to God and those Americans who had little reason to count their blessings. Living as a single woman in an industrial city, she learned first-hand about the sufferings of ordinary Americans. As well as serving as the Troy City missionary, she supported the Women's Temperance Union, campaigning to end the social evils of drink, and the Fresh Air Fund, a charity that arranged country excursions for poor urban children. She also worked for the less obviously deserving, including prisoners and prostitutes, regularly visiting them in jail and speaking for them in court. She was on vacation in Ocean Grove, a New Jersey seaside resort run on Christian principles as a permanent camp meeting, when it was reported that her arrest was imminent and a lengthy prison sentence likely.

A former keeper at Matteawan, William E. Hopkins, accused of helping Perry in his April escape, had confessed and implicated her in the crime.

Newspapers were filled with speculation about her conduct and character. Acts that had once won her the respect of fellow Christians and, at worst, the mild scorn of sceptics, were now condemned as reckless or even corrupt. The police claimed that if any criminal convinced Amelia Haswell of his or her desire to lead a better life, she would help them avoid arrest by whatever means she could, in defiance of the law. Her relationship with Perry was described as 'mysterious', and the age difference between them became a constant theme in reports that bordered on character assassination. Although he clearly saw her as a 'Mother', detectives and reporters repeatedly insinuated that she was romantically infatuated with him. The sweeping criticism extended to her 'not very prepossessing' appearance. She was described as 'taller than the average woman, inclined to stoop', with 'a sallow complexion', and as being obliged 'to wear glasses'. The *Sun* struggled to be more positive: 'She is an intellectual looking woman, but would hardly be considered handsome.' Whatever her answer to possible criminal charges, Amelia Haswell had already been found guilty of being less than a perfect model of femininity.

In truth, she was undoubtedly naïve and unworldly in her dealings with Perry and the other troubled or damaged men and women she tried to help. She was a woman of unshakable faith and utterly binding principles who was prepared to battle with authority and bend man's law if it conflicted with her totally sincere interpretation of God's. She was formidable as a foe, as the Pinkertons had discovered, and, as Perry knew and sometimes exploited, ever faithful as a friend. She was not in love with Perry in the simple sense implied by those who sniggered, but she certainly loved him. She was undoubtedly taken in at times, too easily convinced by his romantic stories, too keen to see the best in him, but she was no fool. When she indulged Oliver Perry, it was a mother's indulgence of a wayward son. He may not always have been sincere when he called her Mother and listened to her advice, but Amelia Haswell took her motherly duties seriously.

Amelia Haswell's interest in Perry was clearly prompted by her Christian faith and social conscience, but there was definitely a more personal bond between them. They were worlds apart in background, age and general temperament. Yet, like Perry, she was passionate, eloquent and impetuous. She may have been a little infatuated with the charismatic, damaged young man who walked into her class, but she may also have recognized something of herself in him. Was she drawn to the young robber because he reminded her of a part of herself? Be that as it may, her impetuosity and unworldliness eventually landed her in serious trouble.

William Hopkins had been arrested when detectives working for American Express had uncovered a second escape plot by Perry while still at Matteawan. He had apparently bribed a keeper to help him and confided in him that Hopkins had provided the keys that had been used in the earlier escape. The keeper informed Allison, Perry was held in solitary confinement until he was sent to Auburn and Hopkins was arrested.

Hopkins was in his forties, with a wife and children and a serious drinking problem. Confronted with the evidence against him he admitted his guilt and, after some prompting, implicated

Amelia Haswell. He said that in the fall of 1894 she had sent him a parcel of jewellery that Perry was giving him as a reward for his help in his planned escape, which included providing the keys, a file and blank keys and unlocking the cell of Maguire, whom Perry had brought into the plan because he was a skilled jeweller. Hopkins also confessed to telling Perry he would leave clothes and a pistol at an agreed spot near a local racetrack, but that instead he had got roaring drunk in the village. His testimony revealed that Perry had planned his escape even more carefully than had been thought. It also suggested that he had a rather respectable accomplice. According to the Matteawan authorities, Haswell had visited Perry regularly, bringing him religious reading matter. The prisoner had, they said, spoken often of the spiritual solace she brought him. Now they suspected that her support had been more practical.

Hopkins had already sold the jewellery, which he thought was from Perry's haul in his first train robbery, so detectives were sent to search jewellers and pawn shops. Soon a watch, two rings, one set with a two-carat diamond, the other a 'beauty' with a fourteen-carat diamond, were returned to American Express. What was Amelia Haswell doing with these in the first place, let alone sending them to a keeper as a bribe?

There is no record of exactly what, or how, Perry was told about what was happening to his 'Mother', but his own circumstances had taken a turn for the worse. Still driven by his compulsion to escape, made worse if anything by his glimpses of the world, he was discovered smuggling sand from the exercise yard. He had been filling his pockets when the guards were not looking, and storing it in his cell to make a sand bag to use as a weapon. When it was found in a surprise inspection, he was once more placed in the dungeon. On release he was held in solitary confinement in his gloomy cell in the basement corridor, now occupied by condemned men for whom there were no death cells. He was the only prisoner in his row who had not been sentenced to death.

While Amelia Haswell stayed in Ocean Grove, no move was made to arrest her because this would have required extradition proceedings that would have revealed prosecution evidence. As soon as she returned to Troy she would be arrested. Understandably, she did not hurry and Ocean Grove's religious services, with congregations of over seven thousand, gave her plenty of spiritual succour. Meanwhile, her friends and associates proclaimed her good character and innocence of any charges that might be made against her. They claimed that, far from breaking the law, she was an honest woman who had been hounded by detectives and the 'old Troy police ring', a byword for political corruption.

She remained silent until the enterprising editor of the *Troy Times* telegraphed her at the gloriously named Ocean Queen Hotel to invite her to tell her story. To everyone's surprise, she replied with a letter that was immediately published across the state. In it she acknowledged that she had indeed sent jewellery to Hopkins at Perry's request, but insisted that it was an innocent act. The jewellery, she said, was not stolen but Perry's legal property. Perry had originally asked her to sell his watch because it 'would be old-fashioned, and he would realize more for it now than a few years hence'. Perry also asked her to sell two rings, sent to her after his trial by the Wayne County sheriff. Whether or not what Perry said about the jewellery was true, Amelia may easily, if a little naïvely, have believed that it was not stolen. She had expressed some reluctance after her past experiences, so Perry suggested she send them to a 'friend' called Hopkins who would sell them. He made no reference to Hopkins being a keeper. 'I enquired', she wrote, 'whether he felt sure he could trust this man. I explained that so many would take advantage of his help-lessness.' Perry replied, 'If ever I had a friend this man is one. He feels sorry for me, and would not betray me.'

Haswell eventually agreed and sent the parcel, covering her tracks – almost certainly unwittingly – by letting a friend post it for her. The next she heard of it was weeks after the escape, when Perry, back in Matteawan, wrote asking her to visit him. She did so, with her aunt, and he told her the truth about his deal with Hopkins, complaining that Hopkins had let him down. Instead of telling the police, or even the asylum authorities, Amelia Haswell wrote to Hopkins asking him to return the jewellery and, when he was obstructive, to Perry's father, telling him about what Hop-kins had done so that he could demand his son's property. She was, she wrote, 'indignant to think a keeper would encourage Oliver in wrongdoing', but her desire to protect Perry from further punishment and, possibly, understandable reluctance at being implicated herself, restrained her from following the proper course of action according to the law.

She offered no apologies about her conduct and insisted that in her relationship with Perry 'God knows there is nothing I am ashamed to proclaim from the housetops.' She even claimed that the charge that she had knowingly helped Perry escape was an act of revenge by detectives whom she had defied since 1891: 'All through the period following the robbery, and after the arrest, the detectives kept up their persecution of me. I knew at different times where Perry was in hiding, but I did not choose to betray him. They used all their persuasions, arguments and threats. But his life was in my hands, and I would not give him up.'

If her accusation was contentious, others were even more dramatic. Rumours spread that the campaign against her was being orchestrated by influential men, including Thomas C. Platt. 'Boss' Platt, known as 'The Machiavelli of Tioga County', was a powerful Republican with a reputation for tough, some said corrupt, dealings and a known dislike of reformers like Amelia Haswell. No conspiracy was ever proved but supporters of big business may well have been impatient with the meddling missionary. It was reported that over the past year American Express had lost about $200,000 in robberies and the company was more jealous than ever of its property and reputation.

Damaging rumours proliferated about Amelia Haswell, ranging from complicity in planning the first robbery to hiding the saw in Perry's Bible. But the consequences of being found guilty of the current charges were serious enough. American Express was considering pressing charges for handling stolen goods, the United States Mail could charge her with using the mails for improper purposes, and the District Attorney of Dutchess County, as a representative of the State of New York, could prosecute her for aiding the escape of a felon. While all the possible charges were serious, the latter was a felony for which her sentence, if convicted, would match Perry's: forty-nine years.

The scene was set for a dramatic trial. Amelia Haswell was peacefully arrested when she returned home and, accompanied by her aunt and her brother-in-law, the Reverend John Warren, she was waved off on the railroad journey to the hearing in Poughkeepsie by a large crowd of Christians and reformers. The hearing, to determine if there was enough evidence to hold her for a Grand Jury trial, was so overcrowded that it had to move to a bigger courtroom. Amelia Haswell entered a plea of not guilty. From the start her flamboyant lawyer, Calvin Keach, set his tone by reading the names of all the influential citizens who had offered to stand bail for his client, clearly hoping to establish her good reputation in contrast to the drunken chief witness.

Henry Allison's testimony offered no first-hand evidence of Haswell's complicity in Perry's escape, although he insisted that she had conversations with Perry that could not be overheard. It was clear that the missionary had complained on numerous occasions about Perry's treatment and especially about drunken keepers but, although Allison admitted that he had subsequently sacked one of them, he thought she was generally misguided. Eyebrows were raised when he claimed, 'She told me that Perry had never done anything for which he should be severely punished. He had only robbed an express company, she said, and did not appear to consider that a serious matter.'

Hopkins repeated his allegations and insisted that she had known he was a keeper and written to him as such. He also said that she had advised him not to keep the distinctive watch in case it was recognized.

His evidence might turn out to be untrue, and his reward of immunity from prosecution might have made some suspicious of his motives, but it was unsettling for Haswell's supporters. Keach announced that his client wished to make a personal statement but he needed an adjournment to prepare and to subpoena several witnesses. The case was adjourned for one week and Amelia Haswell put up bail of $1,000, signed for by her aunt and her lawyer.

Reactions to the hearing were typified by Judge Robertson of

Troy. He spoke in defence of Amelia Haswell, praising her good work and intentions, but he clearly had reservations. 'You know Perry was a remarkable criminal, exceptionally bright, and the kind of man that many people pitied, believing he could be saved . . . Miss Haswell took a great deal of interest in his case. Some people may think it possible that her zeal made her indiscreet in some respects . . .'

Amelia Haswell was accompanied to the reconvened hearing by a number of well-known religious and political figures, including the candidate for State Treasurer on the prohibition ticket. The forces of reform and redemption were displaying their support. Keach opened the proceedings by reading her lengthy statement. She denied any involvement in Perry's escape, and explained that she had not gone to the police when she discovered what had happened because she did not want to punish Hopkins's innocent family. Even when her actions were legally suspect, she was anxious to explain, sounding rather like Perry himself, that her moral motives were sound.

At the core of her statement, and of her recent attitude towards Perry, was her obvious sense of responsibility, even guilt, for the heavy sentence he was serving. Having personally persuaded him to plead guilty at his trial, believing according to her Christian principles that it might lead to clemency, she had been deeply shocked at the severity of his sentence. Now, defensively, she stressed that she had done her duty and suffered persecution as a result. 'I firmly believe', she argued, 'that if I had not done voluntarily all that I could to detect and convict Oliver Curtis Perry of that crime, he never would have been convicted.' For her pains she had been hounded by detectives who had made threats 'that they would never rest until they got me in prison'.

163

She closed by touching on what interested many people most of all. 'It has been commented on much in public prints and private gossip, that I felt a deep interest in Mr Perry. I confess I have and still do, as is common with my lifework in the field of trying to reform the wicked of the earth. There is no sentimental false sympathy in my heart toward this man or any other. . . . What is the mission of a missionary unless it be to raise the fallen and stop others from falling?'

At the end of her statement affidavits were read and witnesses, including Haswell's aunt, were called to support her story. Finally William Hopkins took the stand. He had arrived late, and his replies to questions were often non-committal or confused, giving the impression that he had been schooled by the detectives but had forgotten his lines.

Keach moved that his client be released as there was 'not one scintilla of evidence to show her guilt' and a heated exchange began about whether Perry as a thief or Hopkins as a law-breaking keeper was less reliable. Finally the Recorder inter-vened. In his apparent anxiety to conclude the hearing without assuming any responsibility, he sounded like a latter-day Pontius Pilate. 'Although I might discharge this defendant, the District Attorney would still, of course, have the right to present the case for indictment . . . I will not bear any of the burden and will hold the defendant to await the grand jury's action.' Amelia Haswell was granted bail at $2,000, paid by her aunt. To the waiting press she spoke only briefly: 'So much of it is over. I shall continue to place my trust in God.'

The Grand Jury met at the beginning of October and was as decisive in judgment as the Recorder had been hesitant. Amelia Haswell's months of anxiety were swiftly ended as the jury found no grounds for indictment and the case was dismissed. While there would still be whispers about the propriety of her relationship with Perry, the missionary had convinced at least some of the public that she was no felon. Predictably, the dismissal was barely reported by the newspapers that had splashed the accusations across their pages. Amelia Haswell herself felt totally vindicated and declared her intention to continue the work that had led her to court. A few days later, the *Troy Times* published her own lengthy account of her trials, entitled 'A Pure Heart's Triumph', which concluded: 'I have never had such sympathy for the poor and oppressed and erring as I have today, and I can assure the world at large, as far as is in my power, they will have a warmer friend than ever before in Amelia E. Haswell.'

CHAPTER 16

'Oblivion where he belongs'

O N 17 SEPTEMBER, while Amelia Haswell was waiting for the Grand Jury hearing that would clear her name, an extraordinary and terrible event in Auburn transformed Oliver Perry's life. Late in the evening a keeper heard a moaning noise in his cell and went to investigate. When he peered through the door he saw Perry holding a piece of wood with what looked like two nails stuck through it. As the horrified keeper watched, Perry jabbed the nails again and again into his own eyes.

Shouting for help, the keeper struggled to wrangle the improvised weapon from the prisoner. Soon more keepers arrived with the prison physician, but they could barely restrain Perry, who seemed determined to keep stabbing his eyes even though the pain was so intense it had forced him to cry out. Eventually they wrestled him to the ground. Fearful that even in this state Perry might try to escape if taken to the hospital, the keepers pinned his arms and marched him, still struggling, to an isolated cell in a new prison building that was not yet occupied. There he was knocked out with chloroform.

Both his eyes were severely lacerated, but Conant Sawyer, the physician who had committed Perry, believed that the sight in one might be saved. When Perry woke he continued to struggle, so Sawyer kept him heavily sedated. By the end of September, Perry finally agreed to his eyes being treated and the physician was able to work without administering sedatives. Sawyer managed to preserve some of the sight in one eye but Perry was still in real distress, shouting his demands to anyone who came near. He wanted attention, he wanted better conditions and, above all, he wanted to go home. But he would not be going home, whatever he had hoped and wherever home might have been.

Perry had made a blinding machine with a piece of wood and two large saddler's needles, the sort used in the prison workshop. He had shown initiative and ingenuity in making use of everyday objects and material from his first escape attempt in 1892 to the sandbag episode a few weeks before this. Now, for reasons he would not reveal, he had turned this skill to terrible, self-destructive ends. As a result he was blind in one eye, had only limited vision in the other, and was soon to be declared insane once more.

On 1 November Dr Sawyer completed a new Certificate of Lunacy. In his accompanying letter to Dr Allison he noted that after a brief 'docile' period when he first returned to Auburn, Perry had been 'insolent, very talkative'. He went on to describe his unruliness and self-mutilation. But the horrors of Perry's condition had not diminished his physician's sense of humour, or of self-preservation, as he noted: 'In my last interview with him, he said that his next act would be to kill a prison official – the Deputy Warden and myself are special objects of his dislike and I have no special desire to gratify him in this direction.' The following day Perry was taken back to Matteawan.

Two months later he snapped again. But it was not a doctor or keeper that he attacked. Once again he tried to destroy his own eyes. This time he got hold of a small piece of broken glass, about the size of a 10-cent piece, placed it under the eyelid of his sighted eye, and rubbed until it was past saving. He had completed the terrible work begun in Auburn and would never see again. It was evidently the act of someone who was seriously disturbed, but why would a man who had only weeks before been planning an escape decide to destroy his own eyes?

Perry's first explanation, some time later, of why he had blinded himself was that he had been trying to win his freedom. He argued, in conversations leaked to the press, that because a blind man could pose no threat to society, the Governor might be merciful and set him free. It was, in other words, a logical, if terrible, extension of his compulsion to escape, to be free, at any cost. Was this the reason he did it? The trauma of prolonged sensory deprivation had clearly triggered a psychological collapse that made blinding himself seem a logical, if desperate, answer to his problems. If so, it did not work. Far from winning the Governor's sympathy, his act condemned him as hopelessly insane. And while he may have believed, at the time or in its aftermath, that he might gain something from his self-mutilation, the impulse behind it was certainly a distorted response to trauma.

There were undoubtedly other subconscious catalysts. Amelia Haswell, his 'Mother', was being tried, harassed and ridiculed for being in love with him. The analogy with Oedipus who blinded himself when he discovered that he had been incestuously in-volved with his own mother seems all too obvious. Haswell certainly believed that he had been affected by her situation, but it was probably part of a context of mounting pressure and increasing isolation that contributed to Perry slipping into another breakdown where his destructive logic of escape took control. Although it is often overlooked, Oedipus was marked for tragedy not just by his incestuous relationship with his mother but by his murder of his own father. It was not Amelia Haswell's love that Perry longed for, but his father's. The man who had rejected him in childhood continued to dominate his life. If he had once hoped to win his father's attention, even admiration, by robbing trains, now he had brought shame on him.

There may have been yet another catalyst. Self-blinding is almost totally confined to Christian cultures, and is associated with expiating sexual guilt by following, all too literally, scriptural commands to pluck out the offending eye. Predictably, it is Christian men in traditional communities who are racked with guilt about homosexuality who have most often destroyed their eyes. Could Perry have been reacting to guilt or shame about sexual relationships or encounters, either voluntary or forced, in his boyhood or more recently?

As always with Perry, the truth is elusive. His persistence in completing the blinding months later suggests that he was in the grip of a combination of guilt, self-loathing, fear and hope. It is quite possible that he was so desperate for freedom that he was ready to sacrifice his sight, and the blinding was, in one sense, an ironic victory. He had obliterated the sight of bars, uniforms and guards, and the men in power would never again be able to deprive him of daylight as a punishment. The dungeon would hold one less horror.

In the end, all the reasons for Perry's act will never be known. Throughout his life, he and others would reinvent that terrible moment to suit new purposes and arguments. The simplest and most convincing explanation was in a letter he wrote to Conant Sawyer. It suggests an extraordinary desire to exert control over his life, even at the most terrible cost, a desire that would define the rest of his life: 'I was born into the light of day, against my will of course. I now claim the right to put out that light.' As his relationships with his 'Mother' and father were threatened, Oliver Perry returned to the darkness of the womb to be reborn. And, most moving of all, he did so on his own birthday.

Today the Matteawan Asylum buildings are part of Fishkill prison, a medium-security institution surrounded by high fences whose razor-wire catches the light. The Superintendent's turreted quarters are boarded up, judged unsound, but some of the old wards and guards' quarters are still accessible. There are few objects left from the old asylum days, although correction officers remember finding strange medical instruments that were swiftly discarded or dispatched to museums. But one original feature is being recycled: the stained-glass windows that once decorated the Superintendent's rooms are being removed by inmates, under supervision, and placed in their dormitories. 'So the men can have a better view,' an officer remarked. Fishkill is also pioneering a new scheme called 'Puppies in Prison', and inmates can be seen walking dogs in the yard. In an ironic twist of history, the men in Perry's old 'home' are training seeing-eye dogs for the blind.

When Perry's blinding was leaked to the press, the reporters who had been mesmerized by Perry in the past thrilled their readers with accounts of his degeneration into madness. One insisted that 'sensible people are tired of Perry, and wish him to sink into oblivion where he belongs'. His shocking transformation seemed complete and as he struggled to cope with life as a blind man in an asylum, he was consigned not quite to oblivion but to near obscurity. The daring, debonair robber was forgotten and the blind 'lunatic' soon began to disappear as well.

In July 1896 Edward Clifford, who had captured Perry on the shore of the Hudson River, fell victim to his success. Clifford was popular, a decent, hard-working ex-policeman who had quit the force rather than get involved in corrupt politics. But he could not cope with the new prosperity and celebrity he acquired by capturing Perry. He lost his job because of excessive drinking and then shocked everyone by shooting the man who sacked him. Clifford was tried, found guilty of murder in the first degree, and sentenced to death by a familiar figure from the Jersey City legal farce, Justice Lippincott. His attorney, who had acted for Perry, tried once more to exploit loopholes in the law but the verdict was confirmed.

But there would be a long wait in jail for Edward Clifford, as appeals on the basis of temporary insanity continued, funded by popular benefits organized by none other than Chief Kelly. Clifford was finally hanged on 8 May 1900. If the four-year delay was long by the standards of the time, his execution was certainly cruel and unusual punishment: the drop failed to break Clifford's neck and it took him eighteen minutes to die of slow strangulation.

Perry also seems to have had a lasting impact on one of his Jersey cellmates. Paul Genz had finally been given the death sentence he had hoped for before Perry's arrival in the jail, but had rediscovered the will to live. Had his encounter with a man who fought so hard for freedom encouraged him not to give up so easily on life? His lawyers certainly used some of the same techniques as Perry's to get a reprieve, but it was only temporary. Just before he died, in 1897, like Perry he tried to stab himself in the eye. Was he genuinely deranged by fear or trying to feign

172

insanity to save his life? In the end he faced the hangman calmly, but, like Edward Clifford, he took a long time to die: after the 'drop' he lived, hands clenching and unclenching, for fourteen minutes. Years later it was revealed that this was a signal to an opponent of capital punishment who wanted proof of the cruelty of hanging.

Perry, meanwhile, gradually regained some psychological balance. Dramatic as his breakdown had been, like the first episode that had taken him to Matteawan, it subsided. He would always be volatile, prone to violent mood swings and paranoia, but he remained intelligent, rational and capable. Little is known about his daily life in Matteawan but there are clear signs that he was not a broken man. He had occasional visits from Amelia Haswell, and he showed his determination once again, this time by overcoming the handicaps of blindness and imprisonment to write. He had always enjoyed writing when he was allowed pencil and paper. Now he had to rely on someone else to do the writing but when he was able to find a transcriber, he had an outlet that would become essential to his survival.

In October 1897, about two years after his return to Matteawan, a local newspaper published one of Perry's poems, noting that the one-time robber was 'considerable of a poet'. There is no surviving copy of the entire poem but a fragment remains on a torn newspaper. It told a conventional tale of a naughty boy's progress into a life of crime and ended with a defiant assertion that:

> I don't intend to serve this out
> Or even let despair,
> Deprive me of my liberty
> Or give me one grey hair.

The conclusion was intriguing. Surely as a blind man, certified once more as insane, he was not planning another escape? He was obviously not suicidal. So how was he planning to avoid serving out his sentence?

The plan soon became clear. Perry, the celebrity outlaw, hoped to use the press to engage public sympathy for an appeal to be released as a blind man who could do no harm. The poem was sent to the paper by one of Perry's supporters, probably Amelia Haswell, who also relayed his renewed allegations of abuses in the asylum. It was a sensible enough idea, but by now the press and public were more interested in Perry the character than Perry the protestor or Perry the poet. Since his return to the asylum he no longer made the front pages. Instead he was now a curiosity, almost a grotesque, to be paraded on the pages of the illustrated supplements published with weekend editions.

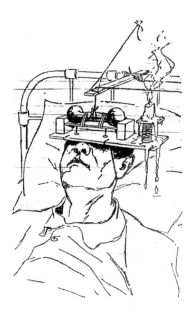

The *New York Tribune's* interpretation of Perry's 'Blinding Machine'.

The most extraordinary feature was in the *New York Tribune* in 1899. In it Perry described his blinding. Contrary to the official report, Perry claimed that he had devised an intricate blinding machine: 'I thought it out very carefully. I was very ingenious, even as a child.' He described constructing a blinding machine with wood, nails, cord and a candle, all smuggled into his cell or made from gifts, including a small dumbbell, meant for exercising, sent by friends. He had, he claimed, put sharpened nails through a piece of herring box, at exactly the right distance to pierce his eyes, and used the dumbbell to weight the board. Then he rigged up a pulley system above his bed that used a burning candle to release the weighted board so that it would drop into his eyes. Then, he said, he took some opium that he had obtained from a friend, lit the candle and waited for the machine to do its work.

Perry claimed that the Auburn officials had suppressed the story of his machine in order to avoid publicity. The apparatus, which he described in extraordinary detail, sounds impossible to construct in a prison, even for a man of Perry's evident ingenuity, but it is possible that he had managed to conceal the equipment he described in his cell, given the vagaries of prison security at the time. Even so, he was almost certainly embellishing the truth, hoping to turn the traumatic event that had labelled him a madman into a story of skill and daring, to recall, if not rival, those of his robberies. The compulsion to display his intelligence and skill that accompanied his masochistic recklessness was evidently as strong as ever. In the past it had charmed and impressed, now it merely seemed to prove his lunacy. The paper that printed his story even concluded that Perry's 'bump of self-esteem is, so to say, affected with elephantiasis, so that he loves notoriety with a consuming passion. And he has sought it in spectacular ways that would have fed the soul of Tom Sawyer.' Once Perry had been able to use the press even as it used him. The relationship was no longer mutually beneficial.

If Perry had not been judged an insane fantasist, his arguments easily dismissed as deranged, his criticisms of the institutions in which he was held might have found a more receptive audience. As the century drew to a close, an increasing number of people felt that the American dream was being turned to nightmare by unregulated business, political indifference and corruption, and a lack of welfare for the poor. New York's prisons came under mounting pressure from reformers, as the sheer number of convicts made primitive conditions intolerable. To some the prisons were a moral affront, to others examples of old-fashioned inefficiency in a system that gave powerful posts to friends and political allies rather than the able or experienced. Liberals and pragmatists alike pressed for curbs to the power of wardens and superintendents who ran them like private kingdoms. Over the coming decades there would be bitter battles over the correctional system, but in 1900 drastic measures were needed to avoid the immediate threat of violent insurrection.

Matteawan may have had medical aspirations, but it was no exception and by 1900 was a cause for real concern. Designed to hold 550 patients, it now housed 719. Henry Allison officially reported that conditions were dangerous: about 200 patients slept in corridors, and as there was inadequate housing for keepers, many were obliged to lodge outside, leading to security problems. Rumours of the state's solution, moving men to a new asylum within the grounds of Clinton prison in the village of Dannemora in the far north-east, just fifteen miles south of the Canadian border, made matters worse. Inmates dreaded being sent into what sounded like total isolation and panic ensued. In October a crowd of patients attacked their keepers in a mass escape attempt; although order was eventually restored, seven men got away. The following month, the first group of patients was transferred to the new asylum. This was designed to hold men who, like Perry, had been certified and, some might argue, driven insane while serving sentences; Matteawan would now only hold women and men judged insane at their trial. Sheer numbers meant that the transfer would be done in groups over the next year.

Perry, meanwhile, was continuing, with the assistance of friends, to seek public support for a pardon from the Governor. In 1901 a selection of his poetry was published in the *New York Journal*, William Randolph Hearst's rival to Pulitzer's *World*, the paper that had previously got the best Perry stories.

One poem, called 'Sweetheart', was addressed to an anonymous 'friend', a young woman whose identity is still unknown. The 'sweetheart' was possibly one of Perry's younger Christian supporters, possibly a friend of Amelia Haswell's, but she may have been an invention. Perry was still adept, even in an asylum, at tapping into the concerns of his audience. This poem neatly recalled the lost comforts of romance and home that Perry had once hinted at as the catalyst for his crimes:

> I often feign to be with thee,
> And to talk with thee and chat,
> But letters are no use to me,
> I am sightless – you know that,
> Yet the light I cannot moan,
> Nor your pretty eyes to meet,
> But break the bar and let me home,
> To your heart so pure and sweet.

The second poem was dedicated to his father:

> O father, list ye to my prayer,
> That tho' I oft did blunder
> I hope once more to be with thee,
> Ne'er again to break asunder.

While the sentiments, like those in the first poem, may have been designed to appeal to tender-hearted readers, there is a directness about the verse, despite its conventional language, that suggests it was heartfelt. Perry had angrily refuted rumours that his father had been terrified that his son would hunt him down when he escaped from Matteawan and clearly still yearned for his support.

The other poems were more explicitly concerned with his desire to be pardoned. One was addressed to the Governor, Republican Benjamin Odell, the other, the best of his poems, to an even higher power, calling on the 'Great Light divine' to:

> Flash down into this earthly hell
> Where lying brutes their libels tell
> And then, O, Christ, if it be right,
> Show me a friend of holy might
> Present some one from the outside world
> Who shall not cry, 'Demented, absurd'.

But demented and absurd was precisely what most people believed Oliver Perry to be, whatever his true condition. His campaign to be pardoned gained little momentum and a publicized fight with a fellow inmate damaged his cause. Its timing could not have been worse. Reformers had long argued that because when judged insane a convict could be held well beyond the end of his original sentence, even for life, he had little

178

incentive to good behaviour. Finally, in 1901, a bill was passed to grant insane convicts the possibility of commutation of sentences. Perry's poems might have elicited public sympathy, but any official record of misconduct, even provoked, could ruin his chance of proving his sanity and winning his freedom.

The following spring he tried to make his case in person, when Governor Odell visited the asylum. Dr Allison met the Governor and his party, which included members of his family as well as state officials, at the ferry and escorted them on a tour of the institution. Just before his visit Odell had issued pardons for two Matteawan inmates, raising the hopes of many patients. The visitors asked to see the most notorious inmates, including Perry. Asked to present themselves for 'inspection', the patients seized their chance. First Quimbo Appo, a well-known old Chinese man, sent to Matteawan after a series of grisly murders, asked for a pardon so that he might return to China. When Odell refused, Appo reportedly became threatening and was dragged away. Perry tried a more diplomatic approach, shaking the Governor's hand and presenting a petition, signed by many of his supporters, for his release. Odell listened politely but, according to a report, 'left him with little hope'. The Governor finally fled when a Polish woman tried to show him the marks of the hypodermic needle on her arm that she claimed had driven her mad. Appo died in the institution, but some of the other hopeful patients did leave Matteawan before too long. On Wednesday, 5 June 1902, thirty-five men, including Perry, now thirty-seven years old, set out on the long railroad journey not to freedom, but to Dannemora.

Mountain Bughouse 216

T HE RAILROAD journey upstate from Beacon to Plattsburgh, the nearest stop to the village of Dannemora, is
truly spectacular. First the train runs alongside the wide
Hudson River as it moves
in stately fashion to the
state capital, Albany,
then passes through the
foothills of the Adiron-
dack wilderness until,
hours later, it reaches
the lakes of the North
Country. It seems to
move forward in space

but backward in time, as the buildings of successive generations
give way to ancient forests and mountains, a landscape barely
marked by its human inhabitants. Slowly but surely the train
climbs until it is hugging a cliff wall high above the chain of lakes
that mark the way to Canada. Nervous passengers, advised not to
look down, stare ahead instead, only to see the front of the long
train implausibly near the edge of the next bend in the cliff.

Plattsburgh sits on the last and largest lake, Champlain. On one side are the jagged heights of New York's High Peaks, on the other the blue Green Mountains of Vermont. It is the site of one of the decisive naval battles of the Revolutionary War, but here such recent events seem inconsequential. Rumours persist that a prehistoric creature still swims in the deeps of the lake. This is a New York as far removed from the metropolitan and industrial visions of the nineteenth and twentieth centuries as it is possible to imagine, but its sublime beauty has, inevitably, a dark side. As one nineteenth-century visitor commented, 'One is likely to become maudlin with the beauty of it all . . . to be possessed of an urgent desire to wander on and on.' Even today, an unprepared rover in these forests, the last remnant of those that once covered the whole state, may never return home.

When Perry and his fellow patients were transported here, the route would have been the same and the landscape similar. There are new houses, of course, but the wilderness is protected and few choose to live in such isolation all year round. In the long winters that can last into April, the temperature drops well below freezing; heavy snows cut off towns, villages and houses, and break power supplies, plunging modern residents back into an earlier way of life. Perry's train journey would have been much slower and far less comfortable. Even now there is only one train a day and one track in each direction, so a deer on the line or sudden bad weather can bring the service to a halt. A century ago visiting officials, with every comfort available to them, complained bitterly of the privations of a trip to Plattsburgh. Prisoners travelled in the most basic of conditions and even in the summer it would have been a miserable experience. To a blind man even the beauty of the landscape could offer no relief.

Dannemora State Hospital (Courtesy of Special Collections,
Feinberg Library, State University of New York at Plattsburgh).

Dannemora was far away from the friends and supporters who
helped Perry stay in touch with the free world. Visiting Matteawan may not always have been easy for Amelia Haswell and her
fellow reformers, but the trip to the distant Adirondacks was
daunting indeed. Perry knew that he was facing the greatest
isolation of his life. The reputation of Clinton prison, within
whose grounds his new asylum stood, was fearsome, as its
nicknames reveal: 'Little Siberia', 'the Northern Bastille', the
'Dark Hole of Calcutta'. Since the prison opened in 1845, its
remote location had fostered a regime that seemed indifferent to

183

regulation. Rumours of terrible abuses led to investigations that would culminate in 1903 with the state hiring Pinkerton agents to go undercover as prisoners. The threat of ending up in Clinton had discouraged Perry from turning himself in after the first robbery and now he would be doubly confined within its grounds. Some may have found a bleak justice in this eventual journey.

Clinton, today still a maximum-security prison housing more than 2,500 men, is one of the most imposing correctional institutions in the United States. To those outside the state its name has little resonance, but once seen it is never forgotten. At night its lights shine clear across to the neighbouring state of Vermont, in daylight it is equally daunting. Clinton's sheer size and immense, solid perimeter wall, totally enclosing the world of the prison, manage to upstage its dramatic backdrop of dark wooded mountains and dwarf the small village of Dannemora that grew up around it. Clinton's convicts once laboured in rich iron ore mines, while the village people found work in the prison and later in the asylum. The work was hard and poorly paid. Even in the 1940s asylum attendants received low wages and only two weeks' vacation a year. Extraordinarily, they were obliged to draw lots for when they could take it, with losers having to take precious holidays in deepest winter.

In 1896 the Superintendent of Prisons, the Warden of Sing-Sing and Henry Allison of Matteawan had visited Dannemora and chosen it as the site for a new asylum. It is hard now to imagine how such a remote location, far from most patients' families and friends, can have seemed a good choice, but the decision was both well intentioned and expedient. Like Matteawan, it was a rural, supposedly restful, location, with cold, clear air that gave Clinton

184

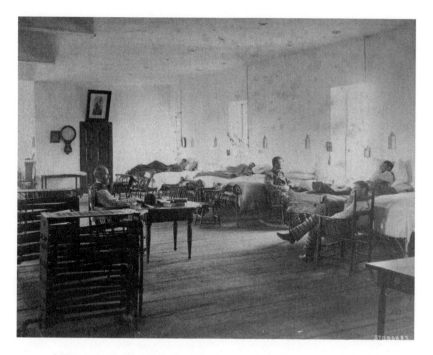

A Dannemora Ward during Perry's time there (Courtesy of Special Collections, Feinberg Library, State University of New York at Plattsburgh).

the highest survival rates in the state of prisoners with tuberculosis. It also had a supply of free convict labour to build the new institution.

The completed asylum was celebrated in the press as 'A Comfortable and Ornamental Structure, and Credit to the State'. Its opulent entrance is unchanged, with an elegant hallway and sweeping staircase of dark, highly polished wood. An early visitor could have easily felt that he or she was entering a well-appointed retreat. But the building that is now a medium-security annexe to the main prison was then known as the 'mountain bughouse' and the bugs' accommodation was less than salubrious. Today most of the men sleep in dormitories, as if they were in a particularly

185

shabby boarding school, but some, such as sex offenders and others who need to be segregated for their own safety, still inhabit the 'rooms' that once held the criminal insane: stone cells with high windows that even now, with heating, are chilly reminders of life beyond the polished surface. Like Matteawan, this institution has moved on, but its past is visible in odd corners. Prisoners queue to see the doctor outside cold tiled rooms where the original inmates were once 'treated'. In the basement is a row of bare stone cells, formerly used to hold the most unruly men. Nearby stands a large steel cage with wide-spaced bars. Now it stores broken furniture, but its design suggests it would have been ideal for administering the notorious water treatment used across the state in Perry's day. Here men who could not be controlled in any other way could, like Perry when he attacked James Shaw in Auburn, be blasted with high-pressure water hoses until they were subdued. The force drove men against the bars and made many lose control of their bowels.

Perry should logically have disappeared in Dannemora, as he all but did in Matteawan. Few traces of convicts declared insane were preserved and most that were are forbidden to the public. But digging in the Dannemora archives revealed a case file full of Perry's correspondence and writings. There are letters from supporters and government officials, and on dozens of pieces of paper, from neat lined sheets to small torn scraps, and always written in pencil, Oliver Perry's own writings. Unlike the letter from Lyons, these are not, of course, in his own handwriting. As in Matteawan, he dictated all his letters and poems to other inmates, whose varying degrees of literacy are poignantly revealed. One or two wrote in careful copperplate, but most struggled to spell even simple words and were defeated by Perry's sometimes ambitious vocabulary. Intriguingly, each note is signed 'Oliver C. Perry' with a similar flourish and large, proud capitals, suggesting the blind prisoner was still determined to sign his own name. Although Dannemora threatened Perry with the greatest isolation of his life, it has left the fullest record of his thoughts, revealing a man of extraordinary determination and spirit.

If the Matteawan authorities breathed a sigh of relief when Perry went north, those in Dannemora may have had greater confidence that they could cope. The new building was not overcrowded and was certainly less vulnerable to escape attempts. And Perry seemed to be a spent force. Times had changed, new stories occupied the press, and how much trouble could one blind madman cause? The staff in the new hospital would also have been well prepared for Perry, as their first Superintendent was Dr Robert Lamb, the physician and amateur photographer from Matteawan. Dr Lamb had done rather well for himself. As well as being promoted to the new post, he was highly respected in state government circles. In the summer of 1902, when Perry arrived, he was travelling in Europe for the New York Department of Prisons, to explore new approaches to criminal identification. He went first to Paris to study under Alphonse Bertillon, the deviser of the Bertillon method of identification by measurement, then on to England to research the even newer technique of reading fingerprints. But if the Superintendent and his staff assumed that Perry would be easier to manage than he had been in his previous institutions, they were badly mistaken.

The person who knew Perry best, who had stood by him through all his, and her own, trials and tribulations, was Amelia Haswell. Determined to bridge the great distance between them,

187

she wrote to Dannemora with extraordinary regularity: long letters to Perry with religious cards, newspaper clippings and brief notes to the Superintendent accompanied by money to buy 'comforts' for her friend. Her greatest gift, was, in her eyes, the reminder of his hopes for a better life to come, but she did all she could to make his present life more bearable. Every couple of weeks she sent money for small items, each winter she sent money for flannel underwear or blankets to help him survive the terrible cold, and each Christmas she sent a gift. All too often these were judged inappropriate and returned, much to his, and her, disappointment. But it was her letters, often the only friendly contact Perry had, that were his real lifeline. Communication with the outside world was one of the most precious privileges for the men in Dannemora. It was also one of the easiest to control and silence from a patient often meant that the privilege had been withdrawn as a punishment. Perry's silences could last for many months and his friend's ensuing anxiety was exacerbated by the distance between them.

Amelia Haswell was neither rich nor in good health, but she was determined to visit Perry in his first summer in Dannemora. Perhaps unwisely, she wrote to him about her plan, only to find that ill health prevented her. Her own eyes had become diseased, and one was removed that year in an emergency operation. The experience deepened her sympathy for Perry, but her understanding was no consolation. Although she reassured him she would make the journey at a later date, and did manage to visit him some years later, his disappointment when the visit was postponed was acute. As Amelia Haswell knew, to a man with little to look forward to, and who had felt betrayed and unwanted since infancy, few things hurt as much as a broken promise. There is no record of how Perry responded to this disappointment. But he was already preoccupied with the miseries of his new home and about to embark on a potentially fatal campaign against one aspect of the Dannemora regime: food.

Food had long been something of an obsession of Perry's. After a childhood of neglect, poverty and abuse, he was always anxious, sometimes paranoid, about what he ate. Food had been the trigger of many incidents in Auburn and Matteawan and in Dannemora it was the catalyst for his next dramatic act. It started with his usual, and undoubtedly accurate, complaints about his rations. Food in all prisons was bad: often stale, sometimes maggoty, and rarely nourishing. Organized and casual 'scams' meant that better items might be creamed off, while contamination by staff or inmates was an ever-popular trick.

One of Perry's more light-hearted criticisms was a sarcastic four-page long 'Bill of Fare' describing a week's meals. This included breakfasts of 'cracked rice mush with watered molasses' or 'cornmeal mush', dinners of 'pea soup well watered', 'beef stew with mighty little meat' and 'fresh fish and unpared potatoes no longer than hen's eggs. No gravy and about two mouths of fish', and suppers of 'Apple sauce well watered', and 'five prunes floating in water'. 'The meals', Perry concluded, 'consist of mush, mush, mush, or slush, slush, slush.'

While few can have relished their rations, Perry had additional reasons for complaint. He had been suffering for years from the combined effects of the rupture discovered soon after his arrival in Auburn, and of later beatings, that made it hard for him to digest many foods. As a blind man he also had physical difficulties in eating some foods, and an increased vulnerability that

189

gave him a deep suspicion of what he was eating and a desperate desire to get some control over it. Using his ability to turn other people's logic to his own advantage, as he had in court and in the press, he argued that as he had been judged insane, and so in need of care, he should be given better food than that provided for ordinary prisoners. No concessions were made, so, convinced that he had nothing to lose, he took a dramatic step. On 19 November 1903 he announced that unless his requests for better food were granted he would stop eating altogether. The authorities refused to listen, so he refused all food. Oliver Perry was on hunger strike.

CHAPTER 18

'When I am yelling for freedom'

DAYS PASSED, Perry began to weaken, and still he refused to eat. Without food, death would be a certainty before long. But was he really determined to die rather than compromise? He was certainly not suicidal. A man like Perry, as he had proved when he blinded himself, could have found a quicker way to die. There was no audience watching or waiting for the outcome. Although he was genuinely angry about the conditions he and his fellow patients endured, unusually, given his past mania for publicity, he did not seem to be trying to attract the attention of the press or the public. In his letters to Amelia Haswell and others he made no reference to the hunger strike as a public protest, only mentioning the particular concerns he wanted addressed by his keepers. Just as his reasons for blinding himself remained unclear, so Perry's motives in taking his hunger strike so far were never fully explained, but he was undoubtedly driven by the reckless, masochistic impulsiveness that characterized his adult life. He was trying to assert his will, at any cost.

In years to come similar situations would test prison authorities across the world. Some prisoners have stopped eating as a suicidal protest, refusing to sustain a life no longer worth living.

Others, like the British suffragettes and Irish Republicans, have used their own bodies as weapons in a battle for political change. Today, the legal and ethical dilemmas of treating a prisoner who refuses food are complicated by the gaze of the media, but the central question remains: can someone be forced to live? In the closed world of the asylum in 1903, the doctors had an answer. When Perry was near death, they strapped him to a table, pushed a tube up his nostril and poured a mixture of eggs and milk into his stomach.

When it was clear that the doctors could end his hunger strike by force, Perry changed tactics. He was determined to win some control over his life, so if his food was served according to his requirements, he would eat. If not, he insisted, the doctors would have to tube-feed him or watch him die. In effect he forced his own force-feeding. From his cell he issued constant written requests and complaints. Sometimes he included his fellow inmates, with whom he seems to have been quite popular, as he had been in the past, in his requests. But usually his demands were personal: Oliver Perry was still a determined individualist. His demands often read like an imperious customer dealing with room service in a bad hotel. He refused food because it was inferior to that served to the keepers, or had been tampered with, such as milk that he claimed was watered down after the cream had been skimmed off for the staff. He rejected food that was stale, like a cake sent by Amelia Haswell and delivered so late it had dried up.

Sometimes he specified what he would like to eat, in bills of fare that read like poignant reminders of real food he had once enjoyed: '*Breakfast*. Two hard fried eggs turned over; and boiled or fried potatoes or hash. *Dinner*. Fried Beefsteak, or carved

One of Perry's bills of fare.

Roast Beef, or fresh fish together with boiled or mashed potato and gravy. Also macaroni and beans when prepared. *Supper.* Two hard fried eggs turned over; and fried potatoes or hash.'

Only rarely did Perry win any concessions from his doctors and keepers and many notes revealed the harsh reality of his situation. He often begged the doctors to warm through the mixture that they pumped through his nose into his stomach or to reduce its volume so that it caused him less pain. Although sometimes he ate regular food in his room from a metal plate, and his weight remained quite stable, Perry was forcibly tube-fed, sometimes for weeks at a time, for the rest of his long years in Dannemora.

His attempt to take control of his own life was not confined to eating. After years of complaining about being forcibly drugged, he tried to manipulate the use of medication. He warned his doctors that if his suffering became too much to bear, he would shout all night until they administered a knockout injection and gave him some 'oblivion'. As with the tube-feeding, he tried to turn punishment into treatment on demand. Some months later he extended his campaign even further. Insisting that as a man judged 'insane' he should not be forced to wear the degrading clothing of a prisoner, particularly distressing for a man once known for his style, he tore off all his clothes and demanded decent attire. When this was refused he went naked, wrapping himself in a blanket only when visitors arrived, anticipating by over half a century the actions of political prisoners in Northern Ireland. Occasionally he would wear underclothes, if he felt that he had been well treated. Going naked was no casual gesture. Perry was housed in a room with no heating and in winter the temperature was well below zero, day and night.

It would be hard to argue that a man who imposed such a regime on himself was sane, but his writings, preserved by the authorities he fought, reveal that while he was clearly prone to paranoid fears and compulsions, his intellect and reason were as sharp as ever and he had sensitivity and subtlety as well as a violent temper. His behaviour also prefigured that of some more recent prisoners who, after extreme bouts of destructiveness and delusion, have, in better surroundings, recovered completely.

Coincidentally, just weeks after New York's greatest train robber started his hunger strike, Thomas Edison, inventor of the electric lights that had illuminated Utica in 1891, thrilled America with the first real 'feature film' to be shown in the nation's vaudeville theatres: *The Great Train Robbery*. At twelve minutes, this was the longest, most dramatic moving picture ever, telling the story of bandits robbing a train. While the action took place in the 'West', it was filmed in studios and on the railroads in New York and New Jersey. Edison publicists boasted that New York's own 'frontier' train robberies could only enhance the film's appeal to eastern audiences. A dramatic scene in which a robber fired his gun straight at the shocked but delighted audience showed just how powerful this new medium would be, with crime a favourite subject as it had been in the dime novels of the 1890s.

It was, of course, one Perry would never experience. Life in an asylum for a blind man must have been at best tedious, at worst terrifying. There was no work or education and, although he made some friends, he was frequently housed with the most irrational and disturbed men. But, with difficulty, he had sustained his own love of writing. He was dependent on others to read and write for him, and the only way to get another patient to do so was by paying him with tobacco. When this worked, he could hear letters and books and dictate his own thoughts. But when his keepers or doctors wanted to punish him, they could easily stop him buying tobacco, or simply lock his door. His supporters, and state officials, repeatedly advised the doctors that letting someone read and write for him could only help alleviate his situation and their own, giving him some mental stimulation to distract him from his complaints. One governor even sent word that Perry should be allowed notepaper to write to him. But time and again, the response to his unruly behaviour was to deprive him of this outlet. The officials' actions may well be understandable – Perry must have been infuriating – but they made the problem worse.

His many notes and letters, from the periods when he was allowed to write, testify to his desperate need to communicate, to find a voice that could not be silenced by drugs or double-doored cells. He also continued to write poems, which he had transcribed into a little book that was his prize possession. The poems were generally protests or appeals for sympathy. Some were religious in theme, with conventional messages of promised renewal and redemption designed to appeal to his supporters. Some expressed more personal and tangible hopes.

One written in 1904, called 'My Prospective Friend', was addressed to a new physician, Dr Charles North, who had recently arrived in Dannemora from a post in Matteawan. The physician was reported to be a fine amateur actor and shared Perry's love of music: an accomplished violinist, he even started a patients' orchestra. If Perry had known him in Matteawan, he gave no hint of their relationship in his poem, but, as he had so often, he was pinning his hopes on one man:

> Oh! Doctor Nord; if thou only
> Let me tell my stomach's tail [sic]
> It will reveal how very lonely;
> Veryly [sic] do I moan and wail;
> Ere long I pray that thou may find
> Room in thy heart for one whose [sic] blind.

196

The Patients' Orchestra at Dannemora (Courtesy of Special Collections, Feinberg Library, State University of New York at Plattsburgh).

Dr North's reaction to his welcoming poem is not known but he would occupy a place in Perry's thoughts for over a decade. In the coming years Perry would repeatedly accuse him of both systematic corruption and personal vindictiveness, and North would block all attempts to review Perry's case. None of Perry's accusations was investigated and many of North's practices, that seem harsh or insensitive today, were common at the time. Two examples reveal North's rigidity and Perry's frustration.

First, a few years after his arrival, North refused Amelia Haswell's request to be allowed to send Perry a mandolin for Christmas. She and some of his other friends hoped would that this would help occupy and cheer Perry who, like the physician, had always loved music. But North was unmoved. Perry remembered the decision for the rest of his life. Years later he reminded his friend that the Superintendent allowed some patients to buy beer 'but when I was anxious to drink in a few notes from a mandolin which you and

197

others desired to send me, oh! that was different and yet he has never suggested any occupation for the mind'. To mark another Christmas, Amelia Haswell hoped to send Perry a ring. In her accompanying letter to Dr North she acknowledged her impulse might seem odd, 'but when you consider how few things one can send a blind man, and knowing how much he used to prize a ring and as some one suggested it, I acted upon it. It is inexpensive (not solid) and I thought whether in the circumstances you might allow it.' North again refused. He may simply have been following the letter of the law, but his decisions appeared insensitive and short-sighted to Amelia Haswell who believed some kindness would encourage Perry to cooperate with his doctors. To Perry they appeared to be the work of a vindictive man bent on persecuting him.

Returned letter from Amelia Haswell.

Whatever the rights and wrongs of both men's behaviour, Perry's 'prospective friend' swiftly became his most hated 'adversary', a personification of the brutality, indifference and cruelty of the system. To make matters worse for Perry, towards the end of 1904 Henry Allison died and Robert Lamb returned to

Matteawan as Superintendent, leaving a vacancy in Dannemora that Charles North hoped to fill.

Perry's fear about North's likely promotion was evident in a letter to Amelia Haswell, urging her to start a new petition to the Governor for his parole to a regular asylum near his friends. Amelia Haswell was working hard on his behalf, sending stories to the press. As his hunger strike had changed into a long-term campaign, Perry had turned his attention to getting out of Dannemora. But, aware of his damaged reputation, he had evidently decided that 'escape' to an asylum for free men was his only real hope. He wanted her to publicize it in the press because, as he noted with his ever acute understanding of the power of the press, 'President Roosevelt says that the only way to work quick reforms is through the public newspapers and he is right.' By this time, even Cole Younger, a killer as well as robber, had been paroled and pardoned. But he, unlike Perry, had been a model prisoner, had never complained and had certainly never been certified insane. Perry's letter, accompanied by a poem that combined religious sentiments with scathing references to North's 'crooks', was annotated 'Not mailed owing to the many false statements referring to other patients, which if true would have no relation to Perry's affairs. C.H.N.'

But Amelia Haswell kept trying on his behalf, even telling the *New York Evening World* that he had blinded himself for her sake. She claimed that for a man who had always chosen an outdoor life, being confined was torture, and whenever he glimpsed the sky he was driven to attempt to escape. If he could no longer see, he would no longer be tempted; if no longer tempted, he could not disappoint her again. The story was a 'hook' to draw press and public attention to Perry's present situation explained in an excerpted letter from the prisoner.

He described a brutal and mean regime, with men stealing blankets from one another in order to endure the harsh winter conditions. In a move calculated to appeal to Christian reformers, he also drew attention to the lack of religious services for many months, because the attendants used the only suitable room for their weekly dances instead. The image of attendants dancing while their damaged charges were deprived of the consolations of religion was surely bound to appal the respectable reader. 'Is this a hospital in reality?' asked Perry. 'Shame upon all Christian taxpayers who know and still allow this degrading and brutalizing mismanagement to continue.' The stories were most probably true, but, as ever, Perry did not miss a trick in spinning them to appeal to his readers. He had declared years before that he was no longer a believer, but he knew that his most faithful supporters were.

Amelia Haswell kept trying to explain Perry's behaviour to his doctors in the hope they would understand and help him. 'Oliver is naturally quick and fiery and impulsive, and his intentions might be the best, but when brought to the test of patient waiting and forbearance, in this he was sorely lacking, not having learned self-control in his past life it is not so easy now.' 'This would be no evidence of insanity to me,' she added, rather naively, 'for I know it was his natural temperament.' She was at pains to show she was sympathetic to the doctors. 'I can understand how Oliver might be a very trying patient – but when I attempt to put myself in his place, imagine my being blind among lunatics, and no way of diverting my mind, it would be enough to drive a sane man insane.' She repeatedly, but unsuccessfully, urged the Superintendent to try a new approach: 'Such men are used to cuffs and

200

blows and curses, but kindness in time I believe will touch the hardest heart.'

Whatever the miseries of his life, and the restrictions imposed by his doctors, Perry had retained three distinctive characteristics from happier days: a love of music, a concern for his personal appearance, and an almost childish sweet tooth. Inmates were generally allowed to receive carefully vetted gifts, and also money to purchase goods through the steward. Amelia Haswell duly sent money, usually $2, every few weeks, so that Perry could do so. Many of his requests were refused, but they reveal his tastes. At the end of 1904, for example, he hoped to purchase a 'twenty-five cent harmonica made by M. Hohner in A or D key', 'granulated sugar', a 'pound of raisins', and a 'pound of stick peppermint candy'. In a later note, that may reveal the heightened senses blindness brought, he asked for '2 jars of scented cold cream – 20c, 2 envelopes of sen sen [breath perfumes] – 10c, 4lbs of roasted peanuts for 50c, shiff of keenans [tobacco] – 20c, 2 plugs of Climax – 20c, 1lb of B & J peppermint drops – 20c, 2 coconuts, Adams wintergreen flavored gum – 25c.'

Perry's sweet tooth, and the occasional treats he was allowed, contributed to another of his problems. He had been suffering from the sharp torment of constant toothache for years. Campaigns at the time to allow prisoners to purchase toothpowder show that dental hygiene was non-existent in correctional institutions. Eventually his teeth were in such a bad condition that eating, even when he wanted to, was a near impossibility. Amelia Haswell offered to pay for them to be replaced with dentures. After protracted negotiations with the dentist who worked for the hospital, a set was produced, but it was shoddy and ill-fitting. Perry was infuriated, but retained his sense of humour. He wrote to the dentist, accusing him of using inferior materials, knowing that when the dentures broke 'you could rest securely in your position as a respectable citizen and say "Oh! I can't help it, the poor fellow is crazy and has probably been trying to take a piece out of his iron bedstead, or something of that sort."' In the end Amelia Haswell demanded her money back and Perry's teeth were forgotten.

But Perry had also retained his ability to make friends among his fellow prisoners. One wrote to him from New York City:

Friend Oliver,

I wrote you in a poem that I would remember you. I am out, and as I thought about my promise to-day, I count [sic] help writing this letter. Is Miss A. Haswell sticking to you still, I know she cares a good deal about you and I hope you still respect her in your heart.

How is Supt. Lamb and Dr. North, the nurses, attendants and the boys. How is your health and let me know if possible everything worth knowing about yourself.

Friend Oliver I am in good health, getting stout and doing well. 'The unexpected often happens' and I experienced it as never before when I was told to pack up and be good to myself. Well, I never in all my life felt so happy; liberty was sweeter, the air was better, food tasted different, and in fact nature seemed a smiling; everything was good with the exception of the Devil, the same old Satan.

Cheer up and be of good courage, don't worry, for you ought to know worry has not done anybody good. Oliver the unexpected in your life may happen some day, if not in this world perhaps in the next. I hope it will be for the better. Good old New York town has changed greatly; for old time sake I took a car to see the city; first I went through the subway by local and express, then I took a ride on the Third Ave. Elevated Road, then the surface roads as the Third Ave., Madison Ave, and horse car. One fine day I went to Coney Island, and I must say it was greatly changed for the better. Gee if I told you one quarter of what I saw it would fill a good sized book. Dear old Coney Island was still waiting for me, and I was glad to see it looking so well. I enjoyed myself greatly and left early, because my money gave out. I could stay there all day, it was so good, with the bands of music playing and the people so happy also so many new things that was interesting and your money going, gee it was all to the good.

Not wishing to bore you with a long letter I will cut it short by wishing you God's luck, also all them that I have mentioned in this letter.

I remain,
your friend,
Hyman.

Hyman Epstein had been Perry's fellow inmate and, it seems, friend, although this is the only record of their relationship. Epstein's own story was a strange one. In 1901 the twenty-one-year-old Jewish New Yorker had been sentenced to two years in prison. In Auburn he converted to Christianity but his behaviour was interpreted as religious mania and he was declared insane. After a spell in Dannemora where he befriended Perry, he was sent, at the end of his sentence, to the asylum on Ward's Island in Manhattan where he was to be held indefinitely. His family made no attempt to aid him as they refused to accept his conversion as the act of a sane man, while the asylum authorities insisted that he was insane because he claimed to have 'seen Jesus Christ'. Epstein seemed doomed to remain incarcerated indefinitely. So one September morning in 1903 he slipped away from the guards, crept to the riverbank and started swimming across the East River to freedom. Powerfully built, he was making good progress against a swift current when a policeman in a patrol boat spotted him. Assuming he was an unfortunate sailor who had fallen overboard, the patrolmen tried to rescue him. Epstein attempted to dodge the boat but eventually gave himself up.

He was taken to the police court in Harlem, where he explained his story to the magistrate. For the first time, almost miraculously, somebody in authority believed him. The magistrate, impressed by his rationality, declared that it was an outrage that he had been locked up in an asylum. It was, he said, no crime for a sane man to attempt to escape from such confinement. The asylum physician's explanation did not impress the magistrate: 'I have seen a number of religious persons who have contended that they have seen Christ, and they were not insane, either.' He declared Epstein sane, and announced that he would spend his own money to help him gain his freedom. Eventually a Supreme Court writ was issued against the asylum to show cause for Epstein's detainment, and in due course he left Ward's Island a free man.

Perry may have lost a friend but he was now just as determined to escape. In June 1906 he wrote a letter of appeal to the new Governor, Republican Frank Higgins, accompanied by an acrostic poem called 'Chief Executive'. Composing acrostics, a form he used many times, was quite a feat for a blind man who relied on the help of men whose literacy was rarely developed. The challenge was clearly something Perry relished but this time the ambition of the poem's content, begging for a chance to prove his worth as a reformed man, was let down by the form. In an unusual lapse, either he or his transcriber thought 'Governor' only had one 'r', and the first letters of each line consequently spelled out 'Honorable Govenor [sic] Higgins'. What Higgins would have made of the poem, or appeal, will never be known, as the authorities decided it was unacceptable and marked it 'Don't Send'. Undaunted, Perry kept up a sustained campaign to convince politicians and government officials that his case should be reviewed, writing to successive governors and members of the Commission in Lunacy responsible for overseeing the state's institutions. Just as each new doctor would receive a poem, so each time a new man took up public office, he would hear from Dannemora State Hospital 216.

Perry's keepers heard his complaints even more loudly, as a special Fourth of July poem called 'A Parody' revealed. Written to be sung to the music of 'Marching through Georgia', it commemorated a protest that Perry seems to have particularly enjoyed:

How the turkeys gobbled when they heard me yell so loud;
How the Doctors wondered that I was never cured;
How the village people all gathered in a crowd
When I was yelling for freedom.
(Chorus)
Hurrah! Hurrah! come give a shout with one;
Hurrah! Hurrah! I know you would be free,
And so I hope to make it, to live in good old Troy.
For I am working so hard boys.

205

How the 'Bugs' did curse that time O yes it was a fright;
How they damned and double-damned the man who's out of
  sight;
How they would have choked me all in my sightless plight
When I was yelling for freedom.
(Chorus)

How the Doctors suffer when they see one with a friend;
How they long to queer me when money they do send;
How they try to starve me, no solace to extend
When I am yelling for freedom.
(Chorus)

Someone, presumably a doctor, wrote on the poem, in red ink,
'Illustrative of Perry's Egotism'.

CHAPTER 19

'O God, how much longer?'

IN AUGUST 1907 the men of Dannemora rioted for the first time. Only five years after opening, the asylum was already so overcrowded that some of the most dangerous men were housed in a dormitory, allowing them to collaborate in planning what turned into a desperate siege. They improvised weapons by getting hold of some sash weights and breaking up several beds and a steam radiator. Guards used ammonia fumes, then resorted to turning the high-pressure water hose on men who appeared through the windows, and finally to shooting. The order was only to kill if absolutely necessary, but when the riot was finally quelled, it was discovered that one patient, Isaac Dubois, had died from gunshot wounds. In the past, Perry would surely have been at the centre of any dramatic event, but this time he was not involved. A blind man would have had little chance of taking part in such a protest, and Perry spent his time composing letters and poetry to demand a better life.

Sometimes his protests were personal: on 1 January 1907 he dictated a mordant, and prophetic, acrostic spelling out 'Unhappy New Year'. But increasingly he attacked the asylum regime more formally. That same year he sent a letter via a local clergyman to the Reverend John Warren, Amelia Haswell's brother-in-law, who, he hoped, would in turn forward it to the new Governor, Charles Hughes. The elaborate chain was devised to overcome possible censorship. His complaints now were not only about brutality or cruelty, but about serious financial corruption, and, for a certified lunatic, he displayed inside knowledge of the institution as well as a keen understanding of the contemporary political context.

He was clearly anxious about how he would be read – 'I shall try not to make a misstatement as I realize that it would reflect upon my sanity or veracity' – but adamant in his critique of conditions and corruption. Perry evidently hoped that Governor Hughes, in his opinion 'no machine man', would condemn the doctors who 'graft at the expense of their patients'. After cataloguing petty abuses and contrasting asylum conditions with those in the neighbouring prison, he turned to accusations of corruption, from 'petty graft' to serious allegations.

He claimed that 'a summer residence at the lake' had been 'finished off with lumber from our new chapel and dining room' and 'provisioned from our store room to feed Supt. Collins, Dr Lamb and all their friends who wish to visit these mountains'. Hospital employees were too busy working on this camp to look after patients, he wrote, because 'Dr North's principal desire is to make a good showing before the Albany authorities and at the same time graft for himself.' Although the Adirondack forests were under pressure, because of the demand for newsprint, 'camps', lavish vacation homes that combined rural style and real luxury, were increasingly fashionable as retreats for Vanderbilts and Rockefellers. Some survive today as expensive hotels and restaurants serving local delicacies like wintergreen ice-cream. The irony of Perry's observations about the use of prison timber and labour to build such a 'residence' was, in the circumstances, remarkably understated.

While the Dannemora doctors fed their horses on good oats, wrote Perry, their patients lived on 'mush' and 'like Oliver Twist the mush eaters are crying for more'. He offered a catalogue of petty actions by the doctors that seem trivial, but must have seemed unbearably cruel to men with little pleasure in life. One prohibited gifts or purchases of handkerchiefs or soap because he considered the official provision adequate, and of cheese, because 'he don't like the smell'. Another banned peanuts because 'once upon a time some unfortunate happened to drip a few peanut shells upon the floor'.

Corruption and indifference, Perry insisted, had led to the neglect of patients. In the hospital the already basic bathroom facilities had been allowed to fall into disrepair, 'so now we have but two seats and one urinal for about a hundred men [in his section]. Sometimes a man will urinate in the sink where we must stand to wash.' One urinal had, he claimed, been removed and installed in the summer camp, while broken combs provided for general use were rarely replaced, a 'brush hung for over two years until the hairs wore down to the wood', and only 'two roller towels for so many men, some of whom are diseased, makes it seem very unsanitary'. While he dwelt at length on the degradations of poor hygiene, the terseness of the ex-reformatory boy's most serious allegation is perhaps telling: 'There is little classification and young fellows from Elmira reformatory are herded in dormitories with old-time criminals who frequently seduce the weaker ones under the promise of candy, etc. I know several who

209

commit unnatural crimes in two and three ways during the day as well as at night.'

Perry seemed genuinely concerned about the situation of all the men in Dannemora and his letter reads as a heartfelt protest about conditions and corruption rather than a calculated pretext for a private plea. He had clearly managed to follow what was happening in American politics and saw his situation as part of a greater picture. He was particularly impressed by President Roosevelt, who had made some moves against systematic corruption. His admiration for the President may have been increased by the many parallels in their lives. Roosevelt may have been born into affluence rather than poverty, but he was, like Perry, a puny child who made himself an athlete, an easterner with a taste for western adventure, and a man of charisma, courage and determination. He also happened to be a champion of simplified spelling.

But the conclusion to Perry's protest letter was deeply personal and concerned with the psychological and physical torments of his daily life: 'O God, how much longer? I am harassed by day and haunted in my nightly dreams. I pace up and down and sing or chant in order to keep from talking to myself about my troubles.' His mental misery was exacerbated by his physical conditions: 'I have been not let out in God's sunshine for over four years yet Dr Macdonald will not leave my door open as he does that of others so that I can get some reading done [by allowing a patient to enter and read to him]. No warmth will reach me in this cold room and I feel the strain upon my mind.' He ended by begging his friend to send the letter to the Governor, but also with a more immediate request, to help him get a hot-water radiator that he could use to warm through the tube-feeding mixture and ease his aching stomach and kidneys.

210

It is difficult to imagine what the Governor might have made of the letter. Hughes was a tough but progressive Republican, described by Roosevelt as 'the bearded iceberg'. But Perry's complaints would go unread. A year later John Warren was writing to Dr North for news of Perry, as he had heard nothing from him.

Perry's writings, by and large, make depressing reading, in the topics and their tone. His complaints were usually justified but his own inflexible attitude and refusal to conform meant that he and his keepers were almost always at loggerheads and his harsh, self-imposed regime of near-starvation and nakedness took its toll. It is easy to believe that he was a broken man, old before his time, sustained only by a determination to beat the system. But two poems, still sealed up in small envelopes in his file nearly a hundred years later, reveal with almost shocking clarity that he was not always gloomy or hopeless. They were written not long after a visit by Amelia Haswell and some of her friends from Troy, and were confiscated and sealed by disapproving staff in Dannemora. The first was marked 'Obscene Poem, given to Dr R. S. Lepes, September 11 1907':

> There once was a pretty young miss
> Who thought it the acme of bliss
> To frig herself silly
> With the stem of a lily
> Then sit on a sunflower to piss.

The records reveal nothing, but this tiny scrap of grubby humour suggests a side to Perry that would otherwise have been totally obscured. Was the poem specially designed to impress or offend

211

Dr Lepes personally, was it about someone in particular or was it just a moment of fun? Whoever or whatever it was for, it shows that inside the damaged man, now approaching his forty-second birthday after fifteen years in prison, was a funny, rude teenager who had never quite grown up.

The second poem, called 'Sweet Maiden', and dismissively marked 'Obscene "poetry"', was more romantic, the 'obscenity' that caused the doctors to confiscate it evident only in the hopeful request of the acrostic.

> My eye is on my charming dove
> Athwart the space between our love.
> You cannot dodge me now my dear,
> Indeed you are a warming cheer.
>
> So now be good and by your smile
> Light up my hopes for a little while.
> Either be good or by your glance
> End all my hope of one small chance.
> Pretty red lips have drawn me on,
>
> Why not be like the loving swan?
> I long to fold you in my arms
> That I may feel your inner charms.
> Hark! Now and hide this rhyme away,
>
> Yet do not fail to read each day
> Or you may quite forget to dwell
> Upon the love which I would swell.

Composed by a Bug
And
Written by a Mug

July 17th Nineteen hundred and in love.

Again, there is no way of knowing to whom the poem was addressed. The 'sweet maiden' may have visited with Amelia Haswell, or have been another patient's visitor, a female employee, or even a figment of Perry's imagination. The poem suggests that, if only in his imaginings, he was still capable of passion, and that, in his imagination, he was not blind. Like the limerick it is cheeky, hinting at a brighter dimension to Perry's life in the period after Amelia Haswell's visit.

In fact, Perry had started to try to conform to the asylum rules and there seemed to be some hope that he might settle down. He had been influenced by one of the young doctors who struggled to work with this most difficult of patients in an already tough job. Amos Baker was one of the few who showed Perry real kindness. Although Amelia Haswell was ever faithful, her repeated exhortations to trust in God did little to cheer Perry. And although he repeatedly asked for news of his father and sent messages begging him to visit, Perry's own family had effectively abandoned him. The only contact he had in all his years in Dannemora was a summons from his paternal grandmother's lawyer. His grandfather had died without leaving a will and his widow, Sarah Emily, Perry's step-grandmother and aunt, was issuing summonses against all other possible claimants to the small plot of land in the Irish Settlement, including Perry. The farm itself had burned down and the land was worth about $300 in total. Dr

North was paid a fee of $1 for serving the writ that deprived Perry of his only inheritance. It was the last recorded contact Perry had with his family.

So the impact of a thoughtful doctor was considerable. His were small gestures, but they meant everything to his patient, who wrote a jaunty 'Toast to St Patrick and Dr Baker' as a thank-you when the physician had got him some pie, a favourite food. Baker arranged for him to have a water glass, an attendant's urinal, much easier for a blind man to use than a regulation chamber pot, and even some old carpet for his cold room. He also promised that he might find him a small table, so that he could eat more easily.

At last, Perry seemed to have found someone in authority he could trust. In letters to friends he wrote proudly of the 'confidence' Dr Baker reposed in him and it seemed possible that, with this encouragement, he might conform enough, by eating in his room and wearing clothes, to convince the authorities he deserved a second chance.

In the spring of 1908 that chance seemed close at hand. A letter to Dr North from Cornelius V. Collins, Superintendent of Prisons, indicated that he was convinced that Perry deserved a trial return to prison, a possible step towards eventual freedom, 'I have received the letter enclosed with your communication from Oliver Curtis Perry and am pleased to know that he shows a disposition to continue obedience to the rules. I trust you will give Oliver such personal attention as it is possible because as soon as your judgment would permit I should like to give the fellow a trial once more in the prison, as I am inclined to think that the change might benefit him temporarily at least.' Collins favoured some prison reform, and had voiced his concern that 17 per cent of prisoners had become insane. He also, coincidentally, lived in Troy and had been collared on several occasions, including once when trying to board a train, by the indomitable Amelia Haswell.

The letter that seemed to put Perry's vision of freedom within his grasp was sent on 1 April, and while it was undoubtedly genuine, it had no more effect than a cruel hoax. Two days later Collins wrote to North again: 'I have no doubt the statement relating to Perry is true in every respect. My only idea was to encourage him in every possible way to obey and respond to even a part of the institution discipline and this apparently is being done.' North had utterly rejected the idea that Perry was, or would be, fit to return to prison. Collins made another attempt to judge for himself but, as Perry commented, the doctors did little to enable their patient to make his case: 'My door was suddenly thrown open, I knew strangers were present, yet no word was spoken; so after an embarrassing silence I said, "Do you want to exhibit me like an animal or will you introduce me", Dr Mac-Donald then spoke but walked away with his visitors. I afterwards learned that they were two members of the Parole Board. Perhaps this circumstance has helped to check Mr. Collins but put yourself in my position. It is only common courtesy to speak to a convict when visitors are ushered into his presence. In my blindness I thought it was some Attendant letting a stranger steal a look at me.' The result of the 'interview' was not in Perry's favour. To add insult to injury, the bad news came in a letter from the Commissioner mistakenly addressed to the 'Hon. Curtis Perry'. The error wounded Perry, as he told his friend, because it 'puts me on a par with lunatics who are always proud of such distinctions'.

Condemned to stay in Dannemora, he found his life increasingly unbearable, although, with Baker's support, he went on trying to conform. He continued writing and even had a poem published in the *Star of Hope*. This was a remarkable prison newspaper, founded in 1899 and published by prisoners in Sing-Sing, featuring the writing of convicts across the state, that served as a means of building a sense of community as well as giving individual prisoners a voice. Perry's acrostic poem on 'Independence Day' was identified only by his prison number 'DSH 216'. Few, if any, who read the conventional patriotic verses would have known that they were written by the notorious train robber.

Perry's success encouraged him to submit another poem later the same year but his second submission, a more polemical piece, signed 'Mountain Bughouse 216', was not published. The *Star of Hope* was an invaluable voice for the prisoners of New York State, but it had to be diplomatic. Calls for reform had to be reasonable and the insane were risky allies. In the coming years they would reap little benefit from the growing efforts to treat their sane fellows with some respect.

In 1909 Amos Baker left Dannemora to take up a post at Matteawan. The repercussions were dramatic. Perry felt abandoned once again and, when some of Baker's 'concessions' were rescinded, his battle with the authorities recommenced. He soon wrote to the Reverend Warren in evident distress: 'I am now in an isolated room with two doors so that no one can hear my cries or talk to me. I defecate ['deprecate' in his transcriber's version] upon the floor in one corner and lie in the other like a wild beast.' He had been moved to the isolation cell as a punishment for what might today be called a 'dirty protest', defecating on the floor of his cell.

The protest began accidentally when the hospital sewer had

become clogged and the water closets were out of use. A blind man's sense of smell is more acute than a sighted man's, so that night, rather than use his open urinal vessel, which he could not empty until the morning, Perry defecated on some paper that he wrapped into 'a neat appearing package', and asked the night watchman to place it in the water closet. The man agreed but instead, as a cruel trick or stupid joke, slipped it back into the room. Finding it later, Perry threw it out of his window.

When he heard of the incident, a furious Dr MacDonald had Perry put in a 'north room upon the violent ward', isolated from the patients who sometimes helped him, and surrounded by a more 'irrational class of insane people'. When MacDonald also ordered that he be made to use a regulation pot, rather than the attendant's urinal Dr Baker had let him use, Perry snapped and smashed the cell window. From then on, his furniture removed as a precaution against his using it to make weapons, he defecated in his cell as a protest, as many other prisoners would do in the future, and refused to eat. He told John Warren that he was prepared to suffer any degradation rather than lose his hard-won privileges without a fight: 'I shall continue to exist just like a wild beast until they exhaust their animosity and terrorize the other patients, at which time I hope to be returned to my quarters and furnishings.'

Perry's brief truce with his keepers was over.

CHAPTER 20

'Out of His Living Tomb Speaks Oliver Curtis Perry'

OUTSIDE DANNEMORA Perry seemed to take on an almost mythical status. In 1908 *The Railroad Man's Magazine*, favoured reading of trainmen and rail fans alike, had featured his story in the latest of its series on 'Great American Train Robberies', written by Burke Jenkins. After noting the exploits of 'our redoubtable gentlemen of the road and paperbacks, the James and Younger boys', the author insisted that it 'remained for the effete East to produce what was probably the boldest railway bandit that ever existed – Oliver Perry.' The author noted that Perry was living out his days in a pitiful condition but Perry's doctors insisted on his health, strength and difficult nature, leading to a new image in the popular press, 'the Samson of Dannemora'.

Independence Day

Dannemora State Hospital 216

J ustice sails on every breeze
U nder our soldiers' flag:
L ong live the Yankees who appease
Y ou boys who do not lag!

F ollowers of our Yankee boys
O 'er mountains, vales and dales,
U nite and mingle heartfelt joys
R emote from bloodstained trails.
T o-day we see a peaceful land,
H allowed by our Savior:

N o one could find a folk more grand
I n good and square behavior.
N ational pride is soaring high,
E ach warrior shoots his guns
T hroughout the land where maidens shy
E 'en though they love these sons.
E very one should shout the day,
N ew vigor to inspire:

H urrah! for Uncle Sam, I say!
U nfurl the flag and fire!
N e'er cease to eulogize that soul
D estined to lead the free:
R emember how he reached the goal
E 'er sought by you and me.
D on't fail to do your very best,

A nd if the call should come,
N ot only speak but fight for rest
D espite the grapeshot's hum.

E vents have shown that we would vault
I nto a war for right,
G iving the foe no chance to halt
H owever fierce his might.
T riumphant nation! peaceful sight!

Perry's poem in the *Star of Hope*.

Perry in Dannemora.

One reporter explained the new analogy: 'Like Samson he has been shorn of the things he had, like Samson he blinded himself in his remorse, like Samson he feels about him only prison walls, like Samson he is the strongest man inside those prison walls – a veritable giant in stature and but for his sightless eyes a perfect physical specimen of manhood.' The new name was attractive, flattering even, although the extraordinary exaggeration bore little relation to Perry's actual physical stature and condition. The line-drawings in the press showed not a biblical giant but an almost classical figure, swathed in a sheet with a bandage across his eyes, looking more like blindfolded justice or Tiresias, staring blindly into a future only he could foretell.

Inside the asylum Perry was increasingly isolated from meaningful contact with the real world. He kept appealing to state officials for his case to be reviewed. Each time they had to judge the word of a criminal lunatic against that of a respected doctor, and each time the review concluded with, at best, a request that he be given a reader. He did gain some concessions, including, eventually, a ruling that a doctor be given the task of reading to him so that he no longer had to bribe a fellow patient. But, although he kept battling, some of the ties that bound him to life and other people started to break.

First his book of poetry disappeared. Although he could not

read its contents himself, it was a powerful symbol of his resistance to the grim reality of incarceration. One day, he could not find it in his cell, and nobody would tell him if it had been stolen by another inmate or confiscated. He was devastated and begged Amelia Haswell to help. She asked Dr North to have the book found because writing was therapeutic: 'I have always encouraged his composing rhyme, as I thought it would help divert his mind. . . . If I was blind and had no way of diverting my mind, I am not sure I would have a mind to divert very long.' A month later she wrote again. Perry was evidently heartbroken. Eventually North replied that even if the book was found, he would be reluctant to return it to Perry in his 'present condition'. He was in no mood to compromise.

Amelia Haswell was infuriated by Dr North's intransigence but she was even more stern with Perry who, she felt, was letting himself down. She warned him, in an eleven-page letter, that his disobedience, particularly his persistent refusal to wear clothes, condemned him in the eyes of the officials who would decide his fate. Choosing a biblical analogy, as usual, she reminded him, perhaps unwisely, of the fate of Nebuchadnezzar, 'who did not give God the glory for any of his blessings'. Might he not, she asked, rather idealistically, take his mind off his sufferings and try to do some good by influencing others? She signed off 'A Friend "in storm and sunshine"'.

But something had snapped. Perry did not read her letter: not because it was confiscated or because he had no reader, but because he refused it. His faith had always been in his Christian friends rather than in Christ, and for him God personified justice and right in this life, not the promise of eternal redemption. Now the missionary's exhortations to trust in God rang hollow. He wanted to win his freedom in this life, not the next. Although her tireless support for Perry stemmed from real love and compassion, Amelia Haswell's letters are often heavy going for a reader who lacks her faith, and her model of patient suffering was one that could not have been less likely to appeal to the rebellious Perry, always more Lucifer than Christ. To Perry she was, and would remain, a friend, but her advice, always less welcome than her practical help, was now almost a torment.

Dr North lost no time in informing her that Perry was unwilling to read any more of her 'fanatical letters'. Her distress was obvious. She replied, defensively, that she was a busy woman with far too many souls to care for to spend her time working to help someone who was not willing to be helped. But, however wounded she felt, Amelia Haswell was no quitter, as she wrote: 'I cannot believe God permitted me to go through the persecution I have trying to befriend Oliver, unless some good must come from it some way, sometime, somehow.' Amelia Haswell continued to write to Oliver Perry and he later referred to her with affection, but after more than twenty years their relationship would never be quite the same.

In February 1912 another link between Perry and the world was broken. Perry had rejected his 'Mother'; now the father who had rejected him died. Oliver H. Perry slipped on a frozen sidewalk outside his home and fell, fracturing his skull. He was carried inside bleeding, as his daughter had been decades before, and died without regaining consciousness. After his death, Perry's stepmother Sarah went on to run a boarding house, while his half-brother took over their father's business. In an ironic twist, given his relatives' risky lives, Claude's son, Perry's

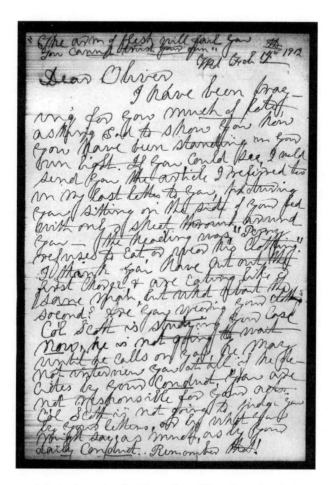

A letter from Amelia Haswell to Oliver Perry in 1912

nephew, became a successful insurance agent. They excised Oliver Curtis Perry from family memory.

Amelia Haswell wrote to see how Perry, who 'always seemed to have considerable affection for his father and grieved because he did not visit him', had taken the news. She wrote that Perry's attitude had always surprised her, as she knew about his rejection just when 'he needed a parent's love'.

There are of course no records of how Perry took the news, but there are signs of a change in his behaviour. Oliver H. Perry's early rejection had done irreparable damage to his son, sparking an anxiety about rejection and a compulsive need to prove himself that would contribute to his crimes and his inability to cope with prison. Perry senior's recent apparent indifference had caused him real distress. But the father's death seems to have given the son a form of release. In 1913 the reporter for *The World* who had interviewed him after the Matteawan escape was allowed to visit him and found a very different man. He was still maintaining his tough regime in protest at his conditions but now seemed to have found almost an inner calm after the repeated storms of his prison life.

Perry recognized the reporter's voice as he approached his cell and said, 'I suppose I have to make my toilet,' as the keeper unlocked his door. His 'toilet' consisted of wrapping a white band over his eyes, wrapping a towel around his loins and putting on a pair of very short prison socks. Despite the temperatures, which sometimes dropped to thirty-five below, Perry lived naked and kept the window of his room wide open day and night. 'You know,' he explained, 'I can't stand the kind of underwear they give me here. I feel very happy this way. I never catch cold. I used to suffer from colds when I was outside, but since I got rid of my clothes I am in perfect physical condition.' The report described a man who, however strange his appearance, was calm and good-humoured. He entertained his visitors by reciting his own poetry, committed to memory. The loss of his book, like the loss of his father, no longer caused him the sharp pain that had driven him to react with such self-destructive violence.

One by one he had stripped away all the trappings of his prison

224

existence. He refused to wear the signs of his convict status, or to feel them against his skin, just as he resisted the institution's other regulations and regimes. While his self-blinding may have been a desperate return to the womb, his defiant return to an elemental state was almost a rebirth. Once the unwanted boy had sought status and comfort in the fine clothes and jewellery that he could only get through crime. Like the era he lived in, he had followed the dangerous dream of extreme individualism and material gain at any cost. Unlike the robber barons, who had bent the law with impunity, he had broken it, and lost his freedom. Now, in the brutal society of the asylum, he found another way of being, with no possessions and little respect, but a stronger sense of self-worth than he had ever had. He had turned the terrible conditions of the dungeon into a pared-to-the bone way of life.

He still hoped to be freed from Dannemora, but had accepted that he would never be seen as normal and wanted only to be sent to an asylum near his friends. The father whose love and acceptance he had never been able to win was dead and the adolescent struggles with authority, triggered by his childhood, seemed to have been played out. It is hard not to see, in the naked blind man standing in the icy wind that whistled through his cell, a fusion of raging Lear and sightless Gloucester, granted new insight through suffering.

Perry's struggle to be pardoned and sent to an asylum near his friends momentarily caught the attention of the Governor, John Dix, but, as so often happened with Perry, he seemed more fascinated by the man than his case and made no intervention.

Outside the confined world of the asylum, the free world was convulsed by conflict. The Great War raged across Europe, while the United States debated the rights and wrongs of this battle between old imperial powers. J. Pierpont Morgan lost no time in extending 500 million dollars' credit to the allied powers, but his investment in the conflict failed to raise American confidence in intervention. In New York State the battle was still being waged between those who sought to preserve the old order of patronage, particularly strong in the rural north-east, and those who argued for a regulated meritocracy to usher in a modern age of professionalism and progress. Prisons were an obvious target for both sides as numerous commissions, enquiries and investigations revealed. Accusations of financial impropriety and corruption flew to and fro in the legislature and the press, hitting reformers and conservatives alike, including Cornelius Collins who was indicted by Grand Jury for larceny and forgery. The Democratic Governor, William Sulzer, founded a 'Prison Reform Commission' that championed the ideals of the 'New Penologists', radical thinkers with ambitious ideas about what prisons could achieve. Thomas Mott Osborne embarked on his undercover operation in Auburn, exposing the horrors of the dungeon and the degradations of prison life. He and others, who had experienced the miseries of working as keepers, went on to become enlightened wardens, trying to build better regimes. There were many setbacks, but gradually some of the worst excesses of the old penal regimes were brought to light. Yet, as usual, Perry and his fellow 'patients' in what was now known as a State Hospital saw little change in their conditions.

1917 was the twenty-fifth anniversary of Perry's final train robbery. To mark it, his life story, in his own words, was published in a number of papers, melodramatically headlined by one 'Out of His Living Tomb Speaks Oliver Curtis Perry'. The story, from rejection by his parents to his robberies, self-blinding and recent protests, was a familiar one. It couched a final appeal, not for freedom, but for compassion. He knew that it was impossible to lift what he called 'the brand of insanity at this time', but was anxious to reassure those used to sensational tales of his bad, mad behaviour that he was not 'the same old Oliver Perry of years ago'. In his skill as a communicator he was very much the old Perry, pointing out the harshness of his sentence before making his appeal to be sent to a civic asylum near his old friends: 'Unless the Governor extends his humanity, I will have to serve twenty-four years and five months more, whereas a man who takes a life gets twenty years. Murderers have been in prison a dozen times before, yet they obtain a parole after twenty years of service. My simple prayer is that my sentence be reduced. The State Lunacy Commission would then have the power to transfer me to the Hudson River State Hospital at any time.'

That year America finally joined in the war that would cover the fields of France and Belgium with the graves of young men. But at the close of 1917 Perry was still to be found in his 'living tomb' at Dannemora.

He would, however, outlive the man he called his 'adversary in chief'. In December Charles North was killed by a murderer called Chris Reichert, who had been declared insane in Sing-Sing. Unlike Perry, he was judged to be no threat and made a 'trusty', so North was relaxed as he visited the carpentry workshop and talked with him about a toy he was making. But when he turned away to leave, Reichert plunged a chisel into his back. The Superintendent bled to death on the floor.

North was succeeded by his assistant, Dr John Ross, but if Perry hoped, as he so often did, that the change might be for the better, he was swiftly disappointed. Ross had a difficult task, running an ever more overcrowded and under-resourced institution. The war had made it almost impossible to recruit attendants, and, echoing Perry's 1895 assessment of the difficulty of obtaining able employees, he appealed for better pay. But nothing changed, and in the summer of 1919 he and his staff were publicly accused of maltreating their patients. The charges were identical to those repeatedly made by Perry only to be ignored, ranging from keeping inmates on an inadequate diet, 'doping' them to make them appear insane to visitors, and failing to release sane men, to causing the death of two inmates in brutal assaults by attendants. This time the complaints were voiced not by a patient, but by a lawyer whose brother was an inmate. The newly elected Democratic Governor Alfred Smith swiftly ordered a formal enquiry into conditions at the institution at which witnesses testified to harsh conditions and brutality. One ex-inmate was direct in his judgment of the Superintendent: 'Dr Ross will go the same way Dr North did. He will be killed by some one of the men. He treats men worse than dogs.'

The investigation, although welcomed by progressives, brought no radical change, and Dr Ross remained in post, while Governor Smith, a principled reformer, was caught up in a seesaw battle for New York with the sardonic Republican Nathan Miller. While Smith eventually created the Department of Corrections and transformed New York's social policy, Miller's conservatism was more in tune with the nation's intolerant, introspective post-war mood. Fear of potential enemies within, of 'reds', in the wake of the Russian Revolution, of immigrants, often assumed to be radicals, and of African Americans, who were moving north to escape continuing persecution, made it hard to work for change. The desire for 'normalcy' made it almost impossible to champion difficult causes.

In a strange synchronicity the year that Perry's chief adversary died also saw the death of his staunchest friend. On Sunday, 14 September Amelia Haswell died at the age of seventy-one. She had caught a cold that developed into pneumonia. The courageous campaigner who had risked her reputation for her principles died in the year when the women of New York were finally given the vote. She may have been naïve, even deceived by him at times, but she had been Perry's friend and champion for over thirty years. In years to come, in an ironic twist to the rumours that had dogged their relationship, she would be transformed in popular myth into his sweetheart: a pretty, but insipid, young Sunday School teacher called Amy. There is nothing in Perry's records, of which very few were preserved after the Great War, to give any hint of how he reacted to the news of Amelia Haswell's death. It is not even clear that he was told that she had died. In a sense, her death would have finally made him the orphan he had always seemed to be.

It is easy to assume that Perry was now totally alone, and he had certainly withdrawn, at least in part, from the world in which he was forced to live. But one letter, sent from the 'Natawanda Club' in New York City, suggests that he was still capable of kindness and even fun:

Dear Friend Oliva Perry, Will you please write to me and let me know if I could help you getting out of the bughouse. If you want me to get you out I will promise to do anything that is in my power. As I have friends on both side. Republicans and Democrats. Hoping to hear from you soon. As I don't forget a pal. Aspecially [sic] as slept next room as you play music aluminum bucket for two night and gave me something to

229

eat a couple sandwiches and tobacco to chew. As I still remain
your true Pal. Charles Isola.

Isola, as the reference to his politician friends implies, was a petty
New York Italian gangster whose career, bound up with the new
age of crime ushered in by Prohibition, had brought him briefly to
Dannemora. There he had met a living embodiment of a different
era of crime and the outlaw and the gangster had become friends.
But his offer to help Perry never reached him. Letters from ex-
prisoners had been banned.

In the aftermath of the Great War and the terrible flu epidemic
that devastated the nation, political struggles continued to occupy
the men charged with oversight of the most vulnerable of prisoners. In 1921, after a bitter argument, Dr Charles Pilgrim, Head of
the State Hospital Commission, resigned, complaining that the
Republican administration had restored 'something like pre-war
conditions', while Governor Miller defended New York's 'splen-
did care' of the 'mentally afflicted'.

Amelia Haswell's death made it difficult for Perry to contact
the press, if he wanted to, but the newspapers were filled with
stories of gangland crime anyway. The new celebrity criminal was
a sharp-suited gangster with a machine-gun and a moll, not a
train robber with a revolver and a missionary. The few articles
that appeared were grotesque, inaccurate caricatures, one describing Perry as 'an insane animal with a terrible lust for blood'.
Another, in February 1924, announced 'Perry, Noted as Outlaw,
Fighting Death in Prison'. The article retold the story of his past
robberies, but gave no details of the threat to his life and almost
no sense of his present. Perry had survived so long against the
odds that he was almost an embarrassment. In an age when the

stories of villains like Al Capone and clean-cut heroes like Lindbergh, the farm boy turned aviator, offered neat moral lessons, even his younger self was out of place. Perry won his fight with death, but he had been forgotten.

Four years later, after a life as quiet as Perry's had been turbulent, the other central character in the original drama bowed out. On 18 December 1928 Daniel McInerney died. That same year Governor Smith set his sights on the Presidency but lost to Republican Herbert Hoover, who confidently predicted an end to poverty. Hoover had come to public attention as the wartime head of the Food Administration, encouraging Americans to eat less with suggestions like 'Meatless Tuesdays' and 'Wheatless Wednesdays'. It is tempting to wonder what Perry might have made of his ideas. Post-war New York seemed, as it had in the Gilded Age, a glittering place of new products and unprecedented pleasures, designed now for the masses not the few. Entertainment had become a boom industry and New York was at the forefront. Country dwellers may have seen their local markets close and farmers leave their land, but a trip in a family motor car, once a sign of unattainable wealth, could take them to a picture palace.

Gloversville might not be the centre of the nation's glove-making any more, but one of its new companies, 'Shine Enterprises', ran seventy-eight picture-houses across the state, where the movie-star heroes and heroines fuelled new fantasies. Outside the walls of the Dannemora State Hospital, the unspoiled wilderness became a favourite filming location. Although the era's chronicler F. Scott Fitzgerald would call it 'the greatest, gaudiest spree in history', few realized that the spending was underpinned not by solid economic growth but by unprecedented speculation.

America was gambling with its future as Oliver Perry had done once before.

The optimistic President was worried about one growth industry: crime. Gangsters thrilled moving-picture audiences as once outlaws like Perry had gripped newspaper readers. But in reality, the prohibition of alcohol turned many ordinary men and women into petty criminals, and battling the big business of organized crime put intolerable pressure on the law enforcement agencies and the prison system. The good times had offered little to those in prison, and at the close of 1928 and in the summer of 1929, the men of Auburn and Clinton fought back against their miserable conditions in the most violent riots ever seen. Auburn was all but destroyed by fire, the Warden taken hostage, the Principal Keeper and eight prisoners killed. The riots spread across the state and beyond. Then, as order was restored in the prisons, and before the enquiry that would establish new security grading and a parole system, 24 October 1929 turned into a Black Thursday and America's great Depression began. In the Mohawk valley, men started digging for Perry's treasure, unaware that the man they thought had buried it there was still alive.

Oliver Perry died at 6.32 a.m. on 5 September 1930, just days before his sixty-fifth birthday. He had served thirty-eight years of his sentence and had spent nearly forty-five years in institutions, fighting for his freedom. The cause given on his death certificate was 'Strangulated Left Inguinal Hernia', while contributory causes were listed as an operation, conducted in the hospital three days earlier, a chronic heart infection and chronic mental condition.

The operation may have been to correct a hernia, or to remedy a different problem, such as appendicitis, inadvertently causing a hernia by cutting through the abdominal wall. No record survives and no autopsy was conducted. But in either case, weakened by decades of abuse and struggle, his body had, it seems, quite literally snapped. It is a poignant coincidence that Perry almost certainly died from the same injury that he had suffered after his dramatic chase through the snow.

The death certificate suggests almost nothing about his life. It states that his birthplace, original occupation and marital status were unknown. One statement stands out, the only suggestion that he belonged, or wanted to belong, to anyone at all: his father's name, 'Oliver H. Perry'.

Perry's death was barely noticed. One newspaper reported the passing of 'Charles Curtiss Perry', while another simply commented, 'No relatives have been located. So, Perry, inoffensive youth who turned out to be one of the most desperate bandits of his time, lies in a felon's grave.' In the press which had used him, and which he had used in return, Oliver Perry was a forgotten man: an outlaw in an age of gangsters. Nobody thought to dramatize his story as they would those of the outlaws he was judged to have 'outdone': in the cinemas, the new tales of the Old West had no place for a New Yorker, no matter how daring his crimes. But Oliver Perry had, and has, an afterlife.

In the hospital itself, he left such an impression that attendants who first worked there years after his death swore they had known 'Old Blind-Eye Perry'. In the stories of his daring crimes that sent Depression-era treasure-seekers out to dig for gold in the hills, in the careful narratives by railroad aficionados, in cartoons and in bedtime stories, traces of Perry survived.

Fittingly, his name has also been written into the landscape of the Mohawk valley near the site of his first robbery. Although the hunt for his treasure has ended, boys and girls in Utica still know of a special place to go, to be alone, to hide, to get away. It is one of those exciting but scary places that become the landmarks of remembered childhood. 'Perry's Cave', where he hid after the robbery, is now the only physical memorial to a man who was once one of America's most notorious, most wanted men: Oliver Curtis Perry.

I PUT OFF visiting the Dannemora graveyard for a long time. While I was looking for Oliver Perry, I didn't want to see his grave. Eventually, feeling that I had to, I wrote to the prison authorities and asked if I might visit it and take a photograph. After some negotiation they agreed, but warned me that it would not be easy to find. There are no names on the gravestones of men who died in the Dannemora State Hospital, only numbers, those allotted when they entered the institution. I reminded myself that it was probably a matter of confidentiality, or economy, rather than indifference. But there was something terrible about the fact that these men, cut off for so long from family and society, should, in the end, still have only institutional identities.

The graveyard for Clinton prison is by the main road, easily accessible to visitors. The final resting place of the prisoners judged insane is, as they were, hidden from public view. Their bodies could be claimed for private burial, but those whose families could not, or would not, come for them were interred in a remote part of the grounds. It occurred to me as I drove with a prison official from the hospital buildings, past the prison farm to the edge of the forest that sweeps up the

235

mountainside, that I was one of very few people who had visited the graves of these unwanted men. I thought of Perry asking to be buried 'alongside dear Blanchy', and of the respectable monument, standing tall in the Syracuse cemetery, that now holds all the family but one.

We passed a small area designated as the Jewish burial ground, then continued on foot across rougher terrain. My guide was friendly and apologetic. They had been trying, he explained, to restore the prison graveyards and had made good progress with the main cemetery. But this one, in a fitting parallel to the history of New York's prison reform, was the last to be renovated. We walked to a sloping field of scrubby grass, where the roots of fir trees tangled across stones the size of house bricks. This was the graveyard. Some of the grass had recently been cut, possibly for my visit, and I could just about discern that the stones were in rows, but only a dozen or so were visible, standing a few inches clear of the earth. These were the graves of the unclaimed men. I had spent years searching for Perry and now I was looking again. I rubbed the earth from half-submerged stones and peered to decipher numbers eroded by decades of rain and ice. But there was no sign of 216.

On the slope above the stones, under tree roots that have gradually snaked downwards, and soil carried by spring mudslides as the snows of winter melt, lie more graves. There men buried by the guards have been buried again, and the stones, the markers of their prison identities, covered over. As I wiped the earth from my hands and walked among the tangled roots, I suddenly found myself smiling. For a man who had fought the system so ferociously that he sacrificed his own body and mind to have been found, finally, in an allocated plot, identified for ever by his prison number, would have seemed like defeat. Instead his body has been covered by the wildness of nature as it reclaims the land from the state. Perry has escaped one last time.

It seemed a fitting, and open, conclusion to my search. Just as his boyhood home had disappeared, enveloped in the broadleaf woodland of the Mohawk valley, so his grave had been subsumed within the darker forest of the Adirondacks. The traces of his life that I had found in the years of looking had brought me closer to him than I had ever expected, but he was still out of reach. The daring robber I had set out to find turned out to be America's broken dream boy, an unwanted child determined to make his mark in a society whose passions and problems he epitomized. His daring crimes that had first caught my eye had made him an instant celebrity, but it was his long struggle to survive, to preserve his identity in a system designed to reduce him to a number that had commanded my respect. I had found the courage, strength and spirit that I had looked for in an outlaw lover, riding free across the Western landscape of my fantasy, in a man who was confined in institutions almost all his life. And looking for the man of my dreams had changed me.

Instead of restoring my imagined scene of childhood innocence, or transporting me into a romantic fantasy, my search had taken me into a darker, harsher world. But there I encountered someone with more determination to savour even life's bitter pleasures than I could have imagined. In the years after I first saw his picture, Oliver Perry had charmed, shocked, infuriated and moved me, as he had the men and women he encountered in his lifetime. In my research I had tried my best, as they had, to pin him down. At times I came quite close to knowing something of what, and who, he was. I saw him at his best and at his worst. But he always escaped. I could never make him mine. And, in the end, I was glad that I could not.

In my strange relationship with Oliver Perry I learned that no matter how much we yearn to belong, to possess and be possessed by anyone, parent, forbidden sweetheart or wanted man, in the end we are alone. When we are children and when we are grown, our desires must always leave us wanting.

Acknowledgements

I COULD FILL another book with the names of all the people who have helped in my search for Oliver Perry and in my efforts to tell his story. These acknowledgements are only a suggestion of my gratitude to them all. While it feels like a minor betrayal of Perry's memory, I must first thank the Department of Correctional Services of the State of New York, especially Superintendents William Mazzuca, Daniel Senkowski and Hans Walker, Deputy Superintendents Paul Annatts and Jimmie Harris, Plant Superintendent Dale Gordon, Lt G. Wilkerson, Faculty Historian Michael Pettigrass, Correction Officer Michael O'Sullivan and Dr Leonard I. Morgenbesser. Whatever happened in the past, the current representatives of New York's Correctional Services could not have been more courteous or helpful. I would also like to thank the staff of the New York State Archives, especially Dr William Evans and Dr James Folts, who helped me locate Perry's records and writings. Dr John R. Sellers and Mrs Nan Ernst, of the Library of Congress, kindly allowed me to work with the Pinkerton National Detective Agency archive before cataloguing.

The following individuals, in New York and further afield, all gave me invaluable help and encouragement: Rebekah Ambrose, Peter Bedrossian, Joe Bendle, Ruby Biswas, Michael V. Carlisle, Doreen Chaky, Beverly Choltco-Devlin, Dorothea Cooper, Phil Cubbin, Barbara Dix, Thomas G. Eldred, Andi Evangelist, Deborah J. Ferrell, Carlton Gilroy, Malcolm Goodelle, Hope V. Hatch, Edward Knoblauch, Virginia LaGoy, Michael Martin, Nancy Martin, Eileen McHugh, Rick Miller and the National Association for Outlaw and Lawman History, Sharon O'Brien, Roy O'Dell, Jeanette Shiel, Tom McCarthy of the New York Correctional History Society, Wayne Miller of the Feinberg Library, Joan Van Voorhis, Paul Paciello, Richard Palmer, Emma Parry, Joe Price, Mat Rapacz, Ruth Rosenberg-Naparsteck, Wendy Scalfaro, Joe Sim, Daniel Smith, Debra Staley, Gina Stankivitz, and Kelly Yacobucci-Farquahar. I would also like to thank colleagues and students, too many to list, at Liverpool John Moores University for their support and suggestions.

I have very special memories of my research in upstate New York because of the good company, hospitality and kindness of Mark de Lawyer, Dawn Capece, Marta Zimmerman, Larry-Ann Evans, Robert Weiss and Ann Rowland and David. Without the enthusiasm and encouragement of James Friel and Peter Wheeler, the passionate advocacy of Jane Turnbull, and the skill and sensitivity of Alexandra Pringle, Chiki Sarkar and their colleagues at Bloomsbury, my obsession with Oliver Perry would have remained a private matter.

A NOTE ON THE AUTHOR

Tamsin Spargo was born and raised in Cornwall. She worked as a reporter, then as an actor, before embarking on her current career as a cultural historian. She is Reader in Cultural History and Director of the School of Media, Critical and Creative Arts at Liverpool John Moores University. Her academic works include *The Writing of John Bunyan, Foucault and Queer Theory* and *Reading the Past: Literature and History.*

A NOTE ON THE TYPE

The text of this book is set in Linotype
Sabon, named after the type founder,
Jacques Sabon. It was designed by Jan
Tschichold and jointly developed by
Linotype, Monotype and Stempel, in
response to a need for a typeface to be
available in identical form for mechanical
hot metal composition and hand
composition using foundry type.

Tschichold based his design for Sabon
roman on a font engraved by Garamond,
and Sabon italic on a font by Granjon. It
was first used in 1966 and has proved an
enduring modern classic.